D1499818

Nutrition for the Prime of Life

The Adult's Guide to Healthier Living

Nutrition for the Prime of Life

The Adult's Guide to Healthier Living

Hugh J. McDonald, D. Sc.
and
Frances M. Sapone, M.D., M.S., R.D.

INSIGHT BOOKS

PLENUM PRESS • NEW YORK AND LONDON

Library of Congress Cataloging-in-Publication Data

McDonald, Hugh J.
     Nutrition for the prime of life : the adult's guide to healthier
  living / Hugh J. McDonald and Frances M. Sapone.
        p.   cm.
     Includes bibliographical references and index.
     ISBN 0-306-44503-4
     1. Middle aged persons--Nutrition. 2. Aged--Nutrition. 3. Aging-
  -Nutritional aspects.   I. Sapone, Frances M.   II. Title.
   RA784.M395   1993
    613.2--dc20   93-2613
                                                                    CIP

ISBN 0-306-44503-4

© 1993 Plenum Press, New York
A Division of Plenum Publishing Corporation
233 Spring Street, New York, N.Y. 10013

An Insight Book

Printed in the United States of America

To my loving wife, Avis E. McDonald

—Hugh J. McDonald

To Nicholas LaPonte, attorney, friend, advisor, who gave me
moral support throughout the preparation of this manuscript

—Frances M. Sapone

Acknowledgments

To Avis E. McDonald, Ph.D., R.N., who edited and typed the manuscript, and provided constant encouragement and practical support, we express our deep appreciation.

During the preparation of the manuscript, we were helped by many other people. A number of professional colleagues assisted us by their good-natured willingness to discuss the merit of including or omitting certain topics, and the appropriate length and depth of presentation. To all these friends, we say thank you for the constructive suggestions.

We acknowledge the major support given us by the staffs of the library of the Stritch School of Medicine, Loyola University, Chicago, and the Skokie Public Library, Skokie, Illinois, by their obtaining copies of many hard-to-find scientific papers that were necessary to complete the manuscript.

Hugh J. McDonald
Frances M. Sapone

Preface

Speaking of obesity, the late Jean Mayer, former chancellor and president of Tufts University and one of the country's foremost authorities on nutrition, said, "Knowledge is not sufficient for cure, but its acquisition is a necessary step." We feel that Dr. Mayer's statement has broad application to dietary change. To put good dietary habits into practice, one must learn the basic principles of a healthful diet and the essentials of sound nutrition practice. *Nutrition for the Prime of Life* has the potential to be an effective tool in this educational process.

Recent surveys conducted by the American Dietetic Association indicate that the public's nutrition knowledge is inadequate, especially with regard to the prevention of chronic diseases that are often associated with dietary habits—for example, cadiovascular disease. This book provides information that older people, and health care professionals working with them, need to know about the role of nutrition in the prevention and treatment of chronic disease. Additionally, the importance of exercise is also discussed, because it works synergistically with sound nutrition practice to maintain good health and ideal body weight.

The first four chapters of the book deal with the demographics of aging in the United States and the controlling factors in aging; the foodstuffs of life: carbohydrates, fats, and proteins; the vitamins and minerals; and the changes in nutrient intake, digestion, and metabolism that occur with aging. One chapter deals with the problems of the digestive tract and the role of fiber and water; another deals with the interrelationship between diet and dental health, an issue important to older people. Nutrition-related diseases, including atherosclerosis, high blood pressure, heart attack and stroke; diabetes mellitus; cancer; arthritis and gout; and nutritional anemias, are explored in some detail. The next four chapters deal with weight control and the benefits of exercise at all ages; drug–nutrient interactions; guidelines for healthy living; and the question of whether nutrition can alter the aging process. An appendix provides, in tabular form, some basic reference materials that readers may find helpful, and a glossary of less familiar words.

The nutritional needs of the older person are an active area of research. Much remains to be learned about how nutrition and aging interact. It is not too early, however, to disseminate what is already known and to present what can be learned by discussing current research efforts. It is hoped that readers will acquire some new insights into the role of nutrition in the health and fitness of the older person and that they may become interested enough to question their own diets and confident enough to make nutritional changes when advisable. The authors believe that almost every reader will find some nuggets of useful knowledge and that they will become more discerning in evaluating the very large amount of nutrition information in the lay press.

The information in this book is intended to be a guide to good nutrition for the older person and not a substitute for the advice of a physician.

Hugh J. McDonald
Frances M. Sapone

Chicago, Illinois

Contents

1

Aging in the United States and the Nature of the Aging Process

Like most industrialized countries, the United States is growing older demographically. According to the U.S. Census Bureau, there are, in this country, more than 31 million men and women who are 65 years of age or older, and it is expected that their numbers will increase to 40 million by 2010 and to more than 65 million by 2030. Life expectancy at birth is now 78.6 years for women and 71.6 years for men (WHO, 1991), as compared with about 47 years at the beginning of this century (NCHS, 1988). The average age and the proportion of the older population are also increasing. People older than 65 now make up 12 percent of the population, compared with 4 percent in 1900, and are expected to increase to 21 percent by the year 2030.

Men and women who survive to old age can now expect still more years of life than in the past. To illustrate the point, people reaching age 65 in 1984 had an average life expectancy of an additional 17 years (19 years for women and 14.5 years for men), and life expectancy at age 65 has increased 2.5 years since 1960 (NCHS, 1986). The increased life expectancy for older Americans is reflected in an even more rapid growth in the population older than 75 and older than 85. According to the present trends, it can be expected that within the next 10 to 20 years, almost 50 percent of the population in the United States will live at least until their 80th birthdays (Brody and Brock, 1985).

As we see around us, especially in the large cities, the pressing

1

needs of some elderly individuals, it is easy to overlook the fact that many older persons are enjoying their later years. They are unencumbered by family responsibilities and have money, leisure, and adequate health to pursue the activities that interest them. According to Ellen Farley, senior vice president of Donnelly Marketing, located in Chicago, men and women 50 years old and older control more than half of all the discretionary income in the United States, about $130 billion. Also, 70 percent of all personal wealth, $7 trillion, is owned by household heads age 50 and older (Chicago Tribune, 1991). These facts contradict the popular notion that most older people are poor, lonely, and ill. About 65 percent of the elderly are actually relatively free of major problems. Among noninstitutionalized elderly persons, the number living in poverty fell from 35 percent in 1959 to about 12 percent in the late 1980s (Holden, 1988). These statistics should buoy the spirits of young adults, who, from so much that they see and read, might be led to envision their own later years as depressing.

Poverty has not, of course, disappeared in this country; it is much more prevalent among minorities and women, particularly widows (Hurd, 1989). Some studies have not shown any association between income and nutrition (Slesinger *et al.*, 1980) while other studies (Fanelli and Woteki, 1989) found median intakes of energy and some nutrients were considerably lower for 65- to 74-year-old participants who were below the poverty line.

Definition of Aging

A good deal is known about the growth, development, and nutritional needs of people from conception to maturity. The scientific community, however, has not made much progress in understanding the mechanisms by which the human body normally ceases to grow on reaching maturity, begins to show the signs of aging, and all too soon starts an inevitable decline. We have not made much progress in either slowing or preventing this series of events.

Scholars in different fields view the aging process in different ways. Biologists, for example, tend to explain aging by discussing changes that occur at the cellular and molecular level. Psychologists describe changes occurring before physical maturity as "differentiation of the individual," while those that occur after physical maturity are described as "aging." Sociologists speak of the aging process in terms of changes in role or role functions.

Aging is a phenomenon that is easily observable in all living things, and many of its consequences are readily evident during life. This discussion will be concerned principally with humans.

Aging can be defined as the process of growing old or maturing through progressive changes related to the passage of time. In biological terms, it is due in part to a failure of body cells to function normally as they once did, or to produce new body cells to replace those that are malfunctioning or have died. Although this definition describes the biological process, it does not explain why people age. Normal cell function may be lost through malnutrition, infectious disease, exposure to environmental hazards, or genetic influences. Among body cells that exhibit early signs of aging are those that normally cease dividing after reaching maturity. There is no precise method for determining the rate or degree of aging. A number of theories attempt to explain why people age, but no one of them has been accepted as the primary cause by all scientists who study these processes.

Theories of Aging: Why Do We Grow Old?

In general, cells appear to be subject to both an endogenous aging process arising within the cell (e.g., genetic effects, and the presence of substances called free radicals) and an exogenous aging process arising from outside the cell (i.e., the environment). Environmental factors that promote or accelerate aging include lack of nutrients, disease, the impact of cosmic rays, effects of hard labor, extremes of heat and cold, and lack of stimulation due to disuse.

In all theories that attempt to explain the why of aging, there is agreement that at a certain point the cells can no longer replenish their constituents. In the living human body, when some cells cease to function, other cells that are dependent on them also cease to function. This gradual slowing down of cell function over the years partially explains the decreased energy needs of older people. The following paragraphs highlight a number of theories of aging.

The wear-and-tear theory maintains that the human body simply wears out with constant use, as might be expected of any complex machine. Aging is believed to be the result of gradual deterioration of organs necessary for life.

The autoimmune theory postulates that aging is caused by flaws in the mechanism of protein synthesis. Alterations of enzymes, for example, may result in defects in one or more of the steps in protein synthesis. The body's immune system will then react to the poorly crafted protein molecules as if they were of foreign origin and will produce antibodies to counteract them. The complexes that form between the antibodies and these less-than-perfect proteins will accumulate in cells as useless debris. It has been proposed that this accumulation of deposits in joints may play a role in the development of arthritis, which is associated prominently with the later decades of life.

The waste-product theory, which is related to the autoimmune theory, proposes that a variety of metabolic waste products or debris, containing damaging substances, build up within the cells and interfere with their function. An example might be the production of partially completed protein molecules.

According to the free-radical theory, the aging process is related to the presence of highly reactive fragments of molecules called free radicals. These charged molecular fragments arise from a variety of reactions [e.g., the spontaneous attack by oxygen on the polyunsaturated fatty acids found in membranes (discussed in the section of Chapter 6 devoted to cancer, especially the role of the mineral selenium, of vitamins E and C, and of beta-carotene)], but also from the impact of cosmic rays. Cosmic rays are streams of highly penetrating charged particles that continually bombard the earth from outer space. When the impact geometry of the incoming cosmic stream and a molecule in a cell of the body is right, highly reactive free radicals may be formed.

The newly spawned free radicals seek out other molecules to latch onto, thereby leading to increased death of cells and eventually impairing their function. The cells in which these reactions occur, as well as those that depend on them, then die. This theory (Harmon,

1986) is probably better developed in scientific detail than any other and provides plausible explanations for such diverse topics as evolution of life, aging, and many disease processes. It also provides a theoretical base for the judicious selection of diets and antioxidant nutrients (selenium, vitamins E and C, and beta-carotene) as a means of increasing the average healthy life span.

The hypothesis that oxyradicals play a major causative role in the aging process and that endogenous antioxidants may neutralize these bad effects, thus leading to longer life spans, has received considerable theoretical and experimental support (Cutler, 1991). Humans have the longest life span of any mammalian species and consume more energy over their life spans on a per weight basis. Aging rate is related to metabolic rate (i.e., the rate at which oxygen is utilized per unit weight of tissue). Since the rate of oxygen metabolism is positively correlated with the rate of oxygen radical production, it is reasonable to believe that active oxygen species may be important as a causative factor in aging. If this is true, then various strategies acting to decrease the toxic effects of active oxygen species might represent a class of longevity-determinant processes. Cutler "tested" the prediction by comparing the tissue concentration of various endogenous antioxidants (superoxide dismutase, vitamin E, carotenoids, uric acid, and vitamin C) in several primate species including human, orangutan, chimpanzee, gorilla, gibbon, and rhesus monkey and in the horse, cow, goat, rabbit, deer mouse, rat, and field mouse. A positive correlation with life span was evident for superoxide dismutase, vitamin E, carotenoids, and uric acid, thus providing support for the oxyradical hypothesis of aging. The results for vitamin C were more complex; plasma concentrations showed no correlation, and some tissues like liver showed an increase in vitamin C for short-lived species. On the other hand, brain tissue, including that of humans, did show a significant positive increase in vitamin C concentration.

The error-in-copying theory maintains that the messages that control the orderly behavior of the cells gradually become so full of errors that the cells can no longer function normally. A closer look would reveal that cells lose their ability to interpret the DNA genetic code and therefore synthesize their proteins incorrectly. As faulty proteins or reduced amounts of protein are produced, cell and organ functions that depend on these poorly minted proteins also falter, and organs elsewhere in the body may be affected adversely.

The biological-clock theory supposes that the program spelled out at conception in the genetic material eventually runs out, simply ending all functions. The programmed genetic determination of the life span operates not only at the level of the individual, but also within the various species, thus determining that one species will live longer than another. Scientists have hoped that it might be possible to determine the site of the biological clock, decipher its mechanism, and learn how to control it, thus turning off the changes associated with aging.

There is some experimental evidence to support the biological-clock theory (Hayflick, 1975). Hayflick found that human embryo cells, *in vitro*, are unable to go on dividing into daughter cells without limit. They are limited to about 50 to 55 replications, with an average of 50, before deterioration sets in. Hayflick proposed that the cell nucleus is the site of the biological clock of aging. The finite capacity of human embryo cells for replication offers support for the idea of a genetically programmed life span of human embryo cells and a biological clock that influences the process of aging.

According to the nutrition theory of aging, minimal eating has a major effect on extending a person's life span. Minimal consumption of food definitely prevents obesity and consequently decreases disease-related deaths. Life insurance underwriters take very seriously the idea that obesity is directly related to higher mortality rates from the major degenerative diseases such as atherosclerosis and cancer. Additional factors that may influence aging include ethnic eating habits, social class, living conditions, and individual eating habits.

In experiments using rodents and other animals, as long as the diet is not deficient in any required nutrients, caloric restriction of protein or fat has been shown to prolong the life span, to retard most aspects of biologic aging, and to improve resistance to age-related diseases such as cancer, atherosclerosis, and diabetes. This result has been replicated many times (Masoro, 1985; Weindruch and Walford, 1988) since it was first described in the 1930s (McCay *et al.*, 1935). Although the underlying mechanisms are unclear, dietary restriction provides the best model now available to study the phenomenon of decelerated aging.

Mortality

Most investigators have thought of mortality largely in terms of the Gompertz Law, proposed by Benjamin Gompertz in 1825, which holds that mortality rates increase exponentially with age (Barinaga, 1992). According to the law, it would be expected that for any species the death rate would climb dramatically in very old age, effectively capping the life span. Until 1992, the law appeared to hold for humans, where chance of death doubles roughly every 8 years during most of adulthood, and also for all other species that have been studied.

Recently, however, conformity to the law began to look very weak when Vaupel and co-workers, in Denmark, analyzed Scandinavian census information, known for its reliability, for a group of people they call "the very old"—for example, human beings older than 85 or so (Barinaga, 1992). Their chance of dying did not continue to increase exponentially into later years.

Since human data are likely to include countless uncontrolled genetic and environmental variables, Vaupel and his collaborators (Carey *et al.*, 1992) took a new approach to test the law. They used an experimental animal that they could grow in the millions, keep under controlled conditions, and follow precisely enough to record each death. They studied millions of medflies and took a census every day, counting each fly that died. They were surprised to find that the likelihood of death peaked at about 15 percent when the flies were between 40 and 60 days old—a very old age for a fly—and then decreased. The most geriatric flies of 100 days or older had only a 40 to 60 percent chance of dying on a given day, less than they had when they were only 20 days old. That is to say, mortality rates were found to level off and decrease at very old ages. The new results, in other words, do not conform to the Gompertz rule. Instead, they undermine the long-standing notion that death rates of all species increase automatically with age.

Vaupel proposes that death rates are not driven by an absolute limit to life span, but rather that they reflect a collection of causes of death, to which some individuals are more susceptible than others. Like fruit flies, he says, "people are different from each other in terms of their vulnerability to mortality."

Human Longevity

Although there is no consensus as to which, if any, of the proposed theories of aging is correct, there is general agreement that many factors play a role in determining how long a person can expect to live. Factors that affect the chances of living a long life, other than disease, are environment, eating habits, level of physical activity, social roles, social environment, marital status, and attitude toward aging.

The presence of modern technology in a country is an important factor in determining longevity. In general, the more technologically advanced the society, the longer the life expectancy at birth. Life expectancy means the probable number of years a person will live after a given age, as determined by the mortality rate in a specific geographic area. It may be individually qualified by the person's condition, rate, gender, or other demographic factors. Active life expectancy at any specific age is the average number of years of life remaining in an independent state, that is, free from significant disability, for a population of individuals (Olshansky *et al.*, 1990).

Since the midnineteenth century, the human population has experienced a near doubling of the expectation of life at birth, from 40 years to near 80 years. Today many people live to be 100 years old or older, and as of 1990, the oldest verified age that an individual had survived was just over 120 years.

Some experts now tell us that human beings may have extended life about as far as it can go (Olshansky *et al.*, 1990). They say that the era of rapid increases in human longevity has come to an end, at least in developed countries. Other experts disagree with this conclusion (Barinaga, 1991).

Most of the mortality declines and increases in life expectancy that occurred early in this century were a result of rapidly declining neonatal, infant, and maternal mortality, due to control of infectious and parasitic diseases. The mortality rates in younger and middle-age groups are now so low in the United States that the complete elimination of mortality before the age of 50 would increase life expectancy at birth by only 3.5 years. Thus, the potential for additional increases in longevity relies on progress in dealing with diseases of the elderly.

Although a segment of the population has survived to older ages from ancient times until this century, only small improvements were made in extending life for the population aged 50 and older. In the last 25 years, however, in the United States, age-adjusted death rates from the major cardiovascular diseases declined by more than 34 percent (U.S. Bureau of the Census, 1988). Moreover, most of the declines in mortality and gains in life expectancy during this recent mortality transition were achieved in the elderly population. Life expectancy at birth in the United States has increased from 47 years in 1900 to about 75 years in 1988 (Olshansky *et al.*, 1990).

Having noted such rapid advances in the extension of life during the last 100 years, researchers are asking how long this can continue and what factors might contribute to future gains in life expectancy. These questions are of great importance because they address estimates of the size, proportional distribution, and health of the elderly population in the future.

A related issue is whether further declines in mortality would lead to an increased active life expectancy or an expanded period of frailty and dependency. Unless active life expectancy is improved from present levels, the combination of population aging, a larger-than-predicted elderly population, and possible shifts in the distribution of frailty conditions among the very old would have a very serious adverse impact on government-funded programs such as Social Security and Medicare. Even if science could eliminate heart disease and cancer, which account for nearly 50 percent of all deaths in the United States, it is unlikely that the average life expectancy at birth would increase much beyond 85.

In the past, investigators have based speculations about the upper limits of human longevity on observation of past trends in mortality; that is, they extrapolated from actuarial tables by estimating how death rates would change if, say, the incidence of heart disease were halved. Olshansky and colleagues (1990) reversed the process by asking themselves how much mortality rates would have to be reduced in order to increase average life expectancy to 120 years. They discovered, from their computer calculations, that even large reductions in current death rates in the United States would result in only small increases in life expectancy. As an example, if through some miracle of medical science and risk avoidance, no one ever again died before reaching 50 (thus eliminating more than 12.4 percent of all deaths), the increase in average life expectancy at birth would be only 3.5 years.

A kind of built-in biological limit seems to be programmed into the cells of the human body. In the landmark laboratory experiments of Hayflick (1975), discussed earlier in this chapter, it was found that human embryo cells were limited *in vitro* to about 50 to 55 replications, with an average of 50, before deterioration set in. This planned obsolescence on nature's part makes a certain amount of evolutionary sense. It has been stated that survival of the fittest rewards only those who reproduce, not those who reach old age, and biologically speaking, once procreation is over, human bodies are expendable.

To combat cellular aging, scientists working in this area agree that the best way is to postpone its effects at the molecular level. Basic research is underway in several laboratories to explore the mechanisms that cause human cells to wear out and to try to find the genes that cause the major degenerative diseases of old age, such as arthritis, osteoporosis, and Alzheimer's disease. This work would produce a double benefit; it would extend life expectancy and help to make the extra years worth living. Researchers, however, have no idea when, or if, breakthroughs will take place. Findings reported in 1990 (Yankner *et al.*) and 1991 (Kowall *et al.*) on Alzheimer's disease may indicate such a breakthrough, and these findings are potentially a major advance in preventing and controlling the disease.

Aging and Nutritional Status

As people grow older, a number of changes affect nutritional status. They may be described as biologic or physiological, psychological, economic, and social changes. Not all individuals are affected to the same extent, however, and many older people enjoy very good health until an advanced age. In general, among older people there is a greater occurrence of chronic disease, a greater use of medications, and a life-style requiring minimal physical exercise. Letsov and Price (1987) theorized that many of the consequences of aging may actually be caused by these other factors. The important role of physical exercise in the health of older people has been reviewed (Smith et al., 1988). Weight gain in adult life probably results from greater decreases in energy expenditure rather than any increase in food intake, which actually seems to decline with age (Bray, 1990).

Physiological Changes with Aging

The physiological changes associated with aging include the alterations in structure and function of the body that occur over a lifetime (Zarit, 1980).

As cells age, the changes they undergo become evident in the organs and tissues of which they are a part. Changes in the skin and hair are among the most visible. The ages of people are often estimated by the degree of visible wrinkling of the skin and the degree of graying of the hair. As people grow older, wrinkles develop because of a loss of the fat underlying the skin, a loss in its elasticity, and a decrease in the number of blood vessels that supply the skin. All of these changes are also affected by the long-term effects of exposure to the ultraviolet rays of the sun and the drying effects of wind and cold. For a large percentage of the population, the hair naturally and gradually turns gray and eventually white, and for many men, the hair on the head thins out, and baldness, to a lesser or greater extent, occurs. Other changes that are often not quite so evident include decreasing stature and change in posture, decreasing visual and auditory acuity, slower response time, and increasing susceptibility to disease.

Older people often complain that food lacks taste or smell, and there is evidence to substantiate the claim that the senses of smell, and possibly taste, do decrease with age (Smith et al., 1988; Chauhan *et al.*, 1987). These changes reduce the pleasure of eating and may lead to decreased appetite as well as impaired utilization of nutrients and limitations of function.

Dental problems are common in the older population and decrease the ability to chew certain foods (see Chapter 7). They may be a result of poor oral hygiene, loss of teeth, or inadequate professional dental care. In any case, poor teeth or poorly fitted dentures, necessitating the use of soft bland foods that are easy to chew, further exacerbate the problem. Physical disabilities such as diminution of vision may make eating less pleasant. Although the decreases in basal metabolic rate and physical activity, noted in some studies, reduce nutrient needs, older people may still consume insufficient kcalories and essential nutrients (McGandy, 1986). Decreased physical activity also may predispose individuals to the development of osteoporosis (see Chapters 8 and 11).

There is a decrease, with age, in the secretion of hydrochloric acid and of digestive enzymes by the stomach (Russell, 1986). There is also a decrease in the secretion of digestive juices by the pancreas and small intestine. These conditions give rise to inadequate absorption of nutrients from the intestinal tract. Malabsorption can also be caused by interactions with medications commonly prescribed for older persons (Hathcock, 1987; also Chapter 9). It is still uncertain whether these changes contribute to nutrient deficiencies in older people and whether such changes are related more to the use of medications, to poor health, or to a sedentary life-style than to age itself (Letsov and Price, 1987).

Since liver cells regenerate themselves throughout life, loss of liver cells with aging is not a great problem. Even with good nutrition, however, fat gradually infiltrates the liver, reducing its work output (Mayer, 1974). The liver's response to moderate levels of blood glucose load is reduced. The reasons may be that the blood is not pushed strongly enough by the heart to reach the pancreas, so that it fails to send its insulin message to the liver, or that there may be fewer glucose-responsive cells in the pancreas (Strehler, 1977).

The volume of blood that the heart can pump decreases as the heart and blood vessels age. The arteries lose some of their elasticity, and the amount of blood entering the network of capillaries in the various organs of the body decreases. Deposits of cholesterol and fat may form in the walls of the arteries, and diffusion of calcium salts into the deposits or plaques may make them relatively hard and inflexible. Since all organs and tissues depend on the circulation of the blood for nutrients and oxygen, degenerative changes in this system may affect all other systems in a critical fashion.

A decrease in the flow of blood through the kidneys gradually decreases their efficiency in removing nitrogen-containing compounds and other wastes from the blood and maintaining the right amounts of salts, glucose, and other valuable nutrients in the body fluids. As less blood is pumped into the minute blood vessels of the kidneys, the network of capillaries decreases in size, causing some kidney cells to be deprived of their nutrient and oxygen supply and to die. Because both the heart rate and the volume of blood pumped into the kidneys depend in large measure on the muscular activity of the person, this degenerative process can be retarded by a regular program of physical exercise.

During aging, the ability of the brain to direct the activities of the body decreases. In humans, brain cells stop reproducing within the first two years of life. From that time onward, they maintain themselves without further cell division. Although thousands of cells die each day, the loss is not readily noticeable. However, over a lifetime, the loss becomes evident in the slowing of reflexes and in the distorted messages directed to other organs. The human adult compensates partially for this loss with a greater amount of stored information, knowledge, and good judgment. Since nerve cells are not replaceable, any damage resulting from accidents may diminish mental ability permanently. Hearing loss, visual impairment, loss of the senses of smell and taste (Chauhan et al., 1987), and loss of the sense of balance are all evidence of impaired cell function.

The Skeletal System and Aging

The bones and muscles in the human skeletal system, like the components of the body's other organ systems, undergo changes with the passage of time. They provide shape and stability to the body and endow it with freedom of movement from one place to another. As people age, bone and muscle mass may be diminished, stature may be shortened, muscle power may be lost, joints may stiffen and ache, and mobility may become limited. For people older than 65 years, arthritis and allied bone, joint, and muscular conditions are among the commonest of all disorders. Although these diseases involving the bones and muscles of the body very seldom directly lead to death, they have often been the cause of chronic, recurrent muscular and joint pain in older people. The good news is that medical help is now available to alleviate much of the discomfort and suffering.

In other parts of this book, especially Chapters 6 and 11, musculoskeletal problems, osteoporosis, osteoarthritis, rheumatoid arthritis, and gout are discussed in some detail, with an emphasis on how nutrition may affect their initiation and control.

Psychological Changes and Aging

Psychological factors that affect the nutritional well-being of the older person may be even more important than the physiological influences. They include behavioral changes, changes in self-perception, and reaction to physiological changes. Many older people experience feelings of depression and inadequacy and a loss of self-worth (Letsov and Price, 1987). Spouses, friends, and even children may have died, and family members may no longer reside nearby. Physical disabilities may prevent the individual from carrying on activities once taken for granted. Feelings of isolation, loneliness, depression, and even anger are not uncommon among the elderly and often affect the intake of food. Many older persons find it difficult to prepare and serve a meal with any semblance of style when they have to eat it alone. In a study conducted over four decades ago, the diets of isolated elderly persons were found to be much poorer than the diets of socially gregarious older persons (Davidson et al., 1962). Closely related to psychological aging is what is called functional aging, which refers to the capacities of individuals to function in society, as compared to those of others of the same age (Birren and Renner, 1977). Psychological age is influenced by the condition of the body, such as the cardiovascular and renal systems, and by changes in the brain that affect memory, motivation, and emotions (Birren and Renner, 1977).

Of the psychological factors affecting nutrition, the most common one is depression (Garetz, 1976). Of all psychiatric diagnoses, depression is most strongly correlated with increased morbidity and mortality, regardless of the age of the subjects (Widgor and Morris, 1977; Nielson *et al.*, 1977) and is most often related to chronic disease and to poverty, which are not uncommon among older persons. At least 30 percent of noninstitutionalized men and women older than 65 live alone (Todhunter, 1976; AARP, 1985). Neither institutionalized nor solitary living necessarily induces depression, but such life changes may be associated with poor self-esteem, which can lead to significant negative changes in eating patterns (Letsov and Price, 1987). Although depression is one psychiatric disorder that can be treated successfully, recent advances in therapy have not been disseminated to health professionals widely or rapidly enough to make the greatest impact (NIA, 1987).

Economic and Sociologic Changes and Aging

Although many older individuals are doing very well indeed, older Americans as a group have a lower economic status than other adults in the United States (U.S. Senate, 1987/88). Despite the fact that the percentage of older persons living below the poverty line, which was 12.4 percent in the later 1980s, decreased substantially over the past two decades, poverty continues to be too high (Holden, 1988). The decline in income most often follows retirement, because nearly half of the nation's full-time work force (about 42 million) have no retirement income except that provided by Social Security (Chicago Tribune, 1991). The effects of inflation on relatively fixed incomes, death of a wage-earning spouse, or failing health (U.S. Senate, 1987/88) are other factors weakening the financial stability of older families and individuals, and imposing economic restraints. Income and health status have been found to be important determinants of life satisfaction in the older population (Chatfield, 1977). Low income may also be a risk factor for inadequate nutrition in older individuals (DHEW, 1974).

Sociologic changes with aging refer to the roles and social habits of individuals in society as they age. Included are changes in norms, expectations, social status, and social roles, and they are evaluated principally on the expected kind of behaviors established by the group. Age-graded expectations of behavior are influenced by the culture and by the person's biological and psychological characteristics (Hall, 1980).

Although most older Americans do not live in institutions, older Americans as a group are more likely to be institutionalized temporarily or permanently (Kane, 1984). Despite the fact that institutional food is likely to meet minimal standards for nutrient content, factors such as lack of choice or limited day-to-day variety may increase the risk of inadequate consumption. Many residents of nursing homes consume a therapeutic diet (NCHS, 1981) that may further discourage adequate intake. An important issue for demented institutionalized individuals is not that the menu is inadequate, but that they may not consume the food (Sandman et al., 1987).

2

The Foodstuffs of Life

Scientific knowledge of nutrition and food chemistry, in conjunction with modern food technology, is responsible for producing in this country a rich eclectic array of natural and convenience foods that are a marvel to many visitors from abroad (Clydesdale, 1991). The food is attractively packaged, and preparation is now so simplified and shortened that nutritious meals of high quality for the whole family are within the reach of most consumers. Good food can make life more enjoyable. In addition to selecting our grandparents with care, having a working knowledge of foods and their preparation, combined with moderation in consumption and adequate exercise, are essential if we are to remain trim, be fit, and live a long life.

Although each member of a family requires the same basic foods, the preparation and the quantities needed will vary with age, physical activity, and other factors, for example, chewing ability. Older persons should have a balanced diet of protective foods, but with fewer kcalories. A variety of foods is more important because the senses of taste and smell diminish somewhat with age, causing some foods to be unappealing (Smith et al., 1988; Chauhan et al., 1987).

In order to furnish nourishment for the body, foods must contain substances that function in one or more of the following ways: (1) they must provide energy for the body (i.e., they must contain substances that can combine with oxygen to release energy required for the body's activities); (2) they must supply substances for the building and/or maintenance of body tissues; and (3) they must provide specific substances that function as regulators of body processes. Many foods can fulfill more than one function because they are mixtures of a number of substances. Any chemical substance found in foods that functions in one or more of the three ways outlined above is a nutrient or foodstuff. The nutrients include carbohydrates, fats, proteins, vitamins, minerals, and water. Vitamins and minerals are discussed in Chapters 3, 4, and 8, and water, in Chapter 5.

Carbohydrates, fats, and proteins, sometimes called fuelstuffs, are the principal nutrients that provide energy for the body. If alcoholic beverages are consumed, they too are a source of energy. These substances all contain carbon and hydrogen, which can combine with the inhaled oxygen to form carbon dioxide, which is exhaled, and water, which is eliminated in the urine. In the process, they release energy. They belong to the great division of chemical substances known as organic compounds, all of which contain carbon and hydrogen (and sometimes other substances such as oxygen, nitrogen, sulfur, or phosphorus) and are combustible. Substances such as carbon, hydrogen, oxygen, nitrogen, sulfur, and phosphorus are referred to as elements and are but a few of more than 100 primary substances that cannot be broken down or separated by chemical means into any other substances. Organic compounds such as the fuelstuffs are so important, both in foods and in the body, that some knowledge of their nature and occurrence is necessary for any intelligent study and understanding of nutrition.

The chemists and biologists of the nineteenth century, particularly Justus von Liebig (1803–1873) of Germany, gradually worked out the nutritive properties of many foods. They found that protein, which contains nitrogen, is the most essential, and the human body can survive on it alone. The body cannot make protein from carbohydrate or from fat, because these substances do not contain any nitrogen, but it can make the necessary carbohydrates and fats from materials supplied by protein.

Energy

Energy may be defined as the ability to do work. The human body requires energy to perform myriad functions, including the pumping action of the heart in circulating blood; the movement of the diaphragm in breathing; the support of physical activity such as walking, working, and talking; growth, as in the biosynthesis and maintenance of new tissue; the maintenance of body temperature at 98.6 °F or 37 °C; lactation; and many other special activities of a living person. Energy is provided principally by the carbohydrates, fats, and proteins of the diet, but if alcohol is consumed, it must be taken into account because of its relatively high caloric value.

In chemistry and physics, the usual unit for measuring energy is the calorie, the amount of heat required to raise the temperature of 1 gram of water 1 °C. In the United States, food energy, on the other hand, is usually measured in kilocalories (thousands of calories) and is abbreviated to kcalories, kcal, or much less frequently, capitalized as Calories (SGR, 1988, p. 54). In speaking these words in relation to nutrition, they are generally pronounced simply as calories i.e., the "k" is silent, but when written or printed on paper, they should be prefaced by the letter "k" (SGR, 1988, p. 54).

The energy value of foods, that is the energy released when 1 gram combines with oxygen during metabolism in a sort of flameless fire, is known as the heat of combustion or fuel factor. The values for each of the three principal energy-producing nutrients and for alcohol are

> 1 gram of carbohydrate, 4 kcalories
> 1 gram of protein, 4 kcalories
> 1 gram of fat, 9 kcalories
> 1 gram of alcohol, 7 kcalories

Carbohydrates

Carbohydrates are compounds of carbon, hydrogen, and oxygen. With rare exceptions, they contain two atoms of hydrogen for each atom of oxygen. Since this is the same two-to-one proportion as in water, they are called carbohydrates. With but few exceptions, they are synthesized in the leaves of green plants, from carbon dioxide absorbed from the air and water obtained through the root system of the plant. Sunlight is necessary for the synthesis to occur. Sugars and starches are important carbohydrates formed in this way. Common sources are potatoes, cereals (such as wheat, rice, oats, and barley), fruit, cane or beet sugar, honey, syrup, molasses, and flour products (such as bread, rolls, cakes, pastries, macaroni, noodles, spaghetti). Carbohydrates can be subdivided into three groups. They are known as simple sugars or monosaccharides (i.e., one sugar group per molecule); disaccharides (i.e., two sugar groups per molecule); and polysaccharides (i.e., more than two sugar groups per molecule). A molecule is the smallest part of a compound that can exist independently. The divisions are important to an understanding of nutrition because the more complex carbohydrates, when eaten, must be broken down into the simple sugars of which they are composed before they can be absorbed and utilized by the body.

The carbohydrates most important in nutrition and the divisions to which they belong are as follows:

1. Glucose, fructose, and galactose—monosaccharides or simple sugars.
2. Sucrose, maltose, and lactose—disaccharides or double sugars.
3. Starch, glycogen, and cellulose—polysaccharides or complex carbohydrates.

Because most sugars are very soluble in water, they are the form in which plants transport carbohydrates, in the sap, from one part of the plant to another or sequester it for temporary use in the juices of the stems and fruits; hence, glucose, fructose, and sucrose are found chiefly in plant juices and in fruits. The sweet taste of green peas and corn is due to the presence of sugar that is later converted to starch as the immature seed ripens; in some fruits (e.g., bananas), starch is present in the unripe fruit and turns to sugar on ripening. Carrots, beets, winter squash, turnips, sweet potatoes, and even onions are vegetables that contain appreciable amounts of sugars. In the United States, sugar for table use and cooking is obtained chiefly from the juices of sugar cane and beets.

Chemically, cane sugar, beet sugar, and maple sugar are all sucrose. The sugar derived by chemical treatment of cornstarch, a process known as hydrolysis, is glucose. Fructose and glucose occur in honey in about a 50:50 ratio. The sugar maltose, formed as an intermediate product during the digestion of starch in the body, is also found in germinated grains (called malt), especially from barley, and in products from partially hydrolyzed starch, which are major components of malted breakfast cereals and malted milk. Lactose, which occurs in the milk of all mammals, is secreted as a source of energy for the young of the species. On digestion, lactose is broken down (hydrolyzed) into equal parts of glucose and galactose. Disaccharides must be broken down into the simple sugars comprising them before they can be used by the body.

Starch is formed in plants by the union of many hundreds of molecules of glucose and is the carbohydrate stored in the form of granules in their seeds, tubers, or roots. Such large molecules have no sweet taste and are not soluble in water. When subjected to moist heat, as in cooking, starch granules absorb water, swell, and are ruptured, forming a colloidal solution, which is more easily digested. Before starch can be used as a source of energy in the body, it must first be broken down into molecules of glucose, of which it is composed. Major sources of starch are grains and all products made from them, such as breads, breakfast cereals, macaroni, cakes, legumes (beans and peas), and some tuber and root vegetables, such as potatoes and sweet potatoes.

Glycogen at one time was called "animal starch" because it is the polysaccharide stored in selective animal tissues in some ways analogous to the storing of starch in plant tissues. Only moderate amounts of glycogen are stored in the liver and muscle tissues, and it is used up during periods of muscular work or fasting. When needed, it is broken down to yield glucose molecules, which are then oxidized in the body to yield energy. Since animals have limited ability to store carbohydrates, very little of it is found in foods of animal origin, such as muscle meats.

Cellulose is also a polysaccharide composed of glucose units, but is practically indigestible by man. The glucose molecules are attached to each other in a way different from that in starch or glycogen, and man lacks the digestive ability to break it down into glucose molecules. It makes up the bulk of the structural or fibrous parts of plants (leaves, stems, roots, and seed and fruit coverings) and also the cell walls. Because it remains undigested, cellulose adds dietary fiber to the food residues in the intestinal tract and promotes their evacuation in the feces. This topic is discussed in detail in Chapter 5.

Foods Rich in Carbohydrate

Starch from corn is almost pure complex carbohydrate. Highly milled rice or wheat flour is more than two thirds starch, but also contains about 7.5 to 11 percent protein. Dry peas and beans contain approximately 60 percent starch and more than 20 percent protein. Soybeans contain less starch and more protein and fat. The grains, such as wheat, corn, rice, oats, rye, barley, and dry products made from them, are rich in starch (45 to 85 percent). Potatoes, cereal puddings such as rice and those with a cornstarch base, cooked legumes, and cereals have a higher and variable water content, so may range in carbohydrate from 10 to 20 percent.

Foods with high sugar content (60 to 100 percent) include table sugar, honey, syrups, candies, jams, jellies, preserves, and dried fruits (dates, figs, raisins, prunes, apricots); others containing appreciable amounts are ripe fresh fruits (9 to 23 percent) and traditional soft drinks (9 to 12 percent). Taken in considerable quantities, these last two sources may contribute appreciable amounts of energy (kcalories) to the diet.

The main contributions to the diet of carbohydrate-rich foods may be summarized as follows: They provide an economical energy supply, may furnish some proteins, minerals, and vitamins (grains and legumes), add flavor to foods and beverages (sugar, fruits, and berries), are pleasant to the taste, are relatively easy to prepare, and can be stored for long periods without refrigeration. Complex carbohydrates (whole grains, bread, potatoes, legumes, bananas, and dry ready-to-eat cereals) are digested over a period of hours and so satisfy hunger for a longer time than the simple sugars.

Lipids and Fats

Lipids are a large class of natural, fatlike substances, such as fats, oils, and waxes, that are lighter than water and insoluble in it, but are soluble in organic solvents such as ether, chloroform, and benzene. The word "lipid" does not describe a specific chemical substance, but a convenient category of substances based on solubility.

Simple fats, which represent a subgroup of lipids, are the most important lipids as far as human nutrition is concerned. They are formed by the union of three molecules of substances called fatty acids with one molecule of another substance called glycerol. Each fatty acid is a chain of carbon atoms to which hydrogen atoms are attached. At the end of the chain, where it is attached to the glycerol molecule, there is an acid (carboxyl) group. As the chain becomes longer, the fatty acids become less soluble. Examples of fatty acids are butyric acid, a four-carbon chain found in butter, and linoleic acid, an 18-carbon chain found in corn oil and soybean oil.

Unlike the carbohydrates, fats contain much less oxygen per molecule in proportion to the amount of carbon and hydrogen. They are a highly concentrated store of potential energy and, when metabolized in the body, combine with more oxygen and release more energy than either carbohydrates or amino acids from protein. They represent the chief form in which animals and people store energy for future use.

Some plants store fats in fruits, seeds, seed germs, or nuts, as evidenced by such common dietary liquid fats as the following oils: corn, soybean, cottonseed, olive, peanut, canola, sunflower, safflower, and sesame. Foods high in fat include butter, lard, fatty meats and fish, cream, whole milk and whole milk cheeses, and egg yolk. Butter fat, fish oils, and the fat in egg yolk are examples of fats that also serve as carriers for fat-soluble vitamins, for example, vitamins A and D.

The physical properties of fats are important in nutrition and are related to their composition. Because fats are insoluble in and lighter than water, if mixed with it, they will float to the surface on standing. Each fat has a characteristic melting point. Those that are liquid at body temperature are more easily digested than those that have higher melting points. As used in nutrition, the word "oil" simply means a fat that is in a liquid state at room temperature. Solid fats, such as butter and lard, melt on slight heating, whereas mutton and beef fat (suet) have the highest melting point among the meat fats, all of which are solid at room temperature.

The difference in consistency, that is relative softness or hardness at room temperature, is reflected in the melting points of the fats and, in large part, is due to differences in the kinds of fatty acids incorporated into the structure of the fats. Fats that are liquid at room temperature, such as vegetable oils and fish oils, contain fatty acids whose hydrocarbon chains have double bonds between some of the carbon atoms in the chain, a condition referred to as unsaturated. These oils can be changed to saturated fats by the addition of hydrogen, accomplished in the presence of a catalyst such as powdered nickel. A catalyst is a substance that influences the speed of a chemical reaction without itself being used up. The addition of hydrogen to liquid fats, a process called hydrogenation, is utilized to produce vegetable shortenings. Margarine, a solid product, may be prepared from corn oil, a liquid, by the hydrogenation process and the addition of coloring and flavoring agents, plus vitamins A and D. It is evident that liquid fats (oils) generally contain unsaturated fatty acids with one or more double bonds. Solid fats contain saturated fatty acids; that is, they will not hold any more hydrogen. Coconut oil is an exception to the general rule in that it is a liquid at room temperature, but the principal fatty acid in its molecule (myristic acid) is saturated. Palm and palm kernel oil also have high percentages of saturated fatty acids (see Table 2.1). Further discussion of saturated and unsaturated fats will be found in Chapter 6, which deals with atherosclerosis and cardiovascular disease.

Linoleic acid, a common unsaturated fatty acid, is found in high concentration in oils obtained from flax seed, corn, cottonseed, peanuts, and soybeans. It is called the essential fatty acid because it is required for the complete nutrition of the human body. Linoleic acid cannot be synthesized by the body and must therefore be supplied from the food we eat.

In the United States, the fat content of the average diet has increased from 32 percent of total kcalories in 1910 to more than 37 percent (13 percent being from saturated fat) at the present time (SGR, 1988). About two thirds of these fats are derived from animal sources, and one third, from plant oils. When incorporated into foods, fats provide prized flavor and satiety value. The flavor varies with the kind of fat used, individual preferences being based largely on habit. The satiety value of fats depends on the fact that they slow

Table 2.1. Fats and Oils Comparison Chart

Product (1 tablespoon)	Saturated fatty acids (grams)	Cholesterol (milligrams)	Polyunsaturated fatty acids (grams)	Monounsaturated fatty acids (grams)
Rapeseed oil (canola oil)	0.9	0	4.5	7.6
Safflower oil	1.2	0	10.1	1.6
Sunflower oil	1.4	0	5.5	6.2
Peanut butter, smooth	1.5	0	2.3	3.7
Corn oil	1.7	0	8.0	3.3
Olive oil	1.8	0	1.1	9.9
Hydrogenated sunflower oil	1.8	0	4.9	6.3
Margarine, liquid, bottled	1.8	0	5.1	3.9
Margarine, soft, tub	1.8	0	3.9	4.8
Sesame oil	1.9	0	5.7	5.4
Soybean oil	2.0	0	7.9	3.2
Margarine, stick	2.1	0	3.6	5.1
Peanut oil	2.3	0	4.3	6.2
Cottonseed oil	3.5	0	7.1	2.4
Lard	5.0	12	1.4	5.8
Beef tallow	6.4	14	0.5	5.3
Palm oil	6.7	0	1.3	5.0
Butter	7.1	31	0.4	3.3
Cocoa butter	8.1	0	0.4	4.5
Palm kernel oil	11.1	0	0.2	1.5
Coconut oil	11.8	0	0.2	0.8

SOURCE: *Eating to Lower Your High Blood Cholesterol.* NIH Publication No. 89-2920; U.S. Dept. of Health and Human Services, Public Health Service, National Institutes of Health, Washington, DC. Reprinted June, 1990.

down the rate of digestion and the emptying time of the stomach; meals that contain considerable fat remain in the stomach for a longer time and so prevent the early recurrence of "hunger pangs" that occur when it is empty.

Cardiovascular diseases are those involving the heart and blood vessels, including angina pectoris, heart attack, hypertension, stroke, and intermittent claudication or severe pain in calf muscles that occurs on walking. Most people who suffer from these diseases have developed widespread fatty plaques on the inside surfaces of the arteries, a condition referred to as atherosclerosis. Although atherosclerosis is a multifactorial disease, there is strong evidence that a diet high in saturated fat and cholesterol is a major factor in its etiology and that lowering the dietary levels of these two substances may retard or even reverse the progress of the disease. Based on this information, several major health-related associations, including the American Heart Association, have recommended a change in diet aimed at lowering dietary cholesterol and saturated fat in the hope of reducing the risk of heart attack. As a sound basis for healthful living, it is advised that the intake of total dietary fat be reduced from the current average of approximately 37 percent to a level of no more than 30 percent of total kcalories, and in particular, that the intake of saturated fat be reduced. In addition, it is recommended that the consumption of fruits, vegetables, and whole grains be increased, that the use of salt-cured, salt-pickled, and smoked foods be used only in moderation, and that if alcoholic beverages are used at all, they should also be in moderation. Cholesterol is biosynthesized naturally by the body and also enters the blood from foods such as eggs, butter, bacon, and bakery goods, to name only a few. Atherosclerosis and allied problems such as high blood pressure, heart attack, and stroke are discussed in greater detail in Chapter 6.

When the intake of fuel foodstuffs exceeds current body needs for energy, the excess is stored in the form of fatty tissues, usually under the skin, or about the hips and/or waist. In the early ages of mankind, when a full meal might have had to suffice for several days, a comfortable deposit of fat might have served a useful purpose as a reserve store of fuel to be drawn on in time of prolonged hunger. Moderate deposits of fatty tissue do serve to support organs and protect them from injury, and to prevent undue loss of heat from the body surface, since fat is a poor conductor of heat. An overfed person continues to store fat he may never need to use as body fuel. Such excessive fat deposits cause undesirable weight gain and place an undue strain on the heart and other vital organs. Life insurance figures show that overweight people have a lower life expectancy than those who maintain normal weight for their height and age (SGR, 1988).

Actually, in some instances, fat deposits in the human body may be either advantageous or disadvantageous, according to whether they are moderate or excessive and even, to some extent, depending on their location, that is to say whether the fat is deposited over the hips or over the belly (Ostlund *et al.*, 1990). In more mundane words, as women grow older, they tend to put on weight around the hips, while men are more prone to larger bellies. It appears that it is not so much how fat a person is, but where the fat is located. Fat around the hips is associated with reduced risk of heart disease, while belly fat is associated with increased risk of heart disease.

Fatty Foods

Some typical fat-rich foods that are almost pure fat or very high in fat are oils of plant origin (such as olive oil, corn oil, cottonseed oil, sunflower seed oil) and butter, margarine, and shortenings such as lard. Foods whose fat content may range from 20 to 50 percent include full-milk cheeses, fatty meats and poultry, chocolate, nuts, and peanut butter. Olives and avocadoes are the only common fruits that are fairly rich in fat.

To summarize the positive qualities that can be associated with fat and fat-rich foods, they are useful in the diet for three main reasons: first, as a concentrated form of body fuel; second, for flavor and satiety value; and third, as carriers of the fat-soluble vitamins.

Lipoids

These substances resemble fats in physical properties, for example, their insolubility in water and a fatty feel to the touch. They are usually associated with fats in the body and are important nutritionally. The class of compounds known as sterols falls into this category. Cholesterol is a specific example. It has a very important role as a major risk factor in the etiology of atherosclerosis, which is discussed in Chapter 6. Cholesterol is important as a precursor (i.e., a sort of mother substance) for vitamin D, the sex hormones, and several important hormones produced by the outer layer of the adrenal glands, which are adjacent to the kidneys. It is also an important constituent of all cell membranes.

Proteins

Proteins are larger and more complex molecules than either carbohydrates or fats. They contain the elements nitrogen (approximately 16 percent), carbon, hydrogen, oxygen, and often smaller amounts of sulfur, phosphorus, iron, iodine, copper, and zinc. They are the chief constituents of all the cells of the body and are essential for the growth, maintenance, and repair of tissues. They are components of skin, hair, and nails as well as connecting and supporting tissue. Plants can synthesize proteins from simple nitrogen-containing substances and water from the soil, combined with carbon dioxide from the air. Some plants, such as clover, are even able to utilize the nitrogen from the air directly because of special organisms attached to their root systems. Man and animals, on the other hand, must obtain their protein from plants or from other animals that, in turn, have obtained it from plants. Proteins are involved in an array of functions such as the catalysis of biochemical reactions in the body (enzymes), the control of metabolic processes (hormones), the transportation of oxygen in the blood (hemoglobin), the body's defense against infection (antibodies), the transmission of nerve impulses (nerves), muscular activity (contraction), and regulation of the genetic material [deoxyribonucleic acid (DNA)].

The large molecules of the proteins are essentially a kind of "mosaic" made up of large numbers of relatively simple nitrogen-containing compounds called amino acids, which are sometimes called "the building blocks of life." Adding to the complexity of the picture, many different amino acids may be combined in a single protein molecule, linked together in an intricate pattern characteristic of the individual protein. Twenty different amino acids are commonly found in proteins, and each molecule of a protein may contain several hundred of these units. It should not be surprising then, that there are thousands of different proteins, special ones assembled by each plant or animal species for specific purposes. Animals and people must break down the food proteins by digestion to yield the amino acid units from which they are built, and then reassemble them in such a way as to make the specific protein characteristic of their particular muscle tissue, gland tissue, blood, or skin.

Although the body must get its nitrogen in the form of amino acids provided by the digestion of food proteins, not all of the 20 amino acids have to be furnished by the food. Some of the simpler ones can be formed in the tissues from what we might call the scraps left over when other amino acids are used. These nitrogen-containing fragments are united with some simple substances formed in the course of tissue oxidation of carbohydrates, and thus the nucleus of one amino acid may be used to build another. Certain amino acids that cannot be synthesized in the body, or are made in inadequate amounts, must be supplied in the food and are called essential amino acids. According to the 1989 edition of the *Recommended Dietary Allowances* (RDA, 1989), nine amino acids are listed as essential for humans, but the number for other species may be larger or smaller. The list for humans is histidine, isoleucine, leucine, lysine, methionine, phenylalanine, threonine, tryptophan, and valine.

Proteins that furnish a well-balanced and complete mixture of amino acids, suitable for tissue building, are said to be of high biological value. Other proteins, which may contain only small amounts or none of one or more amino acids, are said to be of lower biological value, partially incomplete, and incomplete or deficient (according to whether they are low or completely lacking in some special amino acid).

Proteins can serve as a source of energy for the body whenever an insufficient amount of carbohydrate and fat is provided in the diet to meet the body's needs for energy. The primary use of proteins, however, is for building or repair of tissues; hence, they are necessary for growth and are needed in relatively larger amounts by children, young people, and pregnant women.

Protein in Foods

Although protein is a very valuable substance for both plants and animals, it is not required or stored in large amounts. In contrast to carbohydrates and fats, which can be stored in various places in the body, either as glycogen in the liver and muscles or as fat in the fat depots when consumed in amounts exceeding the immediate needs of the body, neither proteins nor amino acids are stored. When proteins are eaten in amounts exceeding the immediate needs of the body, the excess amino acids are stripped of their nitrogen in the liver, and the hydrocarbon residues are converted either to glucose and stored as glycogen in the usual places, or further converted to fat and stored as such. The message, then, is that an adult in normal health can use a rather modest and steady amount of protein-containing food each day, but cannot store excess amounts of protein or amino acids for later retrieval as can be done with carbohydrates and fat. Even foods that are relatively rich in protein contain only one sixth to one third protein (e.g., 16 to 33 percent in most meats, legumes, nuts, and cheeses). Milk contains small amounts of all three fuel foodstuffs, as well as several minerals and vitamins, but when taken with cereal products, may contribute appreciably to the protein supply when used in quantity.

In general, the proteins in foods of animal origin are superior in quality or of higher biological value than those in vegetable foods (i.e., they furnish a better balanced and more complete mix of amino acids). However, the proteins in one food can supplement those in another in their amino acid contributions. Even the incomplete proteins in many vegetable foods contribute valuable amino acids, and some vegetable proteins (e.g., those in soybeans and peanuts) are of high biological value.

For adequate growth in childhood, the protein in the diet should come from a wide variety of foods, and as much as one third of it should be of high biological value, usually furnished by foods of animal origin such as meat, fish, poultry, eggs, milk, and milk products. Older persons, too, need a balanced diet, with adequate protein but fewer kcalories. Variety becomes important because taste, smell, and other sensations diminish somewhat with age, and appetite may require stimulation (Chauhan et al., 1987).

Protein Quality

Proteins in food vary widely in the efficiency with which they can be used in the body, a characteristic referred to as the quality of the protein. The quality is dependent on the kinds and amounts of amino acids present in foods. A complete protein is one that contains all the essential amino acids in sufficient quantities for maintenance of the body and a normal rate of growth. It may or may not contain the nonessential amino acids. Such proteins are described as having a high biological value. Eggs, meat, poultry, fish, and milk all contain complete protein although not identical in quality. Soybeans, wheat germ, and dried yeast have a biological value somewhat less than that of proteins from animal sources. Proteins deficient in one or more essential amino acids are called incomplete proteins. Zein, one of the proteins from corn, for example, lacks tryptophan and lysine; gelatin also lacks tryptophan and contains no valine or threonine.

When the protein in food is of poor quality, the body discards many of the amino acids as far as protein synthesis is concerned. The amino groups of the amino acids, the parts of the molecules that contain the nitrogen, are stripped of their nitrogen in the liver, and the nitrogen is then excreted in the urine as urea. The remainder of the amino acid molecules are converted to glucose and fat. The amount of urea excreted in the urine can thus serve as a measure of the number of amino acids that are wasted, that is, not utilized to build protein. The protein in egg white has been selected as reference protein by the Food and Agriculture Organization of the United Nations and the World Health Organization. It represents a standard of high quality to which other proteins can be compared and is assigned a value of 100. On this scale, milk protein has a value of 60. When a person drinks milk, only 60 percent of the amino acids in its protein is utilized to build human protein; the other 40 percent ends up being used for energy purposes or being stored in the body as glycogen or fat.

The digestibility of proteins varies widely and thus influences the bioavailability of the amino acids. The protein in egg white is very digestible since 97 percent of the amino acids are freed for absorption in the gastrointestinal tract. The proteins in meats, poultry, fish, and milk are also digested very well. Wheat and corn proteins are not far behind, but legumes and other vegetable proteins are digested less readily. Cooking usually improves digestibility (e.g., when milk is heated to prepare evaporated milk or powdered milk). The roasting of peanuts also improves their digestibility, and the controlled mild heating of soybeans is found to improve protein quality by increasing the available methionine, an amino acid, as compared to raw soybeans, in which the available methionine is somewhat low. Mild heating also inactivates an enzyme in navy beans and soybeans that inhibits the important digestive action of trypsin in the stomach.

Complementary Proteins

The four essential amino acids most often in short supply in plant proteins are lysine, methionine, threonine, and tryptophan. To make effective use of such proteins, several courses of action are feasible. They may be fed simultaneously with small amounts of a complete protein, mixtures of several plant foods may be prepared to yield all the required amino acids in suitable amounts, or synthetic amino acids may be added to the food to correct the deficiency.

If plant proteins are fed together with a small amount of animal protein, the quality of the mixture may be improved a great deal. Some typical combinations of plant and animal proteins that supplement or complement each other are cereal and milk; macaroni and cheese; eggs and toast; meat, cheese, or egg sandwiches; and peanut butter with whole wheat bread.

Fuelstuff Status and the Older Person

Total energy expenditure in the human body includes the energy expended at rest, in physical activity, and as a result of energy production by the cells of the body. These components, in turn, are affected by several variables, including age, body size and composition, genetic factors, energy intake, physiological state (e.g., growth, pregnancy, lactation), coexisting pathological conditions, and ambient temperature (RDA, 1989).

National dietary and food-consumption surveys have reported lower energy intakes among older persons than among younger adults (DHEW, 1979; DHHS, 1983; USDA, 1984), a finding that has been supported by several smaller studies. A convenient rule of thumb states that a 5-percent reduction in caloric needs per decade occurs from age 55 to 75, and a 7-percent reduction per decade, after age 75. The decline in energy expenditure is attributed to reduced physical activity and to a decline in basal energy metabolism as a result of a reduction in lean body mass with age. As the number of active cells in each organ decreases with age, a reduction in the body's overall metabolic rate ensues.

Despite the fact that it is difficult to interpret dietary intake studies of older Americans because of methodological problems, existing studies consistently reveal decreases in energy intake with age that may also be influenced by income, race, food preferences, and drug use (SGR, 1988, p. 605). A low-calorie diet may not impair health as long as the nutrient density of the diet is high and can provide adequate amounts of essential nutrients (SGR, 1988).

The fact that the level of obesity among older persons is increasing, as indicated by higher weight-for-height with age (Frisancho, 1984), awaits a complete explanation. Whether the inconsistency between reported low energy intake and increasing body weight is due to loss of height with age (Bowman and Rosenberg, 1982), lack of physical activity, measurement errors, or inappropriate standards has not been settled.

Nature has not provided any clear physiological signal, other than hunger, as to whether or not a person should ingest particular proteins, carbohydrates, fats, vitamins, or minerals. It sometimes does provide such a signal as thirst when water is required, although the signal often weakens in later years. The main dietary sources of energy are carbohydrates, along with fat and protein, and the principal dietary carbohydrates are sugars and complex carbohydrates. The sugars include monosaccharides, such as glucose and fructose, and disaccharides, such as sucrose (table sugar), maltose, and lactose (milk sugar). Complex carbohydrates (polysaccharides) include starches and dietary fibers. It is important for older people to use a variety of complex carbohydrate foods because of the fiber that they contain, the slow release of glucose that they provide, and the many vitamins and minerals that they contain. Surveys reveal that older people too often omit fruits and vegetables from their diet, partly because of the cost, but also because of the difficulties of preparing and storing them.

Protein

The nutrient requirements of the older person are basically the same as those of the younger adult (RDA, 1989, p. 58). The same nutrients are essential throughout the life cycle (carbohydrates, proteins, fats, minerals, vitamins, and water), but the relative amounts will vary depending on the person's age, gender, level of activity, and individual needs. The concept of individual needs, dubbed "biochemical individuality" by Roger Williams, the discoverer of pantothenic acid, a B vitamin, is most relevant for the elderly, since such a large percentage of them have one or more chronic disorders that contribute to their individual nutritional needs. The older person has to obtain the essential amino acids from less food, so it is important that the protein be of high quality (i.e., meat, fish, eggs, milk, and milk products). Adequate complex carbohydrates should be included in the diet to protect the protein from being used for energy. There is very little consistent data available on which to base recommendations for protein intake in older people. Nutrient requirements for older people have been derived largely by extrapolation of data on young adults (Guthrie, 1988; Wright et al., 1991; Morley, 1986).

A review of the earlier literature on the protein requirements of man was published by Irwin and Hegsted (1971). Later studies on protein requirements for healthy older persons were published, with inconsistent results (Zanni et al., 1979; Uauy et al., 1978a, b; Cheng et al., 1978; Gersovitz et al., 1982; Munro et al., 1987). The current recommended dietary allowance for reference protein (egg, meat, fish, or milk) is the same for elderly adults as for young adults, 0.75 g/kg (RDA, 1989). For a man weighing 174 lbs and a woman weighing 138 lbs, this translates into 2.1 and 1.7 oz of pure protein per day, respectively. For foods (meat, fish, etc.) containing protein, and using the most generous conversion factor of 6, this amounts to about 12 oz for men and 10 oz for women per day.

There is some evidence to indicate that the efficiency of nitrogen utilization is reduced by gastrointestinal problems, infection, and metabolic abnormalities, thus causing increased nitrogen excretion.

If nitrogen balance is indeed affected by such factors, older people on marginal intake would be vulnerable. Low intake of protein by older people can often be traced to the high cost of meats, insufficient use of milk and milk products, dental problems such as poor chewing ability, inadequate absorption of nutrients from the intestinal tract, and a poor understanding of elemental nutrition principles.

Fat

As stated earlier, caloric requirements of older people generally decrease with increasing age. The caloric intake should be in balance with the energy expenditure. If, however, a person's caloric intake was not excessive during earlier decades, it does not have to be reduced because of increased age alone. The objective of caloric restriction is to prevent overweight and obesity. If fewer kcalories are needed, less fat and carbohydrates should be eaten.

To stay within the limited energy kcalorie allowance recommended for older adults, it would be difficult to obtain the vitamins and minerals that come from protein-rich complex carbohydrate foods if too high a percentage of the kcalories were derived from the fat. On the other hand, if fat kcalories are restricted too severely, the fat-soluble vitamins and essential linoleic acid may be deficient.

The role of dietary fats in the development of heart disease, obesity, and cancer is discussed in other chapters of this book. Suffice it to say that a decrease in the average consumption of fat by Americans from its present level of approximately 36 percent of kcalories appears desirable (RDA, 1989). Following a comprehensive evaluation of the evidence, the Food and Nutrition Board's Committee on Diet and Health recommended that the fat content of the diet not exceed 30 percent of caloric intake, that less than 10 percent of kcalories should be provided from saturated fatty acids, and that dietary cholesterol should be less than 300 mg per day (NRC, 1989).

3

Nutrient Requirements
Vitamins and Minerals

For many centuries, in fact, from the time of Hippocrates, foodstuffs were believed to contain a vital substance without which they were unsatisfactory as foods. The nature of the vital substance was never well defined. This was the generally held view until about 1827 when the English physician, William Prout, suggested that organic foods could be divided into three categories, which we would now recognize as proteins, carbohydrates, and fats. For many decades afterward, these three classes of substances, along with water and the ash remaining after burning a food sample, were generally believed to be the only essential nutrients. It was also believed that all proteins were nutritionally alike, that the various carbohydrates and fats were equivalent as far as foods were concerned, and that the best diet for man and animals was one that contained these substances in the highest amounts.

One of the earliest recorded accounts supporting the likely presence of small amounts of unidentified, but essential food accessory substances in ordinary foods was published in 1881, in Germany. In this historic paper, N. Lunin reported on work he had completed in 1881, in Estonia, as part of a doctoral dissertation. He found that mice remained healthy when fed milk alone, but sickened and died when fed an artificial mixture of all the purified substances then known in milk (casein, lactose, milk fat, milk ash, and water in the proportions present in milk). On the basis of his observations, Lunin wrote that other organic substances indispensable for nutrition must be present in a natural food such as milk, besides casein, lactose, fat, and inorganic salts. Unfortunately, because of the general acceptance at the time by the scientific and medical community of Louis Pasteur's theory that diseases were caused by germs, very little attention was paid to the work of the young scientist. In fairness to the prevailing sentiment among investigators of that period, no rational explanation had been proposed as to why a minor food component should play such a vital role in the life of experimental animals.

As we look back on the situation from our present vantage point, it is evident that the science and techniques of chemistry were not yet an adequate part of the training and laboratory skills of investigators who were becoming interested in nutrition and food sciences. It would be more than three decades before they would be so equipped.

Actually, in ancient times, medical lore promoted particular foods based on empirical tests as having the power to prevent or cure specific diseases (e.g., Hippocrates, himself, advocated eating liver as a cure for night blindness). We now know, of course, that liver is an excellent source of vitamin A. Many centuries later, during the days of sailing ships, a disease now called scurvy was a major problem on long ocean voyages. As the disease progresses, the capillaries become fragile, gums bleed, teeth loosen, wounds heal with difficulty, and eventually the person weakens and dies. Not infrequently, more than half of a ship's crew was lost. Since ships lacked refrigeration, they carried nonspoilable food, such as salt pork and unleavened bread, made in hard, large wafers and known as hardtack. For hundreds of years, the possible connection between the rations of the sailors and the disease failed to occur to the providers of the food.

On his second voyage to Canada, the French explorer Jacques Cartier sailed up the St. Lawrence river and spent the winter of 1535–1536 at the site of the present city of Quebec. Many of his men were stricken with scurvy, and 25 died of the disease. Some friendly Indians suggested that the men prepare and drink a tea made by steeping the growing tips of the arbor vitae tree (*Thuja occidentalis*) in hot water. They did as directed, and the scurvy was cured. Very much later, it was shown that the needles of this tree contain about 50 mg of vitamin C per 100 grams.

More than 200 years later, in 1753, the Scottish naval physician James Lind published a treatise on scurvy, reviewing the incidence of the disease and reporting on experiments he himself had conducted on sailors. By adding small amounts of fresh fruit and vegetables to the sailors' diet, he was able to reverse the course of the disease and to cure severe cases within a week. Citrus fruits were the most effective. By 1795, the British Admiralty ordered that sailors be provided a daily ration of fresh lime juice, and scurvy ceased to be a major problem. To this day, British sailors are sometimes referred to as "limeys" and the Thames area in London where the crates of limes were stored is still called Limehouse.

A century later, in 1891, Admiral Takaki of the Japanese navy replaced the monotony of rice on his ships by a broader diet. As a result, the scourge of the disease known as beriberi was brought under control in the Japanese navy.

Between 1905 and 1912, F.G. Hopkins in England carried out a series of investigations on rats very similar to those described earlier by Lunin. His experimental results were published in detail in 1912. When he added about a third of a teaspoonful of milk for each rat per day to their diet of purified protein, fat, and carbohydrate plus necessary minerals, the rats lived, rather than died. An alcoholic extract of dried milk allowed the animals on purified diets to live and grow, but the ash from milk was not effective. By these later tests, Hopkins demonstrated that, since the vital unknown food accessory factors dissolved in alcohol, they were organic in nature, because inorganic substances would not have been soluble in alcohol. For establishing that substances we now call vitamins really exist, Hopkins was later to share a Nobel prize with Eijkman, whose work is discussed subsequently.

Vitamins

The pace of research in the field of essential accessory food factors increased steadily in several European countries and the United States. The contribution of a young Polish biochemist, Casimir Funk, then (1911) working at the Lister Institute of London, proved memorable in several ways. He was trying to confirm the results reported much earlier by a Dutch physician, Christiaan Eijkman, that an elusive substance in rice bran had the ability to cure the condition, often fatal, known as beriberi. It was endemic in the Netherlands Indies at that time and even today, when its cause is known, beriberi still kills thousands of people every year. Funk extracted from rice polishings a white crystalline substance that had the power to cure beriberi. He thus confirmed what, at that time, was only a hypothesis, that disease (particularly beriberi) could be caused by the lack of a dietary constituent. He proposed that a lack of specific essential accessory food factors was the cause of beriberi, scurvy, pellagra, and finally rickets and, in 1912, introduced the word "vitamine" to describe them (Funk, 1912). In 1920, the word was shortened to "vitamin" to avoid the inference that all essential accessory food factors were varieties of the chemical substances known as amines. Funk, incidentally, wrote the first complete treatise on vitamins (1914), which was reprinted in English in 1922. Within a few years following the publication of Funk's vitamin hypothesis, there was a sustained effort underway in this general area of research by individual investigators in many laboratories throughout the world. They reported on further studies aimed at proving the presence of elusive accessory food factors necessary for the growth and reproduction of animals, all with ever-increasing sophistication and specificity of action.

The initial discovery of vitamins cannot be credited to any one person, but can be shared by several investigators from different countries who over a period of about four decades, beginning in 1880 with the work of Lunin, laid the groundwork. The actual discovery of the individual vitamins, their isolation, and their synthesis extended from 1921, with the discovery of vitamin B_1 (thiamin), to 1955 with the synthesis of vitamin B_{12} (cobalamin). The overall effort is one of the proudest achievements of biochemical and nutritional research. In this brief account, only the names of the major players and their contributions have been included.

Vitamin deficiency diseases due primarily to an inadequate dietary supply of specific nutrients are now relatively rare in the United States and other developed countries, although they remain common in many developing nations. However, these deficiencies are encountered secondary to numerous pathologic conditions both in this country and elsewhere.

The practical benefits to people flowing from the basic scientific research on vitamins has helped in a major way to ensure a healthier population. This accomplishment is made evident by the constant setting of new athletic records in every field of sport, year after year, and the ever-increasing length of the useful life span in countries where the knowledge is applied.

What is a Vitamin?

Vitamins are organic substances, other than essential amino acids or fatty acids, that are necessary in small amounts in the diet of man and animals for normal growth, maintenance of health, and reproduction. With but few exceptions, they cannot be synthesized by the body, at least in sufficient quantity, and must therefore be obtained from the diet or from dietary supplements.

Vitamins are a heterogenous group of substances that bear almost no resemblance to each other either chemically or in their physiological action. A vitamin must always be defined with respect to a given animal or to man. To illustrate the point, vitamin C is a necessary substance for all animals; however, most animals synthesize it. Man, other primates, and the guinea pig, on the other hand, are unable to synthesize vitamin C. For them, vitamin C is, therefore, a vitamin, but for other animals it is not. Vitamins are not energy sources for the body, but rather catalyze energy release from carbohydrates, fats, and proteins. No single food contains all the vitamins in adequate amounts.

Vitamins can, most simply, be divided into two categories based on the physical property of solubility either in water, on the one hand, or in oil, fats, or fat solvents, on the other. The water-soluble vitamins are vitamin C and the B complex or B complex vitamins, which number eight separate and distinct compounds. The B complex vitamins have little in common except that they are soluble in water; all contain nitrogen, and they are all present in relatively large amounts in the liver.

The fat-soluble vitamins A, D, E, and K are found dissolved in the fat of plants and animals. They are absorbed from the gastrointestinal tract along with fat so that anything that interferes with fat absorption, such as the long-time use of mineral oil for constipation or the condition known as steatorrhea (fatty stools) may lead to a deficiency. Since fat-soluble vitamins are stored in the body and are not readily excreted, there is a danger of excessive accumulation when they are ingested in large amounts. This is particularly true for vitamins A and D.

Naming the Vitamins

During the early days of discovery of the individual vitamins, naming them presented some problems because very little was known about their chemistry. They were designated by the letters of the alphabet based either on the order of their discovery or on the first letter of a word readily associated with their role in nutrition [e.g., vitamin K, from the initial letter of the German word for coagulation (koagulation); vitamin K is involved in the coagulation and regulation of blood clotting]. As the individual substances making up the B complex were gradually shown to be specific chemicals, they were named vitamin B_1, vitamin B_2, and so on. Efforts were later made to drop the combined letter and number designation of the B vitamins because it suggested a common structural or functional relationship that, in fact, did not exist. In chemistry and biochemistry, the simple chemical names of the individual substances are now generally used to designate the vitamins, but in nutrition, names such as vitamin C, vitamin B_6, and vitamin B_{12} are still used. Because the formulas are easier to type, there has, in recent years, been a tendency to drop the subscripts and to write them as follows: B_6 becomes B-6; B_{12} becomes B-12.

The last of the known vitamins to be discovered (1948) and isolated as a pure crystalline substance (also 1948) was vitamin B_{12}. It was synthesized in 1955. Since that time, scientists have been able to produce normal growth, good health, and reproductive capacity in laboratory animals by feeding them a synthetic diet containing all the now known nutrients. Also, in treating certain diseases, patients have been maintained for months on nothing but nutrients and fluids given intravenously. The intravenous, or parenteral, solutions consist of water, glucose, electrolytes, amino acids, fat, vitamins, and minerals. The possibility of discovering a new vitamin seems remote, but with the increasingly refined experimental techniques and instrumentation now available to biochemists, it can never be dismissed.

How Vitamins Work

A catalyst is a substance that speeds up a chemical reaction without itself being used up in the reaction. Most of the essential chemical reactions taking place in living tissues require catalysts if they are to occur at a sufficiently rapid pace to be beneficial. The special types of organic catalysts that promote these reactions are called enzymes and coenzymes, the latter acting to aid enzymes in accomplishing their tasks. They often need to be present only in very small amounts because they function repeatedly; they are not used up, but do wear out, and hence have to be replaced on a fairly regular schedule. This is done automatically by biosynthesis in the living body.

Many of the vitamins are present in the body as parts of enzymes and coenzymes that are required to promote some essential reactions. Consider the chemical changes that occur in the products of food following digestion and absorption. The fate of the absorbed food products is either to be incorporated into the body structure or to release energy. The reactions occur in individual cells, each of which contains hundreds of enzymes that catalyze these changes. The majority of these enzymes require the help of coenzymes, most of which are vitamins or vitamin complexes. If the vitamins are not available to form the coenzymes, the sequence of chemical reactions will not proceed, and the product whose change is blocked will accumulate in the tissue or blood. The accumulated intermediate product may be partly responsible for the symptoms associated with the lack of a specific vitamin.

Provitamins are substances that are chemically related to a vitamin, but that have no vitamin activity until they are converted into the active form in the body. Some examples are carotene, an orange hydrocarbon found in carrots, sweet potatoes, and leafy vegetables, which is converted to vitamin A in the intestinal wall; tryptophan, an amino acid that is converted to niacin in the liver; and a substance known as 7-dehydrocholesterol, which is converted to vitamin D when the skin is exposed to the ultraviolet rays from sunlight.

Vitamins in Foods

For several decades (1870–1905), the existence of vitamins escaped the attention of the few investigators who were working in the very neighborhood, scientifically speaking. This happened, first, because the vitamins are present in foods at such low levels compared to carbohydrates, fats, and proteins (i.e., on the order of micrograms to milligrams). Second, the great variety of foods consumed by people for centuries in various countries throughout the world usually provided enough vitamins to prevent a health disaster, so there were no opportunities to become aware of the importance of the mysterious minor food ingredients. It is true that in time of famine, in cities under siege, and during long sea voyages, when the choice of foods was severely restricted, disease ensued, but it took a long time to awaken to the idea that such strange diseases might be due to a lack of some substances in the food. Third, the amounts of these substances in foods were too low to have been easily detected by chemical skills and scientific instrumentation available at the time.

One of the important objectives of food processing is to increase the storage life of the product. Wheat, for example, is refined to yield white flour, partly because whole-grain products have poor keeping qualities. As white bread made up an ever-larger fraction of all bread consumed, poor health due to deficiencies of various vitamins became more evident in the general population. In order to meet these deficiencies in the diet, the U.S. government initiated a program in 1941 to enrich white bread by the addition of thiamin, riboflavin, niacin, and iron. Shortly thereafter, various manufacturers of breakfast cereals began to enrich their products by addition of these same nutrients up to the level found in the whole grains. The legal standards of enrichment upgrade the levels of thiamin, riboflavin, niacin, and iron close to or even above (riboflavin) the levels found in whole wheat bread, but some B complex vitamins and minerals other than iron are also removed by high milling, and they are not replaced.

Vitamin Supplements

Most well-read people today agree with the thesis that, in adult life, good health and a long life depend on, among other important factors, an adequate supply of all required vitamins. Unfortunately, this situation has given rise to an undue concern over the vitamin content of the food they eat. Some promoters of vitamin supplements have mined this concern by creating doubts as to whether adequate amounts of vitamins can be obtained from everyday common foods. As a consequence, this general concern has spawned a $3 billion per year industry in vitamin sales directly to consumers (SGR, 1988).

Although a so-called well-balanced diet will undoubtedly supply all the vitamins healthy people need for the maintenance of good health, some situations may put them at an increased risk for vitamin-insufficiency states. Among those at risk are alcoholics, pregnant women, surgical patients, the elderly in general, people on low-calorie diets, and strict vegetarians. It is sensible in these cases to give consideration to vitamin supplementation, but only after prior consultation with a physician to rule out serious ailments with overlapping symptoms.

During the past three decades or so, there has been a growing tendency to use certain vitamins in megadoses, that is, exceeding ten times the recommended dietary allowances (RDA, 1989). Some reasons given for doing so are to protect against catching a cold, and to live longer and feel better (Pauling, 1986) with vitamin C. Other situations calling for the use of vitamins at megadose levels include the use of large doses (1.5–3 grams/day) of nicotinic acid to lower blood cholesterol levels in human subjects, as first reported by Altchul *et al.* (1955). Later, Canner *et al.* (1986) reported that the administration of nicotinic acid was associated with a reduction in recurrent heart attacks and in long-term total mortality. The nicotinic acid decreases total and low-density lipoprotein (LDL) cholesterol concentrations and increases high-density lipoprotein (HDL) cholesterol concentrations. Although extensively studied, the mechanism of the lipid-lowering effect of nicotinic acid is not yet known. It does not appear to be related to any vitamin coenzyme function because nicotinamide does not have a similar effect, although as vitamins, they are interchangeable. Another example is the treatment of skin disorders with derivatives of vitamin A. These situations, however, most definitely require medical supervision.

Minerals

Like vitamins, minerals are normally present in relatively small amounts in the average diet. The word "mineral," as used in nutrition, refers to inorganic elements (i.e., elements other than those most characteristic of organic compounds, namely, carbon, hydrogen, oxygen, and nitrogen). They are generally found in the noncombustible fraction of food (i.e., the ash that remains when food is burned with oxygen), are widely distributed in nature, and play a vital role in metabolism. They serve as necessary body regulators and essential constituents of body parts and organs. Water, proteins, fats, and a small amount of carbohydrate account for 96 percent of the weight of the human body, and the inorganic elements make up the remaining 4 percent. They range in amount from calcium, which makes up about 2 percent of the average body weight, to elements like iron, copper, cobalt, zinc, and chromium, which are present only in trace amounts.

The list of essential elements now includes calcium, phosphorus, magnesium, sodium, potassium, sulfur, chlorine, chromium, cobalt, copper, fluorine, iodine, iron, manganese, molybdenum, selenium, zinc, and boron. Aluminum, bromine, arsenic, nickel, silicon, strontium, and tin occur consistently in the human body, but there is as yet no generally accepted proof of need. Some of these trace elements that have no essential function gain entrance to the human body through contamination of food, water, and air. Strontium, for example, in the radioactive form, strontium 90, is found in the atmosphere following atomic bomb explosions. It may be carried by the wind for hundreds of miles and contaminates water and food sources, such as milk from cows who eat grass in contaminated areas. The use of the milk poses a hazard for humans because the strontium is laid down with calcium in bones and teeth, although strontium itself is not known to serve any useful purpose for humans.

The term "mineral" or "dietary mineral" is sometimes reserved for those elements that are required in amounts greater than 100 mg/day, while "trace element" is used to designate those that are required in amounts less than 100 mg/day. Under this classification, dietary minerals include compounds of calcium, magnesium, phosphorus, sodium, potassium, sulfur, and chlorine, while trace elements for humans include iron, iodine, copper, manganese, zinc, molybdenum, selenium, fluorine, cobalt, chromium, and boron. Although it has been reported that calcium (RDA, 1989, p. 176) and iron (Pilch and Santi, 1984; Dallman *et al.*, 1984; DeMaeyer *et al.*, 1985) are the two elements most likely to be in short supply in the United States, there is now some concern expressed about possible spotty excessive intakes of iron, from combined intakes of iron-enriched bread, breakfast cereals, and iron supplements (Selby and Friedman, 1988; Stevens *et al.*, 1988).

The importance of an element in body functions bears no direct relationship to the amount present in the body. A trace of an element such as iodine or zinc, for example, can make a critical difference in the health of a person.

Iodine, which is present to the extent of only 0.00004 percent of body weight, is an essential constituent of thyroid hormones. The hormones are iodine derivatives of the amino acid, tyrosine, and regulate the rate of metabolism in all cells of the body. Zinc is present to the extent of only 0.002 percent, yet, as an essential component of the enzyme carbonic anhydrase, it plays a vital role in the maintenance of life. During the very short time of about one second that the blood courses through the capillaries of the lung, it has been estimated that the single atom of zinc associated with a molecule of the enzyme carbonic anhydrase makes contact with more than half a million molecules of carbonic acid. The result is that the carbonic acid molecule is split into one molecule each of water and carbon dioxide. Because of the rapidity of the enzyme's action, the carbon dioxide is freed rapidly enough from its compounds to leave the blood during that brief moment, when it is separated from the air by an extremely thin membrane. The body's ability to purge itself of carbon dioxide through the exhaled air is therefore dependent on the presence of these critically located zinc atoms.

No single food contains all the essential minerals. A diet selected from all the basic four food groups should, however, be adequate to maintain good health in a person free of disease. Among the criteria that must be met for a mineral to be considered essential are marked improvement in the health and growth of experimental animals on addition of the mineral to a purified diet, and unmistakable evidence of deficiency symptoms must follow on removal of the suspect element from a diet containing adequate amounts of all other required dietary constituents.

Functions of Minerals

Minerals are required for several purposes:

1. The functioning of muscle and nerve cells, the permeability of cell membranes and the normal operation of all cells depend on a proper balance, in the form of salts, of the diverse minerals.
2. They play a primary role in the controlled flow of tissue fluids in the body.
3. Several mineral compounds (salts) are of prime importance in controlling the acidity and basicity of body fluids.
4. Certain tissues, such as bones and teeth, have a high mineral content, especially of calcium and phosphorus, which accounts for their hardness and rigidity.
5. Some mineral elements become parts of specialized physiological compounds (e.g., the iron in the hemoglobin of the blood and the iodine in thyroid hormones).
6. Many metallic elements in their ionic form, such as manganese, magnesium, and potassium, are essential components of important enzyme systems in metabolism.

Minerals are not an energy source for the body, but rather, as is the case with vitamins, may catalyze biochemical reactions involving the breakdown, biosynthesis, and rearrangement of molecules of carbohydrates, fats, and proteins, as well as release energy.

The Later Years

Vitamins

Although the levels of specific vitamins in the elderly are often reported to be low, there is no generally acceptable evidence that the need for vitamins increases with age alone. A deficiency of vitamin A and C in older people, for example, has been reported a number of times. The deficiency, however, may have little to do with an increased need of the vitamins, but rather may depend on the relatively high cost of foods rich in vitamins A and C, such as fruits and vegetables, and the large volume of the food that has to be eaten in order to acquire the necessary vitamins, simply more than many older people can consume. Marginal intakes of vitamin C can, of course, readily be changed to a full deficiency by the effects of infection or trauma. The mental confusion sometimes seen in older people may be due to a deficiency of the B vitamins rather than to a loss of brain function (Mayer, 1974). The vitamin E in convenience foods, so much used by the elderly, is partly destroyed by the heat of processing and by oxidation, thus contributing to a deficiency.

Conditions other than elimination of certain food groups from the diet may also lead to deficiencies of vitamins in older people. Laxatives are often used daily, thus reducing the transit time through the intestinal tract so much that the vitamins do not have adequate time to be absorbed. When mineral oil, which is not absorbed by the gastrointestinal tract, is used as a laxative, the problem is further exacerbated because the fat-soluble vitamins A, D, E, and K dissolve in it and are eliminated in the feces. Last, many older people do not get out in the open very often or long enough and therefore fail to benefit from the vitamin D produced by the action of sunlight on the skin.

Some nutritionists believe that the recommended intakes of particular vitamins in the 10th edition of the RDAs (1989) are too low. This is especially so for vitamins E and C. A. Verlangieri, director of the Atherosclerosis Research Laboratory at the University of Mississippi, is reported as having shown that suboptimal daily levels of both vitamins, which he defines as less than 200 mg of E and less than 1000 mg of C, can promote a breakdown in the lining of arteries and can lead to the formation of lesions that collect cholesterol and may block blood flow. He is, moreover, quoted as follows: "By not raising the recommendations, we're underselling the preventive effect of some of these vitamins" (Verlangieri, 1990). J. B. Blumberg of the Human Nutrition Research Center at Tufts University is quoted as follows: "We know enough about the role diet plays in reducing the risk of chronic disease to qualify separate RDAs for older Americans" (Blumberg, 1990; see also Blumberg, 1992). In the same article, critics are said to cite research indicating that older Americans need greater amounts of vitamins B_{12}, which plays a key role in the prevention of anemia, and vitamin B_6, which is necessary for protein synthesis.

The current edition of the *Recommended Dietary Allowances* lists the two top categories of adults as 25 to 50 years and 51 years and older. For the vitamins, the recommended allowances for the two groups are essentially the same, except for thiamin and riboflavin, which are listed in terms of total caloric intake. No evidence that thiamin requirements are increased by aging was observed in a 3-year study of 18 young and 21 old male adults (Horwitt *et al.*, 1948). Also, Iber *et al.* (1982) considered that the thiamin RDA of 0.5 mg per 1000 kcalories is sufficient for those older than 60 years, and this was officially adopted with the provision that a minimum of 1.0 mg/day is recommended, even for those consuming less than 2000 kcalories daily. The recommended allowance for riboflavin for people older than 50 years is 1.4 mg/day for men and 1.2 mg/day for women. In a review of the vitamin requirements of elderly people, Suter and Russell (1987) reiterate that for many vitamins, the available data are limited, and that some subgroups of older people may require higher amounts of vitamin D (those lacking sun exposure) and vitamin B_{12} (persons with chronic gastritis with atrophied mucosa and glands).

It has been suggested that RDAs based only on age may be misleading and that formulas for calculating allowances should include coefficients for specific diseases and laboratory test results (Schneider *et al.*, 1986). Unfortunately, the necessary data for such an approach are simply not available.

Minerals

Iron-deficiency anemia, a disorder prevalent in later years, is characterized by a decrease in hemoglobin in the blood to levels below the normal range. Low levels of hemoglobin may stem from a diet low in protein, as described in Chapter 4, but may also be traced to low levels of iron in the diet. This situation can result from lack of sufficient red meat in the diet and is exacerbated by low intake of fruits and vegetables. An abundance of fruits and vegetables assures a good level of vitamin C, which in turn aids the absorption of iron (Gillooly *et al.*, 1983). Other factors leading to iron deficiency include poor absorption of iron from the food due to lowered secretion of hydrochloric acid in the stomach, chronic blood loss due to the use of medications like aspirin, or to conditions such as stomach ulcers or hemorrhoids. Some dietary and medicinal substances like calcium phosphate, phytic acid from whole-grain breakfast cereals and bran, antacids, and polyphenols in tea may all cause substantial decreases in iron absorption.

Calcium is another mineral often lacking in sufficient amounts in the food during the later years. Serious loss of bone can occur, especially in women who are following a sedentary life-style, before they are even aware of it. Milk is one of the best sources of calcium, but to have any potential for a positive effect, about 5 cups per day (low-fat or preferably skim) would ordinarily be required. Such a suggestion is not likely to generate much enthusiasm among older women, very few of whom use much fresh milk at all because of associated gas problems. For individuals without lactose intolerance, alternatives are powdered skim milk, which can be stirred into many foods, or the use of calcium supplements. This whole issue is discussed in some detail under the topic of osteoporosis (Chapter 11) and of lactose intolerance (Chapter 5).

According to an international study involving more than 10,000 people (Intersalt, 1988), the hypothesis that salt contributes to high blood pressure may be overstated. It has been found that only about half of the people who suffer from hypertension find that their blood pressure is actually influenced by their salt intake. For the rest of the population, there does not appear to be any direct relationship between consumption of salt and hypertension. For people in general, on the other hand, there is no supportable evidence that even very small amounts of salt lead to sodium deficiency (Page, 1976, 1979). It would then seem prudent for older people to lean toward reducing salt intake because of the prevalence of hypertension and congestive heart failure in their age group and the long-standing, if not always proven, association of salt with those conditions. Because many convenience and processed foods, especially the canned soups commonly consumed by older people, are loaded with salt, it would be preferable to use fresh foods as much as possible.

States of mineral insufficiency are likely to be more prevalent than states of vitamin insufficiency. People at increased risk of such insufficiencies include the elderly, pregnant women, vegetarians, persons on certain medications such as diuretics and people living in areas where the soil is deficient in specific minerals. Although vitamins are generally present in foods in similar amounts throughout the world, minerals may be scarce in the soils of certain regions and plentiful in others. This difference is reflected in the agricultural products from the various regions.

In South Dakota, the soil is rich in selenium, while in Ohio, in parts of China, and in New Zealand, the soil is very poor in selenium. In animal experimentation, several diseases have been found to be caused by simultaneous deficiencies of selenium and vitamin E, and they can be prevented or cured by supplements of either selenium or vitamin E, singly (NRC, 1983). Also, Cohen (1987) reported that when selenium was added to the diet of rats and mice, following the administration of known carcinogens, there was a reduction in the incidence of cancer.

A considerable amount of epidemiologic evidence suggests that cancer mortality goes up when the selenium content of soil and thus of crops grown on them goes down (Shamberger et al., 1976; Shamberger, 1986). Shamberger and colleagues found that Rapid City, South Dakota, had the lowest overall cancer mortality rate in the United States, while Ohio had a rate nearly double that of South Dakota.

If a person living in a region where the soil content of selenium was low were contemplating the use of selenium supplements, it would be advisable to discuss the matter with a physician. Overdosing with selenium supplements poses a very real toxic potential. It would be imprudent and nutritionally unwise to consume routinely more than the 70 micrograms upper limit of the Food and Nutrition Board's 1989 safe and adequate daily dietary intake.

Vitamins, Minerals, and Immunity

A double-blind, placebo-controlled study of 96 men and women, 65 years and older, living independently, and in good health, was conducted by Chandra (1992). The subjects took modest amounts of vitamins and minerals for one year. The daily oral supplement contained vitamin A 400 retinol equivalents; beta-carotene, 16 mg; thiamin, 2.2 mg; riboflavin, 1.5 mg; niacin, 16 mg; vitamin B_6, 3.0 mg; folate, 400 micrograms; vitamin B_{12}, 4.0 micrograms; vitamin C, 80 mg; vitamin D, 4 micrograms; vitamin E, 44 mg; iron, 16 mg; zinc, 14 mg; copper, 1.4 mg; selenium, 20 micrograms; iodine, 0.2 mg; calcium, 200 mg; and magnesium, 100 mg. The placebo contained calcium, 200 mg, and magnesium, 100 mg.

At the end of the year, the subjects receiving the supplement of vitamins and trace minerals were found to have markedly fewer infections and stronger immune defenses than those who did not receive them. The amounts of various nutrients were similar to the recommended nutrient intakes in Canada and RDA in the United States, with the exception of vitamin E and beta-carotene, which were about four times the upper quartile of usual intakes.

Table 3.1. Vitamins for Humans: A Summary

Vitamin	Principal functions	Results of deficiency	Characteristics	Principal sources
		Fat-soluble vitamins		
Vitamin A (retinol) provitamin, carotenes	Formation and maintenance of skin, hair and nails. Required for normal eye function and maintains visual acuity in darkness. Aids in resistance to infections. Beta-carotene may help to prevent lung cancer in smokers. Analogs of vitamin A used to treat acne and other skin problems.	Increased susceptibility to infection and cancers, especially of skin and mucous membranes. Retarded growth and faulty tooth formation. Night blindness.	Withstands usual cooking temperatures. Toxic in large amounts, resulting in painful joints; sometimes loss of hair. Carotene, in excess, may cause yellow discoloration of skin but is not harmful.	Whole milk, low-fat or skim dairy products, egg yolks. Most yellow and orange fruits and vegetables. Dark green (especially leafy) vegetables. Fish liver oils. Fortified margarine and cereals.
Vitamin D D_1, calciferol D_2, ergocalciferol; ultraviolet radiation of plant sterol. D_3, cholecalciferol; sunlight on skin changes 7-dehydrocholesterol to D_3.	Controls absorption of calcium and phosphorus from intestinal tract. Calcification of bones and teeth.	Poor utilization of calcium and phosphorus in bone and in formation of teeth. Rickets in children and osteomalacia (bone softening) in adults.	Relatively stable at refrigeration temperatures. Associated with vitamin A. Toxic in large amounts. Above normal amounts of calcium in the blood. Symptoms include nausea, anorexia, confusion, diarrhea, weight loss, frequent urination. D_3 formed in skin on exposure to sunlight.	Fortified milk and butter, egg yolk. Fish liver oils, and liver. D_3 from exposure of skin to sunlight.

Vitamin E group Tocopherols	Antioxidants, particularly in preserving lipid configuration of cell membranes, protecting l-noleic acid and perhaps other unsaturated fatty acids. May protect vitamin A and carotenes from destruction in the intestinal tract. Shown to improve immunity.	Red blood cell hemolysis. Loss of creatinine in the urine. Decreased immunity.	Heat stable in absence of air. Deteriorate on exposure to light and on contact with iron and lead. Relatively nontoxic in humans (RDA, 1989) as compared to vitamins A and D. Related to action of selenium.	Wheat germ and wheat germ oil. Soybean, peanut, cottonseed, and corn oils. Lettuce and other green leafy vegetables. Rice and rice germ. Margarine, butter. Egg yolk. Nuts, legumes.
Vitamin K Menadione, a synthetic water-soluble analog	Required for synthesis of prothrombin and other blood-clotting factors.	Reduced plasma concentrations of blood-clotting factors, especially prothrombin, resulting in predisposition to hemorrhage.	Stable in air when protected from light. Diphosphate ester is water soluble and widely used clinically. Deficiency may follow prolonged antibiotic therapy or as a result of a defect in fat absorption. In infants with low birth weights, large doses of menadione produce toxic accumulations of bilirubin in brain tissues.	Dark green plants such as kale, spinach, cabbage leaves. Animal products such as liver, pork, cheese, and egg yolk. Intestinal synthesis by bacteria, after first few days of life.

(continued)

Table 3.1. Vitamins for Humans: A Summary (continued)

Vitamin	Principal functions	Results of deficiency	Characteristics	Principal sources
		Water-soluble vitamins		
Vitamin C (Ascorbic acid)	Required for the formation of intercellular cement substances of many tissues including skin, dentine, cartilage, and bone. Important role in healing of wounds and bone fractures. Makes iron available for hemoglobin and maturation of red blood cells. Influences conversion of folic acid to tetrahydrofolic acid, a physiologically active form.	Moderate: Lowered resistance to infections. Tendency of gums to bleed. Severe: Loose teeth, gingivitis, scurvy.	Probably most easily destroyed of all the vitamins; severe losses occur in food processing when open kettles are used due to easy oxidation, also loss when cooking water discarded. Traces of copper or iron hasten destruction due to oxidation. Increased requirement in fevers, infections, wound healing, and in cigarette smoking and long-term aspirin use.	Citrus fruits, strawberries, tomatoes, cantaloupe, potatoes. Fresh vegetables (e.g., broccoli, spinach, asparagus, cabbage).
B Complex Thiamin (Vitamin B$_1$)	Integral part of the coenzyme, thiamin pyrophosphate (TPP), required in the citric acid cycle. Required, as TPP in the hexose monophosphate shunt pathway for glucose metabolism resulting in the generation of the five-carbon sugar, ribose, needed for synthesis of ribonucleic acid (RNA).	Loss of appetite, impaired digestion of carbohydrates. Fatigue, apathy, neuritis. Memory loss. Edema of extremities, beriberi. Alcoholism is most common cause of deficiency in the United States.	Heat labile at temperatures near boiling point of water, particularly in alkaline solutions. Destroyed to some extent in irradiation processes for food preservation. No indication of toxicity from thiamin use. Possibly less efficient use by elderly.	Lean pork, other meats, organ meats, fish, poultry. Whole-grain or enriched cereal products and bread. Wheat germ, soy beans, peanuts, and other legumes. Dairy products, eggs. Green vegetables, fruits.

Vitamin	Function	Deficiency/Symptoms	Stability	Sources
Vitamin B₆ Group (Pyridoxine)	Essential coenzyme in metabolism of amino acids. Required for conversion of tryptophan to niacin and glycogen to glucose. Porphyrin and heme synthesis. Linoleic acid metabolism.	Anemia, neuritis, dermatitis around eyes and mouth. Anorexia, nausea, vomiting.	Inactivated by heat (especially pyridoxal and pyridoxamine), by light, ultraviolet radiation, alkali, and air.	Poultry, fish, beef, liver, ham, egg yolk. Bananas, wheat germ, whole-grain cereals, soybeans, oats, beans, peanuts, corn, and yams.
Niacin (Nicotinic acid, nicotinamide)	Component of two major coenzymes: (1) nicotinamide adenine dinucleotide (NAD), and (2) nicotinamide adenine dinucleotide phosphate (NADP). Both are required in releasing energy from metabolism of carbohydrates, fats, and proteins. Both are components of the citric acid cycle and the electron transport system required to produce adenosine triphosphate (ATP).	Early signs include fatigue, listlessness, headache, and loss of appetite and weight. Sore tongue, mouth, and throat. Nausea, vomiting, diarrhea. Characterstic symmetrical dermatitis on hands, forearms, feet, legs, and neck. Pellagra, mental confusion, dizziness, poor memory, dementia, and death.	Stable to heat and light, acid and basic solutions, and to air exposure. Tryptophan, an essential amino acid, can be transformed into nicotinamide by body tissues; vitamin B₆ (pyridoxine) is required for this conversion. Corn contains bound forms of niacin, which are released by treatment with lime.	Meat, poultry, and fish are better than plant products, on the basis of preformed niacin as well as because of their tryptophan content. Milk, whole-grain or enriched cereals and breads, rice bran, and tomatoes. Yeast, peanuts, and peanut butter are among the richest sources.

(continued)

Table 3.1. Vitamins for Humans: A Summary *(continued)*

Vitamin	Principal functions	Results of deficiency	Characteristics	Principal sources
Pantothenic acid	Component of coenzyme A (CoA), which is essential in metabolism of carbohydrates, fats, and protein. Component of acetyl coenzyme A (acetyl CoA), which is (1) a precursor of cholesterol and steroid hormones; (2) provides acetyl groups for acetylcholine, a neurotransmitter; and (3) is required in synthesis of heme for hemoglobin and cytochromes	No evidence of spontaneous deficiency in humans. No RDA set.	Widely distributed. About half of pantothenic acid is lost in milling process for grains. Relatively nontoxic.	Foods from animal sources such as lean beef and beef liver, eggs, milk. Wheat bran, broccoli, peanuts, lima beans, sweet potatoes.
Biotin	Coenzyme of certain enzymes that catalyze carboxylation and decarboxylation. Especially important in the conversion of pyruvic acid to oxalacetic acid, which in turn combines with acetyl CoA to form citric acid, thus drawing acetate into the citric acid cycle to generate energy (ATP).	Seborrheic dermatitis of infants younger than 6 years. In adult humans, it is necessary to feed large amounts of avidin, from raw egg white, to produce symptoms of biotin deficiency. Symptoms include anorexia, nausea, vomiting, inflammation of the tongue, mental depression, and a dry, scaly dermatitis. May ensue after prolonged use of antibiotics.	Reasonably stable to heat and to mildly acidic conditions, but in the free state, is susceptible to oxidation and to destruction by alkali. Intestinal bacteria produce biotin that can be used by the human host. Doubtful whether any but most severely deficient diet would cause a biotin deficiency in humans.	Egg yolk, organ meats, milk. Soyflour, cereals. Cauliflower, nuts, legumes.

Riboflavin (Vitamin B₂)	Constituent of several enzyme systems involved in intermediary metabolism and the resultant release of energy. Particularly important are the two coenzymes, flavin mononucleotide (FMN) and flavin adenine dinucleotide (FAD). Riboflavin is required in the conversion of tryptophan to niacin in the body.	Growth retardation. Cracks at the corners of the mouth. Inflammation of the lips (cheilosis), and the tongue becomes smooth and purplish (glossitis). Dry and scaly skin. Eyes may itch, become sensitive to light, and bloodshot. Often scaliness, greasiness, and fissures in the folds of the ears and nose. Vegetarians may have inadequate intake unless milk is used.	Relatively stable to heat, acid, and oxidation, but unstable in basic solutions. On irradiation with ultraviolet rays or visible light, it undergoes decomposition. Although widely distributed in food, it is present in only small amounts in the most commonly eaten foods.	Dairy products, eggs, meats, poultry, fish. Green vegetables, wheat germ. Fortified grains, cereals, and bakery goods.
Folate (Folacin, folic acid)	Serves as a coenzyme for single carbon transfer, such as the methyl group, –CH₃. In this role, it is involved in the synthesis of serine, thymine, purines, methionine, and choline. Plays a role in the formation of hemoglobin	In humans, results in megaloblastic anemia. Folacin will cure the anemia and glossitis of pernicious anemia, which is due to a vitamin B₁₂ deficiency, but will not help the more serious neurological symptoms.	Obtained in large measure through its synthesis, by bacteria, in the colon. Deficiency frequently found among the old, chronic invalids and alcholics. Easily destroyed by heat in acidic solutions. Deteriorates when	Fresh green leafy vegetables, asparagus, fruits, and whole wheat bread. Meat, fish, poultry, and eggs. Dry beans, peas, nuts.

(continued)

Table 3.1. Vitamins for Humans: A Summary (*continued*)

Vitamin	Principal functions	Results of deficiency	Characteristics	Principal sources
Folate (*continued*)	(the porphyrin group). Blood cell regeneration in pernicious anemia, but not control of its neurological aspects.		food is stored at room temperature.	
Vitamin B$_{12}$ (Cobalamin)	Required for normal growth, for maintenance of healthy nervous tissue, and for normal blood formation. Involved in nucleic acid synthesis in all body cells, but especially so in red blood cells because of the enormous rate at which they are developed. Important catalytic role in metabolism of folic acid.	Pernicious anemia. Fatigue, confusion, apathy, lack of appetite. Skin may have a lemon-yellow tint; tongue may be sore and beefy red.	Contains the element, cobalt, in a trivalent state; no other cobalt-containing organic compound has been found in nature. Only vitamin to contain a metal as an integral part. Unstable in hot basic or acidic solutions. Nutritional deficiency due to inadequate dietary intake is rare. Deficiency may occur from a strict vegetarian diet devoid of meat, eggs, or dairy products. Alcohol interferes with absorption.	Liver, especially beef and pork. Lean meat, oysters, fish, eggs, milk, and cheese.

Table 3.2. Minerals for Humans: A Summary

Mineral	Location and principal functions	Results of deficiency	Characteristics	Principal sources
	I. *Macronutrients essential at levels of 100 mg or more per day*			
Calcium	99% in bones and teeth. Calcium in body fluids essential for transport across cell membranes. Calcium also bound to protein. Required for normal blood clotting.	Retarded bone calcification, osteomalacia, osteoporosis.	Absorption decreases with age; hindered by lack of vitamin D, antacids, diuretics, phytic acid, lack of exercise.	Milk and milk products, canned sardines and salmon with bones, shrimp, green leafy vegetables (e.g., kale, broccoli). Calcium-precipitated tofu.
Phosphorus	About 80% in bones and teeth. Functions in metabolic processes and neurological function. Important to pH regulation.	May lead to osteomalacia	Excessive use of aluminum hydroxide antacids may cause phosphorus deficiency.	Milk, egg yolk, cheese, meat, fish, poultry, whole-grain cereals, some soft drinks.
Magnesium	About 50% in bone. Remaining 50% is almost all inside body cells with about 1% in extracellular fluid. Functions as an activator of many enzymes. Involved in nerve and muscle irritability.	Uncontrolled neuromuscular activity. Magnesium tetany in alcoholics.	Deficiency following gastrointestinal losses and in alcoholism.	Whole-grain cereals, nuts, meat, milk, green vegetables, legumes.
Sodium	30–45 percent in bone. Major mineral of extracellular fluid, and only a small amount is inside cell. Regulates body fluid pH and body fluid volume.	General lethargy and debility.	Possible factor in etiology of hypertension. Deficiency may occur from profuse sweating, prolonged vomiting, or diarrhea.	Table salt, seafoods, animal foods, milk, eggs, fish, baking soda, and many antacids. Abundant in most canned foods except fruit.

(continued)

Table 3.2. Minerals for Humans: A Summary *(continued)*

Mineral	Location and principal functions	Results of deficiency	Characteristics	Principal sources
Chloride	Major mineral of extracellular fluid, functioning in combination with sodium; serves as an enzyme activator; component of gastric hydrochloric acid. Mostly present in extracellular fluid; less than 15% inside cells.	Marked loss of chloride can result in hypokalemic alkalosis.	Excessive losses in diarrhea, sweating, or vomiting.	Common table salt, seafoods, milk, meat, eggs.
Potassium	Major mineral of intracellular fluid, with only small amounts in extracellular fluid. Functions in regulating pH and cell membrane transfer. Necessary for synthesis of carbohydrates and protein. Regulates neuromuscular excitability and muscle contraction.	Low potassium levels affect heart rate.	Deficiency may be due to some diuretics, prolonged diarrhea, or vomiting.	Fruits, milk, meat, whole-grain cereals, vegetables, legumes.
Sulfur	Bulk of dietary sulfur present in sulfur-containing amino acids needed for synthesis of essential metabolites. Constituent of all protein. Sulfur also functions in thiamin and biotin and as inorganic sulfur. Forms high-energy compounds that make it important in transfer of energy; necessary for collagen synthesis.	No deficiencies known. Only if lacking in protein to the point of severe deficiency will vital sulfur-containing amino acids be lacking.	Sulfur available to body primarily as a component of the amino acids methionine and cystine. Highest concentration in hair, skin, and nails.	Protein foods (meat, fish, poultry, cheese, eggs, milk, legumes, nuts).

Iron	About 70% is in hemoglobin; about 26% stored in liver, spleen, and bone marrow. Iron is a component of hemoglobin and myoglobin, important in oxygen transfer; also present in certain enzymes.	Nutritional anemia is major manifestation. Indicated by low hemoglobin level and small red cell size.	Absorption decreases with age; meat and vitamin C improves absorption. High-fiber diets, antacids, and tea decrease absorption. Use of iron utensils increases supply. Supplements may be required for elderly.	Liver, meat, poultry, fish, egg yolk, legumes, whole or enriched grains, dark green vegetables.
Zinc	Present in most tissues, with higher amounts in liver, muscle, and bone. Constituent of many enzymes and insulin; of importance in nucleic acid metabolism.	Reduces taste and smell; retards wound healing. May play a role in osteoporosis.	Supplement exceeding 15 mg/d may aggravate marginal copper deficiency.	Milk, liver, shellfish, herring, wheat bran (widely distributed).
Copper	Found in all body tissues; larger amounts in liver, brain, heart, and kidney. Constituent of enzymes and blood. May be integral part of DNA or RNA molecule. Aids in absorption and utilization of iron in hemoglobin synthesis.	Deficiency is rare.	Required along with iron to prevent anemia. Zinc interferes with absorption of copper. Copper cooking utensils catalyze destruction of vitamin C.	Liver, shellfish, whole grains, cherries, legumes, kidney, poultry, chocolate, oysters, nuts.

(continued)

63

Table 3.2. Minerals for Humans: A Summary (*continued*)

Mineral	Location and principal functions	Results of deficiency	Characteristics	Principal sources
Iodine	Constituent of thyroxine and related compounds synthesized by thyroid gland. Thyroxine regulates rate of energy metabolism.	Primary cause of simple goiter.	At present, excess is greater problem than deficiency, due to iodine use in sanitizing agents and food additives. Substances present in turnips, cabbage, rutabaga, broccoli, brussels sprouts interfere with iodine uptake; inactivated by adequate cooking.	Iodized table salt, seafoods, water, and vegetables in non-goitrous regions.
Manganese	Highest concentration is in bone; also relatively high concentrations in pituitary, liver, pancreas, and gastrointestinal tissue. Constituent of essential enzyme systems. Activates many enzymes involved in urea formation, carbohydrate oxidation, protein metabolism, bone development.	Deficiency not demonstrated in humans because of abundant supply in edible plant materials.	May be required for best utilization of thiamin.	Beet greens, blueberries, whole grains and cereal products, nuts, legumes, fruit, tea, coffee.
Fluoride	Present in bone. In optimal amounts in water and diet, reduces dental caries and may minimize bone loss.	Increase in incidence of dental caries.	Moderate levels in bone may reduce losses of calcium at menopause. Under conditions of immobility, incidence of osteoporosis may be lower for persons using fluoridated water. Some evidence for reduction of periodontal disease.	Drinking water (1 ppm), tea, coffee, rice, soybeans, spinach, gelatin, onions, lettuce.

	Function	Deficiency	Comments	Sources
Molybdenum	Constituent of an essential enzyme, xanthine oxidase, and of flavoproteins.	Naturally occurring deficiency in United States not known with certainty.	Requirement so low it is easily furnished by common U.S. diet. Supplements not recommended: excess molybdenum associated with copper loss in urine.	Legumes, cereal grains, dark green leafy vegetables, organ meats.
Cobalt	Constituent of cyanocobalamin (vitamin B_{12}), occurring bound to protein in foods of animal origin. Essential to normal function of all cells, particularly cells of bone marrow, nervous system, and gastrointestinal system.	No evidence that intake of cobalt is ever limiting in human diet.	Only known nutritional function of cobalt is as an integral part of vitamin B_{12}.	Liver, kidney, oysters, clams, lean beef, poultry, milk; variable in vegetables and grains.
Selenium	Associated with fat metabolism and vitamin E; spares vitamin E. Antioxidant, especially in cell membranes; stored in liver and kidney.	Keshan disease, a cardiomyopathy.	Associated with vitamin E in preserving lipid configuration in cell membranes.	Whole grains, meats, sea foods, milk; vegetables, variable, depends on selenium content of soil.
Chromium	Associated with glucose metabolism. Increases effectiveness of insulin in glucose utilization.	Impaired glucose tolerance in presence of normal concentrations of insulin.	Reported to improve impaired glucose tolerance in some studies of mild diabetes and in middle-aged subjects with impaired glucose tolerance.	Brewer's yeast; pork kidney. Corn oil, clams, whole-grain cereals, meats, drinking water variable.

Arsenic, tin, nickel, vanadium, silicon, boron: May be essential, but no RDA established.

4

Nutritional Status of the Older Population

An adequate diet for people of any age provides all the necessary nutrients in the amounts required by the body to maintain optimal health. Although individual eating habits differ widely, a guide to nutrient needs of most Americans is provided by two guidelines, the *Recommended Dietary Allowances* (RDAs) and the basic four food groups. The food groups are discussed in Chapter 10, and relevant nutrients listed in the RDAs are reviewed here, particularly in their relation to the older person.

The Food and Nutrition Board of the National Research Council, National Academy of Sciences, was established in 1940. Its initial purpose was to make sure that the population was adequately nourished during World War II, and one of its early functions was to recommend quantities of nutrients that should be provided to the Armed Forces and the general population. These recommendations led to the development of goals for intake of nine specific nutrients that would meet the known nutritional requirements of men, women, and children of varying ages. The first RDAs were adopted in 1941 (Roberts, 1958) and have been published every five to ten years since 1943. New experimental data are reviewed, and both the RDAs and background scientific information regarding nutrients and their functions are updated.

The RDAs are defined in the latest edition (RDAs, 1989, p. 10) as "the levels of intake of essential nutrients that, on the basis of scientific knowledge, are judged by the Food and Nutrition Board to be adequate to meet the known nutrient needs of practically all healthy persons." Specific RDAs have now been established for protein, 11 vitamins, and seven minerals. The guidelines are appropriately used only for normal, healthy people and not for individuals with special nutritional needs. They are not minimal requirements or necessarily optimal levels of intake, but are meant to be safe and adequate levels, incorporating generous margins of safety to accommodate the variability in requirements among people.

The diet for the older person should contain adequate energy, all essential nutrients, and certain other dietary factors to sustain health and vitality. The macronutrients include carbohydrates, fats, and proteins, which are sources of energy as well as of the essential (linoleic) fatty acid, and amino acids that either cannot be synthesized in the body or are synthesized in amounts inadequate to meet body needs. The micronutrients include the vitamins and minerals necessary in small amounts. Fiber, which does not fall into either of these categories, is nonetheless beneficial for good health and is discussed in some detail in Chapter 5.

The required amounts of the different micronutrients depend principally on gender, body size, degree of physical activity, state of health, and age. After at least five decades of living under a wide variety of external conditions and stresses, however, the nutritional needs of individual people can be as different from each other as are the persons themselves. What follows is a review of current knowledge regarding mainly the micronutrients and the needs of older persons.

Nutritional Survey Findings

A serious problem in nutritional status assessment of older people is the lack of correlation between dietary intake data and clinical and laboratory methods of assessment. Collection of dietary data from older persons for epidemiologic analysis based on recalling particular foods eaten and how much over a specified period is complicated by an increased prevalence of forgetfulness, which may result in underreported nutrient intakes (Beaton, 1985). It is a~ difficult to separate behavioral changes in dietary intakes from the effects of aging processes on dietary and nutritional status. As an example, older persons may change food habits for financial reasons, or for health reasons, such as deciding to buy less meat or to adopt a low-cholesterol diet by omitting bacon and eggs from their grocery lists. Several comprehensive national surveys that included people older than 60 years have been carried out, and all of them have identified a substantial proportion of older men and women who fell below the recommended dietary allowances for kcalories, as well as for protein, vitamins, calcium, and iron (Bidlack *et al.*, 1986). However, estimates of obesity from body measurements generally show an increase in percentage of body fat for both sexes as age increases, and the Ten-State Nutrition Survey (DHEW, 1972) found obesity to be a major problem, especially in women.

The findings of diminished caloric intake and increased obesity are difficult to reconcile; however, it is well established that body composition changes in older people. The extremities lose fat, which is redistributed to the trunk, and lean body mass is lost; thus, the term obesity in older populations may need redefinition (SGR, 1988).

Energy

National dietary and food-consumption surveys conducted during the 1970s consistently reported lower energy and food consumption intakes among older persons than among younger adults (SGR, 1988). Although it is difficult to interpret dietary intake studies of older Americans because of methodological problems, the studies that have been made always reveal decreases in energy intake with age that may also be influenced by income, race, food preference, and drug use (SGR, 1988). A low-calorie diet may not impair health as long as the nutrient density of the diet is high and provides adequate amounts of essential nutrients.

The increasing level of obesity among older persons, mentioned earlier, as indicated by higher weight-for-height levels with age, calls for an explanation (Frisancho, 1984). Whether the inconsistency between reported low energy intakes and increasing body weight is due to errors in measurement, inappropriate standards, loss of height with age (Bowman and Rosenberg, 1982), or lack of physical activity has not been agreed on.

Protein

Deficiency of protein is rare in this country except in alcoholics, in families at the lowest poverty level, and in a very few elderly people who live alone and whose diet tends toward tea and toast. In true protein deficiency, muscle mass decreases, and edema, with accumulation of fluid in the abdominal cavity, occurs because of drastic reduction of plasma albumin, the primary protein in the blood.

In a 30-day continuous metabolic balance study of seven men and eight women older than 70 years who consumed RDA levels of protein and energy, it was found that about half were unable to maintain nitrogen balance on this level of protein (0.8 g of protein/kg/day). This means that more nitrogen is being lost in the urea of the urine than is being supplied by the protein in the food that is eaten. The results suggested that higher intakes were required to meet protein requirements of older persons (Gersovitz et al., 1982). The protein allowance for adult men and women was not changed in the 10th, 1989 edition of the RDAs. Because the RDA for protein includes a generous margin of safety and because clinical measurements have rarely found signs of protein deficiency among healthy older people, it cannot be concluded from the data on hand that people with intakes below the RDA are protein deficient or that they would benefit from additional intake of protein.

Calcium

Loss of calcium-containing bone mineral and a higher incidence of fractures occur in older people, especially Caucasian women, compared to younger persons. Bone is turning over in a continuous process of resorption and formation. In children and adolescents, the rate of formation of bone mineral predominates over the rate of resorption, but in later life, resorption predominates over formation. As a consequence, in normal aging, there is a gradual loss of bone (Arnaud, 1988). The age-related loss of bone calcium is discussed in considerable detail in Chapter 11, which deals with bone health and osteoporosis. Reduced efficiency of intestinal calcium absorption may be due to age-related changes in gastric acidity, and/or interaction of intestinal constituents such as fiber, bacteria, and other nutrients.

The RDAs for calcium of 800 mg/day (RDAs, 1989) may not be sufficient to maintain calcium balance in populations consuming western-type diets (Recker and Heaney, 1985). Some older people may have reduced calcium intake because they avoid dairy products containing lactose, to which they have an intolerance. Dawson-Hughes and co-workers (1990) reported that postmenopausal women who took a daily allowance of 800 mg of calcium, in the form of calcium citrate malate, stopped the slow erosion of bone from their hips, wrists, and spine (Dawson-Hughes *et al.*, 1990).

Iron

The interest in iron deficiency stems, to some extent, from evidence that it is the most common nutritional deficiency in the United States (Pilch *et al.*, 1984) and worldwide (DeMaeyer *et al.*, 1985). It is also the most common cause of anemia throughout the world. Weakness, fatigue, and pallor are primary symptoms.

Iron stores normally increase throughout adult life in men and after menopause in women (Pilch *et al.*, 1984), and nutritional iron deficiency is not common in these groups (Zauber *et al.*, 1987). In elderly people, anemia is more often associated with chronic inflammatory conditions, such as arthritis, than with iron deficiency (Yip *et al.*, 1988). Factors that could predispose to iron deficiency in these groups are conditions such as bleeding ulcers and colorectal cancers. Use of aspirin may result in intestinal blood loss by impairing platelet aggregation. It was found in one study that an aspirin tablet (300 mg) taken three times a day for a week increased intestinal blood loss to 5 ml/d from a normal average of 0.5 ml/d (Pierson *et al.*, 1961). Comparison of older subjects who took iron supplements with those who did not showed no clinically significant differences in the biochemical measures of iron status (Garry *et al.*, 1985).

Because iron stores or reserves increase with age, studies that examine only dietary intake of iron in older people need to be interpreted cautiously. Low dietary iron intake at one time does not necessarily increase the risk for anemia because iron may still be available from body stores and because absorption increases when intake and stores are low. In addition, the type of iron and other components of a meal, such as vitamin C, also influence the amount absorbed.

The two major sources of dietary iron are heme iron from the hemoglobin and myoglobin present in meats, and nonheme iron from plants and plant products, from drinking water, and to some extent, from iron cooking utensils. Nonheme iron accounts for the major part of dietary iron intake (Monsen, 1988), but is not very well absorbed. As little as 3 percent of the nonheme iron is absorbed as compared with 23 percent of iron in the heme form (Monsen, 1988). The absorption of nonheme iron from a meal is significantly improved when vitamin C is taken with it (Kuhn *et al.*, 1968), but vitamin C has very little effect on the availability of heme iron.

B Vitamins

A number of studies have indicated a great risk for vitamin deficiencies in older persons on the basis of low dietary intakes, but such deficiencies are not always confirmed by biochemical or clinical results (Garry *et al.*, 1986). Besides, interpretation of biochemical parameters is hampered by lack of data on normal standards for the older population (Kirsch *et al.*, 1987). In their review of the vitamin requirements of the elderly, Suter *et al.* (1987) note that data for many vitamins are limited, and they conclude that some subgroups of older persons may require higher amounts of some vitamins, including B_{12}. They cite chronic gastritis with atrophied mucosa and glands as impairing vitamin B_{12} absorption.

Vitamin C

A human adult requires 10 mg/day of dietary vitamin C, which is also called ascorbic acid, to prevent the onset of scurvy. It has also been shown that the total body pool of ascorbic acid reaches a maximum of approximately 20 mg/kg body weight and that this level can be achieved at a steady state plasma concentration of 1.0 mg/dl

(Kallner *et al.*, 1979). Women require an intake of 75 mg/day, and men, an intake of 150 mg/day, to achieve this ascorbic acid level in plasma (Garry *et al.*, 1982a). This finding was supported by a clinical trial that showed that a daily intake of 60 mg, the current RDA for vitamin C, was insufficient to maintain this plasma concentration (VanderJagt *et al.*, 1987). The clinical significance of maintaining maximal plasma ascorbic acid levels, however, has not yet been fully explored.

The absorption of vitamin C in man is an energy-requiring active transport process. The mechanism for absorption in the intestinal tract and the reabsorption capacity of the kidney are both limited by the load that they can handle. As a result, efficient absorption of vitamin C declines in a dose-related manner (Melethil *et al.*, 1986), and more efficient absorption is achieved by ingesting smaller, multiple doses.

Studies have shown that very few individuals in a healthy elder population exhibit clinical symptoms of hypovitaminosis C (Garry *et al.*, 1982a). They found less than 2 percent of 270 free-living and healthy older persons older than 60 years were at risk for developing clinical symptoms of hypovitaminosis C, as measured by vitamin C concentrations below 0.2 mg/dl. Mean intakes of vitamin C from the diet were 137 mg/day and 142 mg/day for women and men, respectively, approximately 2 to 2.5 times the RDA. In addition, more than half were taking supplemental vitamin C, the mean levels being approximately 600 mg/day.

Low levels of vitamin C in the elderly have usually been explained as being due to low intake, but although a vitamin C supplement of 1 gram/day increased the level in a group of elderly patients, the increase was usually only about one fifth that seen in younger adults (Schorah *et al.*, 1979). This result would seem to indicate that the absorption of vitamin C from the food decreases in the elderly. The plasma levels of vitamin C were determined in healthy persons older than 65 years who were given various amounts of vitamin C (30–280 mg/day) (VanderJagt *et al.*, 1987). The daily intakes required to maintain a plasma level of 1.0 mg/dl were about 150 mg for men and 80 mg for women. Vitamin C consumption at 60 mg/day, the RDA level for adult men and women, was associated with plasma vitamin C levels at or below 0.4 mg/dl in most of the men, a level generally considered the lower limit of normal (Vander-Jagt *et al.*, 1987).

Cigarette smoking is associated with a significant decrease in vitamin C status. On an average, smoking more than one pack a day is associated with vitamin C levels 40 percent lower than those of nonsmokers. In order for smokers to achieve serum levels of vitamin C equivalent to those of nonsmokers, smokers need an additional 65.4 mg of the vitamin per day (Smith and Hodges, 1987).

Many alcoholics have a low vitamin C status generally because of their poor diet, and vitamin C deficiency is common among patients with alcoholic liver disease. Rapid ingestion of alcohol also causes increased excretion of vitamin C (Faizallah *et al.*, 1986) and low plasma concentrations. Vitamin C therapy, using 500–1000 mg/day, has been recommended in the treatment of chronic alcoholics (Piatkowski *et al.*, 1986).

Periodontal disease includes a wide range of pathologic conditions ranging from minor gum inflammation (gingivitis) to severe loss of the bone structure supporting the teeth (periodontitis). Advanced disease results in loosening and eventual loss of teeth. The National Adult Dental Health Survey of 1985–1986 reported bleeding of the gums in 47 percent of persons older than 65. Periodontal disease is a major cause of tooth loss, and efforts to prevent the condition are desirable (Rank *et al.*, 1983).

Because bleeding gums and loosened teeth are classical symptoms of scurvy, due to lack of adequate vitamin C, the vitamin has been associated with periodontal health. This has led to investigations into the relationship between vitamin C and gum disease. A controlled study does suggest a critical role for vitamin C in periodontal health (Leggott *et al.*, 1986). The depletion of vitamin C in humans was associated with increased bleeding of the gums, and a decrease in bleeding was seen with ascorbic acid repletion. Supplements of 600 mg/day were associated with greater improvement than supplemental intakes of 60 mg/day, and inflammation of the gums decreased directly with improvement in the vitamin C status.

It has been reported that large doses of vitamin C when taken with food can destroy the vitamin B_{12} in the food, leading to a deficiency resembling pernicious anemia (Herbert *et al.*, 1974). On repeating the work, using more definitive methods, Newmark and co-workers (1976) concluded that the presence of ascorbic acid did not lead to any destruction of B_{12} in the food. Similar results were later reported by Marcus *et al.* in 1980.

It has been reported, from work done in guinea pigs, that large doses of vitamin C taken regularly over a considerable period can lead to rebound scurvy (Basu, 1985). However, there has been no experimental evidence to support such an effect in humans (Gerster *et al.*, 1988). Investigations in guinea pigs have also been negative or inconclusive (Rivers, 1987).

Vitamin A and Beta-Carotene

In most older persons, vitamin A deficiency does not appear to be a problem. Although both of the National Health and Nutrition Examination Surveys (NHANES; 1971–1974 and 1976–1980) reported that about half of the study population older than 65 had vitamin A intakes at or less than two thirds of the RDAs, only 0.3 percent of the NHANES–I older population had low vitamin A blood levels (Bowman and Rosenberg, 1982). Serum vitamin A data was not available for adults from NHANES–II. Whether the use of vitamin A supplements can account for the observed discrepancy is unknown, but similar data suggest that older individuals can maintain normal vitamin blood levels even with reportedly low dietary intakes (Garry *et al.*, 1987).

The lens of the human eye is approximately 35 percent protein. In contrast to the rapid rate of protein turnover in many organs, the proteins in the lens exist in place for decades. Exposure to light, oxygen, and adverse environmental conditions subject these proteins to aggregation and precipitation, thus forming opacities or senile cataracts, the major form that affects the elderly. Protection of the lens with antioxidants might be expected to be useful (Taylor, 1989). Beta-carotene is a good antioxidant in tissues such as the lens that have a low partial pressure of oxygen (Burton *et al.*, 1984). In line with this hypothesis, high plasma levels of beta-carotene have been found to be strongly correlated with lower incidence of cataract (Jacques *et al.*, 1988a,b).

Vitamin D

It has been reported that older people generally have a lowered vitamin D status. Other groups also showing lowered vitamin D status include chronically ill individuals and those living in institutions with little or no exposure to sunlight. Because the vitamin D endocrine system is the major regulator of intestinal calcium absorption, a reduced vitamin D status might be expected to promote a negative calcium balance in the elderly.

Studies in the United States have reported dietary intakes of vitamin D to be approximately 50 percent of the RDA for older persons (Garry *et al.*, 1982b) and have also reported inadequate intake of vitamin D–supplemented dairy products (Omdahl *et al.*, 1982). However, endogenous production of vitamin D, induced by ultraviolet light, is the principal external factor in maintaining adequate vitamin D status. Because exposure to sunlight activates vitamin D precursors in the skin, it has been recommended that older adults obtain at least a minimal exposure (10 to 15 minutes) two or three times a week (Holick, 1986). Increased sun exposure may help compensate for aging skin's decreased capacity (as much as 50 percent when compared to that of young people) to produce these precursors (Holick, 1986). Moderation in sun exposure is, of course, strongly urged because overexposure is a major risk factor for skin cancer. To compensate for inadequate sunlight exposure due to seasonal variation in northern latitudes, supplements may be necessary (Bouillon *et al.*, 1987).

Vitamin E

A recurring problem for many older people, intermittent claudication, involves pain in the calf muscles that occurs during walking, but subsides with rest. It results from an inadequate blood supply, which is often due to atherosclerosis, arteriosclerosis, or thrombosis of the arteries in the legs. The shortage of blood to exercised muscles can cause weakness, limping, pain, numbness, and fatigue. A study was carried out involving 300 mg/day vitamin E supplementation, an increase in exercise, and a ban on smoking (Haeger, 1974). After two years, the treated group had a 34 percent increase in arterial flow to the lower leg, with no change in the controls receiving dicoumarin (an anticoagulant) or vasodilator drugs. Success in passing a walking test by the patients was 54 percent in those receiving vitamin E versus 23 percent in control subjects.

Vitamin E has been shown to reduce cataract development and damage to the eye in animal studies (Bhuyan *et al.*, 1982). A study involving humans looked into the relationship between plasma nutrient levels and the incidence of several types of cataract (Jacques *et al.*, 1988b). Although the effect was not strong, the investigators found a lower risk of cataract formation was associated with high plasma vitamin E levels. When high vitamin E status was combined with high blood levels of beta-carotene and/or vitamin C, a significant decrease in risk of developing cataracts was evident (Jacques *et al.*, 1988a).

The effect of vitamin E supplementation on the immune response of 32 healthy men and women who were 60 years of age or older was studied in a double-blind placebo-controlled trial. Subjects received placebo or vitamin E (800 mg alpha-tocopherol acetate) for 30 days. The supplementation was found to significantly improve several indices of cell-mediated immunity (Meydani *et al.*, 1990). The authors concluded their paper in the following way: "It is encouraging to note that a single nutrient supplement can enhance immune responsiveness in healthy elderly subjects consuming the recommended amounts of all nutrients. This is especially significant because dietary intervention represents the most practical approach for delaying or reversing the rate of decline of immune function with age."

Epidemiologic studies indicate a lower incidence of infectious disease in elderly subjects with high plasma vitamin E concentrations (Chavance *et al.*, 1985). It has also been reported that population groups maintaining high plasma vitamin E concentrations exhibited a lower incidence of lung cancer (Menkes *et al.*, 1986) and of colon cancer (Knekt *et al.*, 1988).

An informal poll taken during a session of the Oxygen Society at the 1990 meeting of the Federation of American Societies for Experimental Biology revealed that approximately half of the scientists present were taking a supplement of vitamin E, and later inquiry of scientists who conduct research on vitamin E and on free radicals indicated that a significant number take pharmacologic doses of vitamin E (Horwitt, 1991). Some expert scientists in the area of oxygen radicals and human disease have suggested increased use of vitamin E to decrease free radical damage (Cross et al., 1987). Many people have taken large supplements of vitamin E for long periods without any documented evidence of harm (Bendich and Macklin, 1988).

Nutritional Supplements

From a study of the use of vitamin supplements in the United States, it was estimated that at least 37 percent of American adults were using a daily multivitamin preparation (the Gallup Organization, 1982; see also Koplan et al., 1986; McDonald, 1986; Subar and Block, 1990; Medeiros et al., 1991). Higher use of vitamin supplements is associated with older ages, higher incomes, and higher educational levels (Koplan et al., 1986). The second NHANES indicated that the people most likely to take supplemental nutrients are less likely to need them, and those in most need of them are least likely to take them (Koplan et al., 1986). In older persons, vitamin use increased dramatically in the decade preceding 1982 (Garry et al., 1982b; Scheider et al., 1983). Whether or not such supplements improved the health of these people could not be determined from the existing data (Mann et al., 1987).

Some nutritionists believe that the recommended intake for many vitamins and minerals is too low for people older than 65 and should be supplemented. Others hold to the view that they can all be obtained from food if it is selected properly from the four food groups. A middle-of-the-road practical position is based on the level of energy intake. If it is 1500 kcalories or less per day, and this applies to many older people, a combined vitamin–mineral supplement of the common one-a-day kind should be considered.

In a recent article, J. B. Blumberg (1992) from the USDA Human Nutrition Research Center on Aging at Tufts University presents an insightful review of the nutrient needs of people older than 60 years. He points out that the national illness burden has shifted over recent decades from acute to chronic illness, and from younger to older individuals, and that it is easier to prevent morbidity than mortality. A public health implication of this situation is the need to redefine

RDAs by using criteria that address the physiological rate of aging and the risk of associated chronic disease. Recent studies showing a relationship between nutrition and morbidity associated with atherosclerotic cardiovascular disease, cancer, cataract, diabetes, hypertension, and osteoporosis, although not unequivocal, are too compelling to ignore. However, attempts to reduce chronic disease and disability in older adults must, according to Blumberg, accept new guidelines based on less than complete scientific information. Furthermore, RDA reliance on intakes derived exclusively from "normal diets" may have to be reconsidered, especially for the elderly. If the requirements cannot be met readily through dietary intakes typical of older adults, then Blumberg believes that consumption of supplements at rational, defined levels should be endorsed. He presents reasoned arguments for the possible need for increased requirements, with aging, of vitamins B_6, A, D, E, and B_{12}. He also considers the possible need for higher intakes, with aging, of vitamins C and K and folates, as well as zinc, chromium, copper, calcium, and beta-carotene.

5

Dietary Fiber, Problems of the Digestive Tract, and Water

Fiber and water may, at first glance, appear unlikely topics to be discussed together in the same chapter, but these two dietary constituents have much in common. Neither one provides energy for the body, but both influence the way nutrients are absorbed and eliminated. Both of them, acting separately and together, add bulk to the diet, giving rise to a welcome feeling of satiety following a meal.

Nutritionists do not agree on the status of water as a nutrient. It is, however, a tissue-building material. This is evident from the fact that water is a prominent and essential constituent of every kind of tissue, from a solid tissue such as bone to a fluid tissue such as whole blood, which is four fifths water. Some nutrition biochemists classify water as a nutrient because it is chemically incorporated into bone. Other investigators disagree with this decision because, as they see it, water's primary function is to act as a solvent. Since chemical reactions between substances in living things take place only when they are in solution, the materials contained within cells must be kept in solution in order that life processes can go on. In fact, the protoplasm of most cells is about three fourths water.

Dietary Fiber and Problems of the Digestive Tract

The relationships between the consumption of dietary fiber and several human diseases are among the most active areas in nutrition research today. During the last decade, the words "dietary fiber" actually seem to have acquired a subtle aura denoting prevention of disease and connoting good health. Urged on by the advertising of the large cereal companies, the public has joined in the enthusiasm. With the advent of increased research has come the realization that dietary fiber does more than merely provide bulk for the feces. There is abundant evidence that it has a number of important roles to play.

Dietary fiber, which may be described loosely as the nondigestible components of food, is almost entirely of plant origin and provides the supporting structure in the fruit, leaves, and stems of plants. It consists, first, of a variety of complex carbohydrates present in the cell walls of cereals, vegetables, and fruits, and, second, of lignin. Lignin serves as a cementing and strengthening material for the other components in the cell walls of plants.

The most abundant complex carbohydrate in plant fiber is cellulose. It is made up of unbranched chains of 3,000 or more glucose units joined together to form elastic fibers that can take up water and swell. Cellulose makes up about 25 percent of the fiber content of many grains, vegetables, and fruits. Lignin is quite different from cellulose in that it is not a carbohydrate. Its content in plants is quite variable, but an average value of 10 percent of the total fiber is representative for many grains, vegetables, and fruits. The human body itself lacks the enzymes needed to break down or digest either cellulose or lignin, although cellulose can be broken down to a very small extent by bacteria in the intestinal tract. Because of their essential insolubility in water and their indigestibility, cellulose and lignin together are the main bulk-forming components in food.

High- and Low-Fiber Foods

Typical high-fiber foods are fruits, especially if eaten with the skins; cooked and raw vegetables, except potato, unless it includes the skin; legumes, nuts, whole wheat bread, brown rice, breakfast cereals from whole grains [e.g., oatmeal, shredded wheat, dark farina (Wheatena)], and natural wheat bran. Common low-fiber foods are white bread, highly milled breakfast cereals [e.g., white farina (Cream of Wheat)], meat, eggs, cheese, potato without the skin, fats, and milk. Bran makes up about 11 to 16 percent of the whole wheat and composes the outer coating or husk of cereal grains such as wheat or oats. In addition to being a rich source of dietary fiber, wheat bran makes a real nutritional contribution to the diet because it contains many important food factors such as protein, sugar, unsaturated fats, potassium, phosphorus, magnesium, and a variety of vitamins.

Epidemiologic, animal, clinical, and basic science studies generally support the view that dietary fiber is a beneficial component of our diet. It has received the blessing of many health organizations, such as the American Heart Association, American Cancer Society, and American Diabetes Association. It is not, however, a single entity either chemically or physiologically. The subdivision into soluble and insoluble fiber is now widely accepted. Soluble and insoluble fiber have quite different physiological effects, but even within these categories, effects are variable. Perhaps the most important specific attribute of soluble fiber, as reported in many scientific, nutritional, and medical publications, is its potential for reducing serum cholesterol (Kirby *et al.*, 1981; Chen and Anderson, 1986), improving glucose tolerance, and reducing insulin requirements (Anderson, 1980).

The Origins of the Dietary Fiber Hypothesis

An insistent and long-enduring stand in favor of an important role for dietary fiber in maintaining good health goes back, in this country, at least a century and a half. Much of the food consumed by our early forebears was altered very little by technology. When the milling of wheat first began to make available a white flour, almost devoid of roughage or bran, Sylvester Graham (1794–1857), a New England clergyman and vegetarian advocate, was one of the leading people who deplored the diminution of what nature had provided. "Put back the bran," he railed. "The plainer and more natural a man's food," he said, "the more perfectly the laws of his constitution are fulfilled—the more health will be in his body—the more perfect his senses—the more powerful will his intellectual and moral faculties be rendered by suitable cultivation." It all hung together—the right food could end up saving a man's soul! (Deutsch, 1977). He was a fervent, convincing speaker who traveled extensively up and down the Atlantic seaboard. Among other things, he advocated "eating home-baked bread made with coarse, unsifted flour," and "a hard mattress and cold showers" as reasonable prescriptions for a healthy life. In 1837, Graham's lectures first appeared in two large volumes entitled *Lectures on the Science of Human Life*. The ideas they promoted enjoyed wide distribution and acceptance in this country. They became prime health books for five decades, and reformers of many kinds flocked to the Graham movement. Some idea of the sustained interest in his writings may be gained by the realization that a reprinting of his 1837 two-volume work was issued by Fowler, a prominent New York publisher, as late as 1892. His name remains alive today largely because of graham crackers and graham flour, both of which have a high fiber content.

Much of the modern day public and scientific interest in dietary fiber stems from the discerning observations of two medical missionaries, Burkitt and Trowell, working at Makerre Medical College in Kampala, Uganda. They noted the rarity of many "western" diseases in the Africans whom they treated. Among their patients, they seldom observed coronary heart disease, hypertension, diabetes, or, in particular, certain common gastrointestinal disorders such as constipation, diverticulitis, hemorrhoids, appendicitis, cancer of the large bowel, or hiatal hernia. Based on their observations, Burkitt and Trowell developed the "fiber hypothesis." During the 1970s, they popularized their views widely in lectures, medical publications, and books (Burkitt, 1974; Trowell, 1975, 1976, 1981). A high-fiber diet, they believed, might prevent many of the western diseases rarely seen in sub-Saharan Africa, where the diet was rich in relatively unprocessed foods.

Before about 1880, most grain was stone-ground, leaving the healthful germ and bran in the whole-grain flour. With the introduction of steel milling, not only was the bran removed along with the dietary fiber it contained, but most of the vitamins and minerals as well. At the turn of this century, the average person in this country consumed about 225 pounds of flour a year, half of which was whole wheat. Today, the average consumption is less then half that amount and about 95 percent of it is white flour, which contains only about 8 percent of the fiber found in whole wheat bread. It has been estimated that the consumption of cereal fibers in this country declined by 90 percent from 1880 to 1974 (Scala, 1975), during a period when heart disease, diabetes, and colon cancer were increasing in frequency. A reversal in the trend, which continues to the present time, roughly parallels the dissemination of the fiber hypothesis by Trowell (1975).

Soluble Dietary Fiber

In addition to cellulose and lignin, dietary fiber from a limited number of substances of plant origin contains a mixture of components that are soluble in water to a variable extent. The components include gums and pectin, both of which are complex carbohydrates, a fraction called pentosans (made up of polymers of pentoses, which are five-carbon sugars), and a class of chemical compounds known as beta-glucans. The plant gums are any of various amorphous substances, often extruded by plants following an injury, that harden on exposure to air. A typical example is guar gum, obtained from the Indian cluster bean and widely used in the formulation of ice cream and other frozen desserts. Pectin is found in many fruits, and to a smaller extent in some vegetables (e.g., beets and carrots) that form a gelatinous mass when they are cooked. The pectin is the component that causes them to gel on cooling. In the jelly-making process, pectin is added to a solution of fruit juice and sugar to assure that gel formation will occur.

Like starch and cellulose, the beta-glucans are carbohydrate in nature. They are, however, unbranched and composed of about 6 to 12 glucose units joined together in threadlike formation and averaging approximately 10 glucose units each. Because of the variation in the number of glucose units in each specific glucan fiber, it is appropriate to use the term "beta-glucans" rather than "beta-glucan" in referring to this soluble dietary fiber. The type of chemical bond holding the individual glucose units together differs from that in starch and cellulose. Because of the specific way the glucose units are joined, this material is neither digestible, like starch, nor a water-insoluble material of considerable tensile strength, like cellulose.

Structurally, it is like cellulose, but with "kinks" that make it water soluble (i.e., forming a colloidal solution) and viscous. At the present time, oat bran, barley, psyllium seed, and beans offer the best yields of beta-glucans, but the food industry and individual investigators continue to search for alternative economical sources. The highly viscous beta-glucans form about 4 percent of regular rolled oats and 7 to 10 percent of commercial oat bran. Methods have been developed to prepare oat beta-glucans in multipound amounts, which, when partially purified, are referred to as oat gum. Detailed reviews on the chemistry of beta-glucans have been published (Bamforth, 1982; Wood, 1986).

Choosing the Best Dietary Fiber for a Specific Problem

A diet high in nonsoluble fiber is now widely accepted as a treatment for patients with constipation, diverticulitis, or hemorrhoids. Since the effectiveness of the therapy apparently depends principally on increasing the stool weight and softness and decreasing the transit time, wheat bran is a logical choice. Beta-glucans do not seem to play a major role in this situation. On the other hand, the relationship of dietary fiber to the lowering of the level of serum cholesterol and other plasma lipids in cases of hypercholesterolemia, and to reducing the incidence of coronary heart disease, rests largely on the effects of soluble fiber, which contains beta-glucans. Experiments (Kritchevsky, 1974) have failed to demonstrate that wheat bran (lacking in soluble fiber) causes any appreciable lowering in plasma cholesterol levels. Raymond and colleagues (1977), for example, reported that eating as many as nine wheat bran muffins per day had no effect on the plasma lipid in either normal subjects or those with high cholesterol levels. Large quantities of pectin, a soluble fiber, on the other hand, did produce some lowering of plasma cholesterol. When large quantities of insoluble fiber were added to diets, stool weights increased greatly, and intestinal transit time decreased significantly. Bile excretion in the stools was not consistently increased, and cholesterol absorption was not affected.

The popular interest in oat bran as opposed to wheat bran derives from the many animal and clinical studies indicating the specific value of soluble dietary fiber in the regulation of glucose metabolism and reduction of serum cholesterol levels (see Anderson, 1980; deGroot, 1963; Wood *et al.*, 1989).

Although the use of oat bran in treatment of diabetes and high levels of serum cholesterol was reported relatively recently, there is a long tradition of oats as healthy food. Reports of the benefits of oatmeal in the management of diabetes (Allen, 1913) and clinical evidence for its value in lowering serum cholesterol (deGroot, 1963) can be viewed as forerunners of today's voluminous literature on these aspects of dietary fiber. The mechanisms by which the beta-glucans may reduce high blood sugar levels following a meal and lower blood serum cholesterol levels are not certain, but may involve delayed gastric emptying and delayed intestinal absorption. It appears that the viscosity of beta-glucans delays the release of stomach contents into the small intestine as well as slows intestinal absorption of nutrients and cholesterol.

Positive Aspects of Dietary Fiber

Foods containing dietary fiber can make a positive contribution to nutrition because of the lengthy chewing they sometimes require. Eating an apple or a raw carrot stimulates the flow of saliva and digestive juices. The additional time and energy it takes to eat food containing a good deal of fiber results in slower digestion in contrast to readily absorbed high-sugar foodstuffs such as cake.

It has been found that coarse, flaky particles of bran have a greater effect in reducing the gastrointestinal transit time than smaller, fine particles with floury characteristics. The coarse bran has been found to have a significantly greater water-holding capacity. For years, it has been known that increased dietary fiber gives rise to larger, softer stools, partly because it provides a substrate for certain bacteria, normally present in the colon, that are capable of decomposing mixed polysaccharides, and it stimulates their growth. The metabolic products of the fibers themselves have a stimulating effect and so induce bowel movement, while evolved gases, including carbon dioxide, hydrogen and methane, contribute to softening the stools. Low-fiber diets produce small, hard stools that pass through the gut slowly, while high-fiber diets produce large, soft stools that pass more quickly and thus reduce the time the intestinal wall is exposed to toxic substances.

The addition of 30 grams of wheat bran can approximately double the weight of stool from an average of about 100 grams per day in this country to 200 grams. Two factors are related to stool weight: the ability of the fiber to retain water, and the greater amount of bacteria whose growth is facilitated by the presence of the fiber. Addition of wheat bran to a hot breakfast cereal, increasing the crude fiber content from 4 to 6 grams to 6 to 8 grams, restored normal function to 60 percent of the residents of a long-term care facility, most of whom had previously required laxatives (Hull *et al.*, 1980). A study of the relative effects of wheat bran and certain fruits and vegetables has shown that bran has the greatest laxative effect, followed by cabbage. Lettuce and celery have no significant effect, while that of other foods varies. The stools from subjects on cereal supplements are generally heavier than those from subjects taking vegetable and fruit supplements. An interesting finding is that a wheat bran supplement may increase or decrease transit time according to the direction from normality of the original finding, that is to say, it has a regulating effect on both constipation and diarrhea and is not just a laxative.

Dietetic Role in Constipation and Allied Problems

In western countries, feeding habits predispose people to constipation, which can be looked at as part of the price paid for increased consumption of refined carbohydrate foods, for example, the overwhelming use of white bread as compared to whole wheat bread. Low-fiber foods do not promote gastrointestinal motility, but tend to cause intestinal stasis.

Constipation may be described as simple or uncomplicated when there is an absence of any primary medical cause. Simple constipation is much more frequent in the old than in the young. It may be self-induced by a low intake of food, a low intake of fiber-containing foods and of fluids, lack of exercise, ignoring the call for defecation, or a combination of some or all of these factors. It may also be due in part to poor toilet facilities, unfavorable working conditions, or travel.

For about 25 percent of older people, constipation is a problem. They often become overconcerned with bowel habits and many have the notion that a daily bowel movement is essential for good health. Actually, true constipation is characterized by fewer than two bowel movements per week, difficulty and pain with defecation, and possible bleeding. If any of these symptoms occur, a physician should be contacted without delay rather than resorting to self-treatment with laxatives.

The overuse of laxatives is common among older people and may be harmful because of the potential for dependency. Also, when mineral oil is used, it dissolves the fat-soluble vitamins A, D, E, and K in the intestinal tract. Since the mineral oil is not metabolized or absorbed, it is eliminated in the feces, carrying the fat-soluble vitamins with it. Over long periods, serious deficiencies can develop. A deficiency in vitamin A may contribute to the risk of cancer, skin problems, and poor eyesight; vitamin D deficiency may contribute to bone softening associated with osteoporosis; and a shortage of vitamin K may lead to easy bruising and bleeding problems.

The effect of a high-bulk diet on stool output depends on the type of roughage. Cellulose and noncellulose polysaccharides, which can be broken down to volatile fatty acids by bacterial action, may have a laxative effect, while lignin appears to have a constipating effect and indeed has been used for the management of diarrhea. The net effect of foods high in fiber is to increase the size of the stool and enhance peristalsis. For people who have a tendency to constipation, the dietetic approach is generally favored over resorting to medication. They should drink 6 to 8 glasses of fluids daily, develop regular bowel habits, and do some walking every day. Unlike so many laxatives, dietary fiber presents no major problems when taken long-term.

For simple constipation, an old-fashioned remedy utilizes water to initiate action. Water is an excellent lubricant, provided enough of it is taken in a short-enough period that it is not all absorbed from the alimentary tract; it helps to keep the feces soft and bulky. Probably the greatest laxative effect is obtained by taking one or two glasses of plain water, or with a trace of salt or lemon juice added, immediately on rising. It should not be sipped, but taken in large gulps in a brief period. Under these circumstances, the water passes quickly along the alimentary tract and, in conjunction with the breakfast later, stimulates the colon to its normal after-breakfast evacuation.

Appendicitis is an inflammation, either acute or chronic, of the vermiform appendix, a dead-end tube that varies from 3 to 6 inches in length and is about one third of an inch in diameter. The appendix opens off the point where the small and large intestines meet. Symptoms of acute appendicitis are severe abdominal pain, which localizes in the right lower quadrant of the abdomen, along with vomiting and a low-grade fever. As soon as a diagnosis of acute appendicitis is made, surgery is required to remove the infected appendix. Among adults, it is more common in males than in females. Among other contributing factors, the inflammation may be caused by a dry and hard mass of feces that closes off the opening to the appendix and consequently encourages the development of infection. The epidemiologic evidence supports the view that the incidence of the disease drops markedly in the presence of a high-fiber diet.

Hemorrhoids are dilated veins in the mucous membrane inside or just outside the rectum. Because they are easily aggravated by straining on defecation, there is some basis for recommending a high-fiber diet for persons who have this problem. Whole wheat bread provides one choice for many people when supplemented by a portion of natural wheat bran or one of the many bran-containing breakfast cereals. A heaping tablespoonful of natural bran is about five grams, and the amount needed will normally be between 10 and 15 grams; its equivalent in whole wheat bread would be 50 to 75 grams (two to three slices). For the rest of the day, generous portions of green vegetables, salads, and fruits can be recommended. To reiterate somewhat, among the best common sources of fiber are ground whole grains (such as wheat, oats, and barley), beans, broccoli, cabbage, potatoes with skins, and fruits such as apples, apricots, berries, and prunes. Carrots and spinach are generally handled better than cauliflower, cabbage, and brussels sprouts, which can cause gas formation.

Diverticular disease refers to the presence of pouchlike herniations (diverticula) of the wall of the colon, sometimes leading to inflammation (diverticulitis). It affects increasing numbers of people, usually older than 50, and often exhibits few symptoms except for occasional rectal bleeding, which can be severe. There is now considerable epidemiologic evidence from humans as well as animal experiments that this condition may also result from our modern, highly refined low-residue diet. The symptoms of diverticulitis are often relieved by a high-fiber diet. Sufficient evidence supports the theory that the more rapid passage of softer stools through the colon decreases the pressure exerted against its walls and thereby prevents formation and inflammation of diverticula.

In addition to being effective in preventing constipation, hemorrhoids, and diverticulitis, dietary fiber may have a role in preventing cancer of the large bowel, which is rapidly becoming the most common cancer in this country (NRC, 1989). Colon cancers have been prevented in laboratory animals by dietary fiber, and there is good reason to suppose that potential carcinogens in the intestinal contents would be diluted, bound, and more rapidly passed out of the system by a diet high in fiber. However, both epidemiologic and laboratory reports suggest that if there is actually an effect, specific components of fiber, rather than total fiber, are more likely to be responsible. In the only case-controlled study and the only study in which total fiber consumption was quantified rather than estimated from the consumption of high-fiber foods, the investigation "indicated that the incidence of colon cancer was inversely related to the intake of one fiber component—the pentosan fraction which is found in whole wheat products and other food items" (NAS, 1982, p. 7).

Abdominal Discomfort: Flatulence, Heartburn, and Hiatus Hernia

Discomfort in the abdominal area following ingestion of food may have many causes; among them are flatulence, heartburn, and hiatus hernia.

Flatulence, that is, the presence of excessive gas in the stomach and intestines, can be a source of annoyance and embarrassment. Gas-forming vegetables such as cabbage, beans, peas, and onions, carbonated beverages, swallowing air, foods high in fat, and chronic constipation all contribute to the problem. Abdominal distress is also common among people who make large abrupt additions of fiber to their diets. In any case, the discomfort often leads to a habit of constant swallowing in an effort to relieve the distress. Swallowing of air, however, results in more belching and more discomfort. Drugs such as digitalis or aspirin may also be at fault.

A change in eating patterns may relieve functional distress. Highly seasoned food, fatty food, and alcohol, as well as heavy meals should be avoided. Food should be chewed thoroughly, and eating should be unhurried.

A sudden increase of dietary fiber can accelerate the movement of undigested products through the intestine. The normal production of gases during the digestion of foods is usually absorbed through the walls of the intestine and dispersed in the blood. When foods move too quickly through the intestinal tract, however, these gases do not have time to disperse. Although most people adjust to the increased fiber over a period of a few weeks, a gradual increase in the fiber content of the diet is the better approach (Ribakove, 1983).

Heartburn is an uncomfortable, burning, and sometimes really painful sensation in the middle chest that occurs after meals. The heart is not involved, but rather the esophagus, which is the muscular tube about 10 inches long between the throat and stomach. A circular band of tissue, known as the cardiac sphincter, is located in the region where the esophagus joins the stomach and is normally contracted, thus closing off the opening to the stomach. Before food or fluid can enter the stomach, the cardiac sphincter must be relaxed. Though the mechanism by which the sphincter is opened is not clearly understood, most observers consider it to be under autonomic nervous system control. It may weaken and allow the acid and pepsin from the stomach to reflux or backflow into the esophagus, causing irritation. Heartburn is usually worse at night and when a person is reclining after a heavy meal.

Because of the extra fat on the abdomen, obesity increases the chance of food backflowing from the stomach to the esophagus. Since large meals predispose affected persons to reflux, it is advisable to eat smaller meals, but more often. Food should not be eaten less than 2 hours before retiring, since a reclining position increases the tendency for backflow.

Certain foods may impair the functioning of the cardiac sphincter. They include fatty, fried, and spicy foods; peppers; radishes; alcohol; peppermint and spearmint; coffee (regular and decaffeinated); and chocolate. Tomato products and citrus juices do not affect the sphincter, but may irritate the inflamed lining of the esophagus.

Antacids are used to treat heartburn mainly because of their acid-neutralizing effect, but also because they increase the sphincter pressure and thus decrease the backflow. Excessive use of antacids, whether they contain aluminum, magnesium, calcium, or sodium compounds, may be harmful. Older persons are frequently advised to take an antacid or eat a little food every two hours during the day and to take an additional dose of antacid at bedtime. When using an antacid containing a sodium compound, this number of doses may result in a high sodium intake and would, therefore, be ill advised for people with heart or kidney disease.

Loss of appetite and gastrointestinal complaints such as heartburn are sometimes a cause of emotional distress in older people, who often associate such problems with more serious disorders, such as cancer. Conversely, psychological stress and tension can itself lead to stomach and intestinal disorders. Peoples' concerns should not be dismissed lightly, and evaluation for the presence of organic disease by a physician is always in order.

Hiatus hernia describes a condition in which a portion of the stomach protrudes upward into the chest through the diaphragm. The condition occurs in about 40 percent of the population as a whole, but increases with aging; the occurrence varies from 40 to 60 percent of people who are middle-aged and to 90 percent of those older than 70 years. Women are affected more than men. Many people display few, if any, symptoms. In others, bleeding and ulceration of the esophagus may occur.

The major difficulty in symptomatic patients is the backflow or reflux of the acid contents of the stomach into the esophagus. The standard treatment is similar to that for heartburn.

Diagnosis is made easily by x-ray. Surgical treatment is usually unnecessary, and efforts should be directed toward alleviating the discomfort associated with the reflux.

Lactose Intolerance

The inability to digest lactose, the principal sugar in milk (see Table 5.1), occurs in more than half of the world's population. The

Table 5.1. Lactose Content of Selected
Dairy Products

Product	Serving size	Lactose (grams)
Milk	1 cup	11
Low-fat milk	1 cup	9–13
Skim milk	1 cup	12–14
Buttermilk	1 cup	9–11
Cheese		
Cream	1 oz	0.7–0.8
Camembert	1 oz	0.1
Cheddar	1 oz	0.4–0.6
Cottage cheese	1 cup	5–6
Ice cream	1 cup	9
Sherbet, orange	1 cup	4

Source: Walsh, J.O. *Am. J. Clin. Nutr.* 31:592–596, 1978

problem results from lack of the enzyme lactase, normally present in the small intestine. Some medical experts refer to lactose intolerance as the most common of all enzyme-deficiency diseases. Other experts do not agree that lactose intolerance is a disease, but rather consider it a normal genetic variation programmed by thousands of years of cultural and racial dietary habits. If a person's ancestors came from a region of the world where milk is frequently consumed by adults, such as Scandinavia, it is unlikely that he or she will have lactose intolerance. People with ancestral origins in China or sub-Saharan Africa, where milk is not consumed past early childhood, probably have a limit to the amount of milk they can consume without discomfort.

The symptoms of lactose intolerance are bloating, cramps, and diarrhea after the ingestion of milk or milk-containing foods. These symptoms occur when the undigested lactose reaches the colon where bacteria metabolize it into fatty acids. Both these fatty acids and any remaining lactose are very irritating to the bowel. The result is diarrhea. Most individuals with lactose intolerance produce enough of the necessary enzyme to drink a half cup of milk without distress. Studies show that 70 percent of people with this problem remain symptom free even after consuming one cup of milk. However, a few lactose-intolerant individuals produce such small amounts of lactase that even the amount of milk present in a Hershey's Milk Chocolate bar causes distress.

Although lactose intolerance is measured in the laboratory by how much milk the individual is able to tolerate, milk is not the only dietary source of lactose. Lactose is used in a number of fabricated foods, and skim milk powder is added to almost every type of manufactured food product imaginable, from hot dogs to frosting mix. Making the situation more complex, manufacturer's formulations for similar products vary widely. For example, one national brand of creamy vanilla frosting contains nonfat milk, while another national brand does not. This variation in food products makes deciding whether or not to drink a glass of milk based on the amount of lactose already ingested a difficult task. Rather than go through a complicated decision-making process, most lactose-intolerant people avoid milk and other dairy products. They ignore the researchers who proclaim that lactose intolerant individuals can drink a glass of milk with good reason.

Lactose-intolerant individuals may avoid discomfort without eliminating dairy products from their diets. Low-lactose milk (Cheng *et al.*, 1979; Williams, 1989) is available under the brand name Lactaid in most areas of the United States. Lactase has been added to milk to decrease the lactose content by 70 percent. The enzyme itself is also available under the Lactaid name, and it can be used to make milk 100 percent lactose free. Emphasizing cheese and unpasteurized yogurt, which contains active bacterial lactase, as a replacement for milk is another possible solution. For persons unable to tolerate the small amounts of milk sugar present in hard cheeses, lactase is available in tablets, which can be taken as food is eaten. These tablets can also be used when drinking untreated milk.

A number of factors can affect the ability of the gastrointestinal (GI) tract to handle lactose. Age is not a concern once past early childhood. Although lactase production does decline during childhood, paralleling the decrease in milk drinking that occurs at this age, once the individual reaches adulthood, the amount of lactase produced remains constant. The aging process does produce some changes in the GI tract, but a major decline in lactase production has not been demonstrated. If drinking a quart of milk a day was possible at 25 years of age, this amount of milk should not cause diarrhea at 70.

The quantity of fat and sugar other than lactose present in a food may affect the ability of the GI tract to handle lactose. Some lactose-intolerant people have reported the ability to tolerate chocolate milk, but not plain whole milk. The reason for this appears in some cases to be due to the sugar added to the chocolate milk and in other cases to changes in the amount and type of fat. High concentrations of sugar and fat in foods are known to slow the release of stomach contents into the small intestine. Slowing the release of lactose from the stomach gives the limited amount of lactase present time to digest the milk sugar.

Diarrhea from any cause decreases the ability to digest lactose. The enzyme lactase is lost as intestinal contents move through the GI tract more rapidly than normal. Consequently, the diarrhea will increase in severity if any lactose is consumed. Once the diarrhea has subsided, lactose should be avoided for some time until lactase levels in the small bowel have returned to normal. This may take only one day if the diarrhea lasted only a few days. If the diarrhea involved damage to the lining of the small intestine, several weeks may pass before it heals and is again able to digest lactose.

Negative Aspects of Dietary Fiber

As with so many things, there are some negative aspects to the dietary fiber issue, namely, possible adverse affects on mineral absorption. Unprocessed bran fiber and bran cereals contain phytic acid. This substance combines with essential minerals in the diet, including calcium, iron, magnesium, and zinc, to form insoluble compounds that are eliminated in the feces, thus draining away a certain amount of the minerals ingested with food by preventing their absorption from the GI tract. Unprocessed bran contains approximately one percent phytic acid, but the amount in whole wheat bread is greatly reduced because much of it is destroyed by the enzyme phytase while the dough is rising. At the levels consumed in the United States, neither wheat bran nor other fibers appear to pose a serious problem regarding the absorption of minerals for most people. Strict vegetarians and some older people may have intakes of calcium, iron, and zinc below desirable levels. Consuming quantities of wheat bran could compromise their nutritional status.

In addition to the problem of phytic acid, it has been found that starch, protein, and the fiber itself all form insoluble complexes with calcium, iron, and zinc. Although the starch and protein release their bound metals when broken down by pancreatic amylase and trypsin enzymes in the digestive tract, the fiber fails to release the metal until it reaches the large intestine, where it, too, is partly degraded. It has also been found that lignin binds with bile acids and increases their excretion and that vitamin D can bind to the same fiber–bile acid complex and thus be transported through the intestinal tract without absorption. In this way, a high-fiber diet might lead to enough wastage of vitamin D to produce the symptoms of adult rickets. These points should be kept in mind particularly when concerned about older people whose body stores of calcium and iron may already be low. Exposure to sunshine whenever possible should be encouraged, and supplementation may be advisable.

Unsettled Questions

Recently Swain *et al.* (1990) published the results of a study designed to determine whether oat bran diets lower serum cholesterol levels by replacing fatty foods in the diet or by a direct effect of the soluble dietary fiber contained in oat bran. To determine which is the case, they compared isocaloric supplements of high-fiber oat bran (87 grams/day) and a low-fiber refined wheat product (Cream of Wheat) on the serum lipoprotein cholesterol levels of 20 healthy subjects. After a one-week baseline period during which they consumed their usual diets, the subjects were given each type of supplement for six week periods in a double-blind, crossover trial.

Both types of supplements were reported to have lowered the mean baseline serum cholesterol by 7 to 8 percent. The subjects ate less saturated fat and cholesterol and more polyunsaturated fat during both periods of supplementation than at baseline, and the changes were sufficient to explain all of the reduction in serum cholesterol levels caused by both the high-fiber and low-fiber diets. The average blood pressure did not change during each dietary period. The authors concluded that oat bran has little cholesterol-lowering effect and that high-fiber and low-fiber dietary grain supplements reduce serum cholesterol about equally.

Although, on the surface, this appears to be a well-conducted study of normal people, further similar studies using much larger numbers of participants are warranted on both normal and on hypercholesterolemic subjects. It is difficult to square the results of Swain and co-workers with those reported by the majority of other investigators. The discordance may be traceable to the relatively small number of participants in the Swain study. It should be noted also (Bell et al., 1989) that psyllium seed, a good source of soluble fiber, did produce lowering of total and low-density lipoprotein cholesterol levels in a randomized double-blind study in patients with mild-to-moderate hypercholesterolemia. Humble (1991) provided a brief, but balanced review of the literature on the ability of dietary oats to lower blood levels of cholesterol. He commented on the Swain study and the paper by Van Horn et al. (1991), which considers the feasibility of using oats to alter serum lipids among Americans who have elevated levels of total cholesterol.

In this connection, it is in order to mention that a chick-screening model for preliminary testing of the effectiveness of various substances in lowering cholesterol levels has been developed (Newman et al., 1988). The model utilizes six to ten chicks with previously elevated cholesterol, to whom the products are fed for seven to ten days. When products are identified as potentially hypocholesterolemic, larger scale trials can be conducted for more conclusive results. In ongoing investigations on the effectiveness of beta-glucans in barley as hypocholesterolemic agents, the chick-screening model was used. They found that one particular hull-less barley (Washonupana) caused significant reductions in both total (−16 percent) and low-density lipoprotein (−30 percent) cholesterol. The effects were reversed by supplementing the diet with beta-glucanase, an enzyme that hydrolyzes the beta-glucans (Newman et al., 1989). These experimental results confirm that the effectiveness of beta-glucans on serum cholesterol levels is direct.

Water

Water, in its most abundant liquid form, covers 70 percent of the whole earth, and is one of the most necessary substances for the maintenance of all life. It makes up about 50 to 80 percent of the weight of the human body, the wide variations being dependent mainly on body fat content. Deprivation of this nutrient upsets life-supporting processes within the body more rapidly than does a deficiency of any vitamin or mineral. A person can live for months or even years without an intake of some essential vitamins or minerals, but will survive for only a few days if deprived of water. Even mild dehydration may hamper physical and mental performance and cause fatigue. In most western countries, it has been estimated that each persons uses from 15 to 50 gallons daily for personal purposes alone.

For centuries, water was considered an "element," but in 1781, Lord Cavendish of England synthesized it from its elements by exploding a mixture of hydrogen and oxygen gases. He proved that it was a compound of two volumes of hydrogen and one volume of oxygen; hence, it is represented in chemistry by the formula H_2O, which is probably recognized by more people than is any other chemical formula. When perfectly pure, water is colorless, tasteless, and odorless, but all natural waters contain impurities. Although it is commonly spoken of as a liquid, it exists, of course, in the solid state, such as ice and snow, and in gaseous forms, such as water vapor in the atmosphere, and steam.

Distribution

About 60 percent of the total body weight and 70 percent of the lean body mass are made up of water. The proportion will vary from 50 to 80 percent depending on age and the amount of body fat. Every single cell in the body contains water. It is, however, present in widely varying concentrations in different tissues, making up 72 percent of muscle, 20 to 35 percent of fatty tissue, and 10 percent of bone and cartilage. The body of a woman, compared to that of a man of the same weight, contains slightly less water; breast tissue and other more substantial fat deposits are mainly lipid and contain a smaller proportion of water than does muscle tissue. Older women who are both sedentary and obese may be only 50 percent water. There is comparatively little water in fat cells so that the percentage of body water drops as the amount of body fat rises. Exercise also influences the amount of water present in the body. As a person exercises, muscle mass is built, the amount of water increases, and the percentage of body fat declines (e.g., as in a 22-year-old runner who is 70 percent water). Increasing body water by building muscle mass is possible at any age, but it is more difficult at 75 than at 25 years.

Body water is distributed into two major compartments. The intracellular space comprises the fluids contained within the trillions of cells of the body and accounts for about two thirds of the total body water. The extracellular space consists partly of the fluids within the blood and lymph vessels, the juices of the GI tract, the fluid within the eye, the cerebrospinal fluid, and the fluid that fills the spaces between cells in tissues such as muscles, skin, liver, and kidney. It is well to remember that no two cells of the body actually touch each other; they are separated and surrounded by a thin film of tissue fluid. This tissue fluid accounts for one third of the total body water.

The total body fluids add up to about 40 liters. Of this total, the intracellular volume is about 25 liters and the extracellular volume is 15 liters. The volume of the blood is about five liters. It includes the red cell volume (two liters), which is a part of the intracellular volume; the plasma volume (three liters) is, on the other hand, a part of the extracellular volume.

Functions of Body Water

Water plays an important part in a multiplicity of functions; which is why it is vitally important to maintain the proper amount of fluid in the body.

Digestion

Water plays several roles in digestion. It aids in chewing and swallowing fluid and participates in the breakdown of complex carbohydrates, fats, and proteins into their component nutrients. The nutrients then pass through the intestinal membrane and into the blood and lymph, aided by water. Furthermore, nutrients and oxygen are carried to the cells for metabolism by water in the blood vessels.

Metabolism

Water is the medium in which all metabolic reactions occur. For example, when energy is released from the metabolism of carbohydrates, fats, and proteins, or when amino acids link together to form proteins, these substances as well as the minerals, enzymes, and other necessary cofactors are all dissolved in water.

In addition to being a reaction medium, water is a participant in many reactions. The synthesis of carbohydrates, lipids, and proteins as well as the reactions of energy-releasing processes all involve the addition or removal of water molecules.

Solvent and Transportation Medium

Body water is not stagnant; it can and does undergo change from hour to hour. It is circulating constantly and, in so doing, transports many of the dissolved substances such as vitamins, minerals, and macronutrients that it contains, from one part of the body to another. This function is related to the fact that more substances will dissolve in water than in any other liquid.

Excretion

When water leaves the body, as the major component of urine, it carries with it many substances that are no longer needed. Water is necessary for washing out any toxic byproducts or end-products formed during chemical reactions within the body. Many of these byproducts are filtered out by the kidneys and excreted in the urine.

The kidneys are able to handle most toxic components if they are dissolved in water. If the solution becomes too concentrated, however, the toxic products build up, resulting in damage to or malfunctioning of the body. One such toxic component is common sodium found in table salt. An excess of sodium creates a physical need for water; this is the reason a person feels thirsty after eating a salty meal. Other substances that require dilution and thus lead to thirst include alcohol and high-protein foods.

Regulation of Body Temperature

Water participates in the regulation of body temperature. Its evaporation from the skin is the major mechanism utilized by the body to rid itself of extra heat produced during the metabolism of carbohydrates, fats, and proteins. Some of this heat is required to maintain body temperature at 98.6 °F (as measured under the tongue), the temperature at which many enzymes crucial to metabolic processes function most effectively. Because of its ability to conduct heat, water assists in its even distribution throughout the body. Normal metabolism, however, provides more heat than is necessary to maintain normal temperature. If this excess heat is not released quickly, the body temperature will increase to a point where cellular enzymes are inactivated. The evaporation of fluid from the skin requires energy in the form of heat, and the body therefore constantly cools itself by causing water to be lost by evaporation.

The loss of heat through the skin represents about 25 percent of the total caloric expenditure. The water loss is normally 350 to 750 ml per day, but it may be increased under certain conditions, including high temperatures, high altitude, and dry air (RDA, 1989, p. 247).

Other Functions of Water

Water, in the form of saliva, tears, or mucus, serves as a lubricant for the body (e.g., saliva facilitates the passage of food down the esophagus, and in the synovial fluid of joints, water acts as a lubricant).

Within the cells, water may be incorporated in the biosynthesis of new material. For example, glycogen, the form in which carbohydrates are stored, accumulates only in the presence of water, and the deposition of fat involves the accumulation of an additional 20 percent water.

Water Balance

For practical purposes, 1 ml per kcalorie of energy expenditure is recommended as the water requirement for adults under average conditions of energy expenditure and environmental exposure (RDA, 1989, p. 249). Because there is so seldom a risk of water intoxication, the requirement is often increased to 1.5 ml per kcalorie to cover variations in activity level, sweating, and solute load. For men or women older than 50 years, this works out to be about two to three liters or quarts (eight to 12 8-ounce glasses) per day. The actual intake, in the form of drinking water, other fluids, and solid foods, varies considerably, but is ordinarily kept within normal bounds without conscious regulation. Under stressful conditions, when a person is very hot or working very hard, the requirements may double or triple. People get a great deal of their water requirements from food materials (see Table 5.2). Vegetables are 90 to 95 percent water, fruits are 80 to 85 percent water, and meat, fish, and poultry are as high as 70 to 75 percent water.

The total intake is the amount of water entering the body as part of foods, such as meat, potatoes, vegetables, and also as beverages, including pure water, and varies with individual diet preferences. It averages, for adults, about 2,500 ml (2.5 qt) each day. In addition to the water intake from foods and beverages (see Table 5.3), about 300

Table 5.2. Percentage of Water in Selected Foods

Head lettuce	95.5	Peas, cooked	81.5
Asparagus, cooked	93.6	Potatoes, raw	79.8
Watermelon	92.6	Chicken fryer, broiled	71.0
Broccoli spears, cooked	91.3	Sweet potatoes, raw	70.6
Skim milk	90.5	Rice, cooked	70.3
Peaches, fresh	89.1	Beef chuck, braised	49.4
Orange juice	88.3	Beef sirloin, broiled	43.9
Apple juice	87.8	Pork loin, roast	43.7
Whole milk	87.4	Bread	30–35.0
Apples, fresh	84.4	Butter	15.5
Pears, fresh	83.2	Oil, corn	0.0

SOURCE: U.S.D.A. Handbook No. 8.

Table 5.3. Simplified Illustration of Water Balance
in an Adult Person

Intake (ml/d)		Output (ml/d)	
Water and other beverages	1200	Lungs	400
Water from solid food	1000	Skin	500
Water from oxidation	300	Urine	1400
		Feces	200
Total	2500	Total	2500

ml is formed within the body from an average adult daily diet, by the metabolism of carbohydrates, fats, and protein.

The output of water is the amount that leaves the body daily through the urine, skin, lungs, and GI tract. Approximate average figures are in the urine, 1,400 ml; from the skin, 500 ml; from the lungs, 400 ml, and in the feces, 200 ml, or a total of 2,500 ml.

Small imbalances between intake and output, if only temporary, have few consequences. Prolonged imbalances of a minor degree or severe imbalances that occur quickly can be dangerous. If excessive amounts of water are lost and not replaced, the cells become dehydrated. If the amount of water consumed exceeds the amount lost, the excess water is retained within and between cells, thereby causing parts of the body, usually those in the lower portions, to swell. This condition is called edema.

By the time a person experiences the sensation of thirst, there has already been a deficit of body water. Almost colorless urine is a good sign that sufficient water is being taken in. Some liquids are more appropriate and effective than others in supplying water. When the air is hot, the body needs water—not iced tea or beer, but water! Coffee, tea, and alcoholic beverages all have diuretic properties, that is, they increase the amount of water, as urine, lost through the kidneys (Gershoff and Whitney, 1990). The diuretic in coffee and tea is caffeine, and in beer, it is alcohol. As a consequence, these drinks may quench the thirst, but do not replenish the water needed by the body.

Those exercising or working vigorously outdoors have increased need for water. It has been suggested that eight to ten ounces of fluid be taken every 20 minutes during strenuous exercise (Nix and Carlson, 1988). During exercise vigorous enough to cause copious sweating, sodium and potassium are excreted in the sweat in a ratio of about 8:1, respectively. Over time, this situation can cause what is referred to as an electrolyte imbalance in the body. A recipe (Nix and Carlson, 1988) for a homemade electrolyte replacement drink or sports beverage follows: Combine four cups of water, ¼ cut of frozen orange juice concentrate (for flavor and potassium), and ⅔ teaspoon of salt (for sodium). Chill thoroughly.

Special Situations for Older People

In the older person, fluid intake may be less than is needed. Thirst insures adequate intake in the young, but older individuals frequently drink less than is necessary due to decreased sensitivity to dehydration. Additionally, with advancing age, the kidneys are less efficient at conserving water. The urine volume is greater than that in young individuals at the same time that thirst is less able to compensate for this increased loss of water.

Common health problems in the elderly can lead to decreased intake despite the development of thirst. Water may not be conveniently available to individuals with nervous system dysfunction, or arthritis may be severe enough to limit mobility. Individuals with urinary incontinence may voluntarily restrict fluid intake in an attempt to control the problem.

As people age, there is a reduction in total body water. Approximately 72 percent of the total body water is in lean body mass as interstitial fluid (Chernoff, 1990). With the decrease in lean body mass, there is an associated decrease in total body water (Chernoff et al., 1984). There is also a greater likelihood that patients may dehydrate rapidly under conditions of inadequate fluid intake or excessive body or climatic heat (Chernoff, 1990). Signs of dehydration in older people include dry mouth, dry tongue, dry loose skin, sunken eyes, constipation, flushing, fever, personality change, and confusion. Illnesses that cause vomiting and/or diarrhea as well as fever can increase fluid requirements dramatically. It is also not uncommon for older people to limit their fluid intake in the mistaken belief that it will stop diarrhea. Both vigorous exercise that leads to excessive sweating and high-protein diets increase fluid loss. It is vital for elderly people who must cope with these problems to consume extra water to compensate for heavy fluid losses.

Some years ago, a major soup company in this country sponsored research that showed that serving soup three times a day, at the start of each meal, reduces caloric intake. Over time, the individuals on this regimen lost weight. The research project demonstrated that fluid intake can influence, to a considerable extent, how much an individual eats. Frail, underweight elderly people should not be served soup and/or juice at the beginning of a meal. Consuming quantities of liquid at the start of a meal can have a negative impact on their weight and nutritional status. Conversely, overweight individuals can start a meal with juice or a noncream soup to aid in controlling the amount of food eaten.

6

Major Nutrition-Related Diseases of Importance to Older People

A number of diseases take their heaviest toll from among people who are 50 years of age or older. These are chronic diseases that persist over a long period as contrasted to the course of an acute disease, which is generally characterized by a rapid onset, severe symptoms, and a short course. The chronic diseases include cardiovascular disease (atherosclerosis, high blood pressure, heart attack, and stroke), diabetes mellitus, cancer, musculoskeletal problems (osteoporosis, arthritis, gout), and nutritional anemias. A few of them may be prevented, several can be controlled, and some can be reversed through the intelligent application of the appropriate nutritional principles set forth in this chapter, and, in the case of osteoporosis, in Chapter 11.

Atherosclerosis and Cardiovascular Disease

In developed nations, cardiovascular disease (CVD) which includes any dysfunction of the heart and blood vessels, is the most drastic epidemic of modern times. In adults, it is largely a problem of affluent societies. As outlined in the Surgeon General's Report (1988), diseases due to nutritional deficiencies have almost been eliminated in most developed countries. The list includes rickets, pellagra, scurvy, beriberi, xerophthalmia (dry eyes, leading to ulceration and

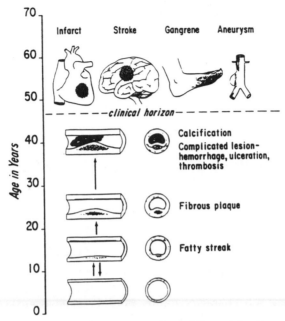

Figure 6.1. A diagrammatic representation of the origination and development of atherosclerotic lesions. The course of events is stage 1, fatty streak, which may first appear in childhood; stage 2, the fibrous plaque, a low-grade inflammatory reaction and a healing response; stage 3, tissue death, calcification, development of new blood vessels in the plaque, and hemorrhage, all predisposing to thrombosis (i.e., the formation of a blood clot), which causes a reduction in the lumen of small arteries and eventually leads to complete blockage of the artery. The whole process may take about 45 years. SOURCE: *Atherosclerosis and Its Origin*, Academic Press, with permisssion.

eventually to blindness), and goiter, caused, respectively, by a lack of adequate vitamin D, niacin, vitamin C, thiamin, vitamin A, and iodine. Unfortunately, they have been replaced by diseases due to dietary excess and imbalance, which now rank among the leading causes of illness and death in this country. These latter diseases are mostly cases of degenerative cardiovascular disease, that is, there is a deterioration of structure or function of tissue involved. They include heart attacks, strokes, congestive heart failure, and some aspects of high blood pressure. The underlying cause is generally atherosclerosis.

According to the American Heart Association (1988), at least 60 million people in the United States suffer from some form of heart or blood vessel disease, and according to the Surgeon General's Report (1988), heart attacks alone were responsible for about 512,000 deaths or 24 percent of all deaths recorded in the United States in 1987. Other heart diseases claimed an additional 248,000 deaths, and stroke claimed 149,000, or a total of more than 900,000 that year. Cardiovascular disease has been the leading cause of death in this country since 1920 and outnumbers deaths due to all other causes, including cancer and accidents (the two other most common ones) lumped together. Prior to 1920, the chief killer was infectious diseases, all now largely controlled.

Despite the grim statistical data, deaths from CVD have declined steadily in recent years. To be more specific, CVD mortality from 1964 to 1985 declined 42 percent. Many authorities believe this resulted from individuals putting into practice some of the recommendations arising out of the vast research on the etiology of atherosclerosis. A simultaneous dramatic decline in the incidence of stroke in the United States has also occurred, many believe because of the good work done by physicians in diagnosing and treating high blood pressure in its earlier stages.

Atherosclerosis and Arteriosclerosis

Atherosclerosis is often confused with arteriosclerosis, which is a generic term used to describe the thickening, loss of elasticity, and hardening of arterial walls (Katz and Stamler, 1953). It is a general aging phenomenon that occurs in all populations. Atherosclerosis, on the other hand, is a disorder characterized by plaques (deposits) of cholesterol, fats, and cellular debris in the inner layers of the walls of medium-sized and large arteries (Figure 6.1). The distribution of plaques is not uniform throughout the arterial tree. The most likely places for plaque formation are at sites of bifurcation or openings of tributaries of smaller diameter, where there is a certain amount of turbulence in an otherwise smooth flow of blood. Although arteriosclerosis and atherosclerosis can exist together, there is no causative relationship between the degree of atherosclerosis and the loss of elasticity (Nakoshima and Tanikawa, 1971).

Atherosclerosis is a degenerative disease, that is, one in which there is a breakdown of structure or function of a tissue. Atherosclerotic plaques (deposits), made up of cholesterol, cholesterol esters, fats, calcium deposits, iron salts, and cellular debris, form in the inner layers of the walls of medium-sized and large arteries. As the plaques develop, the vessel walls thicken in irregular fashion because of abnormal formation of fibrous tissue, the lumen (passageway or channel) narrows, and less blood circulates in organs and areas normally supplied by the artery involved (e.g., the heart, the brain, the kidneys, and the lower extremities).

During youth and middle age, men are more prone to develop the disease than women (e.g., white men between the ages of 30 and 49 are 6.9 times more likely to develop CVD than are white women). The difference diminishes after the menopause. Conventional wisdom relates the protection for women to the presence of sex hormones, the estrogens, but the action is poorly understood. It may even be related to the amount of iron in the bloodstream (Salonen *et al.*, 1992). In the later decades (sixth and seventh), unlike the earlier ones, women are more frequently victims than are men. If the frequency of deaths from CVD is averaged over the entire life span, it is evident that women are affected about as often as men.

Humans are the only mammals who show a marked tendency to develop atherosclerosis. It does not arise spontaneously in animals, although the disease can be induced in many species by force-feeding a diet they would not normally eat. One of the earliest reports is of work done in 1908, when atherosclerosis was produced in rabbits by force-feeding them high-fat diets of milk, meat, and eggs.

Angina, Heart Attack, Stroke, and Hypertension

Heart attacks can be looked on as a complication of coronary atherosclerosis (i.e., fatty thickening of the inner lining of the coronary arteries that encircle the heart in the form of a crown and carry the blood supply and its load of oxygen and other nutrients for the heart tissue). It must be remembered that although the heart (actually the heart muscle or myocardium) pumps all the blood in the body through its chambers well over a thousand times a day, it does not receive any oxygen or other nutrients from it. As the channels or lumens of one or more of the coronary arteries decreases in diameter due to advancing atherosclerosis, an insufficient amount of blood and oxygen reaches the heart muscle, a condition referred to as myocardial ischemia (decreased blood supply).

Angina pectoris (angina), which is characterized by severe pain in the chest, usually radiating to the shoulder and down the left arm, is caused by a poor blood supply to the muscles of the heart due to partially clogged coronary arteries. The pain, which is generally felt during physical exertion, an emotional upset, or after a heavy meal, normally recedes quickly on resting, but will require close medical intervention. Although it is a serious condition, it does not necessarily mean that a heart attack is imminent.

A heart attack (also described as a coronary thrombosis, coronary occlusion, or myocardial infarction) occurs when a blood clot (thrombus), formed either in the vicinity of the plaque or elsewhere in the body, becomes lodged in the narrowed artery and blocks the flow of blood. As a result, the part of the heart that depends on that artery for its blood supply and thus its oxygen and other nutrients is damaged, and the tissue dies. To this is attributed the pain of a heart attack. If the affected area is limited, the heart may continue to function. The alternative is sudden death.

Eight out of ten persons survive heart attacks, and their distress usually disappears in less than a week. In fact, the victim may feel so well that he or she may refuse to follow the admonition to stay in bed long enough, which is a treacherous aspect of the disease. Rest is essential because the heart muscle undergoes certain changes after the coronary artery is obstructed. The person may feel fine, but that part of the ventricle of the heart deprived of nourishment is undergoing changes that need attention. Muscle fibers in this area die and leave a soft spot in the wall of the heart. Completion of the softening process takes from 10 to 14 days, and unless the individual remains quiet during this period, complications may follow. After the 10- to 14-day period passes, the area begins to heal, and by the end of six weeks, the dead muscle fibers are replaced by tough scar tissue. Six more weeks are generally needed for recuperation.

Blood pressure is a measure of the force exerted by the heart on the walls of the arteries, the veins, and the chambers of the heart. It is measured in millimeters of mercury (mm Hg). Two blood pressure numbers are involved. The first and higher number, the systolic pressure, reflects the maximum pressure in the arteries as the ventricles of the heart contract (systole). The second number, the diastolic pressure, reflects the minimum pressure in the arteries during the period of rest between heart beats (diastole).

It used to be said that the diastolic pressure was more important, as it reflects the baseline pressure in the arteries during all but the brief periods when the ventricles are contracting. Recent studies, however, clearly indicate that both pressures are important in predicting the risk of certain diseases, particularly strokes.

The numbers that mark the line between normal and abnormal blood pressure increase with age. In a healthy, young adult, the systolic pressure is approximately 120 and the diastolic pressure is about 80. Consistent, abnormally high blood pressure is indicative of hypertension. Systolic pressure often varies more than the diastolic pressure with age, emotions, exertion, and so on. Most authorities accept a diastolic pressure consistently above 100, in a person older than 60, or above 90, in a person younger than 50, as evidence of hypertension. The World Health Organization sets the upper limits of normal at 160/95.

Most physicians consider elevation of the systolic pressure alone to be less significant than elevation of both numbers or elevation of the diastolic pressure alone. It is quite common for the elderly, in particular, to have a greater increase in the systolic than in the diastolic pressure.

According to the Surgeon General's Report (1988), almost 58 million people in the United States have hypertension, including 39 million who are younger than 65. The occurrence increases with age and is higher for black Americans (of whom 38 percent are hypertensive) than for white Americans (29 percent). Hypertension is a major risk factor for both heart disease and stroke and can seriously damage the kidneys as well. The precise cause of most cases of hypertension is still a matter of speculation among scientists.

A stroke, the risk of which is strongly affected by high blood pressure, occurs when a blood clot or rupture in an artery feeding the brain interferes with blood flow to a part of the brain. Depriving a part of the brain of its normal blood supply results in a loss of consciousness, paralysis, speech defect, or death depending on the site and extent of brain damage.

Cholesterol, Lipoproteins, and Fat

Before the effects of lipids on the incidence of CVD can be discussed, a review of some of the basic facts regarding cholesterol, lipoproteins, and fats is in order because of the important roles they play in the development of the disease. It has become abundantly clear that cholesterol and associated lipids are intimately involved in the evolution of atherosclerotic disease. Whether a person agrees that their role is fundamental or not, it has been obvious for almost two decades that blood lipids can be used as one of the better biochemical predictors of chemical coronary events (Bortz, 1974). In any discussion of atherosclerosis and CVD, the substances called cholesterol, saturated fat, unsaturated fat, and lipoproteins play an important role.

Cholesterol is a soft, pearly white and almost waxy substance and the most abundant sterol in animal tissues. It is found in all animal fats and oils, in organ meats, in egg yolks (the single richest food source), in milk and in other dairy products. There is none in foods of plant origin such as fruits, cereals, peanuts, vegetables, and nuts. More than half of the cholesterol in human blood is synthesized in the body itself at the rate of roughly 800 to 1500 mg daily; the remainder comes from the diet. Of the biosynthesized cholesterol, about 90 percent is formed in the liver and 10 percent, in the intestinal mucosa.

Although cholesterol is a major contributor to the development of atherosclerosis, it serves several vital functions in the body. Approximately 80 percent is used to form cholic acid in the liver, which is then converted to bile salts, which are necessary for the digestion and absorption of dietary fats. Small amounts of cholesterol are used to facilitate formation of the sex hormones (estrogen and pro-gesterone in women and testosterone in men) and the very important adrenocortical hormones. Large amounts are deposited in the horny outer layer of the skin, giving the skin its resistance to absorption of water-soluble substances. Cholesterol also assists in the maintenance of cellular integrity by forming an insoluble cell membrane. Cholesterol concentrations in the plasma may be affected by the amount of dietary cholesterol and fat ingested (Kinsella, 1987). To a certain extent, cholesterol and lipoprotein production are believed to be genetically determined and independent of dietary intake (Grundy, 1986). The major pathways for cholesterol excretion are through conversion to bile salts and elimination in the feces.

Because lipids, including cholesterol, are insoluble in water, they must be united with enough protein to make them water soluble if they are to be transported in the blood. These complex compounds are referred to as lipoproteins. Actually, about 70 percent of the cholesterol that circulates in the blood combines with fatty acids to form substances called esters. Both free (unesterified) cholesterol and its esters combine with protein to form soluble lipoproteins.

The soluble lipoproteins exist in two principal forms. One form, called low-density lipoprotein (LDL) or LDL cholesterol, which accounts for about two thirds or more of the total, appears to promote atherosclerosis. The LDL carries 60 to 75 percent of the total plasma cholesterol. The other form, called high-density lipoprotein (HDL) or HDL cholesterol, appears to protect against CVD. The HDL contains approximately 50 percent protein and smaller amounts of lipid. The LDL and HDL fractions are often, in popular fashion, referred to as "bad cholesterol" and "good cholesterol," respectively. There is increasing evidence that the relative distribution of cholesterol into LDL and HDL is a better monitor of the risk of CVD than is the level of total blood cholesterol. The level of HDL cholesterol alone is generally regarded as a good indicator of the risk of CVD; the higher the level of HDL, the lower the risk. More recently, it has been found that HDL cholesterol can be subdivided into two additional fractions, HDL_2 and HDL_3; of the two, HDL_2 has been more consistently linked with protection from cardiovascular disease (Musliner and Krauss, 1988).

The classification of edible fats into saturated, unsaturated, monounsaturated, and polyunsaturated is important regarding the genesis of atherosclerosis. As explained in a little more detail in Chapter 2, almost all edible fats (lipids) are made up of molecules of a substance called glycerol to which are attached three molecules of long-chain fatty acids. They are referred to as triglycerides. The fatty acids are said to be saturated, unsaturated, monounsaturated, or polyunsaturated. In a saturated fatty acid, every carbon in the chain holds the maximum number of hydrogen atoms. A monounsaturated fatty acid can attach one more hydrogen molecule (H_2) (i.e., two hydrogen atoms (2 H) per molecule), while a polyunsaturated fatty acid can attach two or more hydrogen molecules, each of which contain two hydrogen atoms. The generic term "unsaturated" refers to either "mono-" or "poly-" unsaturated fatty acids.

In the early 1950s, it was shown that ingestion of animal fats increased blood cholesterol levels, and vegetable fats tended to lower them. In the mid-1950s, it was shown that the opposite effects of the two types of fats were caused by their differing degrees of saturation. Animal fats, such as found in beef, pork, lamb, cheese, and butter, are saturated and generally solid at room temperature. Vegetable oils from corn, cottonseed, peanut, soybean, safflower, and sunflower plants, as well as fish oils, are mainly polyunsaturated, and liquid at room temperature. A few vegetable fats high in saturated fat are coconut oil, palm oil, palm kernel oil, and cocoa butter. Except for fats containing stearic acid, a saturated fatty acid, saturated fats consistently raise LDL levels. There used to be a general belief that monounsaturated fats, which are present in high concentrations in olive and peanut oils, neither contributed to the increase nor helped in the reduction of blood cholesterol. More recent research, however, supports the view that they do have a cholesterol-lowering ability similar to that of the polyunsaturated fats, but without the adverse effect of lowering HDL levels, as has been demonstrated for polyunsaturates (Mattson and Grundy, 1985).

The Lipid Hypothesis and Atherosclerosis

An impressive amount of evidence has been garnered to support the hypothesis that the development of atherosclerosis and the consequent risk of CVD rises with increasing blood levels of total and low-density lipoprotein (LDL) as well as low levels of high-density lipoprotein (HDL) cholesterol. According to the lipid hypothesis, the risk of developing atherosclerosis and consequent CVD may be reduced by lowering the levels of total and LDL cholesterol and raising the level of HDL cholesterol.

The Framingham Study

This highly respected study, which is often cited in discussions of the risk factors involved in coronary heart disease, was initiated in 1948 and is named after the town in Massachusetts in which it is being conducted. Known officially as the Heart Disease Epidemiology Study, it has been supported since its beginning by the Public Health Service. It is an ongoing, large-scale, prospective study, which has included more than 10,000 men and women over three generations who were 30 to 65 years of age and in apparently good health at the beginning of the project (Anderson *et al.*, 1987; Castelli *et al.*, 1986). From observations over many years, the importance of an elevated total cholesterol level as a major risk factor for CVD has clearly been established.

The Multiple Risk Factor Intervention Trial (MRFIT)

This was a six-year prospective study for which more than 355,000 men age 35 to 57 without a history of hospitalization for myocardial infarction were screened (Stamler *et al.*, 1986). By comparing the CVD death rates for each five-year age group with the mean total cholesterol levels for each age group, it was evident that the relationship between total cholesterol and CVD death rate was continuous, graded, and strong; moreover, it held regardless of smoking or hypertension status. The data showed that the relationship between the total cholesterol level and CVD is not a threshold one (i.e., there is no minimum level of blood cholesterol at which CVD risk begins). Without doubt, the people at highest risk had cholesterol levels above 240 mg/dl, whereas those at lowest risk had values below 200 mg/dl. However, even the people with the lowest levels were not without some risk. The data emphasized that higher values for blood cholesterol exacerbate the risk of CVD at an ever-increasing rate. In fact, half of the deaths due to high blood cholesterol levels occurred in people whose blood cholesterol was greater than 253 mg/dl.

The data showed that the extra risk associated with progressively higher levels of total cholesterol increases with age. However young men (35 to 39 years) with very high cholesterol levels (greater than 245 mg/dl) are at greater relative risk for dying from CVD than men aged 55 to 57 with similar cholesterol levels.

The data from the study also showed that factors such as smoking or high blood pressure could increase a person's overall risk. This effect can be very important for a person whose blood cholesterol is in the range of 200 to 239, known as the borderline high-blood-cholesterol range. Under these conditions, the presence of two or more risk factors can double the risk for CVD. On the other hand, if no other risk factors such as cigarette smoking, high blood pressure, or severe obesity are present, the MRFIT data show that the overall risk of CVD for men is not increased markedly even when cholesterol levels are as high as 200 to 239 mg/dl.

It should be obvious then that if a person's risk of CVD is to be evaluated, it is necessary to take into account other risk factors that can transform an otherwise innocuous blood cholesterol level into a life-threatening situation.

Analysis of Risk Factors for CVD

Epidemiologic evidence indicates that CVD, like the great epidemics of the past, has a multifactorial etiology (i.e., its origin and development is due to the action of a variety of risk factors, usually working not alone, but in unison with each other for a more devastating effect). During the last four decades, many studies have been conducted to evaluate the prevalence or incidence of atherosclerosis. These have been interspersed with surveys on the fat content of the diet, on blood cholesterol levels, and on the incidence of coronary heart disease among people in different parts of the world. The surveys indicated that levels of blood cholesterol tended to be higher and CVD more common in more prosperous countries with diets rich in cholesterol and fats of animal origin. However, just because two factors occur coincidentally does not prove that one is the cause of the other, and many factors other than dietary fat and cholesterol are known to be associated with CVD. As a result of these many surveys and their detailed analysis, it is now possible to identify a number of apparent biological, demographic, and social differences between so-called "normal" and coronary-prone subjects, and from the various studies there has developed a long list of factors that can be correlated with an increased risk of developing premature coronary heart disease.

Although there are several different ways to classify the many risk factors for atherosclerosis and CVD, one of the simplest is to divide them into two categories: factors over which a person can exercise some control, and other factors over which a person has very little, if any, control. Included in the first category are (1) diet, including the role of dietary cholesterol, total dietary fat, saturated, monounsaturated, and polyunsaturated fats, carbohydrates, and other dietary components such as dietary fiber, alcohol, iron, sodium, potassium, and calcium; (2) cigarette smoking (more than 10/day); and (3) psychological and social factors of lesser importance, such as education, occupation, income, social mobility, personality traits, stress and tension, and physical activity. In the second category (i.e., those factors over which the individual has very little, if any, control), are age, gender, race, family history of cardiovascular disease, and some inherited tendencies toward hypertension, diabetes, and obesity.

Epidemiologic evidence supports the view that cigarette smoking, high blood pressure, and elevated blood cholesterol levels, in decreasing order, are the most significant of the major risk factors (Stamler et al., 1986). Of the three, most physicians consider diet therapy to be in the front line of defense against elevated cholesterol levels. Because no other dietary substances have a greater influence on blood cholesterol levels than saturated fat and cholesterol, the role of these substances and others closely allied to them in the etiology and control of CVD will be considered first.

Pinpointing Hypertensives at Risk for Heart Attacks

About 60 million Americans have elevated blood pressure (SGR, 1988). Although it is associated with heart failure, stroke, and kidney disease, its greatest hazard is its contribution to heart attacks. Because there is no simple and effective way to determine who will be harmed by lack of treatment, physicians routinely give pressure-lowering drugs to all patients who cannot decrease their blood pressure by losing weight, changing their diet, or increasing the amount of exercise.

Building on a suggestion reported in the literature much earlier (Brunner *et al.*, 1973), Alderman *et al.* (1991) determined that a high "renin–sodium profile" (a high level of plasma renin with respect to the level of sodium excreted in the urine) is a useful predictor of myocardial infarction in patients with hypertension. Renin is an enzyme, a normal blood protein. In their prospective study, Alderman *et al.* followed 1,717 patients (mean age 53 years; 36 percent white; 67 percent men) in a program to control hypertension. They determined that a high renin–sodium profile was associated with an increased risk of heart attack, but not stroke.

At the present time, renin–sodium profiling includes the discontinuation of hypertensive medications for four weeks and a 24-hour urine collection. With standardization of assay procedures and some fine tuning, Alderman and associates believe that the renin–sodium profile could identify patients who are more likely to have premature heart attacks and offers the promise of improving the efficiency of antihypertensive treatment by pinpointing those at greatest risk.

Risk Factors for CVD

The Role of Diet

Excessive amounts of cholesterol in the blood, especially when attributed to elevated levels of LDL, has been recognized as a risk factor for coronary heart disease (Grundy, 1986). The National Institutes of Health Consensus Conference (1985) and the National Cholesterol Education Program (NCEP; 1988) have been successful in increasing the public awareness of the significance of elevated blood cholesterol levels. Part of the success is undoubtedly due to the extensive advertising on television, radio, and in print of such disparate food products as corn oil and oatmeal, which are hailed as being effective in lowering blood cholesterol levels, forestalling atherosclerosis, and reducing the possibility of heart attacks and strokes. The beginning of the story goes back about nine decades.

In the first decade of this century, several investigators demonstrated that feeding laboratory animals, especially rabbits, large amounts of cholesterol produced arterial lesions similar to those found in human atherosclerosis. In 1925, it was shown that cholesterol is synthesized in animals. In 1970, studies on rhesus monkeys demonstrated that experimentally produced atherosclerosis lesions could be regressed on a diet free of cholesterol. Since that time, although many dietary studies in humans have been carried out, the results have been anything but uniform. It has been difficult to separate the specific effects of dietary cholesterol, total dietary fat, saturated and unsaturated fats, and even sugar on the etiology of atherosclerosis.

The effects of dietary cholesterol on LDL levels vary among people (Grundy, 1986; Goldberg, 1988). The liver generally attempts to maintain steady cholesterol levels by decreasing its biosynthesis in response to an increased dietary intake. People vary in their ability to adjust to an intake of dietary cholesterol; some exhibit increased LDL levels after cholesterol ingestion, whereas others maintain constant levels of LDL. Dietary cholesterol is present in liberal amounts in animal products such as egg yolk, organ meats (e.g., liver and kidney), and in whole milk and products derived from it, but not in foods derived from plants. Although a desirable daily intake of dietary cholesterol is less than 300 mg, a typical intake in the United States exceeds 600 mg and frequently reaches 900 mg.

In 1988, the American Heart Association and the National Heart, Lung, and Blood Institute published new guidelines for the screening and treatment of hypercholesterolemia (i.e., high plasma cholesterol levels).

A serum cholesterol level greater than 240 mg/dl (Grundy, 1987) is called hypercholesterolemia. This figure is generally cited as the danger point for heart attacks among all persons, irrespective of age. In accordance with this definition, approximately 15 to 25 percent of adults in this country have hypercholesterolemia, which has been reported to be the third most significant risk for CVD (Stamler et al., 1986). P.J. Palumbo, director of clinical nutrition at the Mayo Clinic in Rochester, Minnesota, suggests that older persons can tolerate a higher level of cholesterol and is quoted as saying, "I think 240 is too low as a cutoff point for a healthy older individual" (Stephens, 1991).

Following the two reports of the Lipid Research Clinics Program (1984), it is generally agreed that lowering serum cholesterol levels reduces CVD. It was also demonstrated that reducing LDL, the primary carrier of cholesterol, decreases the risk of CVD. The findings from this large-scale study showed that a 10.4 percent decrease in LDL was associated with a 16 to 19 percent reduction in CVD. Both dietary and pharmacologic interventions reduced serum cholesterol levels.

When blood levels of cholesterol or fats are abnormally high, diet therapy is almost always tried before any drug is prescribed, because it alone is so often successful in normalizing blood lipid levels. Even when drugs are required, a controlled diet should be continued; the effect of diet and drugs together is more effective than either one alone.

Bonanome and Grundy (1988) have demonstrated that in men, a diet high in stearic acid, a saturated fatty acid, does not cause an elevation in plasma levels of LDL, in contrast to a diet high in palmitic acid, also a saturated fatty acid. This suggests that beef and chocolate, which are rich in stearic acid, may not be so bad as previously believed. The same effect may or may not hold for women; the experiments have not yet been carried out. Rosenberg and Shaefer (1988) urge that this study not change the prudent dietary recommendation given to the American public by the Surgeon General: to reduce total fat and calories in our diets.

Blood Cholesterol Levels and the Older Person

For most people, beginning at age 20 and continuing for the next two or three decades, there is an increase in their mean total and LDL cholesterol levels of about 40 mg/dl. Cholesterol levels decrease slightly after age 65, and LDL cholesterol levels continue to show an association with CVD in the elderly, but it is a diminished one (Report of the National Cholesterol Education Program, 1988).

It is comforting to know that the available epidemiologic evidence indicates that as age increases after 44 years, the importance of elevated blood cholesterol level as a risk factor for CVD decreases and virtually disappears after age 65 (Allred *et al.*, 1990). This conclusion is in agreement with the review by Garber *et al.* (1989) of eight studies of elderly men (65 years or older), seven of which failed to find an association between blood cholesterol levels and either CVD incidence or mortality. Because most studies relating heart disease to blood cholesterol level have involved only men, the issue of the relationship in women is not so well defined. Limited data from the Framingham study (Gordon *et al.*, 1977) indicate that the total blood cholesterol is not a significant factor for CVD in either elderly men or women. However, later evidence gleaned from that study (Harris *et al.*, 1988) suggested a trend toward increasing risk for CVD with increasing blood cholesterol levels in elderly women.

The Council on Scientific Affairs' Advisory Panel of the American Medical Association (1983) observed that for both men and women, "there is little evidence to suggest that older patients stand to benefit as much from diet therapy as those younger than 60." The Council suggests that although increased total blood cholesterol is not a risk factor in older people, an elevated LDL/HDL ratio may still be important. This presents a difficulty in that the usual dietary recommendation of reducing saturated fat while increasing the polyunsaturated/saturated fat ratio decreases both LDL and HDL cholesterol levels (Grundy, 1987). In the concluding paragraph of their paper, Allred *et al.* state: "We believe health professionals should be reluctant to counsel elderly patients to give up many of their favorite foods in order to lower their blood cholesterol levels, without any available evidence that such a reduction is beneficial."

Because of the paucity of data on blood cholesterol levels obtained directly from studies on elderly people, there remains a concern among many older Americans as to how high is too high (Stephens, 1991). Most of the data available were obtained from studies conducted with younger men, and these results are extrapolated to an older set of subjects. It has been pointed out that this practice is not appropriate (Fihn, 1987). Now for the first time, a new study sponsored by the National Heart, Lung, and Blood Institute will try to determine at what point the level of cholesterol poses a danger of fatal coronary disease for older people. The study, called CRISP (Cholesterol Reduction in Seniors Program), will be conducted at five major medical schools across the country. Sponsors will study 400 volunteers among men and women age 65 and older with a cholesterol level of over 240 mg/dl, which is the figure generally cited as the danger point for heart attacks among all people irrespective of age.

Controllable Risk Factors Affecting Blood Cholesterol

Dietary Cholesterol

Of all the dietary changes recommended to lower blood cholesterol levels, reducing dietary cholesterol itself probably has the least effect on blood cholesterol concentrations for most people (McNamara, 1987). Considering that absorption of dietary cholesterol averages 60 percent and the rate of endogenous cholesterol synthesis is 11 to 13 mg/kg body weight per day, a reduction in dietary cholesterol intake of 150 mg per day results in a decrease of absorbed cholesterol of 90 mg per day, an amount that is less than 10 percent of the total daily input of absorbed dietary and endogenously synthesized cholesterol.

Fiber

Many studies have shown that an increased intake of dietary fiber, primarily water-soluble fiber, lowers plasma cholesterol concentrations. Most of the studies show that a significant cholesterol-lowering response can be achieved when total fiber is increased to 50 grams per day and soluble fiber to 20 grams per day (Anderson *et al.*, 1988). Some studies have shown that two ounces of oatmeal each day, when the practice is part of a low-fat diet, can result in decreases of five to ten percent in blood cholesterol levels. This decrease is approximately equal to the decrease produced by the low-fat diet alone. The subject is discussed in greater detail in Chapter 5.

Alcohol

Although this has been a controversial subject, the more recent studies indicate a protective effect against CVD when judged by the observation of negative correlations between total alcohol consumption and CVD mortality (Hegsted *et al.*, 1988). Although the deleterious effects of excess alcohol consumption are well documented, including the inference that consumption of alcohol to excess is related to hypertension and high blood triglyceride levels, Hegsted's data suggest that an alcohol intake of one or two glasses a day may significantly reduce the risk of CVD. Rimm *et al.* (1991) reached this same conclusion.

Note, in this regard, that aspirin, a long-time antidote for the side effects of drinking, may actually worsen alcohol's effect, according to Roine *et al.* (1990). They reported finding that aspirin significantly lowered the body's ability to break down alcohol in the stomach.

Roine and colleagues studied five healthy volunteers after ingestion of alcohol (0.3 g/kg of body weight; roughly equivalent to a glass and a half of wine). They found that the blood alcohol concentrations in the fed state, that is, one hour after a standard breakfast, were significantly higher (30 percent) when the subjects received two extra-strength aspirin tablets (500 mg each) one hour before ingestion of the alcohol. The 30-percent augmentation could be the difference between sobriety and impairment. Everyone who uses alcohol, even in moderation, should be aware of this effect.

Although the enzyme primarily responsible for alcohol metabolism, alcohol dehydrogenase, is present in many tissues, the liver has traditionally been considered the principal metabolic site. Frezza and co-workers reported (1990) that the dehydrogenase in the gastric mucosa may contribute substantially to alcohol metabolism, especially when a small quantity of alcohol is ingested shortly after eating. However, gastric metabolism of alcohol is decreased in both men and women with chronic alcoholism. Frezza *et al.* found, moreover, that in alcoholic women, the gastric mucosal alcohol dehydrogenase activity was even lower than that in alcoholic men and that gastric metabolism was virtually abolished. As a result, they concluded that the increased bioavailability of alcohol resulting from the decreased gastric oxidation may contribute to the enhanced vulnerability of women to acute and chronic complications of alcoholism. On a more mundane level, their results provide an explanation for the enduring opinion that men do not usually get as tipsy as women on the ingestion of the same amount of alcohol.

The breatholyzer test for alcohol, utilized by many law enforcement agencies, depends on an analysis of the percentage of alcohol in the exhaled breath. This is a valid procedure because the concentration of alcohol in the breath is related to the level in the blood. There is no mechanism analogous to the role of insulin in controlling the level of blood glucose to control the level of alcohol in the blood. When it is ingested and absorbed, alcohol is cleared from the blood at a slow, relatively constant rate, principally by the liver. More than ten hours are required to clear all the alcohol from the blood of a person who is intoxicated (alcohol 150 mg/deciliter of blood). Physical exercise, such as walking, does not help to reduce the level in the blood, since alcohol is not metabolized to any appreciable extent by muscle tissue.

Vitamin C

Enstrom and co-workers (1992) examined, epidemiologically, the relation between vitamin C intake and mortality in the First National Health and Nutrition Examination Survey (NHANES–I) Epidemiological Follow-up Study cohort. This cohort is based on a representative sample of 11,348 noninstitutionalized U.S. adults aged 25 to 74 years who were nutritionally examined during 1971 through 1974 and followed up for mortality (1,809 deaths) through 1984, a median of ten years. The relation of all causes of death to increasing vitamin C intake was found to be strongly inverse for males and weakly inverse for females. They found that as vitamin C intakes increased from below to above the recommended daily allowances, there was a steady drop in overall deaths and particularly in deaths from heart disease among both men and women. There was no clear relation for individual cancer sites, except possibly an inverse relation for esophagus and stomach cancers among white males. The relation with all causes of death among males remains after adjustment for age, sex, and 10 potentially confounding variables (including cigarette smoking, education, race, and disease history).

Iron

A recent epidemiologic study by researchers in Finland (Salonen *et al.*, 1992) indicates that excess amounts of iron in the bloodstream are associated with increased risk of heart attacks in middle-aged men. Randomly selected men, numbering 1,931, between the ages of

42 and 60, with no obvious evidence of heart disease, were monitored from 1984 through 1989; a total of 51 suffered heart attacks. The amount of iron in the body was determined indirectly by measuring the concentration of ferritin, an iron-storage protein. Analysis of the data showed that the second strongest risk factor, after smoking, was the blood levels of ferritin. For every one percent increase in blood ferritin, there was more than a four percent increase in heart attack risk. The mean ferritin concentration in the study was 166 μg/L. A ferritin level of 200 or more doubled the risk of heart attacks in the study subjects.

It had been hypothesized earlier that iron overload is a major cause of the higher incidence of heart disease in men than in women (Sullivan, 1989, 1991). According to this view, most women are relatively safe from heart attacks until menopause because of the loss of iron in blood during menstruation. However, when women stop menstruating, iron stores start accumulating, and women then change from a protected state to one in which their heart attack rate is much more like that of men.

Coffee

An association between coffee drinking and cardiovascular disease, especially coronary heart disease, has been suspected for a long time. Many studies have been conducted, but the findings have been inconsistent and often contradictory. Some of the studies have found elevated risk of myocardial infarction among men and women with high coffee intakes, but others did not.

The latest clinical two-year study, directed by Walter Willett of the Harvard School of Public Health, was a survey of the coffee-drinking habits of 45,589 U.S. men, all health professionals, who were 40 to 75 years old in 1986 and who had no history of cardiovascular disease (Grobbee et al., 1990). They refer, in their report, to about 40 prior studies that focused on the same problem and stress the precautions they took to achieve validity for their results. They conclude by saying that their findings do not support the hypothesis that coffee or caffeine consumption increases the risk of coronary heart disease or stroke (see Chapter 9). It is evident that three or four cups a day of typical American coffee are safe for virtually everybody, even those with heart disease. By contrast, drinking four or more cups of decaffeinated coffee per day was found to be associated with a moderate elevation in the risk of cardiovascular disease. This finding was unexpected and requires further study. In a recent randomized trial, the consumption of three to six cups of decaffeinated coffee per day did raise the levels of LDL cholesterol, the so-called "bad cholesterol" (Superco *et al.*, 1989).

On the positive side, Diokno and colleagues (1990) report that the consumption of at least one cup of coffee per day was significantly associated with a higher prevalence of sexual activity in women and with a higher potency rate in men. The respondents in the study were men and women aged 60 years and older.

Fish Oils

The fat in certain cold-water fish is rich in two polyunsaturated fatty acids, which are called omega-3 fatty acids. Studies have shown that a diet rich in these fish oils may lower cholesterol levels and in very high doses may also lower LDL and increase HDL (Kromhout *et al.*, 1985). Fatty fish like white tuna, mackerel, herring, and salmon are richer in omega-3 fatty acids than are leaner fish, such as halibut, flounder, and cod. Although fish-oil supplements are available, health professionals generally caution against their use. Eating fish is the preferable way to go.

Exercise

Regular aerobic exercise, which forces the heart and lungs to work harder to meet the muscles' demand for oxygen, has been identified as one of the factors that can lead to improvement in lipoprotein profiles and thus diminishes the risk of premature CVD. Examples of aerobic exercise include brisk walking, swimming, and cycling. The prime benefit derived from such exercise seems to be an increase in HDL cholesterol levels, but there is usually a simultaneous reduction in the level of triglycerides and LDL. There is also some evidence for a lowering of blood pressure and improvement of glucose tolerance. People who exercise regularly tend to be leaner than their sedentary counterparts and are more likely to smoke less, consume less alcohol, and have better dietary habits and lower blood pressure, all of which are associated with lower blood cholesterol levels. To sum up the situation, despite the many positive returns from vigorous, aerobic exercise (see Chapter 8), the NCEP does not view sedentary lifestyle as a CVD risk factor (National Cholesterol Education Program, 1988).

Cigarette Smoking

Epidemiologic evidence indicates that cigarette smoking is now the most powerful exogenous risk factor for CVD (Stamler *et al.*, 1986), but it is probably the most controllable. Smokers tend to have lower levels of protective HDL cholesterol than do nonsmokers. It has also been found that the incidence of heart attacks is three times greater, and death from CVD is five times greater among smokers than among nonsmokers. From an early statistical study of 187,783 men, it was determined that a one-pack-a-day smoker dies of CVD seven years earlier than a nonsmoker (Hammond and Horn, 1958).

Cigarette smoking has been found to be a potent dose-related risk factor for ischemic heart disease in all the cohorts studied (Pooling Project, 1978). Men who smoked more than one pack a day had more than three times the risk of CVD as nonsmokers, while those smoking about a pack a day (20 cigarettes) had more than two times the risk. In general, the risk of CVD rises sharply in anyone who smokes more than 10 cigarettes per day. For cigar and pipe smokers, the risk falls about midway between that of nonsmokers and those who smoke a half-pack per day. Sudden death is the most frequent clinical event associated with smoking, with the excess risk level approaching 70 percent by the time male smokers are 45 years old.

It might be asked, what does cigarette smoking have to do with nutrition? Epidemiologic evidence places hypertension and high blood levels of cholesterol in the second and third places, respectively, after cigarette smoking as the worst risk factors for CVD (Stamler *et al.*, 1986). Epidemiology also shows that risk factors are interactive, and any combinations of risk factors has a greater impact on the risk of CVD than the sum of their independent effects. As a rough rule of thumb, for example, one of the three risk factors doubles the chance of CVD, and two factors cause the odds to be increased tenfold. Since lowering the intake of saturated fats in order to control blood levels of cholesterol is definitely appropriate for discussion, it must also be appropriate to discuss the simultaneous smoking of cigarettes, which nullifies, to a large extent, the good effects of that practice. Stamler *et al.* (1986) and Grundy (1986) have both reported that the combination of high plasma cholesterol levels and cigarette smoking act together in a synergistic manner so that the overall effect is much greater than the additive effects of each risk factor acting alone. Kannel *et al.* (1986) showed that smoking and hypertension compound the deleterious effects of high blood cholesterol, making it three times more likely for a man to die of CVD when all three risk factors—not elevated cholesterol alone—are present.

The effect of smoking is related to dose (i.e., it increases with the number of cigarettes smoked per day). Fortunately, the effects of smoking are, at least partly, reversible, regardless of the duration of the habit, and cessation of smoking is associated with approximately a 50-percent reduction in the risk for myocardial infarction and sudden death. Cigarette smoking is particularly harmful for women who use oral contraceptives.

Less-Controllable Risk Factors Affecting Blood Cholesterol

Male and Female Gender

On average, men experience the clinical manifestations of CVD ten years earlier than women, and myocardial infarction occurs 20 years earlier in men than in women. The CVD rates in women are very low prior to the menopause, but increase after the menopause to approximately the same as those of men or a little greater. The difference is attributed to a protective effect of estrogens in premenopausal women.

Diabetes is a much stronger risk factor in women; women who have diabetes are three or four times as likely to develop CVD as those who do not. Elevated triglyceride levels in women are a significant risk factor, especially in older age groups, but not in men. Also, in women, there is a strong relation between elevated triglyceride levels and low HDL cholesterol levels, but not in men.

Family History of CVD

Members of some families suffer an increased frequency of CVD, which suggests a familial predisposition to the disease. There is also evidence that near relatives of persons who experience a heart attack prior to age 50 are at increased risk of CVD. At this time, there is uncertainty as to whether predisposition is genetic or the result of shared environmental influences (e.g., diet), acquired behavior (e.g., smoking), and life-styles (sedentary or physically active).

Hypertension

Hypertension is defined (SGR, 1988) as a systolic pressure greater than 140 mm Hg and a diastolic pressure greater than 90 mm Hg and can be mild, moderate, or severe. It is considered a major controllable factor for heart disease, and it is the best predictor of stroke in patients older than 45 years. People with systolic blood pressure greater than 160 mm Hg or a diastolic pressure greater than 95 mm Hg are five times more likely to experience a coronary event than people with normal blood pressure. Mild hypertension also poses considerable risk, as exemplified by the fact that most of the coronary events in the Pooling Project (1978) occurred in men with mild hypertension. According to the Surgeon General's Report (SGR, 1988) about 58 million people in the United States have hypertension, including 19 million who are older than 65. The occurrence increases with age and is higher for black Americans (of whom 38 percent are hypertensive) than for white Americans (29 percent).

Diabetes Mellitus

Diabetes mellitus, sometimes shortened simply to diabetes, is discussed separately and at some length later in this chapter. The term is now used for a group of chronic heterogeneous metabolic disorders that have in common an elevation of plasma glucose and often abnormalities in lipoprotein and amino acid metabolism. Diabetes mellitus is a serious risk factor for the development of atherosclerosis, and the association between diabetes and CVD has been well documented in clinical and pathological studies. Even when mild, it presents an increased risk for developing CVD. A common symptom is intermittent claudication (i.e., a severe pain in calf muscles that occurs during walking, but subsides with rest). It results from inadequate blood supply due to atherosclerosis.

Obesity

Although there is very little evidence, except from the Framingham Heart Study, to support obesity as an independent risk factor for CVD, there is evidence that it contributes to CVD risk through an adverse influence on other risk factors. Obesity is directly associated with hypertension, diabetes, elevated triglyceride and serum cholesterol levels (NIH Consensus Development Panel on Obesity, 1985). The NCEP regards "severe obesity" as a CVD risk factor and defines it as excess body weight greater than or equal to 30 percent of the ideal for height and age.

Personality Factors

The classification of people into Type A and Type B personalities is attributed to Friedman and Rosenman (1974). Type A personality is characterized by ambition, competitive drive, enhanced aggressiveness, and a chronic sense of time urgency. Type B personality is the opposite of Type A and exhibits none of these traits. In the Framingham Heart Study, men with Type A personality had twice the risk of CVD, especially if they were white-collar workers. For women, Type A behavior increased CVD risk, whether they were housewives or working outside the home.

Although the NCEP does not identify emotional and personality traits as risk factors for CVD, Type A personality appears to be associated with angina pectoris and sudden death. An acceptable explanation for this association has not yet been suggested.

Diabetes Mellitus

There are references to this disease in the ancient literature of Egypt, China, and India. During the first century, a Greek physician described it as a chronic condition, with persistent, excessive discharge of urine. He called it diabetes, from the Greek work "to pass through." Centuries later, the Latin word mellitus, meaning "honeyed," was added to describe the sugar-laden urine. In its natural course, it is attended by excessive thirst, excessive urination, hunger, weight loss, and lack of energy.

The primary characteristics of diabetes mellitus, often shortened to diabetes, is the elevation of blood glucose, although abnormalities in lipoprotein and amino acid metabolism are not uncommon. The disease usually runs in families, the risk of developing it being roughly proportional to the number and closeness of relatives who have already developed the disease. It is estimated that there are now more than 11 million people with diabetes in the United States (Harris *et al.*, 1987), and the number is increasing by about six percent a year. With its complications, it is the seventh leading cause of death in this country (SGR, 1988) as well as the third leading cause of blindness. The American Diabetes Association states that nearly 20 percent of all Americans older than 55 have diabetes.

Symptoms such as increased thirst, frequent urination, increased volume of urine, persistent fatigue, and drowsiness, all often accompanied by weight loss, may signal the onset of insulin-dependent diabetes. The diagnosis, however, is made chemically, either by persistent fasting hyperglycemia or by a glucose tolerance test. The plasma glucose level is checked after an overnight fast. Then 50 to 100 g of glucose is given to the person being tested, and the plasma glucose level is determined at one half, one, one and one half, and two hours. Normal adults have fasting plasma glucose values below 140 mg/dl. Values do not exceed 200 mg/dl during the test and should be below 140 mg/dl two hours after the glucose has been administered.

Diabetes mellitus exists as two major types. Type I or insulin-dependent diabetes mellitus (IDDM) makes up about ten percent of all cases. People having this type of diabetes tend to develop it during childhood or at least before 30 years of age; it is, therefore, the predominant form of the disease in children, adolescents, and young adults. Type I, or IDDM, develops as a result of the inability of the pancreas to produce insulin. The onset is usually sudden, and the people involved are more likely to be underweight than overweight.

They are unresponsive to oral hypoglycemic agents, require injections of insulin as well as adherence to a modified diet to control the disease, and are ketosis prone. Ketosis refers to the abnormal accumulation of "ketone bodies" (acetone, beta-hydroxybutyric acid, and acetoacetic acid) in the body as a result of a deficiency or inadequate utilization of carbohydrates. Fatty acids are metabolized instead, and the end products, the ketone bodies, begin to accumulate. It is readily made evident by a fruity odor of acetone on the breath.

Type II, or non–insulin-dependent diabetes mellitus (NIDDM) includes the remaining 90 percent of cases, affecting more than 10 million Americans. It usually develops later in life than Type I, generally after 30 years of age and most frequently after 40; in a majority of cases the person is obese or at least overweight. The onset is gradual, and warning signs usually are not present at the time of diagnosis. In fact, people with Type II diabetes are more frequently identified by a screening test for elevated blood glucose than by complaints to their physician about the signs and symptoms of diabetes. Type II diabetes occurs more frequently among women than men. Among women, it is more prevalent among mothers who have given birth to babies weighing ten pounds or more at the time of birth or who exhibit symptoms of diabetes during pregnancy, such as the presence of glucose in the urine (glycosuria), excessive thirst (polydipsia), and frequent, voluminous urination (polyuria). It is a more stable disease and less difficult to control than Type I. By reducing weight and increasing physical activity, the level of blood glucose can be reduced to, or maintained at, normal levels without the need for insulin injections or oral hypoglycemic agents in about 70 percent of cases. Most people with NIDDM maintain normal or greater than normal levels of circulating insulin in response to meals, although they show decreased insulin secretion in response to a glucose stimulus. It would appear, then, that the primary cause of hyperglycemia in these individuals is reduced insulin sensitivity of peripheral tissue rather than reduced insulin secretion. The National Diabetes Data Group has defined specific criteria for the classification of IDDM and NIDDM (NDDG, 1979).

Since non-insulin dependent diabetes mellitus is by far the most common type and frequently occurs in older Americans, the infor-

mation on nutrition and diet in this section will be limited to Type II
diabetes.

The Factor of Overweight

Both Type II diabetes and obesity are characterized by insulin
resistance. It is not surprising, then, that at least 80 percent of
patients with NIDDM are overweight, if not frankly obese, at the time
of diagnosis (SGR, 1988). It was reported more than 50 years ago
(Newburgh *et al.*, 1938) that with reduction in body weight, glucose
tolerance returned to normal, and in the intervening years it has been
shown that, with attainment of blood glucose control, many of the
defects in lipoprotein metabolism also improve. It is obvious, then,
that weight reduction is an effective means of improving abnormalities in both carbohydrate and lipid metabolism. An encouraging
finding is that several studies have shown substantial beneficial
improvements in both carbohydrate and lipid metabolism with moderate weight reduction, that is, without having to reduce to ideal
body weight (Liu *et al.*, 1985; Wing *et al.*, 1987).

Although most experts in the field agree that, with obese or
overweight persons who have diabetes, weight reduction should
have first priority, there are differences of opinion regarding the
nature of the diet. Variations include modest calorie restriction over
longer periods, greater caloric restriction for shorter periods, or
liquid diets of high-quality protein, but low in carbohydrate and fat,
and including supplements of vitamins and minerals, and so on. The
specifics of an enduring weight-loss diet for a diabetic should be
individually formulated by a competent professional, such as a
registered dietitian, in cooperation with the patient's physician, and
should be based on the metabolic abnormalities known to be present.
Moreover, it should incorporate the person's dietary preferences as
well as behavior modification techniques.

Weight loss is helpful in preventing as well as controlling Type II
diabetes mellitus. In 1972, Wood and Bierman estimated that new
cases of diabetes could be cut in half by preventing obesity in middle-
aged adults. Much of the risk of the hereditary form of Type II
diabetes common in the Pima Indians, for example, appears to be
related to their obesity (SGR, 1988, p. 255).

Nutritional Management of Type II Diabetes

Diet, hypoglycemic agents, and exercise are the major means available for treating Type II diabetes. The first treatment of choice for maturity-onset NIDDM is control by diet, but it must be kept in mind that diet and exercise are complementary measures in establishing a caloric deficit. The prime goal is to achieve ideal body weight while maintaining optimal nutrition. Since most people with NIDDM are overweight, usually weight loss is required. Reaching this goal may be associated with a reduction or elimination of the need for oral hypoglycemic agents, improvement or correction of fasting hyperglycemia and glucose intolerance, and reduction of known risk factors for atherosclerotic vascular disease such as excess weight, hypertension, hyperlipidemia, and hyperglycemia. A desirable condition for persons with diabetes is to be leaner than their ideal body weight, since insulin requirements, all other conditions being the same, are based on body size. A second aim of treatment is to prevent excessive glycosuria and hyperglycemia, and the final aim is to prevent the secondary complications of retinopathy, neuropathy, and nephropathy.

Although it is usually thought of as a disease of carbohydrate metabolism, diabetes is also responsible for abnormalities in lipoprotein metabolism associated with an increased development of atherosclerosis and consequent CVD. Because of concern over this situation, dietary recommendations have been made, with intent to reduce the total amount of fat and to increase complex carbohydrates, by both the American Diabetes Association (1987a) and the Canadian Diabetes Association (1981). These recommendations are based on the premise that a decrease in total dietary fat will lead to a reduction in plasma LDL cholesterol concentrations with a resulting reduction in the number of persons who are ill or die from CVD.

Currently the American Diabetes Association recommends that 55 to 60 percent of the kcalories in the diets of persons with diabetes should be supplied by carbohydrates. Unrefined carbohydrates should be substituted for refined carbohydrates, and moderate amounts of sugar may be acceptable as long as desirable weight is maintained and the diabetes is under control. Protein is set at the RDA and makes up about 15 percent of kcalories. Fat should comprise

30 percent or less of kcalories. Distribution of types of fat follows American Heart Association guidelines, and cholesterol is restricted to 300 mg per day or less. Sodium is restricted to 1000 mg/1000 kcalories, not to exceed 3000 mg per day (ADA Task Force, 1987c).

By far the most commonly used method of translating these recommendations into a diet is the exchange system developed jointly by the American Diabetes Association and the American Dietetic Association. In this method, foods are grouped together so that they contain similar quantities of fat, carbohydrate, protein, and kcalories. There are currently seven groups or lists—starch/bread, meat and alternates, vegetables, fruits, milk, fat, and free foods, which provide few kcalories when eaten in designated amounts. The foods within a list can be freely substituted or exchanged for each other in the amounts designated. To use this system, the patient's energy and other nutrient requirements are calculated first, and then food allowances are determined to fulfill the needed amounts of carbohydrate, protein, and fat.

Alternatives in Dietary Management

Although much effort goes into the dietary recommendations developed by the American Diabetes Association and the "Exchange Lists for Meal Planning" undergoes repeated review with revision, the most recent being in 1986, not all experts agree with these dietary guidelines. Diet has been a persistent source of controversy in diabetes care (SGR, 1988; Anderson, 1980). In the 1970s, after numerous research studies verified the benefits of a high carbohydrate, low-fat diet, the American Diabetes Association finally endorsed it. However, not all diabetologists went along with this change. Since the discovery of insulin, the commonly used diet had been a high-fat, low-carbohydrate one. Some experts believed at the time that low-carbohydrate diets provided the best control of diabetes. At present, at least one major diabetes center in the United States still uses the older diabetic diet providing 40 percent of kcalories as fat on a regular basis.

In the late 1970s and early 1980s, an entirely new system of dietary management was developed. Commonly referred to as the glycemic index, this method uses the rise in blood glucose that occurs after ingestion of a food compared with a standard amount of glucose to determine whether a food may be eaten and if so, in what amount. The glycemic index accounts for the fact that food form, fiber type, digestibility, cooking, and preparation of food all affect a food's ability to influence blood glucose levels. It is possible to determine the glycemic index for entire meals as well as individual foods. In theory this seems like an ideal diet, but much work is required before it can become a practical dietary system for most people with diabetes. As it is not possible to predict the glycemic index of foods consistently, much more testing of foods and food combinations is necessary. In addition, using this system requires considerable memorization before it can be put into practice, and not all foods with a low index are necessarily good choices. For example, sausages have an index of 28, while bread has an index of 69, and potatoes, an index of 80, which is nearly the same as that of glucose.

Dietary Controversies

Fats versus Carbohydrates

To reduce the risk of CVD in persons with Type II diabetes, dietary recommendations must take into account the abnormalities of lipid metabolism as well as those of carbohydrate metabolism. Since hyperglycemia appears to predispose diabetics to peripheral and cerebral vascular disease, therapy must include not only the normalization of blood glucose levels, but must be concerned with preventing, delaying, or reducing the onward course of all metabolic complications.

Several studies have shown consistently that the isocaloric substitution of carbohydrate for fat in the diet of persons with Type II diabetes results in an increase in plasma glucose, insulin, total triglyceride, and very low density lipoprotein (VLDL)–triglyceride concentrations and a reduction in HDL cholesterol levels without appreciably affecting total plasma cholesterol concentrations (Coulston *et al.*, 1987; Coulston *et al.*, 1989; Garg *et al.*, 1988). It has also been demonstrated that diets containing conventional quantities of fat, i.e., 35 to 40 percent of total kcalories, in which a portion of the saturated fatty acids is replaced with unsaturated fatty acids, are beneficial (Coulston *et al.*, 1989; Garg *et al.*, 1988). Such diets reduce total cholesterol and LDL cholesterol to the same extent as replacement of saturated fatty acids with complex carbohydrates without increasing fasting or day-long plasma glucose, insulin, and triglyceride concentrations, or decreasing HDL cholesterol concentrations. It has also been demonstrated that the substitution, in the diet, of monounsaturated fatty acids for saturated fatty acids results in beneficial effects on lipid metabolism (Garg *et al.*, 1988).

Simple versus Complex Dietary Carbohydrates

For patients with diabetes, it is usually recommended that the ingestion of simple carbohydrates (monosaccharides and disaccharides) be discouraged, and ingestion of complex (polysaccharide) carbohydrates be encouraged.

A widely held belief is that because simple carbohydrate foods are absorbed readily, they will cause sharp increases in plasma glucose responses. The only study to address the effects of simple and complex carbohydrates fails to support the concept (Hollenbeck *et al.*, 1985). In this study, glucose levels in the blood and urine were increased significantly when diets containing 80 percent complex carbohydrate and 20 percent simple carbohydrate were compared with diets containing 80 percent simple carbohydrate and 20 percent complex carbohydrate. Based on this study, it would appear that advising people with diabetes to decrease their consumption of fruits, vegetables, or dairy products (simple carbohydrate content more than 50 percent) in favor of complex carbohydrates will probably not help to control the level of plasma glucose.

Dietary Fiber

Although the relevance of dietary fiber in human health and disease has been discussed in some detail in Chapter 5, and its role in diabetes has been reviewed by Toma and Curtis (1986), a few specific details and practical limitations for people with diabetes will be described here.

Some of the earlier studies reported that when persons with diabetes were fed high-carbohydrate, high-fiber diets, blood glucose levels remained lower (Jenkins *et al.*, 1976). The effect of the fiber on blood glucose levels was believed to be due to delayed digestion and absorption in the gastrointestinal tract. Whatever the mechanism, some investigators have been able to withdraw oral hypoglycemic agents from people with NIDDM diabetes by requiring a high-carbohydrate, high-fiber diet (Kiehm *et al.*, 1976).

Later published reports showed that optimal hypoglycemic and/or hypolipemic effects required dietary fiber intakes between 70 and 100 grams per day (Simpson *et al.*, 1981; Anderson *et al.*, 1980). These high levels of fiber have not been broadly accepted. Other studies using lower levels of dietary fiber, ranging between 45 and 50 grams per day reported little or no significant benefits in carbohydrate or lipid metabolism (Hollenbeck *et al.*, 1986; Riccardi *et al.*, 1984; Karlstom *et al.*, 1984; Uusitupa *et al.*, 1989). On the other hand, the specific value of soluble dietary fiber from oats in the regulation of glucose metabolism is promising (Wood *et al.*, 1989). A discussion of the clinical significance of dietary fiber in the management of lipoprotein metabolism in patients with diabetes mellitus was published by Hollenbeck *et al.* (1987).

The Place of Fish Oils

Several clinical studies (e.g., Kromhout *et al.*, 1985) have been carried out to determine the protective effects against athero-sclerosis, cardiovascular disease, and stroke of fish diets and fish oils. To state the situation simply, they lower cholesterol levels in the blood and decrease the tendency of the blood to form clots, a combined effect that reduces the risk of a heart attack or stroke. Kromhout concluded "consumption of as little as one or two fish meals per week may be of preventive value in relation to coronary heart disease." The reports of Kromhout and several other investigators gave rise to widespread interest in the possible benefits of the long-chain, polyunsaturated fatty acids (the n-3 series of fatty acids) in fish oils, for patients with diabetes. Relatively recent studies in patients with NIDDM showed a significant decrease in total plasma triglyceride and VLDL–triglyceride concentrations with fish-oil supplements of approximately five grams per day with no change in LDL- or HDL-cholesterol concentrations (Glauber *et al.*, 1988; Schechtman *et al.*, 1988). Unfortunately, both studies demonstrated a deterioration in plasma glucose control at higher doses of fish-oil supplements.

Simple Refined Sugars

Persons with diabetes have generally been advised to avoid foods containing simple refined sugars, such as sucrose. The basis for this guidance was that simple sugars would be absorbed readily, resulting in large swings in plasma glucose levels. It was reported, however, that when a portion of the complex carbohydrate in an individual single meal was replaced by sucrose, no large increase in either glucose or insulin was observed (Bantle *et al.*, 1983; Slama *et al.*, 1984). The intake of moderate amounts of sucrose by people with Type II diabetes over days, weeks, or longer, has been reported to lead to postprandial increases in the levels of plasma glucose, insulin, and triglycerides in addition to increased fasting levels of triglycerides and cholesterol, and decreased levels of HDL cholesterol (Coulston *et al.*, 1987). Confusing the picture is a report (Bantle *et al.*, 1986) that shows no significant differences in metabolic control in patients with diabetes after 8 days of increased sucrose consumption. Because of a clear-cut lack of consensus on this matter, and because the studies of longer duration do show rather consistent deleterious metabolic effects, it would seem appropriate at the present time to limit the intake of sucrose.

Alternative Sweeteners

The American Diabetes Association currently recommends the use of both nutritive and nonnutritive alternative sweeteners in the management of diabetes (ADA, 1987b). However, whether or not they are effective in controlling weight among persons with Type II diabetes or lead to better control of the disease remains to be demonstrated. The principal low-calorie sweeteners readily available in the United States at the present time include saccharin, aspartame, and acesulfame-K. It has been estimated that more than 90 percent of people with diabetes use low-calorie sweeteners, and are likely to ingest greater quantities than are the general population, although the risks and benefits for individuals have not yet been thoroughly investigated over the long term (Crapo, 1988; ADA, 1987d). They can be a help in achieving the balance of diet and exercise that is so essential to a healthy life-style.

Diet and Nutrition in Relation to Cancer

Cancers are populations of cells in the body that have acquired abnormal patterns of growth. Unlike normal cells, they have the ability to multiply and spread without restraint. In the United States, they rank in second place among the leading causes of death. In 1987, the number of deaths due to this disease was 476,700, which was 22.4 percent of the total (SGR, 1988). During the same period, more than 900,000 new cases occurred, and the American Cancer Society (ACS, 1990) estimated that 1,040,000 persons would be diagnosed with the disease in 1991. It is also estimated that 6 million persons now living have had cancer at some point in their lives (ACS, 1990). Environmental factors, of which cigarette smoking is the most commonly recognized, are believed to contribute to as many as 90 percent of all human cases. Cigarettes alone were responsible for approximately one fourth of all the fatal cancers in 1987. Cancer incidence related to diet was estimated, in 1986, at 35 percent (Watson and Leonard, 1986). The American Cancer Society and the National Cancer Institute also estimate that 35 percent of cancers are linked to diet. It is obviously a significant risk factor and one over which we have a good deal of control.

Considerable effort has been devoted to studying the influence of both environmental and genetic factors on the incidence of the disease. From this research, it has become clear that most cancers have external causes, and, in principle, should therefore be preventable. With the exception of skin cancer, people in different parts of the world suffer from different varieties of the disease, depending on their habits, diet, and customs rather than on their ethnic origins. When people migrate from one country to another, they tend to acquire the patterns of the disease that are characteristic of their new homeland. As an example, Japanese residing in the United States develop the spectrum of cancers that is typical for the United States and different from that in Japan.

Factors in our environment that are potential causes of the disease include substances in the air we breathe, the water we drink, the regions in which we live and work, and the foods we eat. Among the factors whose precise effects are difficult to assess are the diets consumed by different groups of people, partly because the foods they eat are so complex. Studies on the association between diet and cancer have focused on the gastrointestinal tract, the breast, and other tissues susceptible to hormonal influence, and, to a lesser extent, the respiratory tract and the urinary system.

It has not been difficult for epidemiologists to demonstrate a correlation between diets consumed in affluent societies and the incidence of cancers in such organs as the breast, colon, and uterus. It has, however, proved to be much more difficult to establish causal relationships and to determine which, if any, of the dietary components is responsible. Similarly, difficulties are encountered in laboratory experiments. As in humans, most animals have a significant occurrence of cancer in old age, and the rates of incidence often appear to be affected by changes in diet. The influence of diet on spontaneous and experimentally induced cancers is not easy to investigate because the underlying mechanisms and molecular biology are still not fully understood. The evidence already at hand justifies some interim guidelines, and they have been published in slightly different versions by several responsible organizations, including the U.S. Department of Health and Human Services, the National Research Council of the National Academy of Sciences, the National Cancer Institute, the American Institute for Cancer Research, and the American Cancer Society.

In attempting to determine which constituents of food might be associated with cancer, epidemiologists have studied population subgroups, including immigrants to the United States, to examine the relationship between specific dietary patterns or the consumption of certain foods and the risk of developing particular cancers. In general, the evidence suggests that some types of diets and some dietary components (e.g., high-fat diets or frequent consumption of salt-cured, salt-pickled, and smoked foods) tend to increase the risk of cancer, whereas others (e.g., low-fat diets or the frequent consumption of certain fruits and vegetables) tend to decrease it.

In the laboratory, investigators have attempted to shed light on the mechanisms by which diet may influence carcinogenesis. They have examined the ability of individual nutrients, food extracts, or nonnutritive components of food to enhance or inhibit carcinogenesis and mutagenesis. A mutagen is a chemical or physical agent that interacts with the deoxyribonucleic acid (DNA) to cause a permanent, transmissible change in the genetic material of the cell.

In 1987, the American Cancer Society published a revised list of dietary guidelines aimed at the prevention of cancer.

1. Avoid obesity.
2. Cut down on total fat intake.
3. Eat more high-fiber foods.
4. Include foods rich in vitamins A and C in the daily diet.
5. Include cruciferous (cabbage family) vegetables in the diet.
6. Cut down on salt-cured, smoked, and nitrite-cured foods.
7. Keep alcohol consumption moderate, if you do drink.

These guidelines, which were developed from both epidemiologic and experimental studies, will serve as a framework around which to develop the story of diet in relation to cancer.

Scientists and clinicians who are authorities on cancer generally agree that the best way to control the disease is to prevent it from starting or to detect it at the earliest possible stage of development when it can be brought under control or stopped more readily. Diet is one of the major avenues of approach to prevention and also one of the easiest to follow.

Dietary Fats, Fatty Acids, and Cholesterol

In 1980, the National Cancer Institute commissioned the National Research Council of the National Academy of Sciences to conduct a comprehensive study of the available scientific information pertaining to the relationship of diet and nutrition to cancer. The committee set up to carry out the task published their report, *Diet, Nutrition, and Cancer* (DNC) in 1982. Of all the dietary factors that had been associated, epidemiologically, with cancers of various sites up to that time, fat was found to have produced the greatest frequency of direct associations, particularly to the breast, the prostate, and the large bowel. The committee concluded that both epidemiologic studies and experiments in animals provided convincing evidence that increasing the intake of total fat increased the incidence of cancer at certain sites, particularly the breast and colon, and, conversely, that the risk is lower with lower intakes of fat.

The data from the studies in animals suggest that when the total fat intake is low, polyunsaturated fats are more effective than saturated fats in enhancing the initiation and development of tumors, whereas the data on humans do not permit a clear distinction to be made between the effects of different components of fat. The committee judged the evidence associating high fat intake with increased cancer risk to be sufficient to recommend that the consumption of fat in the American diet be reduced to approximately 30 percent of kcalories, but stated that the available data, in 1982, did not provide a strong basis for the recommendation (DNC, 1982, p. 92).

The type of fat ingested may affect tumor formation; for example, it appears that polyunsaturated fats such as safflower oil and corn oil, which contain linoleic acid, have the greatest tumor-enhancing effect for mammary cancer (Cohen, 1987). Diets rich in oleic acid (monounsaturated), found in olive oil, also correlate with increased mammary tumor incidence. On the other hand, eicosapentaenoic acid, found in fatty fishes and marine mammals, may protect against the development of the disease (Carroll, 1986). As a matter of fact, populations with relatively high fat intake of these fatty acids have moderate to low rates of breast and colon cancer (Weinhouse, 1986).

Among the most recent published reports (Willett *et al.*, 1990) was a prospective study conducted with 88,751 female nurses, 34 to 59 years old, who completed a dietary questionnaire in 1980. By 1986, 150 cases of colon cancer had been documented. After adjustment for total energy intake, animal fat was positively associated with risk of colon cancer. No association was found for vegetable fat. Processed meats and liver were significantly associated with increased risk, whereas fish and chicken without skin were related to decreased risk. The ratio of the intake of red meat (beef, pork, lamb) to the intake of chicken and fish was particularly strongly associated with an increased incidence of colon cancer. The authors support existing recommendations to substitute fish and chicken for meats high in fat.

In 1992, Willett *et al.* provided evidence against an adverse influence of fat consumed in the diet on breast cancer incidence. Subjects in the study were 89,494 nurses whose diets and incidence of breast cancer were tracked for 8 years beginning in 1980, when the women ranged in age from 34 through 59. No relation was found between dietary fiber intake and the incidence of breast cancer. Although details concerning the effect of fiber on diet are considered elsewhere in this chapter, note that the authors stress that reducing dietary fat is still recommended to lessen the risk of colon cancer and heart disease.

The evidence linking dietary cholesterol or serum cholesterol with cancer risk was reviewed in 1984 (McMichael *et al.*). With increased cholesterol intake, they found a slightly increased risk for colon and breast cancer, but it was not sufficiently strong to infer causation. Regarding blood cholesterol, they reported that preclinical cancer causes a lowering of blood cholesterol, but that naturally low blood cholesterol in men was correlated with increased risk for colon cancer.

More than 4½ decades ago, it was reported that caloric restriction inhibits the growth of both induced and spontaneous tumors in mice (Tannenbaum, 1945). In 1987, it was shown that caloric restriction inhibited tumor growth in rats even when they ingested five times more fat daily than did the controls (Kritchevsky *et al.*, 1987). In the same year, a review of more than 80 studies involving caloric restriction and tumor incidence in mice was published (Albanes, 1987). The results indicated that the carcinogenic potential of dietary fat is markedly enhanced when consumed as part of a high-calorie diet.

Overweight and Obesity

Epidemiologists have provided largely indirect evidence for a relationship between obesity and cancer. In laboratory experiments, the incidence of tumors is lower and the life span much longer for animals on restricted food intake than for animals fed ad libitum.

However, in these studies, all nutrients were simultaneously depressed; thus, the observed reduction in tumor incidence might have been due to the reduction of some specific nutrient, such as fat. It is also difficult to interpret experiments in which caloric intake has been modified by varying dietary fat or fiber, both of which may by themselves exert effects on tumorigenesis. Although neither the epidemiologic studies nor the animal experiments permit a clear interpretation of the specific effect of total caloric intake on the risk of cancer, the studies conducted with animals show that a reduction in total food intake decreases the age-specific incidence of cancer.

Although the evidence is not so clear for human beings, it is thought that obesity itself may increase tumor formation (Desmond, 1987). The strongest association has been demonstrated with endometrial cancer (Willet and MacMahon, 1984, i.e., cancer involving the mucous membrane lining of the inner surface of the uterus). Women with malelike fat distribution over their abdomens are six times more likely to develop breast cancer than those with more traditional fat deposits on hips and thighs (Schapira *et al.*, 1990). The American Cancer Society states that people who are 40 percent over their recommended weight are most at risk for breast, colon, bladder, and uterine cancers.

Why should obesity be expected to have any relation to the incidence of cancer? The answer at present is still quite speculative. One hypothesis is that obesity is directly linked to diets high in fat, which is an important risk factor in its own right. Obesity is also often linked to reduced blood flow because of atherosclerosis, thus making it more difficult for tissue to repair itself. There is also some support for the idea that excess weight reduces the ability of the body to respond to viral and bacterial invasions, as well as ward off other diseases. Environmental toxins such as pesticides are often deposited in the fat of animals, and when the animal products are eaten, the toxins are transferred to the diner. Finally, fats, which are high in kcalories, but low in nutrients, often displace vitamin-rich foods that may help fight cancer.

Dietary Protein

Dietary protein has often been associated with cancers of the breast, mucous membrane lining of the uterus, prostate, large intestine, pancreas, and kidney. However, in western diets the major dietary sources of protein, such as meat, contain a number of other nutrients, and therefore the association of protein with cancer at these sites may actually reflect the action of another constituent, such as fat, which is present in the protein-rich foods. It is important but often difficult to separate the effect of one constituent from the other. When protein intake was adjusted for total caloric intake, no correlation of protein intake to breast cancer was shown (Katsouyanni *et al.*, 1988). In a review of the literature dealing with dietary and nutritional influences on cancer, more than a dozen papers were listed in which protein and meat intake could not be correlated with colorectal cancer (Rogers and Longnecker, 1988).

Dietary Carbohydrate

The principal carbohydrates in foods are sugars, starches, and cellulose. The data on cellulose are discussed elsewhere under dietary fiber. Dietary sucrose has been reported to be without effect on spontaneous tumors in mice when fed sucrose at 10 percent by weight of the diet (Roe *et al.*, 1970) or rats at 77 percent by weight (Friedman *et al.*, 1972).

Armstrong and Doll (1975) correlated per capita intake of foods and specific nutrients with cancer incidence and mortality in 23 and 32 countries, respectively. They reported a significant direct correlation between sugar intake and pancreatic cancer mortality (but not incidence) in women only. No reports of case-controlled studies have, however, appeared since then that support their findings.

Dietary Fiber

The awakening of interest in a possible correlation between the incidence of colon cancer, which is the second most frequent cause of death from cancer in the United States, and diets low in fiber is generally credited to Trowell (1975), who hypothesized that many chronic diseases, including cancer, are associated with a low intake of dietary fiber. Potential carcinogens, whether ingested as part of the diet or produced as a result of digestive processes, are present in fecal material (Desmond, 1987; Willett and MacMahon, 1984). Because fiber adds bulk to the stool, the carcinogens present in the large bowel are diluted, and the transit time in the intestinal tract is decreased. This would be expected to lessen intestinal exposure to cancer-causing substances present in the stool. From one epidemiologic study (Bingham et al., 1979) in which the individual components of fiber were assessed, there was an inverse correlation between the incidence of colon cancer and the consumption of the pentosan fraction of fiber found in whole wheat products. From this it would seem likely that further epidemiologic investigation of fiber would be more productive if the relationship of cancer to specific components of fiber were analyzed.

An issue in human studies is the lack of information about the specific components of dietary fiber and how they may affect cancer risk. Although rodent studies have provided conflicting results, they do support the idea that the type of fiber is important. In those studies that showed a protective effect, wheat bran, a source of water-insoluble fiber, was more consistently associated with lower risk of colon cancer than were other fiber sources (Pilch, 1987). Willett (1989) reported that fiber from fruits and vegetables, but not from cereals, has been consistently associated with a lower risk of colon cancer.

From all the studies reported to date, the evidence for a correlation between dietary fiber intake and the risk of colon cancer is moderately positive.

Vitamin A and Beta-Carotene

A number of epidemiologic studies, roughly from the period 1960 to 1980 suggest an inverse association between ingested vitamin A, or its principal precursor, beta-carotene, and carcinogenesis, particularly lung cancer (DNC, 1982, Chapter 9). Beta-carotene, which is found abundantly in carrots, sweet potatoes, and leafy vegetables such as beet greens, spinach, and broccoli, can act as a provitamin; that is, when ingested, each molecule can theoretically be transformed in the liver into two molecules of vitamin A. But beta-carotene appears to play an additional role in human metabolism quite apart from its vitamin function. It serves as an antioxidant or scavenger by reacting with or trapping free radicals and preventing the possible genetic damage that they can cause (Burton and Ingold, 1984).

Shekelle and co-workers, in 1981, published the findings of a 19-year follow-up study of 1,954 men who worked in a suburb of Chicago, and reported that lung cancer incidence was inversely associated with carotene intake, estimated from the consumption of fruits and vegetables, both with and without adjustment for cigarette smoking. There was a sevenfold increase in the risk of lung cancer in smokers whose carotene level fell in the lowest quartile when compared with those in the highest quartile of intake. In a paper on diet and lung cancer risk (Byers *et al.*, 1987), it was reported that cigarette smokers were about 15 times more likely to develop lung cancer than nonsmokers. No significant association of lung cancer and the intake of preformed vitamin A (retinol) was found based on estimates of foods rich in vitamin A.

In 1987, Desmond reported that beta-carotene had a stronger protective effect against malignancy than vitamin A itself and, in the same year, Kune *et al.* reported an inverse correlation between the intake of beta-carotene and risk. In 1988, Byers published a review of the major studies from the preceding 5 years into the relationship between diet and cancer. He reported that the hypothesis relating carotene to lung cancer was "fairly consistently supported." The available studies on diet and lung cancer, which were reported in 1989, show a consistent protective effect of beta-carotene (Connett; Kune *et al.*; LeMarchard *et al.*).

Although increased consumption of beta-carotene has also been reported to be associated with reduced risk of cancers of the breast, cervix, esophagus, and stomach, the associations are not nearly so strong as they are for lung cancer. A decreased risk of breast cancer was associated with more frequent use of green vegetables (La Vecchia *et al.*, 1987), and an increased intake of beta-carotene was found to be associated with a decreased risk of breast cancer (Rohan *et al.*, 1988).

For esophageal cancer, an association was reported between its incidence and the frequency of consumption of carrots, green vegetables, and fresh fruit (Decarli *et al.*, 1987). The group with the highest carotene intake had one fourth of the risk of developing this cancer when compared with the group having the lowest intake.

Reduced levels of serum beta-carotene were reported to be associated with increased risk in a study of gastric cancer (Gey *et al.*,

1987), and Wald *et al.* (1988) found that a low level of beta-carotene was associated with an increased risk of developing stomach cancer. In summary, there is strong evidence from epidemiologic studies that dietary beta-carotene has a significant protective effect against lung cancer. There is also fairly strong evidence of a protective effect of dietary beta-carotene in cancers of the breast, cervix, esophagus, and stomach. There is, however, a lack of consistent protective effect of dietary vitamin A (retinol) on cancer of the cervix, colon, esophagus, or lung, all of which offers support for the hypothesis that the protective effect of beta-carotene is quite separate from its ability to be transformed into vitamin A (retinol).

Vitamin C

The association of vitamin C (ascorbic acid) with cancer, in epidemiologic studies prior to 1982, is mostly indirect, based on the consumption of foods such as fresh fruits and vegetables, known to contain high concentrations of the vitamin, rather than on actual measurements of vitamin C intake or blood-level determinations. In general, the data suggest that vitamin C may lower the risk of cancer, particularly in the esophagus and stomach (DNC, 1982, Chapter 9). These observations are consistent with the hypothesis that vitamin C protects against gastric cancer by inhibiting the reaction of secondary and higher amines with nitrate to form carcinogenic nitrosamines (Weisburger *et al.*, 1980).

In 1987, Tannenbaum and Wishnok confirmed the inhibition of nitrosamine formation by ascorbic acid and speculated as to its potential value as an *in vivo* nitrite scavenger. The cancer-prevention properties of vitamin C as a nutrient have also been reported in at least two publications during 1987 (Hanck, 1987; Romney *et al.*, 1987). The consumption of vitamin C–rich foods was found by Glatthaar *et al.* (1986), on the basis of epidemiologic studies, to be associated with a lower risk of stomach and esophageal cancers. In a later epidemiologic study involving 11,348 noninstitutionalized adults aged 25 to 74 years, there was no clear relation between the intake of vitamin C and individual cancer sites, except possibly an inverse relation for esophagus and stomach cancer among males (Enstrom *et al.*, 1992).

In addition to blocking the formation of nitrosamines, it has been hypothesized that vitamin C may affect carcinogenesis because of its well-known capability to act as an antioxidant, and also to enhance immune system response (Glatthaar *et al.*, 1986). It may be that the principal benefit of vitamin C, for cancer, is to reduce the risk of developing it rather than to have therapeutic value.

To summarize the relation of vitamin C to cancer, there is fairly strong evidence that vitamin C may lower the risk of cancer in the esophagus and stomach. The effect may be due more to reducing the risk of developing it than to its therapeutic value. In a 1988 review of epidemiologic and experimental data concerning dietary and nutritional influences on cancer, by Rogers and Longnecker, the authors concluded that there seems to be no connection between vitamin C intake and cancer of the lung, prostate, or ovary. For other types of cancer, there is too much inconsistency in the data from different investigators, or too weak a signal, to reach a judgment.

Vitamin E and Selenium

The most active of the various E vitamins, and also the most widely distributed in nature, alpha-tocopherol, is a pale yellow liquid, soluble in fats and fat solvents, but insoluble in water. It is the form used in most of the studies of the relationship of the E vitamins and cancer and is generally regarded as the major lipid-soluble antioxidant in the body.

There has been much concern for many years about the potential risks to human health resulting from the use of nitrate and nitrite as preservatives in meat, fish, and poultry products. They inhibit rancidity, maintain flavor, preserve the pink color of meats and, most important, prevent the growth of botulism spores. Unfortunately, dietary nitrate, naturally present in many vegetables as well as in cured meats, is converted to nitrite by bacteria in the saliva and the salivary plaque. Although neither nitrates nor nitrites have been shown to be carcinogenic by themselves, nitrite can combine with other common nitrogen-containing food substances called amines, especially in the stomach, to form compounds called nitrosamines (NAS, 1981). Nitrosamines are definitely carcinogenic in numerous species of animals in which they have been tested and are associated with tumors in many organs, depending on the nature of the particular amine that reacted with nitrite to form them. The formation of nitroso compounds, and hence their carcinogenic action, has been reported to be partially controlled by a variety of agents, including especially vitamin C and vitamin E (Watson and Leonard, 1986). An important action of both vitamin C (Mirvish, 1986) and vitamin E (Fiddler *et al.*, 1978) is apparently their ability to inhibit nitrosamine formation by competing for the nitrite, thus decreasing the incidence of nitrosamine-induced cancers.

The double bonds in unsaturated fatty acids are especially vulnerable to spontaneous attack by molecular oxygen, resulting in the formation of lipid peroxides and causing the formation of free radicals. The reaction may be initiated by a number of diverse factors, for example, some of the oxides of nitrogen that are present as pollutants in the air, or by the impact of cosmic rays (see Chapter 1, under Free-Radical Theory). Free radicals are very reactive, transient, intermediate compounds, which may appear at low concentrations in biochemical reactions. In peroxidation, their presence is necessary to sustain the chain reaction. They are the real culprits for the pathological consequences of lipid peroxidation, such as being suspect agents in the initial steps of both cancer and cardiovascular disease. Free radicals can act as carcinogens by altering DNA molecules and causing mutations. Peroxidative damage to DNA in rats was decreased by moderate amounts of vitamin E (Summerfield and Tappel, 1984).

Ordinarily the body utilizes a potent enzyme, glutathione peroxidase, which contains the element selenium and is present in most tissues, to destroy peroxides that form spontaneously. An additional safeguard, however, is the presence in the body of scavenging molecules that interact with any free radicals, such as those produced in the peroxidation of unsaturated fatty acids. In humans, the principal scavenger is vitamin E, which interacts with any free radicals produced and therefore inhibits the formation of peroxides and the further generation of more free radicals.

Because of its solubility in oil and fats, vitamin E diffuses into the polyunsaturated fatty acids associated with the phospholipids in all membrane structures. It plays a very important role in preserving the lipid configuration of all membranes and in protecting linoleic acid, and other unsaturated acids, from peroxidation. It may also protect vitamin A and carotenes from destruction in the intestinal tract.

Vitamin E and the element selenium work cooperatively in the control of peroxidation throughout the body. Selenium functions primarily as a critical component of the enzyme glutathione peroxidase, which destroys peroxides present in the cell protoplasm, a semifluid, viscous, water-based medium. Because the effect of vitamin E on peroxide formation is limited primarily to the membrane, both selenium and vitamin E appear to be necessary for efficient removal of all peroxides. From animal experiments, it is clear that many diseases are caused by simultaneous deficiencies of selenium and vitamin E, and they can often be prevented or cured by supplementation with either nutrient alone (NRC, 1983). The data from a clinical study by Salonen *et al.* (1985) suggest that dietary selenium deficiency is associated with an increased risk of fatal cancer, that low vitamin E intake may enhance the effect, and that a decreased intake of vitamin A and beta-carotene contributes to the risk of lung cancer among men who smoke and have a low selenium intake.

Several epidemiologic studies have been published that support the hypothesis that low selenium status may be associated with an increased risk of developing not only cancer, but also cardiovascular disease (Lavender, 1987). In the case of cancer, a number of experiments with rats indicate a protective effect of selenium against tumorigenesis (Combs and Combs, 1986). A review of the selenium–cancer relationship, however, concluded that the protective effect of selenium against cancer in humans is still uncertain, and recommended against the use of selenium supplements (Willett and Stampfer, 1988).

Previous research had shown that vitamin E is a major lipid-soluble, chain-breaking antioxidant in the blood plasma of normal adults. Ingold *et al.* (1987) explored the possibility that the requirement for vitamin E could be met by some other lipid-soluble or water-soluble antioxidant in humans with a severe vitamin E deficiency. They, therefore, measured the chain-breaking, antioxidant activity of blood plasma from severely vitamin E–deficient patients. They concluded that even in cases of very severe vitamin E deficiency, the requirement for this vitamin is not met by any other exogenous or endogenous antioxidant.

In a study in 1987, Trickler and Shklar reported on the prevention, by vitamin E, of experimental oral carcinogenesis in hamsters. The study results showed that vitamin E, given orally or applied to the surface, prevented tumor development. None of the vitamin E–supplemented hamsters had any evidence of tumors after 28 weeks. The researchers concluded that the complete suppression of tumor development in the vitamin E–supplemented animals was convincing evidence that vitamin E was an effective anticancer agent and indicated that, because it is relatively nontoxic, it could be used as a human tumor preventive if this action could be demonstrated in humans.

In 1987, at the University of Toronto, Lemoyne *et al.* demonstrated that pentane output in the breath is a reliable indicator of lipid peroxidation, as pentane gas is a product of lipid peroxidation that can pass from the lungs into the expired air, and is readily measured by gas chromatography. An inverse relationship between pentane output and vitamin E status was demonstrated both in animal experiments and in human subjects.

In 1988, Van Gossum *et al.*, using the pentane-analysis method, further tested the hypothesis that vitamin E is a lipid-soluble antioxidant in cell membranes and functions as a free-radical scavenger to prevent lipid peroxidation. Vitamin E supplementation in 10 normal adult volunteers resulted in a simultaneous increase in the plasma levels of vitamin E and a significantly decreased breath pentane output. It is evident, therefore, that it can reduce lipid peroxidation, which, as mentioned earlier, is associated with free radicals that are believed to cause cell damage, and may lead to both cancer and CVD.

The effect of vitamin E supplementation on the immune response of older healthy men and women was investigated in a double-blind, placebo-controlled study (Meydani *et al.*, 1990). Subjects received placebo or vitamin E (800 mg alpha-tocopherol acetate) for 30 days. It was reported that several indices of cell-mediated immunity were significantly improved with vitamin E. In other words, the immune system of these people, which protected their bodies against all kinds of foreign substances and toxic agents, including bacteria, viruses, and chemicals, were strengthened. It had also been reported earlier that population groups maintaining high plasma vitamin E concentrations had a lower incidence of lung cancer (Menkes *et al.*, 1986).

Taking vitamin E may reduce the risk of oral cancer, according to a report from the National Cancer Institute (Gridley *et al.*, 1992). In an analysis of 1,114 adults as well as 1,268 control subjects, statisticians found that among people who took vitamin E supplements for at least six months, the risk of cancer of the mouth and throat was significantly reduced.

In the face of the substantive positive values or functions that have been attributed to vitamin E, note that, in 1985, Nomura and associates conducted a study of serum vitamin levels and the risk of cancer of specific sites, in men of Japanese ancestry living in Hawaii. They reported that vitamin E offered no protection against any type of cancer. Despite the fact, therefore, that considerable progress has been made in clarifying the role of vitamin E and selenium in the etiology and prevention of cancer, and that of vitamin E in strengthening the immune system, there is still an embarrassing element of inconsistency in the published reports. Obviously, further research will be needed to remove these inconsistencies.

Alcohol

Many studies have related the consumption of alcohol to the incidence of cancer both in animals and people (Doll and Peto, 1981; DNC, Chapter 11, 1982; Byers, 1988; Rogers and Longnecker, 1988). The well-documented increase in the risk for oral, laryngeal, esophageal, and liver cancers from the copious use of alcohol was reviewed by Rogers and Conner (1985) and led the American Cancer Society and other responsible health bodies to warn the public of the dangers of alcoholic beverages.

The epidemiologic evidence regarding the relationship of alcohol consumption to risk of breast cancer is remarkably consistent (Rogers and Longnecker, 1988). Increased risk is evident at very low intakes of alcohol, and the risk generally increases with the amount of alcoholic beverage consumed. Harvey *et al.* (1987) reported that moderate alcohol consumption by women before 30 years of age was more strongly related to breast cancer risk than was consumption at later ages. Of all cases of breast cancer in women consuming an average one-half drink or more of alcohol daily, 29 percent may be attributed to alcohol (Rothman, 1986). Therefore alcohol, which is currently used by about 57 percent of American women, is a potentially important risk factor for one of the most common cancers in females (Rogers and Longnecker, 1988).

Collectively, the data from more than 20 studies suggest that alcohol may be directly associated with moderate risk of large bowel cancer, particularly rectal cancer (Rogers and Longnecker, 1988). For rectal cancer, the association is stronger in males than females, and it appears that alcohol consumed in the form of beer is more strongly related to risk than an equal amount of alcohol in the form of wine or spirits. There also appears to be a statistically significant association between beer drinking in certain countries, but not in others (DNC, 1982, p. 203). These associations with specific beverage types suggest that the effects may be due to intake of different contaminants in the beverages, rather than to consumption of alcohol per se.

When combined with cigarette smoking, moderate use of alcoholic beverages has not been associated with an increased risk of cancer. It has been suggested that the additional effect of drinking, in smokers, is minimal compared with the havoc wrought by cigarette smoking alone. Excessive consumption of alcoholic beverages by smokers appears to act synergistically to increase the risk for cancer of the mouth, larynx, esophagus, and the respiratory tract (Doll and Peto, 1981). Delivery of carcinogens to susceptible tissues may be enhanced with consumption of alcohol (Weinhouse, 1986).

Iron

Stevens et al. (1988) reported on body iron stores and the risk of cancer. The study, based on a large population survey, found a correlation between high body levels of iron and cancer of the colon, lungs, bladder, and esophagus in men. Two lines of evidence provide a biological rationale for the hypothesis that increased body iron stores are associated with an increased risk of cancer (Selby and Friedman, 1988). First, iron can catalyze the production of oxygen radicals, and these may be proximate carcinogens (Cerutti, 1985). Second, iron may be a limiting nutrient for the growth and development of cancer cells; excess iron may increase the chances that cancer cells will survive and flourish.

Stevens et al. (1988) concluded that too little iron is clearly detrimental. However, iron elevated beyond a level necessary to avoid anemia may also have adverse consequences, and iron supplementation for those who are not anemic may be unwise.

Cruciferous Vegetables

Cruciferous vegetables, which are members of the cabbage family, include cabbage, brussels sprouts, broccoli, cauliflower, and kale. In a clinical study, Graham *et al.* (1978) reported that a decreased risk for colon cancer was associated with frequent ingestion of raw vegetables, especially cabbage, brussels sprouts, and broccoli. Similar but less impressive results were obtained for rectal cancer.

Three different derivatives of the chemical substance known as indole have been found in brussels sprouts, cabbage, cauliflower, and broccoli. They have been studied for their effects on chemically induced neoplasia in rodents (Wattenberg and Loub, 1978). When added to the diet of mice, they have inhibited induced neoplasia of the forestomach and pulmonary adenoma formation.

A major inducer of anticarcinogenic protective enzymes was isolated from broccoli (Zhang *et al.*, 1992), and its identity was confirmed by chemical synthesis. It is an isothiocyanate, known commonly as sulforaphane.

Katsouyanni *et al.* (1986) found intakes of cauliflower and cooked or raw cabbage were inversely associated with risk of breast cancer, but the association was statistically significant only for raw cabbage.

In four investigations, reported in an 1988 review by Rogers and Longnecker, dealing with dietary and nutritional influences on cancer, frequent intake of cruciferous vegetables, or cabbage alone, was found to be inversely related to colorectal cancer. On comparison with the relationships found to exist between various other nutrients and the risk of cancer, those between cruciferous vegetables and cancer risk can best be described as moderately strong.

Bacterial Infection and Stomach Cancer

Although stomach cancer has declined steadily during the past 60 years in developed countries, it still claims 13,000 lives annually in the United States. In much of Asia and Latin America, it is very common, and worldwide, its prevalence is second only to that of lung cancer. Until recently, research on environmental risk factors for stomach cancer focused primarily on diet. Now two articles (Parsonnet *et al.*, 1991; Nomura *et al.*, 1991) reached the conclusion that people who develop stomach cancer were more likely to have been infected with *Helicobacter pylori* bacteria 15 or 20 years earlier than those who do not develop it. Spontaneous cures of *H. pylori* have not been documented, and it is likely that infection acquired early persists throughout life.

It is clear, however, that infection with *H. pylori* alone cannot explain the pathogenesis of gastric carcinoma. *Helicobacter pylori* infection is very common, affecting approximately 50 percent of North American adults who are older than 50 years. As only a very small percentage of infected persons will ever have stomach cancer, there must be other critical cofactors affecting risk. Possible cofactors are age at onset of infection and diet. Dietary factors suspected of increasing risks are nitrates and salt, while protective foods include fresh vegetables and fruits, which exert their effects through vitamins A, C, and E, also beta-carotene, for reasons explored earlier in this chapter.

The Future: Predicting Individual Cancer Risk

Epidemiologic methods have been reasonably successful in identifying groups of people who are most at risk of developing cancer, for example, the association of lung cancer to cigarette smoking. When it comes to predicting individual risk, however, classical epidemiology is powerless. The reason is that individuals vary markedly in their responses to carcinogens. As pointed out by Marx (1991), only one in ten cigarette smokers actually develops lung cancer, which is why classical epidemiology is helpless when asked the question every individual most wants answered: What's my risk of cancer?

Because of advances in understanding cancer at the molecular level, researchers are on the verge of being able to make such predictions. For one group, people with a rare, hereditary cancer susceptibility, they already can. Last year's discovery of the gene for Li–Fraumeni syndrome, for example, made screening possible for this condition, which predisposes its carriers to several kinds of cancer. Screening may soon be available for people with hereditary susceptibility to colon cancer (Kinzler *et al.*, 1991; Nishisho *et al.*, 1991). Attempts to find molecular markers (that can, like cancer-susceptibility genes, help detect the individuals at highest risk from environmental exposures) are still in the early stages of development. The new molecular methods are referred to as molecular epidemiology.

In a special issue of *Science* (254:1081–1268, 1991), seven articles explore developments in basic and applied research that are increasing our understanding of the pathways leading to cancer, and the new approaches to prevention and therapy (254:1131–1177, 1991).

Arthritis

Arthritis or inflammation of a joint is not a disease in itself, but is caused by more than 100 ailments. Most commonly, arthritis occurs as osteoarthritis, rheumatoid arthritis, or gout. All three have some relationship to dietary habits, but the relationships are not clear-cut, and there is still considerable controversy about them. More is known about the effects nutrition and diet do not have on arthritis than about the subtle links diet has to the development and prevention of arthritis.

There is no acceptable evidence that folk remedies or other dietary treatments influence osteoarthritis or rheumatoid arthritis. Avoiding orange juice, bananas, raisins, or other dried fruits will not alleviate them. Oil of evening primrose is not a cure, and consuming large quantities may be dangerous. Honey, lecithin, vinegar, and large quantities of vitamins are not treatments. Dairy products do not cause it. In fact, gout is the only type of arthritis with a scientifically proven dietary link.

Gout

Gouty arthritis is due to an inherited metabolic defect that leads to excess uric acid in the blood, a condition known as hyperuricemia. Most, but not all, individuals with this problem develop gouty arthritis. Although dietary modification is used in the treatment of gout, it is not caused by diet (Bollet, 1988). No one can give himself gout; only those individuals who have an enzyme defect or whose kidneys excrete less uric acid than normal develop gout. The typical picture envisioned by most people of the person with gout—the obese, fiftyish man dining on rich food with several glasses of wine—does bear some relationship to the facts, however. Uric acid is produced when purines found in protein-rich foods are metabolized. Foods such as caviar and meat gravies are rich sources, as are some vegetables such as asparagus and mushrooms. Women are rarely affected by gout and usually not before menopause (Natow and Heslin, 1986). In males, the first attack typically occurs between 40 and 50 years of age. Although alcohol consumption does not cause gout, overindulgence or even moderate chronic use may precipitate an attack. Lactic acid produced during ethanol metabolism inhibits secretion of uric acid by the kidney (Drum, 1981).

Attacks of gout occur suddenly, without warning, most often as pain, swelling, warmth, and shiny redness in the large toe. Usually the pain radiates up the leg. The pain is so severe that the person is unable to walk. When hyperuricemia develops, the uric acid can no longer remain in solution in the blood. It precipitates as sodium urate crystals in the tissues of the body. Deposits of these crystals are referred to as tophi and tend to accumulate in the small joints and surrounding soft tissue. In chronic gout, tophi tend to accumulate on the outer edges of the ear and to affect outer joints of the foot as well as fingers, wrists, elbows, and knees.

Gout is usually controllable with medication and diet. Commonly used medications are allopurinol, probenecid, and colchicine. These drugs have allowed liberalization of the diet (Bollet, 1988). Prior to the use of these drugs, protein was limited to 20 to 30 g per day, about half the current RDA, and all food containing purines were eliminated. Currently, only high-purine foods are restricted for most patients, and protein intake has been increased to approximate the RDA (Kalman, 1981). Some high-purine foods (150 to 1000 mg per serving) are broths, gravies, organ meats, anchovies, herring, fish roe, mussels, beer, and wine. Formerly, coffee, tea, and cocoa were eliminated from the diet of gout sufferers because it was thought caffeine, theophylline, and theobromines were metabolized to uric acid (Natow and Heslin, 1986). It is now known that their metabolic products are methylurates that are not deposited as gouty tophi.

Patients with gout should consume 2.5 to 3 quarts of fluid per day to help prevent uric acid kidney stones. If obese, the person with gout should lose weight to help control hyperuricemia. The loss must be slow and gradual. Rapid weight loss and fasting can cause an attack. In these situations, ketones build up in the blood, which causes a further increase in blood uric acid levels.

Osteoarthritis

Osteoarthritis, commonly referred to as degenerative arthritis, occurs because of degeneration of the cartilage in joints. In normal joints, cartilage provides a smooth surface that, when lubricated by synovial fluid, allows bones to glide past each other. When cartilage is damaged, bones are not able to move past each other easily when a joint is moved, resulting in damage to the bone ends. This damage stimulates growth of new bone, but the new bone is abnormal. Spurs, or osteophytes, are formed. Osteoarthritis can result from trauma to the joint or infection. Recently, some families in which arthritis is a common problem have been shown to have an inherited defect in the structure of the cartilage in their joints. Additionally, joints that do not align properly are likely to develop osteoarthritis. However, for most patients with this type of arthritis, the cause is unknown (Roe, 1983). While the age of onset of symptoms is often 50 years of age or above, it frequently begins at a much younger age. At present, whether or not aging is a risk factor is unknown. Obesity and overweight appear to be risk factors because of the added stress on knees, hips, and ankles. These joints are weight bearing and are the ones commonly affected. Surveys of people with arthritis indicate that they are frequently obese, but because arthritis caused limitation of activity, it is unclear which came first, the obesity or the arthritis (White-O'Connor *et al.*, 1989; Simson, 1989). However, because obesity aggravates the condition, it is important for arthritic individuals to maintain normal body weight (Bollet, 1988).

Rheumatoid Arthritis

This form of arthritis is an autoimmune disease that affects the entire body, not just the joints. Patients with rheumatoid arthritis may feel fatigue and have low-grade fever. Loss of appetite can occur when the disease is active, and some patients lose considerable weight as a result. Rheumatoid arthritis causes inflammation within the joint; eventually destruction of the cartilage and bone occurs. The affected joints frequently feel warm and become swollen and painful. The small joints of the hands and feet are usually affected first. Typically, the inflammation occurs in a symmetrical pattern; thus, the same joints on both sides of the body are affected at the same time. It is usual for rheumatoid arthritis to begin in midlife, and it is characterized by periods of remission. During remission, pain subsides and symptoms disappear.

Nutritional therapy in rheumatoid arthritis is aimed at maintaining normal weight and restoring any nutritional deficiencies that might have occurred as a result of weight loss. Furthermore, preventing nutritional deficiencies as a result of treatment is a primary goal. In patients using high doses of aspirin, vitamin C depletion can occur and the vitamin C may need to be replenished (Sahud and Cohen, 1971). Aspirin and other anti-inflammatory drugs can cause gastrointestinal blood loss, and iron supplements may be required to prevent anemia (Vreugdenhil, 1989; Vreugdenhil et al., 1990). Some patients require corticosteroids (see Chapter 9), which increase the risk of developing osteoporosis (Bollet, 1988). Consuming adequate calcium and vitamin D along with regular exercise is important to avoid loss of bone.

Over the years a number of case reports in the medical literature have linked this type of arthritis to certain food allergies (Zeller, 1949; Parke et al., 1981; Denman, 1983). It appears that in some cases, food allergies can cause painful and swollen joints. Whether or not these individuals have a previously unrecognized form of allergic arthritis or specific foods are triggering their rheumatoid arthritis is the subject of considerable debate among rheumatologists. Unfortunately a number of nonscientific publications have used this information to allege that rheumatoid arthritis is due to food sensitivity. They advocate the use of the radioallergosorbent test (RAST) for food allergy and elimination diets. The RAST is almost always positive for food allergy, even in nonallergic individuals, and no research studies consistently link certain food groups, nightshade vegetables (tomatoes and eggplant), for example, to rheumatoid arthritis. It does not make sense for people with this problem to arbitrarily eliminate foods based on a perceived connection. However, if symptoms always become worse after eating a particular food, it is probably prudent to avoid eating it (Bollet, 1988). This decision involves a little detective work, because food as eaten can be very complex. If the family recipe for pasta sauce always worsens the symptoms, the tomatoes cannot be the culprit if raw tomatoes are eaten several times a week without problems. Tomato-based pasta sauces easily contain 25 or 30 ingredients with all the spices, herbs, and other flavorings. Any one of them may provoke a flare-up.

High-fat diets are known to decrease inflammation by altering the amounts of various prostaglandins produced. Polyunsaturated fatty acids have a greater effect on the immune system than saturated fatty acids. Of the polyunsaturated fatty acids, the omega-3 fatty acids found in fish oils have the greatest effect (Meydani, 1988, 1991a). This information led to research experiments in which fish-oil supplements were given to patients with rheumatoid arthritis. These experiments were successful in relieving the symptoms, but when the supplements were discontinued, symptoms returned to prestudy levels. Whether fish oils will be useful in long-term therapy is unknown at present. Immunologists investigating fatty acids and immune function believe that high levels of omega-3 fatty acids in the diet will adversely affect the body's ability to fight infections (Meydani *et al.*, 1991b). These oils not only decrease inflammation, but also decrease the number of white blood cells circulating in the blood, as well as decreasing their mitogenic response, i.e., their ability to multiply in response to a stimulus such as bacteria. At this time it would be ill advised for a person to consume fish oils as a dietary supplement. Emphasizing fish in the diet, however, by serving cold-water fish such as cod and salmon two or three times per week may be of benefit.

Nutritional Anemias

The word anemia literally means "without blood," and it is used in a medical sense to describe a decrease in the number of circulating red blood cells and/or a decrease in the concentration of hemoglobin within these cells. Iron, folic acid, pyridoxine (B_6), vitamin B_{12}, protein, ascorbic acid, vitamin E, and copper contribute to the health and function of red blood cells. Deficiency of any of these nutrients can result in anemia, but nutritional anemias are most commonly due to a lack of iron, folic acid and/or vitamin B_{12}. The others rarely cause anemia, and normal, healthy people eating a varied diet have no risk of developing anemia from the lack of B_6, protein, vitamin C, vitamin E, or copper in the diet. Some members of the general population, however, are at risk of developing anemia from these causes. Alcoholics, strict vegans, especially those following the highest levels of the macrobiotic diet, and others following bizarre diets such as "junk-food junkies" who totally shun fruits and vegetables are at risk from a deficiency of one or more of these other nutrients.

Iron-Deficiency Anemia

A deficiency of iron leads to a type of anemia referred to as microcytic, hypochromic (i.e., small cells that are pale in color). A common occurrence accompanying this type of anemia is unusual dietary cravings called pica. It is not uncommon for a person with iron deficiency to consume large quantities of ice. Ice craving appears to result from the iron deficiency; however, in some cases, pica causes the anemia. In 1981, a case report in the *Annals of Internal Medicine* (Leming et al., 1981) described a 74-year-old woman who consumed large quantities of magnesium carbonate, which binds the iron in the gastrointestinal tract, making it difficult to absorb. This substance is used by gymnasts to keep their hands dry during exercises.

Adult men and postmenopausal women need about 1 mg per day of iron to maintain normal hemoglobin levels. The RDA is set at ten times this amount because only about 10 percent of iron in the typical American diet is absorbed. Heme iron, that is, iron from animal sources such as red meat, is absorbed much better than nonheme iron. The absorption of nonheme iron is increased if accompanied by a source of vitamin C (Hunt et al., 1990) and/or a source of animal protein (RDA, 1989). A number of foods and food components greatly inhibit the absorption of nonheme iron. They include the food additives calcium phosphate and ethylenediaminetetraacetic acid

(EDTA); coffee and tea, soy proteins, egg yolk, wheat bran, and other dietary fiber. Whole grains contain phytates, and spinach contains oxalic acid (oxalate), both of which hinder the absorption of iron. A number of cereals and grain products have iron added to them as a form of enrichment or fortification. Some of these products are designed for vegetarians and people who significantly limit their intake of meat and poultry. Unfortunately, the iron salts used in this process are not well absorbed. They are selected for palatability and shelf life of the product rather than for absorbability.

Iron Deficiency and the Older Adult

Despite the fact that, as discussed in the chapter on vitamins and minerals, iron deficiency is one of the most common nutritional problems, anemia from insufficient iron is more likely to be due to blood loss than to failing to meet the RDA for iron. Bleeding in older people can result from hemorrhoids, hiatus hernia, diverticulitis, ulcers, gastrointestinal cancers, and even untreated gum disease. A number of medications can cause bleeding (aspirin, for example) or hinder absorption of iron, such as the prolonged use or abuse of antacids and laxatives. Chronic diarrhea decreases iron absorption even if the laxative abused does not directly hinder iron absorption. Furthermore, the decrease in gastric acidity that occurs with aging decreases iron absorption. It is important for older individuals to consume adequate vitamin C to compensate for this loss; however, this does not always occur. A low intake of vitamin C has been associated with iron deficiency in the elderly (Roe, 1983), and avoidance of food sources of vitamin C is a common finding in gastrointestinal diseases (Nutr. Rev., 1989), which are more prevalent in older people. Among healthy elderly individuals, low iron intake has been found to be due to a low intake of food energy; in the U.S. diet, iron intake is 6 mg per 1000 kcalories. An inadequate intake of animal protein results in a low intake of heme iron, and high tea consumption results in the impaired absorption of iron. Of course the aged person with few teeth, whose diet tends toward tea and toast or sweets is at significant risk for iron deficiency (Roe, 1983).

While a number of the elderly may be at risk for iron-deficiency anemia, supplemental iron should not be taken unless the diet has been evaluated for iron content. It is possible to consume too much iron, causing toxicity (see Chapter 3), and one of the signs of toxicity happens to be mild anemia. Older adults with even mild hypochromic, microcytic anemia need to have the cause determined before taking iron supplements to rule out life-threatening problems such as colon cancer and to verify that a mild decrease in hemoglobin level is actually due to anemia. Women, even postmenopausal women, tend to have lower hemoglobin levels than men, and blacks, regardless of economic status, have lower hemoglobin values than whites. Aging appears to affect the hemoglobin concentration in men, but not in women. It appears that as the production of androgens (male hormones) decreases with age, the hemoglobin level drops (Natow and Heslin, 1986).

Anemia Due to Lack of Folic Acid and/or B_{12}

Both vitamin B_{12} and folate are necessary for dividing cells. Without these nutrients, the synthesis of DNA is slowed, causing a decrease in the maturation rate of the nucleus of red blood cells. These large immature cells are released into the circulation, resulting in macrocytic anemia. Although either vitamin deficiency can cause this type of anemia, only B_{12} deficiency leads to neurologic damage. The damage occurs because myelin, which insulates nerves, cannot be maintained without sufficient vitamin B_{12}. Vitamin B_{12} is required for the conversion of folic acid to tetrahydrofolate, the form of the vitamin necessary for DNA production. Excessively high intake of folic acid will overcome the decrease in activation that occurs with B_{12} deficiency and correct the anemia, but will not stop the damage to nerves. Daily intake of folate that meets the RDA for this vitamin will not mask pernicious anemia.

Although folic acid was first identified in green, leafy vegetables, it is widespread in foods, being found in most animal products; a number of fruits; dried peas and beans; and beer, because brewer's yeast is a particularly rich source. As a result, folic acid deficiency due to dietary lack was not thought possible until the 1970s (Coleman, 1990). Vitamin B_{12}, however, is found only in foods of animal origin. In theory, strict vegans—those who eat only plant products— are at risk for vitamin B_{12} deficiency. Although these people would seem to need a B_{12} supplement, very few vegans actually develop a deficiency of this nutrient. Nutritionists are not sure of the reason, but certainly the fact that several years' supply of this vitamin can be stored in the liver contributes to their lack of anemia. Furthermore, most grains and cereals have microscopic contamination of animal origin that can be a source of vitamin B_{12}.

Rather than being caused by lack of dietary B_{12}, most anemia of this type is due to a lack of intrinsic factor, a situation referred to as pernicious anemia. Intrinsic factor is produced in the stomach and binds to vitamin B_{12}, enabling the vitamin to be absorbed in the ileum. Individuals with pernicious anemia make antibodies that destroy both the intrinsic factor and the cells that produce it. Without intrinsic factor, the small intestine is not able to absorb B_{12}.

Macrocytic Anemia in Older People

Aging does not appear to increase the need for folate, but a number of factors that occur more commonly among the elderly increase the need for this vitamin or decrease its intake (Rosenberg, 1982). Diseases of the gastrointestinal tract can lead to malabsorption of folate, and people with these problems frequently limit their intake of foods containing both folic acid and vitamin C, which is required for activation of the vitamin (Nutr. Rev., 1989). Many drugs taken by the elderly can induce folate deficiency. These include anticonvulsants, barbiturates, triamterene, a commonly used diuretic, and aspirin in large doses. However, the drug most commonly associated with folic acid deficiency is alcohol (see Chapter 9). In the 1960s and 1970s, folic acid deficiency was reported to be the most common nutritional deficiency in the elderly (SGR, 1988). Avoidance of foods that are the richest sources of folate were found to be a major reason. Foods such as liver, green leafy vegetables, and fortified breakfast cereals were found to be lacking in the diets, frequently because the elderly dislike these foods. One aspect of folate status not usually considered when evaluating the diet is length of cooking. Folic acid is destroyed by long cooking, especially in finely chopped or small foods such as rice and beans. Conceivably, this could contribute to a dietary deficiency in an edentulous elderly person whose diet is limited to soup and pureed foods. A mashed, fresh banana would be helpful in avoiding folate deficiency since folate is very well absorbed from this source (Natow and Heslin, 1986).

Vitamin B_{12} deficiency is most commonly caused by a lack of intrinsic factor and gastrointestinal disease in the elderly. The incidence of pernicious anemia increases with age, affecting 1 in 200 people in the 60 to 70-year-old age group. A secondary cause is the decrease in gastric acidity that occurs with advanced age. The initial digestion of B_{12} requires gastric acid to remove it from food. Unfortunately, dietary supplementation with B_{12} will not correct the problem. These people require a monthly injection of the vitamin (Schilling, 1985). Whether or not all older people should be receiving supplemental vitamin B_{12} is continually debated among physicians and registered dietitians. Those in favor point to the increasing occurrence of pernicious anemia with advancing age and the fact that the neurologic manifestations of B_{12} deficiency are seen in the absence of anemia, particularly in the elderly (Lindenbaum *et al.*, 1988). Once present, neurologic damage is not reversible by correcting the vitamin B_{12} status of the person.

7

Dental Health and Nutrition

Dental disease—caries and periodontal disease—is not a new human illness. Even prehistoric human skulls show evidence of both problems. Man's search for the cause of these dental problems also dates back to ancient times. Greek physicians were the first to recognize the relationship between the consumption of sweet foods and tooth decay. Aristotle advised against eating soft figs, as he felt they were the main cause of rotted teeth. By the fifteenth century, prominent physicians, such as Arculanus, were advising their patients to avoid sweet, sticky foods to prevent tooth loss (SGR, 1988).

Dental caries and periodontal disease are significant health problems in the United States. They are not life threatening unless left untreated for long periods, but they can cause pain, tooth loss, and substantial expense. In 1986, the U.S. Department of Commerce reported that the annual cost of dental care in the United States came to $21.3 billion. The cost of dental disease continues to rise and uses a significant portion of our health care dollars.

Fortunately, most dental disease can be prevented. The incidence of both caries and periodontal disease is declining due to better dental hygiene and care, the use of fluoride, improved nutrition, and decreased intake of cariogenic foods. Over the last 25 years, the percentage of edentulous (without teeth) persons in the population has declined steadily not only because of the prevention of periodontal disease, but because of improvements in the treatment as well.

Changes in Dental Disease That Occur with Aging

Loss of Teeth

Prior to age 35, the primary cause for tooth loss is dental caries, while after 35 years of age, it is most frequently due to periodontal disease. Tooth loss can have a detrimental effect on nutritional status, as toothless individuals frequently limit food choices to those that are easy to chew or require little biting, e.g., a partially edentulous individual may select sweetened applesauce over a fresh apple. By so doing, the person is losing the benefit of the extra fiber in the fresh apple and some vitamin C, while taking in extra sugar and kcalories. At the same time, he is increasing the risk of decay in remaining teeth due to the loss of tooth cleaning that occurs when chewing the fresh apple and the availability of additional sugar to the oral flora.

Although toothlessness has been in steady decline since 1960, it remains a major problem for Americans older than age 65 (SGR, 1988). It is hoped that research into the interrelationships between periodontal disease and nutrition will lead to further declines in the percentage of edentulous persons in the United States.

Periodontal Disease

The percentage of Americans with periodontal disease does not increase with aging once adulthood has been reached, but the severity of the disease does increase. This may be one reason that the number of edentulous individuals increases significantly at 65 years of age. The National Adult Dental Health Survey of 1985–1986 showed that bleeding gums were present in 43 percent of employed adults and 47 percent of people older than 65. The periodontal disease was judged to be severe in 68 percent of the older individuals, but only 24 percent of the working adults had severe disease (SGR, 1988).

Dental Caries

Investigators in dental research have traditionally used the number of decayed, missing, and filled permanent teeth to determine the prevalence of dental caries in the United States. This method works

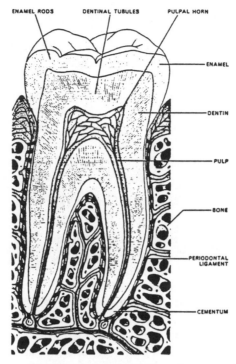

ENAMEL RODS   DENTINAL TUBULES   PULPAL HORN

ENAMEL

DENTIN

PULP

BONE

PERIODONTAL LIGAMENT

CEMENTUM

Figure 7.1. Cross-section of a normal tooth and surrounding anatomical structures. SOURCE: *Dental Science Handbook* by L.W. Morrey and R.J. Nelson, Superintendent of Documents, Washington, DC, 1970.

well with younger people, but older adults lose teeth primarily from periodontal disease rather than from decay. More recent surveys (e.g., the 1987 National Institute of Dental Research survey) have attempted to use the number of decayed and filled permanent teeth surfaces to compensate for teeth missing from other causes. This survey showed that the number of decayed and filled tooth surfaces increases steadily up to about 40 years of age. Additionally, for individuals under 34 years old, dental caries has declined significantly. It was not possible to determine whether dental caries is declining in individuals over age 34, because tooth loss due to periodontal disease prevented meaningful comparisons with earlier surveys (SGR, 1988).

The location of dental decay changes with aging. At about age 60, root decay becomes a major problem. In the 1987 National Institute of Dental Research Survey, 63 percent of adults older than 65 had root decay, but only half of these carious lesions had been filled. Lack of treatment can lead to tooth loss. Root caries results from the greater exposure of root surfaces due to age-related gum recession or periodontal disease (SGR, 1988).

Initiation of Dental Caries

In 1889, an American dentist, W.D. Miller, theorized that dental caries was caused by oral bacteria fermenting dietary carbohydrates, leading to acid production. Acid production lowered the pH, which resulted in dissolution of the enamel (Dennison and Randolph, 1981). This theory was largely ignored until the 1950s when the role of microorganisms in caries formation was considered again (Shaw, 1952). Three classical experiments conducted by Shaw demonstrated the validity of Miller's theory. Feeding a high-sucrose diet to germ-free animals did not result in caries formation; feeding a carbohydrate-rich diet directly into the stomach via a tube did not cause caries formation in animals with known cariogenic oral flora; and a positive relationship was found to exist between carbohydrate consumption and caries formation in humans. Although other theories of dental decay are occasionally promoted, Miller's theory has been well accepted since the early 1950s (Dennison and Randolph, 1981).

Over the last several decades, controversy has centered on whether a specific bacterium will affect a specific site on a tooth and produce caries via acid production at that site or whether a number of plaque bacteria working together cause decay. This is a difficult question to answer primarily because children develop caries on the crown of the tooth, whereas older people tend to develop them at the root following the recession of gum tissue that occurs with aging (SGR, 1988). Although some dental researchers regard these as independent types of caries, and others do not, the bacterium most associated with dental caries is *Streptococcus mutans*, with *Lactobacillus* a close second.

The initiation of dental caries also requires the presence of dental plaque, which adheres to the tooth's surface. Plaque is a clear, gelatinous material formed by organisms in the mouth when sucrose is present. The sucrose is converted to very sticky polysaccharides called glucans. The glucans adhere to the protein covering of the tooth, the pellicle, which is produced by bacterial action on saliva. Dental plaque provides a means for cariogenic bacteria to attach to the tooth's surface as well as a favorable environment for their multiplication (Table 7.1). If not removed by brushing, the plaque hardens, providing a protected environment for the bacteria to produce decay (Dennison and Randolph, 1981).

Although dental caries is due to the dissolution of tooth enamel by acid produced from fermentable carbohydrates by plaque bacteria, a number of factors affect an individual's propensity to develop caries. Two of the most important, dietary habits and fluoride exposure, are discussed in separate sections of this chapter.

Mineralization of teeth, as well as subtle differences in microscopic tooth structure, are affected by heredity and nutritional status before and after birth. If nutritional status is compromised during the development of oral structures, teeth may be prone to caries later in life (SGR, 1988).

Whether or not nutrient intake and nutritional status affect the

Table 7.1. Summary of Dental Caries Formation

1. Food is eaten.
2. Food particles lodge between the teeth or in recesses on the surface of teeth.
3. Sucrose present in food and salivary proteins are turned into plaque by bacteria present in the mouth.
4. The plaque adheres to teeth and is a favorable environment for the multiplication of decay-causing bacteria.
5. Acid is formed from fermentable carbohydrates as the decay-causing bacteria multiply.
6. Acids accumulate on the surface of the tooth, causing the pH to drop.
7. When the pH drops to 5.5, the tooth enamel begins to demineralize, enabling bacteria to invade the tooth.

occurrence of caries in adults is a complex issue. After a tooth erupts into the mouth, the enamel goes through a maturation process in which minerals in food, drink, and saliva are incorporated into the enamel. This process occurs by direct contact with the minerals and is unrelated to nutritional status (SGR, 1988). However, poor nutritional status adversely affects the ability of the immune system to fight infection. Dental caries is a form of bacterial infection and like all infections, caries occurs more frequently in individuals with poor nutritional status. Furthermore, over time, the salivary glands are adversely affected by inadequate nutrient intake.

Saliva has a major role in the prevention of caries (SGR, 1988). It contains substances that directly prevent bacteria from attaching to the surface of the teeth and can cause bacteria to clump together. Clumped bacteria are quickly cleared from the mouth by swallowing, as they lack the ability to attach to teeth. Saliva can contain antibodies to specific oral organisms, and it contains enzymes and proteins that either inhibit bacterial growth or kill bacteria. Another important function of saliva is its ability to buffer the acids produced when fermentable carbohydrates are present, thereby preventing demineralization of tooth enamel (Dennison and Randolph, 1981). Furthermore, saliva supplies calcium and phosphorus for the remineralization of tooth surfaces that have lost minerals from acid attack (SGR, 1988).

Decreases in saliva production that occur with aging or from disease such as Sjögren's syndrome, increase the risk of caries. Individuals with decreased saliva production should use an artificial saliva preparation containing fluoride to help prevent tooth decay (SGR, 1988).

Diet and Dental Caries

Throughout most of the twentieth century, table sugar, i.e., sucrose, has been thought of as the major culprit in dental decay. Until the mid 1970s, most epidemiologic and experimental evidence pointed to sucrose. In the United States, dental caries increased until World War II, paralleling the increase in sugar consumption. During the war years, when table sugar was rationed, the incidence of caries fell, and as the diets of developing nations became more westernized, the incidence of dental caries in those countries increased. Westernization of the diet meant an increase in sucrose consumption and a decrease in the intake of fiber and complex carbohydrates, again pointing to sucrose as the problem.

Attempts to induce caries by adding table sugar to the diets of individuals with little dental decay was dramatic in its action. In 1929, dental researchers observed that a group of children in an orphanage had very few carious teeth, although their diets were nutritionally inadequate. Allowing them to eat three pounds of candy per week dramatically increased the number of caries (Kaplan and Valauri, 1990). One well-known study was conducted in Vipeholm, Sweden after World War II (Gustafson *et al.*, 1954; Dennison and Randolph, 1981). The patients in this study were divided into four groups, each receiving a different diet. Individuals in the study who were allowed to eat snacks of toffee and other candy between meals had the greatest increase in caries, while participants given extra sugar as a sweetened beverage had fewer caries. Adding table sugar and bread to meals did not increase the number of carious lesions. The investigators erroneously concluded that bread and white sugar solutions are noncariogenic. More important, however, they realized that sticky sugars are very cariogenic, but that the amount of white sugar consumed was of little importance. The frequency of sugar exposure determines the likelihood of developing caries. While the results of these studies were valuable, under the guidelines now in place at all reputable health research centers in the United States, permission for such studies would not be granted today.

Later research demonstrated why frequency of sugar consumption is important. Each time the plaque bacteria are exposed to sugar, they produce acid for 20 to 30 minutes. This principle was easily demonstrated by giving a volunteer five sugar-based cough drops to eat at once, which resulted in acid production for up to 30 minutes. Having the subject eat them, one at a time, with 35 minutes between each cough drop, resulted in 2.5 hours of acid production (Dennison and Randolph, 1981). Individuals such as former President Reagan, who was reported to have kept a bowl of jelly beans on his desk in the

White House, munching on one or two several times a day, are far more likely to develop tooth decay than the person who eats a half pound of chocolate creams at one sitting, once a week.

Other investigators began to reexamine the information provided by the Vipeholm study. Clinical observations in the United States of patients prone to develop caries linked frequent use of sweetened coffee, tea, and other sweetened beverages such as cola to their high rate of caries. For the first time, dental researchers realized that other dietary components also influence caries development. The individuals in the Vipeholm study receiving the sweetened beverages did not develop caries, because these beverages were consumed with meals. Even sticky gooey sugars are less cariogenic when consumed as part of a meal. A presweetened breakfast cereal may not cause problems when eaten with milk, buttered toast, tea, and tomato juice for breakfast, but consuming it dry as an evening snack is likely to lead to decay. Sipping sweetened ice tea while munching on caramel corn is an equally poor snack choice.

In the early 1970s, the sugar-consumption patterns in the United States began to change. High-fructose corn syrup became widely available and began to replace refined white sugar in many commercial products. Between 1970 and 1979, the per capita consumption of refined white sugar dropped more than ten pounds per year, and the use of corn sweeteners and honey nearly doubled from 20 pounds to 39.1 pounds per person per year. The caries rate in the United States did not decline as dramatically as expected, and dental researchers began to realize that sugars other than refined white sugar can induce caries. In fact, the so-called natural sugars, honey and brown sugar, may be more cariogenic than table sugar due to their sticky nature (Dennison and Randolph, 1981).

Finally, in the 1980s, investigators again examined the role of starches, which are complex carbohydrates, in caries formation. An article was published in the *Journal of the American Dental Association* revealing the cariogenicity of some starchy foods (Kaplan and Valauri, 1990). Breadsticks, corn flakes, and croissants stayed in the mouth longer than sweets and produced more acid for a longer time period, making the teeth more susceptible to decay. Although the mouth bacteria cannot ferment starches, amylase, an enzyme in saliva, begins to digest the starch, providing a ready source of glucose to the bacteria in the mouth. The knowledge that starches can be cariogenic is especially important to older individuals. The decrease in gum tissue that occurs with aging allows more space for starchy foods to lodge in the mouth, and declining saliva production adds to the difficulty of removing these foods from the teeth.

Anticariogenic Foods

Anticariogenic foods are considered by some dental researchers to be foods that do not cause the acidity of the saliva to rise to a point where tooth decay can occur. Others think of anticariogenic foods only as foods that decrease the ability of fermentable carbohydrates to cause tooth decay.

Foods high in protein or fat do not increase the acidity of the saliva as they are not fermented by oral bacteria, so they are believed to be safe for teeth (Dennison and Randolph, 1981). From a dental viewpoint, snacks of nuts, meats, and some cheeses such as Brie, blue, or mozzarella make good snack choices. However, foods such as these are typically high in fat and kcalories. Furthermore, whole milk cheeses and meats contain significant amounts of cholesterol. Excessive use of these foods as snacks can lead to elevated cholesterol and weight gain.

Monterey jack, Swiss, and cheddar cheese decrease the cario-genicity of sticky, sugary foods (Patoka *et al.*, 1991). Eating them before or after sugary foods buffers the acids preventing the decrease in pH that leads to demineralization of the teeth. They also increase saliva production, which helps to return the pH to normal and cleans the teeth. Fat in these cheeses and other foods decreases stickiness of sugary foods so that less adheres to the teeth (Kaplan and Valauri, 1990).

Hard and fibrous fruits and vegetables may also be helpful in preventing tooth decay. Formerly, crunchy vegetables such as carrots, celery, and green peppers were thought of as nature's toothbrush when eaten uncooked. It was believed that they literally scrubbed the teeth clean of plaque and tartar. In the early 1980s, dental research showed that these foods cannot replace a toothbrush. While they do clean tooth surfaces, they do not remove plaque at or below the gum line. The cleaning action of these foods is thought to be due to their ability to stimulate copious saliva flow rather than their ability to brush away retained food particles (Dennison and Randolph, 1981). Understanding the relationship between fermentable carbohydrates and anticariogenic foods can be helpful in planning a diet that decreases the risk of developing tooth decay. Just rearranging the sequence of foods in a meal and the time of day certain foods are eaten can be very helpful in preventing tooth decay. Ray is a 70-year-old, very active retiree. He has been a "sugaraholic" his entire life and never liked eating three meals a day, but preferred to eat small snacks throughout the day. Since retiring nearly 3 years ago, Ray has developed a problem with root caries because of his eating habits. He brushes his teeth after breakfast and again before bedtime, when he flosses. A diet history reveals problems with foods consumed in the late afternoon and evening. A typical afternoon snack consists of a jelly donut and a glass of cranberry juice cocktail. Dinner is a salad with oil and vinegar dressing, followed by sweet-and-sour pork with rice, picked up from the local carry-out, and tea. In the evening he has another snack of hot apple pie, sometimes with American cheese. Ray munches on the pie over an hour's time.

There are several ways to handle Ray's excessive sugar consumption, but he is reluctant to make major dietary changes since he is not overweight and does not have either diabetes or hypercholesterolemia. Ray and the registered dietitian working with him developed the following plan that requires eliminating only the jelly donut: an afternoon snack of 1 oz of cheddar cheese with cranberry juice cocktail; dinner of sweet-and-sour pork with rice followed by a lettuce salad with at least two crunchy vegetables such as carrots and celery with oil and vinegar dressing, and tea; and eating the apple pie immediately before brushing and flossing in the evening.

Flouridation of Water

At the beginning of this century, it was realized that dental fluorosis in certain areas of Colorado and the Texas panhandle was due to the fluorine naturally present in the water supply (SGR, 1988). The high level of fluorine present in the water in these areas (2 to 6 ppm) causes changes in the enamel as it develops in children's teeth.

Instead of the normal glistening translucent appearance, the teeth acquire dull white patches and may exhibit a brown stain, referred to as "mottling." Pitting of teeth is common, but in extreme cases, the ends of the teeth break off, producing jagged edges. Except in these extreme cases, fluorosis is more a cosmetic problem than a health problem. In fact, the teeth of these children were extraordinarily resistant to decay.

In the late 1930s and the early 1940s, more than 4,000 children in 13 cities were studied to determine the incidence of dental caries and fluorosis in relation to the varying amounts of fluorine in the water supply (SGR, 1988). A sodium fluoride level of 1 ppm was found to provide significant protection against dental caries with no risk of fluorosis. As a result of these findings, a large-scale study of the benefits of fluoridating was begun in 1945. Sodium fluoride at a level of 1 ppm was added to the water of Newburgh, New York; Brantford, Ontario, Canada; and Grand Rapids, Michigan (Nizel and Papas, 1989). Three neighboring cities were chosen as controls. These cities had little natural fluoride in the water, and no fluoride was added. After a period of 10 years, it was found that the children who had been receiving fluoridated water from an early age had about 65 percent fewer dental caries than did the children in the other communities (Shaw *et al.*, 1968; Dennison and Randolph, 1981).

On the basis of the favorable results obtained in the pioneering studies, many municipal governments began to fluoridate their water supplies. By the end of 1985, about 54 percent of the people in the United States had access to fluoridated public water systems. The federal government's objective had long been to have 95 percent of the population served by public water supplies drinking fluoridated water by 1990. That goal has not been reached, but smaller cities and towns such as LaCrosse, Wisconsin, have begun to fluoridate their water supply as recently as 1989.

Extensive investigations have been carried out to determine the mechanism by which fluorine imparts greater resistance to tooth decay. When bones and teeth become calcified, first a crystal structure called hydroxyapatite is formed from calcium and phosphorus. Fluoride ion (F^-), if present, replaces some of the hydroxy group (OH^-) portions of the crystal, resulting in a chemical transformation to crystalline fluorapatite. This fluorapatite is apparently less soluble in acid and more resistant to the cariogenic action of acids in the mouth (Dennison and Randolph, 1981). There is some evidence that fluoride may exert a protective action on the teeth by inhibiting the formation of acid by bacterial enzymes in the plaque on the teeth of persons drinking fluoridated water (SGR, 1988). The plaque contains as much as 250 times the concentration of fluoride that is present in the saliva. Even small differences in the acidity of the plaque will alter the extent to which the enamel may dissolve.

Fluoride's ability to prevent tooth decay is most effective during childhood, but it affects the teeth of adults as well. Adults without exposure to fluoride in childhood experience less tooth decay if they reside in a city with fluoridated water than if they reside in one without fluoridation (Bowden and Stanmeyer, 1977). Their teeth may be protected against decay in fluoride's antibacterial action. However, adult teeth can incorporate fluoride into their structure during the remineralization that occurs after exposure to acid (American Dental Association, 1984). Ample evidence exists to substantiate fluoride's ability to decrease the incidence of tooth decay. Whether or not municipal water supplies should be fluoridated at the present level of 1 part per million is the subject of some debate. When water fluoridation began in the 1950s, it was an economical way to provide fluoride to entire communities. Today about 80 percent of the toothpaste sold in the United States contains fluoride. Fluoride-containing dental rinses are available without a prescription. Infant formula is supplemented with fluoride, and infants are frequently given vitamin/mineral supplements containing fluoride. Commercial food products are frequently prepared with fluoridated water. In fact, fluoride has become so common in our environment that it has been found in water supplies that previously were shown to lack natural fluoridation.

Significant dietary sources of fluoride, in parts per million, are beer (0.15 to 0.86), fresh-water fish without skin or bones (1.00), seafoods including fish (0.4 to 1.6), canned salmon and sardines with bones (7 to 12), tea leaves (less than 5 to 110), brewed tea (0.5 to 1.5), and wine (0.0 to 6.3).

Fluoride is known to be toxic when consumed at levels exceeding 20 milligrams of fluorine per day for several years (RDA, 1989). Symptoms of fluoride toxicity include bone pain, changes in the spine, and digestive problems. The presence of dental fluorosis and the possibility of toxicity has led some communities with very high natural fluoride levels (8 ppm) to defluoridate their water supply. Individuals in areas with fluoridated water typically consume 1 to 2 milligrams of fluoride per day from water and 0.2 to 0.6 mg from food. Though some fluoride is swallowed when using toothpaste and dental rinses, the total amount of fluoride consumed by most individuals is well below toxic levels even in areas with high natural fluoride levels. Both the U.S. Public Health Service and the Surgeon General's report have concluded that there is no association between fluoride and human cancers (APHA, 1991; SGR, 1988).

It must be remembered that fluoride is not a panacea for dental caries. The use of fluoridated water does not allow an individual to forego brushing, flossing, and professional preventive care, nor does it permit a person to have continual exposure of the teeth to sugar and still remain caries free. Other countries, Australia and the United Kingdom, for example, where there is limited water fluoridation or where fluoridation is more recent than that in the United States, have experienced a decline in dental caries similar to the decline in the United States. These declines are attributed to the many advances in dental science, along with the introduction of fluoride into the water supply and alternative fluoride sources (Diesendorf, 1986). Fluoridated water still contributes to the declining rates of dental caries in this country, but it is no longer as important to healthy teeth as it was in the 1940s and 1950s.

Diet and Periodontal Disease

Determining the interrelationships among diet, nutritional status, and periodontal disease is an active area of dental research as the causes of periodontal disease remain to be identified. Like dental caries, it results from the growth of oral bacteria. Bacterial by-products irritate the gum tissue, resulting in gingivitis (inflammation of the gums) and periodontitis (inflammation and destruction of the underlying supportive structures). The first stage of periodontal disease is gingivitis, but everyone with gingivitis does not develop periodontitis. Poor oral hygiene and plaque build-up are considered to be the cause of gingivitis, but why it progresses to bone destruction in some individuals is not known. A number of risk factors are associated with the development and progression of gum disease. Soft diets, lack of saliva, faulty nutrition, and endocrine disorders such as poorly controlled diabetes all increase a person's risk of developing periodontal disease as they promote plaque build-up. Excessive intake of sugary foods has not been directly linked to periodontal disease, but since sugary foods promote growth of plaque bacteria, they should be avoided by individuals with the disease.

The term "faulty nutrition" is yet to be clearly defined for preventing and treating periodontal disease. Healthy teeth and gums require adequate amounts of vitamins A, C, and D, along with calcium, phosphorus, zinc, and iron, yet it is possible to link the disease to a deficiency of only a few of these nutrients. Inducing vitamin C deficiency in laboratory animals can cause gum disease similar to that in humans, but humans develop tooth and gum problems only if the clinical signs of scurvy are present. So-called subclinical deficiency of vitamin C does not appear to be a causative factor in developing gum disease (Rubinoff et al., 1989).

Only diets deficient in protein, vitamin A, and the B vitamins have been clearly linked to periodontal disease in humans. Severe protein–calorie malnutrition that commonly occurs in developing countries is known to cause the disease (Dennison and Randolph, 1981). In the United States, severe protein–energy malnutrition is rare in the absence of disease, but marginal deficiencies do occur. Such deficiencies can affect the immune system's ability to respond to infection and the ability of the oral epithelium to renew itself. Vitamin A is also needed to maintain the integrity of the oral epithelium. As with skin, the oral epithelium provides a physical barrier to bacteria. Marginal deficiencies of these nutrients may influence the severity of periodontal disease rather than cause it. Folic acid appears to prevent experimentally induced gingivitis even in people with normal serum folate levels (Pollack and Kravitz, 1985). Adults with previously recognized gingival inflammation and normal serum folate levels have been successfully treated with folic acid supplements or topically applied folate solutions (Pollack and Kravitz, 1985). Since the plaque was unaffected by the additional folate, the cause of the inflammation was thought to be due to end-organ failure. "End-organ failure" is a technical term meaning either sufficient nutrient does not reach the tissue where the nutrient is utilized or the tissue's ability to utilize a nutrient is diminished. In either case, the organ needs extra nutrition to function normally.

The American Dental Association, being cognizant of the importance of preventing periodontal disease, has issued the following recommendations:

1. Eat a well-balanced diet.
2. Brush and floss at least once a day.
3. Visit a dentist regularly to have teeth professionally cleaned and to detect early signs of gum disease.

Chewing Problems

Tooth loss and the wearing of dentures often lead to significant problems in chewing a number of foods. Individuals with dentures frequently have difficulty chewing fibrous meats such as beef and pork, whereas others complain that chicken, a gelatinous meat, "sticks to my uppers and is hard to swallow." Biting into hard and crunchy fruits and vegetables is another common problem. Foods such as fresh apples, corn-on-the-cob, raw celery, and carrots are frequently eliminated from the diet by these people. Some find cooked fruits and vegetables tasteless both because of the decrease in taste acuity that occurs with aging and the presence of a plastic appliance in the mouth. Difficulty with chewing and the concomitant elimination of a number of foods from the diet lead to digestive problems. Failure to adequately chew starchy and fibrous foods results in large particles that are inadequately moistened with saliva, making them difficult to swallow. Air is frequently swallowed, causing bloating and belching. Decreasing the amount of dietary fiber causes constipation. Fiber supplementation in the form of a fiber laxative such as psyllium hydrophilic mucilloid (Metamucil®) may be needed to restore normal bowel function.

These digestive problems are in addition to the nutritional problems that occur when several foods are eliminated from an individual's diet. Restricting the number of fruits and vegetables in the diet drastically limits the sources of folacin, vitamin A, and vitamin C. Iron and even protein can be in short supply if the amount of meat falls below six ounces per day. Increasing the intake of other protein-rich foods such as milk, cheese, and eggs can supply the needed protein, but iron supplementation may be necessary to prevent anemia. Supplements of other vitamins and minerals should be unnecessary if fruits and vegetables are prepared in a creative manner.

People accept or reject food based on eye appeal, aroma, flavor, and mouth feel. It is important that fruits and vegetables be prepared in a way that is both esthetically pleasing and easy to chew. Quickly stir-frying finely julienned carrots with a little ginger and nutmeg is a more appealing dish than plain boiled carrots. Vegetable purees are acceptable, too, if prepared from fresh vegetables in the French manner rather than as strained baby food served in the jar. Fine restaurants will often serve a scooped-out tomato half filled with pureed fresh broccoli or peas as accompaniment to meat. This is more attractive than just plopping the puree in a bowl. Spending a little time at the local library looking over the fruit and vegetable chapters in a number of cook books is an easy way to find acceptable and appealing preparation methods.

Individuals undergoing oral surgery either for gum disease or tooth extraction have a different type of chewing problem. For a few days they may require a liquid diet, and if general anesthesia is used, a clear liquid diet is normally given first. Typical liquid diets are usually designed to be used for gastrointestinal problems rather than for oral surgery. The salty and highly acidic foods these diets include cause discomfort to people with a mouth wound.

Take, for example, the case of Michelle, who is undergoing outpatient surgery on her upper jaw. This surgical procedure requires general anesthesia, so she will be at the hospital all day and have her first postsurgical meal there. A clear liquid diet is ordered. Her meal arrives and she attempts to eat it. Michelle finds each item causes her pain. The meal consists of a salty, peppery beef broth, lemonade, lime sorbet, and strained orange juice.

A better selection for Michelle's first meal would have been unsalted chicken broth, cranberry juice, raspberry sorbet without seeds, and iced tea with sugar. These milder-tasting foods are much less likely to cause pain. A good rule of thumb to follow when choosing clear liquids: if the food or food ingredient would cause pain to a paper cut, avoid it.

Full liquid diets present problems in addition to those that normally occur with clear liquid diets. Full-liquid diets often cause diarrhea because of the amount of lactose they contain. Diarrhea may occur even in individuals who normally drink considerable quantities of milk because of the antibiotics required after oral surgery. Raw eggs served as eggnog were, at one time, frequently incorporated into full-liquid diets. Recently, the Centers for Disease Control recommended no longer consuming raw eggs because of possible contamination by salmonella. Again, the typical full-liquid diet is designed to rest the gastrointestinal tract rather than the mouth. The sudden lack of dietary fiber causes constipation in a few people, and some foods that do not need to be chewed, applesauce for example, are unnecessarily eliminated.

Dental clear-liquid diets are deficient in most nutrients. Even full-liquid diets may be deficient in trace minerals and some B vitamins. Normal, healthy individuals should not be affected by the nutritional deficiencies of liquid diets when used for a day or two after oral surgery. Those requiring repeated procedures or who are in poor health should be given a liquid food replacement such as Ensure,® Enrich,® or Sustacal®.

8

Exercise, Nutrition, Weight Control, and Physical Fitness

With the advent of prolonged travel in space, the physiological problems of weightlessness and limited exercise encountered by experimental animals and by astronauts have revitalized interest in nutritional aspects of physical activity. When the space shuttle Columbia roared into orbit on June 5, 1991, the American space program resumed an intensive effort to understand the changes that occur when the human body enters the near-zero gravity of space.

Scientists of the National Aeronautics and Space Administration (NASA) suspect that the changes in the body's calcium levels that occur during space flight may result in changes in the neurovestibular system located in the inner ear. This system is extremely sensitive to gravity. A constant stream of positioning data flows from the nerve cells to the brain, which senses the body's relationship to other objects. In space, in the absence of gravity, information sent to the brain from the inner ear and other sense organs conflicts with cues expected from past experience. The result is disorientation and space motion sickness, which can incapacitate an astronaut. The ultimate objective of NASA is to pave the way for future flights to Mars, extended stays in a permanent space station, and other missions that would require astronauts to stay in space for months or years.

Astronauts have also noted that the strength of their muscles deteriorated rapidly in weightless environments unless they exercised. A few hours after the June, 1991, launch of Columbia, the astronauts in Spacelab assembled a bicycle exercise machine. Such exercise compensates for the absence of the minimal physical activity involved in maintaining posture and simple movement against normal gravitational pull on Earth.

On a more mundane level, it has been known for decades that untrained muscles are smaller and weaker than trained muscles. Also, when a broken arm, for example, is immobilized in a cast for several weeks, atrophy, or a wasting away, begins to take place; the muscles weaken, and the bones and joints deteriorate with inactivity. Sedentary people undergo the same kind of atrophy, weakness, and resulting vulnerability to injury, to a lesser degree, of course. In apposition to these experiences, it may be said that appropriate exercise and fitness have maintenance values for the organism, whether human or animal, as a whole. All the available evidence supports the principle that good nutrition and adequate exercise work together in a synergistic fashion to facilitate wellness, i.e., a vibrant state of health.

Nowadays, almost everyone in the United States is aware of the importance of nutrition and exercise. They also are aware to a limited extent that physical activity and good nutrition together play a very positive role in helping to prevent several major chronic diseases. The value of a physically active life-style that is maintained for as long as possible is widely held and admired, if not always practiced.

The record-breaking athlete, like the great painter, musician, or scientist, demonstrates just how far the human species can reach. Each generation of athletes, trained to achieve maximum performance with bodies, minds, and emotions, runs faster, jumps higher, lifts more, and scores better than previous generations. For their events and their eras, champions emerge as the fittest individuals in society. Most people can identify with the athlete and can share the excitement of athletic accomplishments, but few can realistically aspire to such standards themselves. There is, however, an appropriate level of physical activity for each person. At a minimum, this activity should be of the kind, intensity, and frequency sufficient to keep individuals fit for the world they live in.

The principal elements of fitness are strength, suppleness, and stamina. Strength is the basic muscular force required for movement.

Suppleness, or flexibility, is the quality of muscles, bones, tendons, and ligaments that permits full range of movement in a joint. Stamina, or endurance, is the quality that enables a person to mobilize energy to maintain movement over an extended period. Stamina is largely a matter of developing an adequate oxygen-transport system. For the older person, it is normally achieved by sustained whole-body exercise, such as that involved in running, walking, bicycling, and swimming.

In the well-nourished person, of whatever age, physical activity is the most powerful stimulus to the conversion of simple substances in the food eaten into the complex compounds of living matter such as muscle and the associated blood-supply system. Among the benefits to be derived from regular physical exercise of sufficient intensity are an increase in fat-free body mass and hopefully some reduction in body fat stores. An increase in the blood level of high-density lipoprotein (HDL) can be expected, as well as a decrease in triglyceride, total cholesterol, and low-density lipoprotein (LDL) levels. The blood pressure has been reported to be lowered (Martin *et al.*, 1990). Carbohydrate metabolism undergoes a change, reflecting an increased insulin sensitivity in muscle and a greater tendency for glucose uptake. There is also an increased mobilization of free fatty acids from fat-storage tissue and a greater capacity to oxidize free fatty acids within muscle. All these changes are influenced by the type, frequency, intensity, and duration of exercise. The general trends mentioned are associated with regular weight-bearing exercise that exceeds approximately 60 percent of the individual's aerobic power (Buskirk, 1981).

Energy Needs of the Body

Human energy, derived from the food that is eaten, is utilized in three principal ways: to support basal metabolism, for muscular activity, and for metabolizing food.

1. *Energy for Basal Metabolism.* A number of reactions, some physical and others chemical, but all required for the maintenance of life, go on in the living body without any conscious

attention being paid to them. They include the beating of the heart, the inhaling of oxygen from the air, the exhaling of carbon dioxide, the metabolic activities of all the body's cells, the maintenance of body temperature, and surges of nerve impulses originating in the brain, which control the overall operation. The basal metabolic rate (BMR) is the energy expended by an awake individual, lying down in a room at a comfortable temperature, who must have been without food or heavy exercise for at least 12 hours. In this relaxed state, a person needs the least amount of oxygen, and the body's cells generate the least amount of heat. The rate of oxygen consumption can be used as a measure of the BMR, i.e., the rate at which kcalories are spent for these maintenance activities. The BMR is usually expressed as kcalories per hour and represents a surprisingly large fraction (as much as 70 percent) of the total energy requirement for an individual. The BMR is higher in the young, in people with a large surface area, in males, in people with fever or under stress, and in people with an overactive thyroid gland. It is lowered by increasing age and by fasting or malnutrition and is relatively unaffected by physical exercise, after 12 hours of rest.

2. *Energy for Muscular Activity.* As shown in Table 8.1, energy is required for all activity that is dependent on the use of the muscles, such as walking, swimming, playing tennis, dancing, or even talking. The amount of energy expended depends on the amount of weight being moved and the length of time devoted to the activity. The component of the total energy requirement that varies most among individuals is the energy used for exercise or other physical activity. As people grow older, their physical activities generally decline in such a way that their total energy needs, including BMR, decrease about 5 percent per decade, after age 20.

3. *Energy for Metabolizing Food.* The digestion of food, absorption of nutrients, and the metabolic reactions that release energy from the food are all processes that require some energy input. The energy required for the conversion of food into metabolic energy is called the specific dynamic activity (SDA). It usually amounts to about 10 percent of the total

energy needed for both basal metabolism and physical activity. It is less for carbohydrate (7 percent) and fat (4 percent) than it is for protein (30 percent), which requires more processing within the body in order to be broken down. Although SDA varies slightly depending on the relative amounts of carbohydrate, fat, and protein in the diet, it usually ranges from 200 to 300 kcalories per day.

Exercise and Obesity

Of the three energy-producing constituents of foods and of body tissue (carbohydrates, lipids, and proteins), only lipid (fat) can be stored in reasonably large amounts in adipose tissue, that is, connective tissue in various parts of the body that contain masses of fat cells. Carbohydrates and protein in excess of immediate needs are converted largely to fats for storage. During prehistoric days, when deprivation, hunger, and starvation were ever present, the ability to store excess kcalories compactly as fat in adipose tissue was useful to man as a protection against food shortages. This ability later became a handicap in modern, industrialized societies where food is always available, overnutrition and underactivity are prevalent, and very little physical effort is needed to obtain and prepare food for eating. Thus fitness must be considered relative to the time and circumstances.

Under normal conditions in the human body, new lipids are continuously being deposited in the adipose tissue, and depot lipids are being metabolized. When these two opposing processes balance each other, in a dynamic steady-state condition, which they do for the majority of adults, with little or no conscious effort, the total amount of body fat remains relatively constant. If, however, there is an intake of kcalories in excess of metabolic requirements, and no physical exercise is done, the excess will form extra depot lipid that cannot then be used expeditiously. For each nine kcalories of food intake in excess of the body's needs for maintenance and energy, roughly one gram of fat is deposited. Weight gain in adult life probably results from a greater decrease in energy expenditure rather than any increase in food intake, which actually seems to decline with age (Bray, 1990).

In this discussion, the word "overweight" will be used to define a body weight 10 percent or more above the normal age-, or sex-, and height-related "ideal weight," that is, the weight adjusted for height associated with longest survival, a concept first developed by the life insurance industry. "Obesity" refers to a condition in which there is an excessive accumulation of fat in body tissue; it is often loosely defined as a condition 20 percent or more above the ideal weight. It should be remembered that there are occasional exceptions to these definitions, hence the words "loosely defined" in the previous sentence.

Another way of describing various degrees of excess body weight is the body mass index (BMI), which is defined as the weight in kilograms divided by the square of the height, in meters. A BMI of 26 or more is equivalent to overweight. According to this criterion, approximately 39 percent of men and 36 percent of women in the United States have excessive body mass for their stature (NRC, 1989). A healthy weight is often defined as a BMI of about 20 to 25 (Bouchard, 1991). A simple nomogram to facilitate calculation of the BMI is given in the *Surgeon General's Report on Nutrition and Health* (1988) on page 284.

Insurance company data contain an inherent flaw in that they consider body weight per se rather than the relationship between lean body mass and body fat. In the United States, nearly everyone who is overweight is overly fat, so the two terms are used interchangeably. It is, however, possible to be overweight without having excessive body fat. Typically, athletes such as football players are overweight, but they have extra muscle rather than fat.

In a technical sense, obesity is simply the net result of consuming food having a greater energy value than the individual expends. Factors that are believed to contribute to its causation include heredity; overeating; altered metabolism of adipose tissue; defective or decreased thermogenesis (the process by which kcalories from the metabolism of foods are converted to heat); decreased physical activity without an appropriate reduction in food intake; and certain prescribed medications. Of the six factors, which can interact with one another, individuals have some control of only two, overeating and underactivity.

Obesity is one of the most prevalent diet-related problems in the United States. It has been estimated to affect about 34 million adults, aged 20 to 74 (NCHS, 1987), with the highest rates being observed among the poor and minority groups (Van Itallie, 1985). In 1986, population rates of overweight were reported for adults aged 25 to 74 as 26.0 percent of men and 29.4 percent of women (NCHS, 1986). In 1981, 25.6 percent of Americans aged 20 to 74 were reported to be overweight (McDowell *et al.*, 1981). Age-related rates for blacks (36.6 percent) exceeded those for whites (24.6 percent), and those for females of all races (26.7 percent) exceeded those for males (24.4 percent). Although the rate for black males (26.3 percent) was only slightly higher than that for white males (24.2 percent), the rate for black females of 45.1 percent was highest of all—almost twice that of the 24.6 percent for white females (NCHS, 1987).

The 10-year incidence of major weight gain in U.S. adults was estimated by Williamson *et al.* (1990). Persons (men, 3,727; women, 6,135) age 25 to 74 years at baseline were reweighed a decade after their initial examination. The incidence of major weight gain was twice as high in women as in men, and was highest in persons aged 25 to 34 years (men, 3.9 percent; women, 8.4 percent). Initially overweight women aged 25 to 44 years had the highest incidence of major weight gain of any subgroup (14.2 percent). For persons not overweight at baseline (men, 2,760; women, 4,295), the incidence of becoming overweight was similar in both sexes and was highest in those aged 35 to 44 years (men, 16.3 percent; women, 13.5 percent). Williamson and co-workers concluded that obesity prevention should begin among adults in their early 20s and that special emphasis is needed for young women who are already overweight.

The peak overweight rates for men occur from ages 35 to 64, whereas rates for women continue to increase throughout the ages in which they are measured. The percentage of adults classified as overweight increases from a low of 5.5 percent among black males aged 20 to 24 to a high of 61.2 percent among black women aged 45 to 54 (NCHS, 1987).

It is important to know that mortality risk does not appear to be related to weight in a linear fashion. There appears, instead, to be a critical point above which risk increases precipitously. It is also important to know that mortality rates from life insurance company statistics are about the same for formerly obese people as for those who never were obese and that a recent reinterpretation and evaluation of insurance company statistics suggests that many people are healthiest at weights a little above those that were formerly thought to be ideal (see Appendix B, Unisex Weight Table).

Severe overweight increases the risk for elevated blood cholesterol, high blood pressure, and diabetes, and hence for diseases for which these conditions are risk factors, namely, coronary heart disease, stroke, neurologic disorders, and kidney diseases. Severe overweight also increases the risk for gallbladder disease, and may have some effect on certain forms of cancer. Because of these facts, many people in this country try to lose excess weight. According to data from the 1985 National Health Interview Survey, 27 percent of males and 46 percent of females were at that time trying to lose weight by reducing caloric intake, increasing physical activity, or both (Stephenson *et al.*, 1987).

Upper-Body versus Lower-Body Obesity

Women generally have more subcutaneous fat than men, but men suffer a greater cardiovascular risk from a given degree of fatness than women (Bjorntrop, 1983). The distribution of body fat may be an indication of this difference. More men than women accumulate large fat cells in the abdominal region. This distribution around the abdomen, with increased waist-to-hip ratio, is referred to as upper-body obesity. It is associated with increased cardiovascular risk factors such as hypertriglyceridemia and impaired glucose tolerance (Krotkiewski *et al.*, 1983). Lower-body obesity is more typical of women, who tend to accumulate fat in the hips, the buttocks, and extremities, a distribution that does not appear to be associated with increased cardiovascular risk factors (Krotkiewski *et al.*, 1983).

Regardless of gender, a high waist-to-hip ratio predicts an increased risk for cardiovascular disease (CVD) and diabetes (Larsson *et al.*, 1984). A 12-year study of 1,462 women found the waist-to-hip ratio to be a better prediction of myocardial infarction, angina pectoris, stroke, and death than any other anthropometric measurement obtained (Lapidus *et al.*, 1984). In both of these studies, people whose waist-to-hip ratio was in the top 20 percent of distribution (greater than 1.0 for men or 0.8 for women), suffered the greatest incidence of cardiovascular disease.

The waist measurement is the smallest girth at the narrowed area above the navel, and the hip measurement is the largest horizontal girth between the waist and thigh. Both measurements are taken with the subject in a standing position and must be in the same units, usually inches or centimeters. As an example, suppose one man's measurements were waist, 36.5 inches, and hip, 44.0 inches. The waist-to-hip ratio (WHR) is 36.5 divided by 44.0 or 0.82, which is less than 1.0 and therefore out of the high-risk category. Now suppose a second man's measurements were waist, 46, and hip, 41. The WHR is 1.1, and because it is greater than 1.0, it puts him in the high-risk category for CVDs.

The technique is capable of some fine tuning, e.g., the change with age. More recently, Ostlund *et al.* (1990) has also reported on the use of WHR as a predictor of the level of HDL_2, "good" cholesterol in older adults.

Measuring the Amount of Fat in the Living Body

The measurement of body density provides a quantitative technique for determining body fat and fat-free mass. The density is determined from the weight of the body after submersion in water and out of water, using Archimedes' principle (Bray, 1976). Although the technique is not difficult, it requires special facilities and is cumbersome.

A much simpler method, that of bioelectric impedance analysis (BIA) is now available (Segal *et al.*, 1988). Electrodes are applied to one arm and leg, and the electrical impedance is measured. Because impedance is related to the aqueous portion of the body, formulas are used to estimate the percentage of fat in the body. The estimation of body fat using BIA correlates well with values determined from density measurements and is regarded as sufficiently accurate for measuring fat in both lean and obese people.

Theories Regarding the Etiology of Obesity

Most adults maintain a remarkably stable body weight. The mechanisms that govern eating, obesity, and the body's energy balance are much more complex than once thought (Martin *et al.*, 1991).

Some cases of obesity are due to an endocrine dysfunction, but it is estimated that less than two percent of obese people are fat because of such underlying hormonal causes as a disorder of the thyroid or adrenal glands. In this group of people, the basal metabolism is lowered so that weight gain results unless the diet provides fewer kcalories than is usually considered normal. Although overweight tends to run in families, that is to say, obese parents often have obese children, the belief has been that habits of overeating are learned within the family environment because of attitudes toward food and factors of life-style rather than being inherited. Raising a question about this view is that many farm animals are bred for more or less fatness or leanness, and strains of laboratory mice are known to have a predisposition to fatness. Stunkard and his associates published two important papers that go a long way to buttress the importance of genetic influence on human fatness (Stunkard et al., 1986a, b). Their reports, in fact, arrive at the conclusion "that human fatness is under substantial genetic control."

A theory that has been around for a long time pictures the body as having a preferred, preordained weight that may bear little relation to an accepted standard, but one that the individual tends to maintain or to revert to following attempts at weight adjustment. According to the theory, for individuals for whom this situation is factual, attempts at weight loss can be discouraging. There are also a number of theories regarding the etiology of obesity that are based on conjecture that some inherited enzyme or hormone imbalance is responsible for the problem.

In another study, elegant techniques were used to measure thermogenesis, that is, the production of heat by the cells of the body, in humans (Ravussin et al., 1988). Their work supports the view that a particularly low familial metabolic rate at rest is probably the most important contributing factor to a familial predisposition to obesity. The subjects of the Ravussin study were southwestern American Indians with a very high incidence of both obesity and diabetes. Nearly two thirds of the women and about one half of the men in this population are obese.

In the final analysis, the common type of obesity, often referred to as simply obesity, is due to the intake of energy (food) being in excess of the energy output (work), but failure of the normal regulating mechanisms to prevent overeating is, in turn, blamed on genetic or congenital factors. Attempts to demonstrate with human subjects that the metabolic rate in the obese person is lower than that in the lean person, an idea that seems reasonable enough, have failed repeatedly. In other words, the metabolic processes of the obese person appear not to be more than usually economical in the conversion of food energy into work (Owen *et al.*, 1987).

Diet Therapy for Obesity

To lose weight, a person must decrease caloric intake, increase caloric expenditure, or do both. The chief approach to weight reduction involves behavior change related to diet.

In the overweight or obese person, weight loss reduces health risks of many kinds, which is an enticing factor. In theory, weight loss should be accomplished easily, but in practice, traditional diet therapy has not been very successful; people who lose weight tend to regain it (Stunkard, 1987). Consequently, a combination of diet and exercise appears to be the most sensible approach to treatment (Stricker, 1984). Because obesity is a condition requiring continuous attention, any behavior changes required to maintain weight loss must be long-term. Behavior change is now an integral part of broader programs that include nutrition education, exercise, low-calorie diets, and cognitive restructuring (Stunkard, 1987). Such programs form the basis of many commercial efforts that treat large numbers of overweight or mildly obese people in the United States (Brownell *et al.*, 1986).

Estimating Weight Gain and/or Loss

To estimate weight gain and/or loss, let us recall that each gram of fat represents the storage of 9 kcalories of energy. However, body fat is not stored as pure fat; rather, some water is stored with it. As a consequence of this fact, the energy value of each excess gram of body weight represents only 7.7 kcalories.

To illustrate the estimation of weight gain or loss, consider the example of a person consuming 100 kcalories per day in excess of energy requirements. Most people can easily consume this many excess kcalories without being aware of it, because it would require, per day, only 3 teaspoons of butter, a 1-oz square of fudge, or an oatmeal cookie to supply the additional kcalories. At the end of a year, this would represent 36,500 extra kcalories. Since a pound of body fat represents 3,500 kcalories, the individual would gain a little over 10 pounds during a year.

Estimating Weight Gain:

$$\frac{\text{excess intake of kcal}}{3,500 \text{ kcal/lb}} = \text{weight gain in lb}$$

$$\frac{36,500}{3,500} = 10.4 \text{ lb}$$

If such a diet were continued for, say, five years, 50 pounds would be added to the person's weight, which is enough in most instances to bridge the gap between normal weight and obesity. Due to day-to-day variations in physical activity and water balance, small variations in daily gain can, of course, be anticipated.

Before embarking on any weight-loss and exercise program, a check-up from one's personal physician is advised. If nothing of a medical nature is amiss, the first decision to be made should be to determine the desired, as well as feasible, weight loss per week and the number of kcalories allowed per day in order to achieve the expected results. There is merit to settling for a modest, but sustainable weight loss of, say, one pound to two pounds per week. Loss of one pound per week would require reducing the usual daily energy intake by 500 kcalories.

Estimating Weight Loss:

$$1 \text{ lb body fat} = 3,500 \text{ kcal}$$

$$\frac{3,500 \text{ kcal}}{\text{kcal deficit/day}} = \text{no. of days to lose 1 lb}$$

$$\frac{3,500 \text{ kcal}}{500 \text{ kcal/day}} = 7 \text{ days}$$

$$\frac{3,500 \text{ kcal}}{\text{no. of days to lose 1 lb}} = \text{kcal deficit/day}$$

$$\frac{3,500 \text{ kcal}}{7 \text{ days}} = 500 \text{ kcal/day}$$

A simple way of converting the daily reduction in kcalories to loss in pounds per week is to multiply the daily reduction by two and then divide by 1,000. In the above example, this would be

$$\frac{500 \times 2}{1000} \text{ or } \frac{1000}{1000} \text{ or a loss of 1 lb per week}$$

For the serious dieter, it is advisable to have on hand one of the booklets or charts available at leading bookstores that list the caloric value of many foods. One that can be recommended, and is available at a very modest price, is *Calories and Weight, The USDA Pocket Guide*, United States Department of Agriculture, Human Nutrition Information Service, Agriculture Information Bulletin 364; 114 pages; Revised March, 1990. For sale by the Superintendent of Documents, U.S. Government Printing Office, Washington, DC 20402.

When a reasonable and effective intake of food that appears to work has been achieved, a major part of the battle has been won. It now remains, however, to maintain the weight-loss momentum by judicious choice of foods that will supply a full daily complement of required nutrients. Holding as close as possible to one's regular time pattern of eating, choice of foods, and recipes for food preparation (as long as they fulfill the nutritional requirements) and simply cutting down is more likely to succeed than embracing the latest rapid-weight-loss plan. The lowered-caloric diet should be palatable and should allow the use of every-day foods in a reasonable variety and at moderate cost.

This is a time when consultation with a registered dietitian, nutritionist, or physician is recommended. Any acceptable diet for long-term use should contain the recommended dietary allowances of vitamins and minerals as well as the essential amino acids and essential fatty acids (supplements of iron, calcium, and a daily multivitamin tablet may sometimes be advisable).

Food-selection suggestions have been made available by several advisory organizations or groups: the American Heart Association, the American Cancer Society, the Surgeon General's report (SGR, 1988), and *Diet and Health: Implications for Reducing Chronic Disease Risk*, of the National Research Council (1989). The intake of foods that are high in fat should be a primary limitation. Reducing the intake of both concentrated sweets and of alcohol, and selecting protein sources from among low-fat foods will all reduce kcalorie intake. An increased consumption of complex carbohydrates with more vegetables, fruits, and whole grains will contribute more fiber and water, both of which add to a feeling of satiety without adding kcalories. Because it is difficult to increase protein intake much above the level in an ordinary diet, a low-carbohydrate diet is also a high-fat diet, with its attendant risk of elevated blood lipids.

Observations during Weight Reduction

Anyone not grossly obese and about to begin a weight-reducing regimen should be aware that there may not be any drop in body weight for as long as 2 or 3 weeks, even when there is faithful adherence to a calorie-deficient diet. This discouraging phenomenon occurs because as fat is withdrawn from storage sites, water enters the cells to take its place and remains fixed for some time, after which it is released rather quickly. When weight loss is evaluated over a period of two to three months, the hoped-for weight decrease will be observed. Sometimes a period of weight loss will be followed by a refractory period, even when kcalorie intake and output remain unchanged. This phenomenon is due to a changing composition of the body tissue providing the caloric deficit. It is greater when glycogen or protein, with a higher water content, are being used up than when fat is being consumed.

The group approach to weight reduction has been found to have advantages over an individual effort. The regularly scheduled meetings, often weekly, give people an opportunity to share and discuss with one another their problems in losing weight. The members of the group provide understanding, encouragement, and a certain spirit of competition and support to the efforts of the individual person.

Weight Fluctuation and Health Consequences

It has been estimated that at any given time 25 to 50 percent of adult Americans are trying to reduce their weight by dieting (NRC, 1989). The rate of success in losing some weight is fairly good, but the record of keeping it off permanently is not good at all (Berdanier and McIntosh, 1991; Goodrich and Foreyt, 1991; Williamson et al., 1990).

The result is that there are often repeated episodes of weight loss and subsequent regaining of the weight. This variability of body weight has been referred to as "weight cycling" and the dieting pattern that causes it has been dubbed "yo-yo dieting."

Cycles of weight loss followed by weight gain were not perceived as an important biologic issue until Brownell and colleagues called attention to the phenomenon in 1986, as a result of animal experimentation. Lissner and colleagues (1991), including Brownell as senior author of the study, examined the association between variability of body weight and subsequent health outcomes in people. Their study, in 1991, reported on the relation of variability in weight to total mortality, cancer morbidity and mortality, and mortality from coronary heart disease in 1,804 women and 1,367 men from the Framingham Heart Study.

The study considered people to have fluctuating weight if they had one or two large weight losses and put it all back on, or if they stayed relatively slim, but had many smaller ups and downs. It did not determine whether a few large fluctuations were better or worse than many smaller ones. Among the conclusions were (1) The danger of yo-yo dieting to the heart was about the same as staying fat; (2) men with fluctuating weight had nearly twice as high a risk of dying from heart disease as did those with stable weights; (3) among women, the risk was about 50 percent greater.

Exercise and Special Situations

Exercise and Food Selection

In a detailed study of energy intake and gross dietary composition of men and women athletes, compared with control subjects, it was evident that for athletes in training essentially no difference was observed in the percentage of energy derived from carbohydrate (40 to 50 percent), fat (31 to 41 percent), or protein (11 to 17 percent) (Brotherhood, 1984).

A comparison of middle-aged men and women runners with control subjects has been made (Blair *et al.*, 1981). The runners consumed about 600 kcalories per day more than the nonrunners when running 55 to 65 km per week. The percentage consumption of major nutrients, however, was essentially the same. The dietary pattern of many health-conscious exercisers suggests that most are careful with their diets and tend to eat fewer meat items, less fat, and more vegetables and other sources of complex carbohydrates (Buskirk, 1990).

Exercise and Atherosclerosis

Regular aerobic exercise, which forces the heart and lungs to work harder to meet the muscles' demand for oxygen, has been identified as one of the factors that can lead to improvement in lipoprotein profiles and thus diminishes the risk of premature CVD. Examples of aerobic exercise include brisk walking, swimming, aqua-aerobics, cycling, cross-country skiing, skating, stair-climbing, and rowing. The prime benefit derived from such exercise seems to be an increase in HDL cholesterol levels, but there is usually a simultaneous reduction in the level of triglycerides and LDL (NCEP, 1988). People who exercise regularly tend to be leaner than their sedentary counterparts and are more likely to smoke less, consume less alcohol, have better dietary habits and lower blood pressure, all of which are associated with lower blood cholesterol levels. However, despite the many positive rewards from vigorous, aerobic exercise, the NCEP (1988) does not view sedentary life-styles as a CVD risk factor.

Exercise and Mild Hypertension

Almost 58 million people in the United States have hypertension, including 19 million who are over age 65 (SGR, 1988). The goal of antihypertensive therapy is to minimize end-organ damage that can lead to kidney failure, stroke, and coronary heart disease. Although the efficacy of drug therapy in the treatment of hypertension is widely accepted, there has been a continuing interest over the years in the effectiveness of nonpharmacologic therapies such as exercise. Although four previous controlled studies (e.g., Martin *et al.*, 1990) have reported lowered blood pressure to be associated with aerobic exercise training, Blumenthal *et al.* (1991) found that a four-month program of moderate aerobic exercise, without dietary changes, in patients of normal body weight and average level of fitness did not appear to offer much benefit. They concluded that moderate aerobic exercise should not be considered a replacement for pharmacologic therapy in nonobese patients with mild hypertension, but suggested that "a more vigorous exercise program, perhaps over a more extended time period, might be effective."

Researchers at Miami University, in Ohio, have assessed the effects of simple isometric handgrip exercise training on resting blood pressure (Wiley *et al.*, 1992). Isometric exercise describes the situation in which muscles are briefly tensed in opposition to other muscles or to an immovable object. The exercise training consisted of brief handgrip contractions separated by rest periods. People in one phase of the study trained with four, two-minute isometric handgrip contractions with three-minute rests between contractions. The intensity of the contractions was equal to 30 percent of their maximal effort for each day. The exercise sessions were performed 3 times per week for 8 weeks. All 8 trained subjects had a significant decline in both systolic and diastolic blood pressure, with group averages of 12.5 and 14.9, respectively. Seven matched control subjects, who did not train, had no change in resting pressures. The results demonstrate that although training with a simple regimen of interrupted isometric contractions does temporarily raise blood pressure modestly, it leads to a gradual and significant reduction in blood pressure over time. In a second study, reported in the same article, Wiley and associates again demonstrated a lowering of blood pressure in a five-week isometric training regimen with new subjects, and then followed them for an additional five-weeks in which no isometric training occurred. They found that resting blood pressure returned to the pre-exercise levels. These results are sufficiently attractive to justify further investigation regarding the potential use of this exercise model in regulating blood pressure nonpharmacologically as well as to investigate the physiological mechanisms involved in blood pressure regulation.

Exercise and Osteoporosis

Physical exercise appears to play a very positive role in osteoporosis. Bones undergo rapid loss when inactive or immobilized, and prolonged immobility, especially for older persons, results in osteoporosis (see Chapter 11). The best prophylaxis is to remain physically active. Controlled studies have shown that regular exercise can maintain or even increase bone mass in postmenopausal women (Chow *et al.*, 1987).

In a 15-year follow-up epidemiologic study of 1,419 elderly Britons, it was found that the risk of hip fracture increased with decreasing mobility and decreasing outdoor activity (Wickham *et al.*, 1989). In 1991, a report was published on an epidemiologic evaluation of 8,600 postmenopausal women and 5,049 men in a Southern California retirement community for risk factors for hip fractures (Paganini-Hill *et al.*, 1991). Incidence rates were twice as high in women as in men, but in both sexes the rates nearly doubled every five years between 70 and 90 years. Physical exercise was found to be strongly associated with decreasing hip fractures in both sexes.

In the age range from 70 to 90 years, men and women who actively exercised one or more hours a day had about half the risk of hip fractures as those who exercised less than a half hour per day or not at all. Effective exercises included swimming, bicycling, playing tennis, jogging, vigorous walking, dancing, and indoor exercise program. According to Paganini-Hill and her coinvestigators, regular exercise is an attractive method for preventing osteoporotic fractures, including hip fractures, because it is inexpensive, generally suitable for the population as a whole, and it provides other health benefits.

Exercise and Diabetes Mellitus

Physical exercise influences the control of blood glucose levels in both Type I and Type II diabetes mellitus (see Chapter 6). It appears to facilitate the transport of glucose into cells and thus has an insulinlike effect in lowering blood glucose levels. People who do not have diabetes are able, without a conscious decision, to decrease insulin release during exercise and thus avoid hypoglycemia. In contrast, people who receive insulin exogenously are unable to exert this control, and exercise can potentiate the hypoglycemic action of the insulin. This is particularly important when such a person engages in physical exercise at the time when the insulin dose has maximally depressed the glucose level. A program of planned exercise can be very beneficial for a person with diabetes, because it acts to lower the blood sugar, and aids in weight maintenance, but unplanned exercise may be hazardous.

By appropriate timing of physical exercise, some improvement in the control of glucose levels may be gained. For example, if people with diabetes can exercise when the blood glucose level is high, they may be able to lower it by exercise alone. Conversely, if people with diabetes have to exercise when the blood sugar level is low, it is important that they receive additional carbohydrates in order to prevent hypoglycemia.

Exercise, Mineral Balance, and Vitamin E

Iron

It is well known that iron-deficiency anemia impairs oxygen transport and, consequently, aerobic power and performance capacity (Schoene *et al.*, 1983). A number of studies have indicated that between 2 and 5 percent of exceptional athletes have iron deficiency or relatively low body iron stores (Deuster *et al.*, 1986). The percentage is higher for women athletes than for male athletes. Hematuria (blood in the urine) in distance runners is not uncommon, particularly in those running on hard surfaces. Heel strike, rapid perfusion through small blood vessels with rupturing of red blood cells, and mechanical shaking of the kidneys have often been cited as causes for hematuria (Buskirk, 1990).

Proposed causes for iron deficiency include inadequate iron intake, inadequate iron absorption, gastrointestinal blood loss, losses in sweat, and red cell hemolysis with hematuria.

Chromium

That chromium plays a role in vigorous physical exercise in humans is evident from the fact that urinary chromium losses were increased twofold on the day of a 9.66-km run when compared with a rest day (Anderson *et al.*, 1984). Trained athletes have also been found to have lower resting urinary chromium concentrations, but greater chromium losses because of exercise (Campbell *et al.*, 1987).

Vitamin E

In animal studies, exercise appears to increase free-radical concentrations in tissues and is associated with increased metabolism of vitamin E (Packer, 1984; Gohil *et al.*, 1987). In humans during exercise, vitamin E is mobilized, perhaps as a result of the breakdown of fat stores (Pincemail *et al.*, 1988).

Pentane measurement is useful as a measure of lipid peroxidation, which is promoted by the presence of free radicals (Pincemail *et al.*, 1987). The amount of pentane exhaled in the breath is found to be negatively correlated with vitamin E status (Lemoyne *et al.*, 1987); in other words, the higher the vitamin E level in the blood, the lower will be the amount of peroxidation of fatty acids and therefore the lower the amount of free radicals produced that might cause injury to muscle. To reiterate, vitamin E as an antioxidant retards the lipid peroxidation that generates free radicals, which in turn may cause exercise-induced muscle injury.

While pentane production more than doubled in a placebo control group of high-altitude mountain climbers, a group supplemented with 400 mg alpha-tocopherol per day showed no significant change in the amount of pentane exhaled (Simon-Schnass *et al.*, 1987). Under some circumstances it is clear that vitamin E can protect muscle from the damaging effects of exercise-induced free-radical injury.

Exercise and Needs for Major Nutrients

The nutrient needs of active and sedentary persons are similar in composition, but differ in quantity, with the active individual requiring more food-derived energy. A diet containing approximately 10 percent protein, 30 percent fat, and 60 percent carbohydrate is recommended (Buskirk, 1981). The major variable that affects energy expenditure and energy needs is physical activity.

Factors that modify nutrient needs include periods of rapid growth, gender, and aging. More nutrients are needed to support growth and development. Girls generally require fewer kcalories than boys, and women need fewer than men. As people age beyond adulthood, energy needs decrease because of both a gradual reduction in fat-free body weight associated with a lower resting metabolic rate and the reduction in physical activity (Buskirk, 1985).

Physical Activity and Body Weight

Various studies have shown that physical inactivity in adult life shortens life expectancy (Paffenbarger *et al.*, 1986), partly because underactivity without concomitant decrease in food intake can so often result in obesity. The large difference in caloric expenditure between the most inactive and most active occupations, 2,300 to 4,400 kcalories daily, suggests that exercise could help manage and prevent obesity. Obesity may be a disease of inactivity, but that hypothesis has been difficult to prove (Stern, 1984).

Epidemiologic data show relatively low energy intakes to be coupled with increasing body weight, particularly in women (Dennis *et al.*, 1985). The finding is attributed to a decreased activity level.

Another interesting, but as yet unvalidated, aspect of the relationship between physical activity and body weight is the importance of involuntary movement, i.e., spontaneous fidgeting or moving, which varies from one person to another. In one study, for example, in which energy expenditures in unselected subjects were measured, very large individual differences in energy of 100 to 800 kcalories per day, were attributed to differences in spontaneous activity (Ravussin *et al.*, 1986). It is obvious that cumulative effects of physical activity over time could be important in preventing or correcting obesity.

Planning for Fitness

Food-for-fitness fads come and go, but the only way to achieve and maintain physical fitness is through appropriate exercise and eating a balanced diet. A good program of exercise should be consistent with each person's goals and should be realistic in individual and environmental limitations. An almost infinite variety of exercise options can be adjusted to one's needs and desires. For total health benefits to be derived, however, a program should include some form of controlled, continuous, rhythmic exercise, such as walking, swimming, or bicycling, but an exercise program need not be complex or elaborate to be beneficial.

Spot-reducing exercises can be disappointing because a person cannot tailor redistribution of fat through exercise. Fat distribution is primarily determined genetically, so exercise has little effect on it.

Medical clearance before beginning a fitness program involving exercise, weight loss, and diet is wise, especially for the physically inactive or older person. A number of medical conditions are aggravated by physical exertion and should be ruled out before any kind of an endurance program begins. It is prudent to plan a fitness program and present it for comment to a physician who is aware of one's physical condition and past medical history, before actually starting it.

Exercise and Weight Control

For many Americans, increasing the expenditure of energy through exercise may be a more effective way of maintaining health, including desirable body weight, than a reduction in energy intake. Besides promoting fitness, increased physical activity can be planned to permit a more ample intake of food, which in turn makes it easier to comply with the recommended dietary allowances of nutrients.

Exercise can be divided into two classes, anaerobic, such as weight lifting or isometrics, and aerobic, such as walking, cycling, swimming, running, jogging, skating, skiing, and other forms of active sport. In anaerobic exercise, where the objective is generally to increase muscle strength and muscle size, the energy needed is provided without utilization of inspired oxygen. It is limited to short bursts of vigorous activity, and there is a low expenditure of kcalories and no significant cardiovascular benefits. In aerobic exercise, ample oxygen is required for sustained periods of hard work and vigorous athletic activity. During aerobic activity, blood circulation is stimulated, a relatively large number of kcalories are expended, and the efficiency of the cardiovascular system is improved.

Of the many forms of aerobic exercise, walking is the simplest. It does not require any special equipment except a good pair of walking shoes and can, at some level, be undertaken safely by almost everyone, young, old, or overweight (Pender, 1987). Swimming is another excellent choice where conditions such as osteoarthritis prohibit other forms of exercise. Of course, to reiterate, it is advisable to consult with one's personal physician to rule out unknown medical complications before starting any ambitious exercise program, even walking.

As shown in Table 8.1, the expenditure of energy by a man weighing 175 lb and walking briskly (3.5 mph) is roughly 460 kcalories per hour. For a woman weighing 140 lb, the equivalent figure is 370 kcalories per hour. About 3,500 kcalories must be expended by the body to result in a loss of 1 lb. In the case at hand, and provided there is no change in the daily intake of food, the man should show a loss in weight, per hour of walking, of $470 \div 3,500 = 0.13$ lb (i.e., approximately one tenth of a pound). Although this rate of weight loss may not look very encouraging at first, it must be remembered that the only nutritionally valid and lasting methods of losing weight take time and, when compared to the highly advertised fad programs, are hardly spectacular.

Let us now consider another aspect, the cardiovascular effect, of a walking exercise program. At a moderate to fast pace of 3.5 to 4 mph, walking may increase the heart rate by 40 to 50 percent above normal rate. This is sufficient, when done for ½ to 1 hour, at least three times weekly and over a period of at least a couple of months, to stimulate the heart and lungs and increase the uptake and delivery of oxygen to all the tissues of the body. Let us assume, then, that the man (175 lb) does walk at a pace of 3.5 mph for 1 hour, three times weekly, for two months, thus chalking up 24 hours. The loss in weight would be $0.13 \times 24 = 3.1$ lb. For the woman (140 lb), the equivalent figure is $0.106 \times 24 = 2.5$ lb. Over a period of 52 weeks, the overall loss in weight for a man would be $(52 \times 3.1) \div 8 = 20$ lb, and for a woman, 16 lb, both quite significant and more satisfying figures. There are, in other words, two major benefits associated with a vigorous walking program: a satisfying loss in weight combined with gratifying cardiovascular benefits.

In certain situations, a walking program may present some special problems (e.g., the neighborhood may not be safe, or the only suitable time may be after dark). In such cases, a simple non-motorized treadmill with adjustable incline and a braking control can

Table 8.1. Physical Activity and Corresponding
Caloric Expenditure

Activity	Kcalories expended per hour[a]	
	Man[b]	Woman
Sitting quietly	100	80
Standing quietly	120	95
Light activity	300	240
Cleaning house		
Office work		
Playing baseball		
Playing golf		
Moderate activity	460	370
Walking briskly (3.5 mph)		
Gardening		
Cycling (5.5 mph)		
Dancing		
Playing basketball		
Strenuous activity	730	580
Jogging (9 min/mile)		
Playing football		
Swimming		
Very strenuous activity	920	740
Running (7 min/mile)		
Racquetball		
Skiing		

[a]May vary depending on environmental conditions.
[b]Healthy man, 175 lb; Healthy woman, 140 lb.
SOURCE: Nutrition and Your Health: Dietary Guidelines for Americans, 3rd ed. U.S. Dept. of Agric., U.S. Dept. of Health and Human Services. Garden Bulletin No. 232. Washington, DC, 1990.

be a satisfactory alternative. In cases where personal preferences may intervene, it is helpful to remember that in the opinion of exercise physiologists, the aerobic benefits of, say, one mile of walking are roughly equivalent to those from one tenth of a mile of swimming, four tenths of a mile of running, or two miles of bicycling. If a person should wish to lose weight at a faster or slower rate, the walking pace, or the number of hours per week devoted to walking, or both, may be altered. It must be remembered that the expenditure of energy from walking in outside areas is related to the weight of the person involved, to the lay of the land, i.e., whether it is level, inclined, or rolling in character, and even to the direction of the wind.

Contrary to prevailing opinion, the effects of acute exercise in humans are to decrease food intake immediately after exercise (Stern, 1983). For moderately active people, long-continued exercise promotes increased calorie intake.

Besides the loss in weight which occurs, and the possible cardiovascular benefits, walking enthusiasts have, over the years, ascribed a host of additional benefits to a regular, disciplined, walking program. Some of the benefits, for example, are said to be reductions in hypertension (Martin *et al.*, 1990), lowered serum cholesterol and triglycerides, an increased ability of the lungs and heart to take in and distribute oxygen in the body thus increasing physical endurance, an improvement in thinking ability and memory retention, especially in older people, and increasing the elasticity of the blood vessels, thereby decreasing the probability that they will rupture under high blood pressure, which is one of the causes of stroke. Finally, many walking enthusiasts speak of an increased clarity of thought and a sense of well-being following a long walk. The last effect may be related to the release of polypeptide hormones, the endorphins, by a small area of the brain known as the hypothalamus. The release of the endorphins, which seems to be triggered by vigorous exercise, appears to have a mood-elevating effect.

An ideal exercise program combining loss or control of weight with physical fitness is one that is consistent with an individual's goals and realistic in personal and environmental limitations. Many exercise options can be adjusted to meet a person's specific desires and needs. Every physical activity, even restlessness during sleep, is associated with expenditure of energy. In expected total health benefits, however, any program should include some form of a controlled, rhythmic exercise. Walking is presented here as an example of an exercise program that is simple, safe, and adaptable to the needs of almost everyone.

An Encouraging Note: Substantial Health Benefit from Even Minimal Exercise

In an 8-year, 13,344-subject study (Blair *et al.*, 1989), it was shown that even a minimal amount of exercise, such as a brisk half-hour walk once a day, confers significant protection not only from CVD and cancers, but also against death from a wide range of other causes. The study is important because (1) it included both men and women in contrast to earlier, mostly male surveys; (2) it strengthened the evidence that exercise can ward off cancer; and (3) it was one of the largest studies ever done that relied on an objective measure of fitness rather than on the participants' descriptions of how they exercised.

The researchers measured fitness by a maximal treadmill exercise test. They put people on a treadmill, set them walking, then periodically increased first the incline and then the speed of the treadmill until the walkers had to quit. The subjects were grouped into five different fitness levels based on their performance and then followed for eight years. By the end of that time, 283 of the walkers, all of whom were in good health at the beginning of the study, had died. After making allowances for several other health-affecting factors, including smoking, age, cholesterol levels, weight, blood pressure, and family history of heart disease, the researchers found that deaths were sharply higher in the least-fit category than in the second-most sedentary group, more than double for men and almost twice as high for women. In the most-fit group, which included people who regularly ran up to 40 miles a week, death rates tended to be even lower, but the improvement was not so dramatic.

As pointed out by Koplan et al. (1989), the greatest reduction in relative risk made evident by the study of Blair et al. (1989) occurs between the lowest level of fitness and the next lowest level. These data suggest that even a modest improvement in fitness level among the most unfit confers a substantial health benefit. Koplan et al. suggest that physicians should advise their patients to choose an activity, e.g., walking, that is pleasurable (or at least not abhorrent), and they should emphasize that it be done regularly (or at least 3 days per week) and long enough (about 20 minutes) to strengthen cardiorespiratory capacity.

Exercise Carried to Excess

Some people carry exercise to excess, so much so that it almost becomes an addiction. As described elsewhere in this chapter, in regard to a walking program, many exercise enthusiasts speak of an increased clarity of thought and a sense of well-being following a long walk. Other participants, particularly in vigorous, rhythmic activities, report that a good workout diminishes stress and increases a sense of calmness and confidence. These effects may be related to the release of polypeptide hormones, the endorphins, (from "*endo-genous morphine*") by a small area of the brain known as the hypothalamus. They bind to morphine receptors in brain tissue. The most active polypeptide, containing 30 amino acids, is beta-endorphin. The release of the endorphins, which seems to be triggered by vigorous exercise, appears to have a mood-elevating effect.

Because of these pleasant aftereffects, some exercisers find themselves developing a dependency on an exercise routine and become anxious, resentful, and even angry when work or family and social events interfere. A number of reports in the literature attest to the fact that men and women who carry exercise to the point of exhaustion may also experience a suppression of sex hormone production and experience a decline in sexual interest and performance. Unlike other types of addicts, exercise addicts can usually break their dependency and resume full control of their lives by deliberately altering their exercise routines.

9

Drug–Nutrient Interactions

The influence of both prescription and over-the-counter (OTC) drugs on the nutritional status of older adults cannot be overlooked. As a group, the elderly take more medications than any other segment of the U.S. population and, as a consequence, are more likely to experience undesirable side effects, including nutritional problems. Additionally, older individuals are more likely to experience as yet unrecognized nutritional problems due to polypharmacy, i.e., use of multiple drugs, concurrently.

Although several diet–drug interactions had been well known for a number of years, only in the last dozen years has the importance of doing research on this interrelationship been recognized. What began as a simple idea, lumping dietary habits, nutrition, and drugs into one problem, has evolved into separate areas of study. The effects of nutrients on drugs is now recognized as being separate from the effects of drugs on nutrients and nutritional status.

Nutrients can diminish the therapeutic effects of drugs, i.e., nutrient–drug interaction. For example, warfarin (Coumadin®) is an anticoagulant that functions by interfering with the action of vitamin K in blood clotting. Vitamin K intake normally increases during the summer months, which may result in the need for more warfarin to maintain the therapeutic effect; and vitamin B_6 and high-protein diets interfere with the antitremor drug, levodopa, in patients with Parkinson's disease. The term *diet–drug interaction* now refers to the effect of the nonnutrient components of food on drugs as well as the

timing of food intake in relationship to the timing of drug administration. For example, the antibiotic tetracycline is absorbed better on
an empty stomach than when taken with meals, while absorption of
nitrofurantoin, an antibiotic used in the treatment of bladder infections, is increased if taken at mealtime.

In this chapter, only the effects that drugs have on nutrients and
on nutritional status will be discussed. For readers interested in how
diet and nutrients alter the therapeutic effect of drugs, reference may
be made to the book by Roe (1989b), who has written at some length
on the subject. Furthermore, the discussion will be limited to the
major groups of drugs taken long-term by older people. Although
short-term use of drugs such as antibiotics may compromise the
nutritional status of frail individuals, normal, healthy people usually
have sufficient nutrient reserves to withstand these short-term nutritional assaults.

Differences between Older and Younger Adults in Absorption, Distribution, and Excretion of Drugs

In the mid-1980s, Americans older than 65 used about 25 percent
of both the OTC and prescription drugs sold in the United States,
although they made up only 12 percent of the U.S. population. At
least one medication per day was taken by more than half of older
people in 1984, but by 1986, the majority were taking two to five
drugs daily. Females take more prescription drugs than males by a
ratio of three to two. Three hundred seventy-five million prescription
medications were purchased by older Americans in 1984, and they
spent over $4.5 billion on these medications (SGR, 1988). Despite
these facts, most drug studies for safety and efficacy are done using
younger adult males. Americans over 60 years of age experience 40
percent of all adverse drug reactions (Hester, 1991), including nutritional deficiencies, not only because they take more drugs, but also
because changes in the absorption, distribution, and elimination of
drugs occur with aging.

Although physiological changes of aging do affect the structure
and function of the gastrointestinal tract, it still has enormous capacity to absorb small-molecular-weight compounds such as drugs.

However, the rate of absorption can be slowed, giving a drug more time to interact with nutrients within the tract. Changes in body composition that occur with aging include increased body fat and decreased plasma albumin concentration, lean body mass, and body water. Drugs that are fat soluble are retained for longer periods of time as a result of these excess fat stores. Other drugs have a decreased volume of distribution and decreased plasma-protein binding, resulting in effectively increasing the drugs' activity. Drugs are eliminated primarily via the kidney and biliary system. It appears that drugs eliminated by the biliary system are unaffected by aging; however, the kidney's ability to filter blood declines with age, resulting in slowed elimination of certain drugs (digoxin, for example), making more drug available for longer periods (Roe, 1987).

Nutrients as Drugs

During much of history, the sciences that we now know as medicine, nutrition, and pharmacology were intermingled. Treatments for injuries and diseases have often included manipulations of the diet and use of remedies prepared from plants, animals, and minerals. Laurel, caraway, and thyme were used as medicines by the Sumerians, and the Egyptians used garlic, opium, coriander, and mint as both foods and drugs. The Greek physician, Hippocrates, advocated changes in life-style along with proper diet and herbal medicines to improve health. Dioscorides, a first century AD physician, wrote *De Materia Medica*, a reference on the medical use of 500 plants. This reference book was used by physicians until the seventeenth century. In the Far East, the first Chinese herb book was written about 2,700 BC, describing the medical use of plants. Many of these plants are the original source of modern drugs, including morphine from the opium poppy and ephedrine from ma-huang (SGR, 1988).

The science of pharmacology began to evolve in the seventeenth century when a group of scientists, then known as iatrochemists, promulgated the position that chemistry's proper function was to assist physicians to improve health. By the eighteenth century, acute infections were being treated with arsenic and sulfur (SGR, 1988).

Some authorities believe these treatments were the beginning of chemotherapy, while others regard them as examples of quackery. Modern pharmacology is no longer an empirical art handed down from one generation of healers to the next, but rather a science in which pure chemical agents are studied to determine their physiological effects and their roles in the treatment of disease.

As medicine, nutrition, and pharmacology were developing into separate disciplines, medicine's most successful treatments still involved the use of foods to cure disease. Medical scientists in the eighteenth century realized that scurvy was preventable and treatable by the inclusion of citrus fruits in the diet even without being able to identify the specific food factor responsible. Even well into the nineteenth century, specific food and dietary patterns were still being identified as curing disease, e.g., lean meat, poultry, or fish was found to cure pellagra.

With our centuries-old tradition of using foods, and indirectly nutrients, as treatments for disease, it is no wonder that many individuals have difficulty accepting the premise that nutrients can be pharmacologic agents that affect the body in ways unrelated to their nutritional roles.

The Federal Food, Drug, and Cosmetic Act defines drugs as "articles intended for use in the diagnosis, cure, mitigation, treatment, or prevention of disease in man or animals; and articles (other than food) intended to affect the structure or any function of the body of man or other animals" (Federal Food and Drug Act, 1985; Requirements of Laws, 1984). In one sense, nutrients such as niacin and vitamin C, which prevent the development of the classical nutritional deficiency diseases pellagra and scurvy, respectively, are drugs under this law. However, the Food and Drug Administration (FDA) relies on the principle of intended use in determining whether or not a substance is a drug. If a therapeutic claim is made, a nutrient or even a food may be considered a drug, subject to the drug requirements of the Food, Drug, and Cosmetic Act.

Although there is no legal definition of a food or a nutrient, the term *nutrient* is commonly defined as a chemical substance ingested to support growth, maintenance, and repair of tissues (Spallholz, 1989). Using this definition, niacin and vitamin C are nutrients, but these vitamins are also therapeutic when used in the treatment of a vitamin-deficiency disease. Drugs, then, are chemical agents used to prevent or treat disease by altering the structure or function of the body. Nutrients are drugs only when they perform functions other than providing for the normal growth and maintenance of the body.

The National Research Council describes three basic differences between the drug actions and the normal physiologic functions of nutrients. The differences are:

> Doses greatly exceeding the amount of a nutrient present in foods are usually needed to obtain a therapeutic response; the specificity of the pharmacological action is often different from the physiological function; and chemical analogues of the nutrient that are often most effective pharmacologically may have little or no nutritional activity (RDA, 1989, p. 14).

The toxicity of these drug–nutrients must also be considered. Prolonged intake of large doses of preformed vitamin A, for example, results in toxicity and yet has been used in the successful treatment of acne (SGR, 1988).

Niacin is an excellent example of a drug–nutrient meeting two of the three criteria discussed and partially fulfilling the third. As a vitamin, niacin functions in energy metabolism. The need for the vitamin can be fulfilled by nicotinic acid or nicotinamide (see Chapter 3). The active form of the vitamin is nicotinamide, and the body easily converts nicotinic acid to nicotinamide. The human body also has the ability to convert nicotinamide to nicotinic acid, but practically speaking, little nicotinic acid is produced, as nicotinamide is the physiologically active form of the vitamin (McCormick, 1988).

Currently, nicotinic acid is one of the drugs of first choice in treating individuals with elevations in both blood cholesterol and triglycerides. Typically, one to three grams of niacin per day is required to achieve a significant reduction in cholesterol, while the RDA for niacin is only 19 mg for adult males (RDAs, 1989). The way in which nicotinic acid lowers blood cholesterol and triglyceride levels is independent of its function as the vitamin niacin. Most experts believe that nicotinic acid, in high doses, decreases the flow of fatty acids to the liver from adipocytes (fat cells) (Stone and McDonald, 1989). With fewer fatty acids available, the liver produces fewer triglycerides. Furthermore, nicotinic acid increases secretion of cholesterol into the bile (Roe, 1988).

A number of side effects are known to occur with the high doses of nicotinic acid required to reduce cholesterol levels. They include flushing, itching, nausea and diarrhea, hyperglycemia, and hyperuricemia (excess uric acid in the blood). Nicotinic acid is toxic to the liver, and several patients using the sustained-release form of the drug have had liver transplants as a result of liver failure (Mullin *et al.*, 1989). None of these problems is associated with physiologic doses of nicotinic acid or with nicotinamide.

Alcohol

Ethyl alcohol or ethanol is unique in that it is both a nutrient and drug simultaneously. As a nutrient, it provides energy to the body at 7.1 kcalories per gram. Before renal dialysis was widely available, patients with kidney failure were given ethanol to supply needed kcalories. The volume of food these individuals were allowed to consume was extremely small because of restrictions on water, sodium, potassium, and protein. A 1.5-oz "shot" of 80 proof Scotch provides approximately 100 kcalories without any protein, sodium, or potassium and only a small amount of water.

Clearly, though, alcohol is a drug, toxic to the gastrointestinal tract, the brain, and the heart, as well as the liver. Alcohol is detoxified in the liver by the same enzyme system that detoxifies other drugs and toxins. Whether or not cirrhosis is caused by alcohol alone or in combination with some other factor such as malnutrition is still open to some debate, because many alcoholics do not develop cirrhosis. However, it is clear that ethanol profoundly affects the nutritional status of individuals who ingest large quantities.

Chronic alcohol abusers may develop malnutrition by allowing alcohol to displace food, as large quantities of alcohol depress appetite (Lieber, 1989). Even well-fed individuals can develop malnutrition with chronic alcohol use because of its adverse effects on the digestion, absorption, metabolism, utilization, storage, and elimination of nutrients (Alcohol, Health, and World Research, 1989; Lieber, 1989).

In small amounts, alcohol adds kcalories to the diet and stimulates the appetite, which may lead to further increases in kcalorie consumption. As the percentage of kcalories from alcohol increases, the percentage from fats, carbohydrates, and proteins decreases. Since alcohol kcalories are empty kcalories, vitamin A, vitamin C, and thiamin intakes decline below the RDAs. Calcium, iron, and fiber intake, which are already below desirable levels in the diets of many people decline as well. Further, at higher intake levels, alcohol is no longer metabolized as a nutrient, but rather by the microsomal oxidizing system in the liver. This system wastes energy, and much of alcohol's caloric value is dissipated as heat. Research studies in which subjects are given considerable excess kcalories as ethanol fail to produce a weight gain. Weight loss occurred in studies in which 50 percent of the kcalories were given as ethanol and carbohydrate was removed from the diet (Lieber, 1989).

Alcohol can affect the ability of the gastrointestinal tract to absorb nutrients. With chronic consumption, the microscopic structure of the small intestine is changed, limiting the gut's ability to absorb glucose, amino acids, and minerals. This change in structure limits the ability of the enzymes that split disaccharides (see Chapter 2) to function. Lactase, the enzyme that converts milk sugar to glucose and galactose, is the most severely affected. Additionally, alcohol can cause gastritis and ulceration, which leads to blood loss (Natow and Heslin, 1986).

How alcohol affects the nutritional status of individuals who frequently consume smaller quantities of it needs to be investigated further. Research in this group is affected by the fact that alcohol is almost never consumed in pure form. A number of alcoholic beverages contain essential nutrients. In wine, for example, 80 percent of the iron is in the reduced (ferrous) form, which is the absorbable form of nonheme iron. Research on alcoholics who consume wine primarily indicates that this iron is absorbed and can cause liver damage from iron overload (Natow and Heslin, 1986). It would appear, however, that the custom among older Italian immigrants of having a glass of wine with dinner is beneficial to these older individuals.

What may be surprising to some readers is the quantity of alcohol present in a large number of OTC and a few prescription medications (Table 9.1). Many of these medications are antitussive–decongestant liquids for short-term use, but a number of them are vitamin–mineral tonics popular among the elderly. One of these

Table 9.1. Alcohol Content of Selected Medications

Donnagel (OTC)[a]	1.4%	Peri-Colace Syrup (OTC)	10%
Robitussin (OTC)	3.5%	Geritol Liquid (OTC)	12%
Feosol Elixir (OTC)	5%	Geriplex–FS Liquid	18%
Donnagel–PG (Rx)[b]	5%	Comtrex Liquid (OTC)	20%
Fluorigard Anti-Cavity		Organidin Elixir (Rx)	21.75%
Dental Rinse (OTC)	6%	Donnatal Elixir (Rx)	23%
Tylenol, Adult Liquid			
Extra-Strength (OTC)	7%		

[a]OTC, over the counter.
[b]Rx, prescription.
SOURCES: AMA Drug Evaluations, Physicians' Desk Reference, and PDR for Nonprescription Drugs.

tonics, Eldertonic®, is made in a sherry wine base and is 13.5 percent alcohol or 27 proof. This is sufficient alcohol concentrations to stimulate gastric acid production if taken on an empty stomach (Natow and Heslin, 1986).

Alcohol affects the metabolism of protein, carbohydrates, and lipids (see Chapter 2). It increases urinary excretion of nitrogen and decreases the conversion of amino acids to glucose by the liver. The result can be hypoglycemia, even in nonalcoholics. Hyperglycemia may result because alcohol inhibits the body's response to insulin and induces the release of epinephrine, one of the hormones that increase blood glucose levels during times of stress. Fatty acid metabolism is impaired, leading to ketosis and elevation of blood lipids, including cholesterol. High-density lipoproteins (HDL) are also elevated, but the elevation appears to be of a type of HDL that does not protect against coronary artery disease (Feinman, 1989).

Vitamin nutrition probably comes to mind when most people think of alcoholic malnutrition. There is no question that alcoholics with liver disease and/or pancreatitis have problems with their vitamin status, but the effect of alcohol on the vitamin status of well-fed alcoholics is not as clear. A 1953 study of the 16,000 inmates of the House of Corrections (currently, Cook County Department of Corrections, Division 2) in Chicago, found only 14 individuals with nutritional problems related to vitamin deficiencies (Roe, 1985).

Current research is illuminating the subtle ways in which alcohol affects vitamin status.

Alcohol interferes with the absorption of thiamin if the concentration of thiamin is low. Therefore, taking medications containing significant amounts of alcohol at meal times should be avoided, if possible (Feinman, 1989). Vitamin B_{12} absorption is also inhibited by alcohol. While this does not seem to result in nutritional problems for alcoholics (Lieber, 1989), older individuals may already have limited B_{12} stores and a decreased ability to absorb the vitamin. Absorption of the phosphorylated form of vitamin B_6 appears to be decreased by ethanol (Feinman, 1989), and activation of the microsomal oxidizing system by ethanol increases the need for B_6 as well (Lieber, 1989).

Folate is particularly important to the health of the small bowel. Alcohol appears to inhibit folate absorption, which leads to further decreases in folate absorption due to structural changes in the cells that line the small bowel. Structural changes in these cells impair the absorption of fats, glucose, sodium, and water. Although folate deficiency usually occurs in alcoholics consuming large quantities of alcohol, the deficiency is initiated by low folate consumption (Feinman, 1989). Folate is found primarily in green, leafy vegetables, foods that are sometimes lacking in the diets of older people. Malabsorption of fat-soluble vitamins does not occur unless there is a severe folate deficiency, but ethanol can interfere with the activation of vitamin D, leading to osteoporosis (Feinman, 1989). The need for vitamin A is increased when the microsomal oxidizing system is activated in the liver (Lieber, 1989), and serum levels of vitamin E decrease with chronic alcohol consumption (Feinman, 1989).

The direct effects of ethanol on minerals in nonalcoholics are not well defined (Feinman, 1989). Whether or not ethanol directly inhibits calcium absorption has yet to be determined. Ethanol appears to increase urinary excretion of zinc and magnesium. Blood loss due to gastritis can lead to iron deficiency (Lieber, 1989).

Cardiovascular Drugs

Older individuals use more cardiovascular drugs than other age groups, for two reasons. First, despite the fact that the incidence of cardiovascular disease (CVD) has been declining in the United States over the last several years, it is still the number one cause of death and disability for older adults. Second, many of the CVDs afflicting older people are amenable to treatment with changes in life-style and the use of medications. Some individuals do not require drugs to maintain normal blood pressure and cholesterol levels because they have been able to make and maintain the necessary life-style changes. Most people with these problems, however, require continued use of medications. Taking these drugs is a life-time regimen, at the same time that these drugs are increasing one's life span.

A number of cardiac problems are not related to either hypertension or abnormal blood lipid levels, for example, mitral valve replacement due to rheumatic heart disease. These individuals can have an otherwise normal life, but require anticoagulation therapy.

Cardiovascular drugs cause more serious adverse reactions than any other group except psychoactive drugs (SGR, 1988). Not only do they bring about many serious side effects, but they also cause many problems of a lesser nature. Gastrointestinal problems are a particular concern with a number of these drugs, occurring in 10 percent or more of the patients who are taking them. Individuals experiencing gastrointestinal upsets may not be reacting to the drug itself, because as medications are prepared, other ingredients besides the drug component are added. Commonly used ingredients that may cause gastrointestinal problems in susceptible individuals are lactose and cornstarch. Distress due to one of these ingredients can sometimes be eliminated by changing brands of medications or changing the form in which the drug is given.

A typical scenario for this type of problem might unfold as follows: You are a 60-year-old male high school history teacher. It is January, and you have just returned to school after two weeks of vacation (i.e., little exercise and too much rich food). You have gained a few pounds, are not feeling well, and realize that the cough that began before Christmas is still hanging on. You visit your family physician and are given erythromycin (E-Mycin®) for your bronchitis. Because your blood pressure is mildly elevated, and because your blood pressure was also high last October, the physician prescribes an antihypertensive medication.

You have moderate lactose intolerance and are aware that you should avoid diary products while taking an antibiotic such as E-Mycin®, but do not quite recall the reason. By the end of the second day on these medications, you are very uncomfortable due to bloating and diarrhea. You telephone your physician to discuss the problem. He reminds you that E-Mycin® contains lactose and asks if you have been consuming any dairy products that would add to your lactose burden. As you have not, the physician concludes that the problem must be due to the antihypertensive medication. He tells you to stop taking it and to come to the office in a few days when the symptoms have subsided.

During the next few days, two more patients on the same antihypertensive medication visit the physician with complaints of diarrhea. As both of these patients also have severe lactose intolerance, he begins to suspect a formulation change and checks with the manufacturer. The physician's suspicions are confirmed; the tablet now contains lactose.

On your return visit to the physician, the lactose problem is discussed, and your antihypertensive medication is changed to one without lactose.

Antihypertensives

Diuretics

Hydrochlorothiazide (HydroDIURIL® and Esidrix®), chlorothiazide (Diuril®), and chlorthalidone (Hygroton®) are thiazide-type diuretics that increase the urinary excretion of sodium chloride and water along with potassium, zinc, and magnesium (Murray *et al.*, 1991). Long-term therapy decreases glucose tolerance. Furthermore, thiazide-type diuretics can elevate blood triglyceride and cholesterol levels. Most patients on this type of diuretic are given a potassium supplement and are advised to select foods high in potassium. Thiazide-type diuretics may also increase excretion of riboflavin (Murray *et al.*, 1991; Roe, 1989a), and anorexia and gastrointestinal distress can be a problem (Natow and Heslin, 1986).

Furosemide (Lasix®) is chemically similar to the thiazide diuretics. It is more potent and acts for a shorter time. Furosemide increases loss of sodium chloride, potassium, zinc, and magnesium in the urine and increases urinary loss of calcium as well. Cholesterol and triglyceride levels are not elevated by this diuretic. Patients taking furosemide require a potassium supplement (Murray *et al.*, 1991).

Combination Diuretics (Dyazide®, Aldactazide®, and Moduretic®)

Potassium-sparing diuretics are less potent diuretics that eliminate the loss of potassium in the urine. They can cause hyperkalemia (elevated blood potassium level) and are not as effective at controlling blood pressure as the thiazide-type diuretics, so they are usually prescribed in combination with a thiazide diuretic, usually hydrochlorothiazide. People taking this type of diuretic may develop either high or low blood potassium levels, but most individuals on combination diuretics do not have a problem with their potassium levels (Murray *et al.*, 1991). Dyazide contains triamterene, while Aldactazide has spironolactone, and Moduretic is amiloride in combination with hydrochlorothiazide.

Potassium Chloride (K-Lor®, Kay Ciel®, Kaochlor®, and Slow-K®)

Potassium chloride is irritating to the gastrointestinal tract. Ulceration and blood loss can be caused by slow-release forms. Potassium supplements may cause diarrhea, nausea, and vomiting, and decrease the absorption of vitamin B_{12} (Roe, 1989a,b).

Angiotensin-Converting Enzyme Inhibitors (ACE Inhibitors)

Captopril (Capoten®) may cause elevation in serum potassium levels and excessive sodium loss. In the first few months of therapy, captopril can also decrease taste acuity (Roe, 1989a). Both lisinopril (Prinivil® and Zestril®) and enalapril (Vasotec®) can cause retention of potassium and sodium loss, but this does not occur as frequently as with captopril. Gastrointestinal problems, with diarrhea being the most common, have been reported with lisinopril use (PDR, 1991). Dizziness and headache are the most frequently occurring adverse reactions to enalapril (PDR, 1991).

Other Antihypertensive Agents

A number of nondiuretic antihypertensive agents cause retention of sodium and water. Some of these medications can cause problems severe enough to require concurrent administration of a diuretic to avoid edema. Hydralazine (Apresoline®), methyldopa (Aldomet®), prazosin (Minipress®), reserpine (Serpasil®), and terazocrin (Hytrin®) all have the potential to cause edema.

Drowsiness is known to be an adverse effect of clonidine (Catapres®), reserpine (Serpasil®), and methyldopa (Aldomet®). It can be the cause of a decrease in food intake, especially in frail, elderly people. Gastrointestinal distress, a side effect common to these drugs, may also be a cause of decreased food intake. Other common adverse reactions that can have an impact on nutritional status are dryness of the mouth and constipation from clonidine (Catapres®) and nausea, vomiting, diarrhea, and anorexia from hydralazine (Apresoline®). Some individuals experience nausea and diarrhea as part of the "first-dose phenomenon" with prazosin (Minipress®). The most common nutrition-related problems due to methyldopa (Aldomet®) are dry mouth and various gastrointestinal complaints.

Several of these drugs may affect the vitamin–mineral status of patients. Iron absorption is decreased by methyldopa (Murray *et al.*, 1991), and the need for vitamin B_{12} and folate is increased (Natow and Heslin, 1986). This is especially significant for elderly people who may have a decreased ability to produce hydrochloric acid and intrinsic factor. Hydralazine is a vitamin B_6 antagonist, which may cause a depletion of this vitamin (Roe, 1989a).

Beta-Blockers

Beta-blockers are a class of drugs used in the treatment of several different cardiovascular problems, including hypertension, angina, and arrhythmias. Beta-blockers function by blocking the stimulation of the $beta_1$-receptors of the heart. Unfortunately, many other cells in the body contain a similar receptor, the $beta_2$-receptor, and blocking these receptors can lead to some serious problems with side effects. Most drugs in this group have the potential to block both types of receptors.

Individuals taking beta-blockers do not necessarily experience the symptoms that go along with hypoglycemia. They do not sweat, and their heart rate does not increase. Moreover, beta-blockers can block the liver's ability to respond to hypoglycemia and may actually further decrease the blood sugar level. In insulin-dependent diabetics, beta-blockers prolong the duration of hypoglycemia during an insulin reaction.

Other side effects that can be caused by beta-blockers include gastrointestinal distress, fatigue and lethargy, depression, and elevation of serum triglycerides. Some beta-blockers, theoretically, are not so likely to cause these problems. They are the so-called cardioselective beta-blockers. However, this selectivity for beta-receptors appears to occur only at relatively low doses (AMA, 1992).

Cholesterol- and Triglyceride-Lowering Drugs

Cholestyramine (Questran®) and colestipol (Colestid®) are bile-acid–binding resins with troublesome gastrointestinal side effects. Cholestyramine and colestipol frequently cause bloating and constipation. Chronic constipation can cause and/or aggravate hemorrhoids. Furthermore, cholestyramine decreases iron and calcium absorption (Spallholz, 1989; Murray et al., 1991) as well as absorption of B_{12} and folate (Natow and Heslin, 1986). Resins can elevate triglycerides, so their use is limited to individuals with abnormal cholesterol levels (Stone and McDonald, 1989). Since resins function by inhibiting the reabsorption of bile acids, their use can result in fat malabsorption, which impairs the absorption of fat-soluble vitamins. Vitamin supplementation may be necessary (MSD, 1989).

High doses of niacin (nicotinic acid) can aggravate peptic ulcers, leading to blood loss and anemia. Some patients experience elevations in blood glucose and uric acid levels (Stone and McDonald, 1989). Additionally, various forms of gastrointestinal distress are frequent complaints. About 5 percent of patients taking lovastatin (Mevacor®) experience gastrointestinal distress (MSD, 1989), the most common being flatus, abdominal pain, and diarrhea (PDR, 1991). Gemfibrozil (Lopid®) can also cause gastrointestinal problems, and clofibrate (Atromid-S®) increases the incidence of gallstones. They may also cause nausea and vomiting, and, in rare instances, a decrease in taste acuity and an unpleasant aftertaste (Manual of

Clinical Dietetics, 1988). Gastrointestinal complaints are a very rare side effect of probucol (MSD, 1989).

Agents Used in Congestive Heart Failure

Digitalis Glycosides

Digoxin (Lanoxin®) is the most commonly used drug in this group. Occasionally, digitoxin (Crystodigin®) is used by individuals likely to skip a dose of medication. Digoxin has few if any nutritional side effects. Nausea, vomiting, abdominal pain, and/or anorexia are signs of digitalis intoxication, which occurs more frequently in the elderly. A low serum potassium level predisposes to digitalis toxicity (AMA, 1992). There is some question as to whether or not digitalis increases the loss of magnesium, calcium, and potassium (Roe, 1989a). Vitamin D supplements should not be self-administered by persons taking digitalis. They can elevate serum calcium levels resulting in heart rhythm irregularities (AMA, 1992).

Vasodilators

Isosorbide dinitrate, nitroglycerin, hydralazine, and prazosin are discussed in other sections on cardiovascular drugs.

Antianginal Agents: Nitrates

This group of drugs is used in the treatment of angina and can be administered sublingually, orally, or as an ointment applied to the skin. They are also available in a patch that is worn around the clock, releasing a measured dose of the drug. Oral nitrates are also used in treating congestive heart failure. Nitrates are not known to cause nutritional problems directly. Since common side effects include headache and dizziness, a few individuals may decrease food intake as a result.

Antiarrhythmic Agents

For digitalis glycosides, see Congestive Heart Failure (above); for propranolol, see Beta-Blockers (p. 227).

Quinidine compounds (Quinaglute®, Duraquin®, Quinidex®, and Cardioquin®) are irritating to the gastrointestinal tract. Diarrhea, nausea, and vomiting are the most common adverse side effects. Procainamide (Pronestyl®) occasionally causes anorexia, vomiting, and nausea. The most common side effects of disopyramide (Norpace®) include dryness of the mouth and constipation. Nausea, vomiting, gastric pain, and diarrhea may occur. Low blood glucose is a rarely occurring adverse reaction.

Antiemboli Agents

Dipyridamole (Persantine®) is used to prevent emboli after cardiac valve replacement. Dipyridamole can cause gastrointestinal distress and headache. These adverse reactions are usually mild and usually disappear with long-term use.

Warfarin (Coumadin®) interferes with vitamin K–dependent blood coagulation factors, and as a result, changes in the amount of vitamin K in the diet can affect blood clotting. Patients taking warfarin are advised not to change dietary habits, especially the intake of green leafy vegetables. Diarrhea and nausea are rarely occurring consequences of warfarin therapy.

Aspirin has recently been shown to be effective in the prevention of myocardial infarction and strokes due to atrial fibrillation. See Nonsteroidal Anti-Inflammatory Drugs (p. 232) for adverse reactions.

Calcium-Channel Blockers

Calcium-channel blockers inhibit the influx of calcium ions into cardiac and vascular smooth muscle cells. This action makes calcium-channel blockers useful in the treatment of angina, hypertension, and arrhythmias. Calcium-channel blockers are significant for what they do not do. They do not affect blood calcium levels or the metabolism of calcium. Further, calcium itself does not influence the functioning of these drugs. Individuals on calcium-channel blockers should not be on a low-calcium diet.

In clinical trials of verapamil (Isoptin® and Calan®), 7.3 percent of patients reported constipation as an adverse reaction (PDR, 1991).

Nausea and headache were also reported by a significant number of patients. Nutritionally important side effects rarely occur with diltiazem (Cardizem®), except for nausea and headache. Nifedipine (Procardia®) is more likely to cause gastrointestinal distress and headache than either of the other calcium-channel blockers.

Other

In clinical trials of Pentoxifylline (Trental®), 2.8 percent of patients experienced dyspepsia, and 2.2 percent had vomiting. Fewer than 1 percent of patients complained of a bad taste in the mouth (PDR, 1991).

Corticosteroids

Corticosteroids are hormones produced by the adrenal gland as a response to stress. These hormones help the body perform a number of functions that ensure survival. Steroids help to maintain normal blood glucose levels during periods of extreme hunger and starvation. After an injury, steroids signal the body to retain more sodium and water to aid in maintaining blood pressure. Steroids make amino acids available for wound healing and limit the inflammatory reaction that occurs. Inflammation is decreased by blocking the production of prostaglandins, which are the major chemical mediators of the inflammatory response. Their anti-inflammatory property makes steroids useful in the treatment of a number of diseases, including autoimmune disease such as rheumatoid arthritis and systemic lupus erythematosus (SLE), asthma, and allergic rhinitis (hay fever).

Steroids can be administered systemically via injection or tablet; applied topically to the skin; used as eye drops in ophthalmic solutions; used as eardrops in otic preparations; inhaled into the lungs; or even sprayed into the nose. The last two forms of the drug were developed to decrease the risk of adverse side effects that occur with long-term use of steroids in diseases such as asthma. There have been no reports in the medical literature of topically applied steroids causing changes in metabolism, but a few individuals have reported side effects after prolonged use of ophthalmic preparations. These individuals may have swallowed the drug after it drained through the tear ducts, or possibly the drug was absorbed by the mucous membranes of the eyelids.

Currently, patients requiring long-term oral steroids are usually placed on an every-other-day regimen to diminish the metabolic effects of prolonged steroid use. However, this method of administration dos not entirely eliminate metabolic consequences, and some individuals still require every-day dosage.

Steroids decrease the absorption of calcium and phosphorus, increase the retention of sodium and water, and increase the excretion of vitamin C, vitamin K, calcium, zinc, potassium, and nitrogen. Steroids alter metabolism, thereby increasing vitamin B_6, folate, and vitamin D needs. Alterations in metabolism lead to elevations in serum glucose, cholesterol, and triglycerides. Over time, alterations in fat, carbohydrate, and protein metabolism lead to muscle wasting, along with fat deposition, and to weight gain along with a diabetic-like state. Osteopenia, a decrease in the amount of bone, can result if the increased need for calcium, phosphorus, and vitamin D are not met. Steroids promote gastric ulceration and can cause occult blood loss from the gastrointestinal tract, even without ulcer formation.

Nonsteriodal Anti-Inflammatory Drugs

This group of drugs is exactly as described by its name. Each drug in the group has anti-inflammatory properties, but is chemically unrelated to adrenocorticosteroids. Nonsteroidal anti-inflammatory (NSAI) drugs block production of prostaglandins, the major chemical mediators of the inflammatory process, just as steroids do. Drugs in this group are used to control a variety of diseases that involve an abnormal inflammatory process. The inflammation may be temporary, and of a limited nature, such as a sprained ankle, or due to a life-long problem, such as rheumatoid arthritis. The NSAI drugs have the advantage of causing fewer and less severe side effects than steroids, and many of these drugs relieve pain as well. Unfortunately, NSAI drugs cannot entirely replace steroids for all individuals suffering from an inflammatory disease, and some steroid-responsive problems such as asthma can't be treated by this group of drugs at all.

Salicylates

Aspirin is the prototypical NSAI agent. Before the development of the other drugs in this group, aspirin was the drug of first choice for rheumatoid arthritis. Patients took ten to 20 tablets per day. Many individuals on this regimen experienced severe gastrointestinal distress, and 70 percent of patients experienced occult bleeding (AMA, 1981). Even low doses of aspirin can cause gastrointestinal problems and blood loss. Long-term use of aspirin may cause anemia even without producing blood loss. Spallholz (1989) reported that aspirin increases vitamin C excretion and reduces iron absorption.

Choline magnesium trisalicylate (Trilisate®), diflunisal (Dolobid®), and salsalate (Disalcid®) are well tolerated by the gastrointestinal tract compared with the other salicylates. Gastrointestinal bleeding occurred in fewer than 1 percent of patients during clinical trials with diflunisal (PDR, 1991). The most common complaint of patients using salsalate is nausea.

Phenylbutazone (Butazolidin®) is a second-line NSAI drug used when other NSAI drugs have failed and is recommended for short-term therapy only in individuals under 60 years of age. Clinical studies indicate up to 9 percent of patients experience gastrointestinal problems (PDR, 1991). A similar number experience sodium and water retention (Murray *et al.*, 1991). It decreases absorption of folate and increases excretion of protein (Natow and Heslin, 1986).

Other NSAI Drugs

Other NSAI drugs are measured against aspirin by their ability to relieve pain and inflammation. Further, they are compared to aspirin for severity and type of adverse reactions. In general they are as effective as aspirin and cause fewer gastrointestinal problems. However, a number of these drugs can adversely affect food intake due to their effect on the central nervous system (CNS).

Ibuprofen (Motrin®) is also sold as an OTC drug, under a number of different names (e.g., Advil®, Ibuprin®, Medipren®,

Motrin IB®, Nuprin®). It is the most commonly used nonaspirin NSAI drug, and it is well tolerated. The most common adverse reactions are nausea and vomiting. Indomethacin (Indocin®) was one of the first NSAI drugs available. It is used less frequently today because adverse effects can be severe, although they occur less frequently than those of aspirin. Naproxen (Naprosyn®) can cause abdominal pain without damaging the lining of the gastrointestinal tract. Meclofenamate (Meclomen®) is known to cause diarrhea in a significant number of patients. It can also cause fluid retention, but not so much as other NSAI drugs. Tolmetin (Tolectin®) can cause changes in weight with long-term use, and water retention is a problem. Water retention is also a problem with the use of diclofenac (Voltaren®), naproxen sodium (Anaprox®), and piroxicam (Feldene®).

Gastrointestinal Drugs

Digestive disorders, including indigestion, heartburn, flatus, abdominal pain, and constipation, are common problems in western society. Low-fiber diets and sedentary life-style are known to cause constipation. It appears that smoking, drinking alcoholic beverages, life-style, overeating, and use of highly processed foods devoid of fiber contribute to other digestive complaints as well. Aging per se does not increase one's risk of digestive problems, but a number of factors common to older individuals increase the risk of gastrointestinal distress. Health problems such as poorly controlled diabetes can cause abdominal pain and indigestion. Tooth loss and denture wearing can affect ability to chew and cause the swallowing of air. Polypharmacy is probably a major cause of dyspepsia in older individuals, but even single-drug use can cause gastrointestinal problems. Drugs such as NSAI agents and erythromycin are notorious for the gastric distress they cause, and emotional distress due to chronic pain, chronic health problems, or from grief and loneliness can adversely affect gastrointestinal function (Natow and Heslin, 1986).

In fact, constipation and dyspepsia are so common in the United States that many individuals no longer think of the drugs used to treat these problems as drugs at all. Patients frequently do not tell their physicians that they regularly take antacids and/or laxatives. Abuse of these OTC drugs can lead to severe metabolic consequences. Before the availability of bulk-forming agents and wetting agents, laxative dependence was a common problem. However, even wetting agents and bulk-forming agents are not free of adverse effects if they are improperly used. In the older person, constipation may be due to insufficient fluid intake (SGR, 1988). Adding a bulk-forming laxative will make the problem worse unless fluid intake is also increased, and with low fluid intake, a wetting agent may cause dehydration with chronic use.

Antacids

The primary ingredients in antacids are aluminum, calcium, and magnesium compounds (Tables 9.2, 9.3). Each of these compounds can cause significant nutritional problems when used for long periods. Occasional use, or even several weeks of use, such as might be required to heal an ulcer, should not cause nutritional consequences. The most common adverse reactions are constipation and diarrhea. Magnesium compounds cause diarrhea, while both calcium and aluminum preparations cause constipation. On occasion, calcium carbonate has caused fecal impaction. Most of the commonly used antacids are a combination of magnesium and aluminum, which helps to regulate bowel function, but some individuals still have problems with constipation or diarrhea.

All antacids inactivate thiamin, which is unstable in slightly basic solutions. Decreasing gastric acidity inhibits the absorption of

Table 9.2. Single-Compound Antacids

Trade name	Drug name
Alterna Gel®	Aluminum hydroxide gel
Amphojel®	Aluminum hydroxide gel
Basaljel®	Basic aluminum carbonate gel
Rolaids®	Dihydroxyaluminum sodium carbonate
Titralac®	Calcium carbonate
Tums®	Calcium carbonate

Table 9.3. Composition of
Antacid Mixtures

Trade name	Active ingredients[a]
Carmalox Suspension®	AH + MH + CC
Gelusil Liquid®	AH + MH + S
Gelusil–M®	AH + MH + S
Gelusil–II®	AH + MH + S
Maalox Suspension®	AH + MH
Maalox Plus Suspension®	AH + MH + S
Maalox TC Suspension®	AH + MH
Mylanta Liquid®	AH + MH + S
Mylanta II Liquid®	AH + MH + S
Riopan Suspension®	AH + MH

[a]AH, aluminum hydroxide; MH, magnesium hydroxide;
CC, calcium carbonate; S, simethicone.

calcium, chromium, iron, magnesium, selenium, and zinc (Murray
et al., 1991). Some antacids, however, have been shown to decrease
iron absorption selectively. Calcium carbonate can decrease iron
absorption and may on occasion cause steatorrhea. Iron absorption
can also be decreased by magnesium carbonate. Aluminum compounds decrease the absorption of vitamin A and phosphate. Almost
all antacid gels contain a significant amount of sodium.

Agents Used for Acid Peptic Disorders

Cimetidine (Tagamet®) and ranitidine (Zantac®) are H_2-receptor
antagonists that block gastric secretion, making them useful in a
number of gastrointestinal problems including ulcers, gastritis, and
esophagitis. Cimetidine can cause diarrhea and may decrease iron
absorption. A bitter taste can also be a problem (Natow and Heslin,
1986). Overall, ranitidine causes fewer adverse reactions. Sucralfate
(Carafate®) appears to increase the speed of ulcer healing by binding
to the ulcer site and protecting it from further damage. Adverse
reactions rarely occur with this drug.

Antidiarrheal Agents

Bismuth subsalicylate (Pepto-Bismol®) has no known nutritional consequences except for constipation and fecal impaction. Kaolin (Kaopectate® and Donnagel®), however, can interfere with nutrient absorption since it decreases stool fluidity by holding water. Kaolin does not decrease water loss per se. Both loperamide (Imodium®) and diphenoxylate with atropine (Lomotil®) can cause nausea, dry mouth, and abdominal distention, which may lead to decreased food consumption.

Laxatives

Bulk-Forming Agents

Bulk-forming agents may cause anorexia and early satiety if taken close to mealtimes or in high doses. They can cause constipation, impaction, or obstruction if sufficient water is not taken. Methylcellulose is high in sodium, which can lead to water retention. Currently, nearly all brands of bulk-forming laxatives use psyllium hydrophilic colloid, from psyllium seed, as the bulk-forming agent. A number of the bulk-forming laxatives contain large amounts of dextrose and other sugars. Diabetic individuals and persons concerned with sugar intake should select a product without added sugar.

Psyllium-containing laxatives include Correctal Natural Grain Laxative®, Effer-Syllium®, Fiberall®, Fiber Con®, Fibermed®, IIydrocil Instant®, Konsyl®, Metamucil®, Modane Bulk®, Perdiem®, Serutan®, and Syllact.®

Stimulants

In the past, this group of laxatives was widely used and abused. With the availability of bulk-forming laxatives and wetting agents, the use of stimulants has decreased dramatically. A number of these laxatives can cause severe diarrhea leading to dehydration; moreover, they can be habit forming. These problems are associated particularly with cascara, castor oil, and danthron.

Bisacodyl (Dulcolax®) can cause dyspepsia and diarrhea severe enough to lower serum potassium levels. The absorption of sodium and potassium are decreased even without producing diarrhea (Murray et al., 1991). Phenolphthalein (Ex-Lax®) rarely causes dehydration and potassium loss even after prolonged use. It decreases absorption of fat-soluble vitamins (Natow and Heslin, 1986) and may increase fecal losses of sodium and calcium (Murray et al., 1991). Senna pod (Senokot®) rarely causes problems with short-term use. There are no known nutrition-related consequences even with long-term use of glycerin suppositories.

Saline Cathartics

This group of laxatives includes magnesium, potassium, and sodium salts. Magnesium salts (Milk of Magnesia) is the only one used long-term, and its chalky taste can cause nausea. Short-term use does not cause problems for normal healthy individuals, but abuse of this class of laxatives can lead to retention of sodium, potassium, and magnesium.

Lubricants

Lubricants are used to soften the feces and to prevent injury to hemorrhoidal tissue. On occasion olive oil and cottonseed oil are used for this purpose, but these oils can add substantially to caloric intake. Mineral oil (liquid petrolatum) is not absorbed, so it has been the lubricant of choice; however, absorption of the fat-soluble vitamins is decreased by mineral oil. Calcium, phosphate, and potassium absorption are impaired by mineral oil (Murray et al., 1991).

Wetting Agents

Docusate (Surfak®, Kasof®, and Colace®) is the most commonly used wetting agent. Nausea, vomiting, diarrhea, and a bitter taste have been reported. Docusate increases absorption of vitamin A and cholesterol, and decreases water absorption (Natow and Heslin, 1986). These changes in absorption should not affect nutritional status in normal healthy individuals as long as docusate is not abused.

Other

Older individuals with chronic constipation may be placed on low doses of lactulose (Chronulac®). Lactulose is well tolerated, but decreases in serum potassium and chloride have occurred in elderly, debilitated individuals receiving lactulose for six months or longer.

Miscellanous Agents

Metoclopramide (Reglan®)

Adverse reactions that can affect nutritional status include drowsiness, dryness of mouth, constipation, and diarrhea.

Simethicone (Mylicon®)

No adverse reactions have been reported.

Antispasmodics

Antispasmodics are used primarily in the management of functional bowel disorders such as irritable colon. Formerly, they were used in treating peptic ulcer disease and are now used as second-line therapy in a variety of gastrointestinal problems. Common problems that can occur with use of these drugs include dryness of mouth and constipation. Some of the antispasmodics can cause diarrhea, headache, nausea, and drowsiness.

Osteoporosis

At present, estrogen replacement is the first line of therapy for osteoporosis. In the last few years, research on etidronate disodium (Didronel®), salmon calcitonin (Calcimar®), and a fluoride–calcium combination (Fluorical®) have shown promising results. Additionally, calcitriol, the active metabolite of vitamin D, combined with calcium supplements has been used with some success.

Sodium fluoride taken in the doses required in the treatment of osteoporosis can cause gastrointestinal side effects in about 25 percent of patients. Slow-release forms of sodium fluoride and disodium monofluorophospate produce fewer gastrointestinal problems. Etidronate disodium is known to frequently cause diarrhea and nausea, but appears to be tolerated better by individuals with osteoporosis than by individuals with other bone diseases. To be effective, etidronate disodium requires adequate intake of calcium and vitamin D, but should not be taken with foods, antacids, or supplements high in calcium. Salmon calcitonin produces nausea and/or vomiting in 10 percent of patients during the early stages of treatment, but nausea decreases or disappears with continued use (PDR, 1991); it requires supplements of 1.5 g calcium and 400 IU of vitamin D per day to be effective. Calcium carbonate is frequently used as the calcium source. Possible adverse nutritional consequences of calcium carbonate are discussed in the section on antacids (p. 235). Vitamin D increases both serum calcium and urinary calcium, so it is vital that adequate fluid and calcium are consumed. Calcitriol can cause vitamin D toxicity. Headache, drowsiness, nausea and vomiting, constipation, dry mouth, and metallic taste are early signs of intoxication.

Estrogen-replacement therapy (ERT) is well recognized as being effective in reducing bone loss and frequency of fractures during the first five to ten years after menopause. However, unopposed estrogen increases the risk of endometrial cancer, so progesteronelike hormones are usually given with estrogen. This hormone combination is similar to oral contraceptives and has similar nutritional consequences. Estrogen increases sodium and water retention. Oral contraceptives increase serum levels of vitamins A and D, iron, and lipids. They may decrease the availability of water-soluble vitamins and minerals other than iron (Manual of Clinical Dietetics, 1988). Biochemical analyses have revealed that oral contraceptive users have lower than normal levels of folic acid, riboflavin, B_6, B_{12}, and C. For the most part, the significance of these subclinical deficiencies is unknown, but a few women have developed megaloblastic anemia due to folate deficiency (Williams, 1989). At higher dosage levels, oral contraceptives mildly elevate serum glucose.

Other Drugs

Acetaminophen (Tylenol®) is most commonly used to reduce fever and pain. It does not have anti-inflammatory properties like NSAI drugs, but it is sometimes used for arthritis and other chronic pain when NSAI drugs are not tolerated. Only in rare instances does acetaminophen cause loss of appetite or gastrointestinal distress. Acetaminophen does not cause gastrointestinal blood loss, but urinary excretion of ascorbic acid may be increased (Roe, 1989a).

Benzodiazepine

The first benzodiazepine, diazepam (Valium®) came on the market in the 1960s and quickly became the most commonly prescribed drug in the world. In the early 1980s, research studies revealed that continuous use of benzodiazepines for one year or longer resulted in addiction to this class of drugs. As a result, their use fell somewhat, but diazepam remains the most commonly prescribed psychoactive drug in the United States. Today, the numerous benzodiazepines available are used for a number of reasons. Oxazepam (Serax®) and alprazolam (Xanax®) are short-acting benzodiazepines that can be used in the treatment of chronic pain and relieve the accompanying anxiety. Diazepam can be used as a muscle relaxant after an injury and in the treatment of seizure disorders. Lorazepam (Ativan®) is an intermediate-acting drug used to relieve anxiety. Other benzodiazepines such as temazepam (Restoril®) and triazolam (Halcion®) are short-acting drugs used to induce sleep.

Because the benzodiazepines are chemically related, they have similar adverse reactions that can have nutritional consequences. The importance of these adverse reactions depends more on the duration of action of the drug and the manner in which it is used than the fact that it causes a given adverse reaction. For example, benzodiazepines are known to increase appetite and cause weight gain (Williams, 1989). This can be a positive effect in an individual having weight loss secondary to chronic pain, but may be detrimental to individuals who are required to stop exercising after an injury. Increased appetite is of little consequence to those using triazolam for sleep. The hunger it produces is not severe enough to disturb sleep, and the drug is no longer functional by the next morning.

Benzodiazepines are known to cause CNS effects that can lead to decreased food intake due to drowsiness, depression, headache, and nervousness. As stated previously, they can lead to weight gain, but some individuals lose weight (PDR, 1991). Benzodiazepines may cause dry mouth, constipation or diarrhea, and nausea, with or without vomiting.

Bicarbonate of Soda

This common household item, normally used as a leavening agent, it sometimes used as a dentifrice and as an antacid by older adults. While it is an excellent replacement for toothpaste, it is very high in sodium, and even this use can significantly increase sodium intake. A 1984 report in the *Annals of Internal Medicine* discusses the spontaneous rupture of the stomach of a healthy man after taking sodium bicarbonate in water (Mastrangelo and Moore, 1984).

Caffeine

The most commonly consumed drug in the western hemisphere is caffeine. Caffeine is present in both coffee and cola as well as in tea and cocoa. Tea and cocoa also contain related substances, theophylline and theobromine, respectively. Research data points to caffeine as a culprit in many human ills, but much of this information is extrapolated from coffee consumption. Such extrapolations are difficult to make as coffee is such a complex food; coffee aroma alone is made up of over 600 volatile compounds. Furthermore research studies using caffeine itself have not consistently produced the same results. Acutely administered quantities of caffeine to nonusers increases gastric acidity, elevates serum cholesterol, increases renin activity, and has a diuretic affect on the kidneys. In chronic caffeine users, the effects are diminished, raising the question of tolerance (Leonard *et al.*, 1987).

Gastric production of acid and pepsin is increased by caffeine, but both regular and decaffeinated coffee have a greater effect than caffeine alone. Caffeine, theophylline, and theobromine act as diuretics, increasing excretion of sodium and water. However, caffeine is a pressor agent, directly elevating blood pressure. Some studies have shown that caffeine increases blood glucose, whereas others have implicated noncaffeine components of coffee. Both caffeine and theobromine appear to elevate cholesterol levels, and probably triglycerides as well. Coffee consumption above 2½ to 3 cups per day is reported to increase apoliprotein B (Apo B), low-density lipoproteins (LDL), and cholesterol levels (Leonard *et al.*, 1987). More recent evidence, however, indicates that noncaffeine components of coffee are more likely to raise serum cholesterol levels than is caffeine itself. At least in moderate coffee drinkers (three 8-oz cups per day) this probably does not increase the risk for coronary artery disease, because both LDL and HDL cholesterol increase equally (Fried *et al.*, 1992).

Sleep Aids and Sedative-Hypnotics

Over-the-counter, diphenhydramine (Miles Nervine®, Nytol®, Sleep-eze®, Sominex®, and Unisom with Pain Relief®) and doxylamine succinate (Unisom Nighttime Sleep Aid®) are available as sleep inducing agents. Both of these drugs are antihistamines that characteristically produce sedation and cause anorexia, dry mouth and constipation. Drowsiness and other effects may last throughout the next day. These drugs should not be used longer than two weeks.

Prior to the development of benzodiazepines, sedative–hypnotics were commonly used in the treatment of both anxiety and insomnia. With continued use, tolerance to sedative–hypnotics develops rapidly requiring increasing doses to attain the same effect. Furthermore, these drugs have tremendous potential for abuse. Consequently, sedative–hypnotics are recommended only for short-term use. They can cause next-day sedation with a resulting decrease in appetite. When used for a week or two, this effect will not influence the nutritional status of normal healthy people, but can negatively affect a frail, elderly person.

10

Guidelines for Healthful Eating

Deciding what to eat is no longer a simple matter. In the 1950s, there was the United States Department of Agriculture's Seven Food Groups, and that was about it. A good breakfast was considered to be juice, milk, toast, and cereal or eggs. In the southern United States, grits replaced cereal. On weekends, pancakes or waffles might be served. Just about everyone ate the same thing. As the interrelationships among diet, nutrition, and health became clearer, however, many health-related organizations began to develop their own dietary guidelines. Sometimes these guidelines were in conflict with each other or were excessive and premature. For example, in the early 1980s, some nutrition experts were recommending 50 grams or more of dietary fiber per day. This amount may compromise trace element absorption and can cause gastrointestinal distress, depending on the type of fiber consumed. Today most nutritionists consider 30 to 35 grams of dietary fiber an acceptable amount.

Further complicating the situation is the fact that the news media are constantly filled with stories on nutrition–health research. Just during the week around Labor Day, 1991, three research studies were released. The USDA announced evidence that 1,300 mg of calcium per day may be the best treatment for premenstrual syndrome (PMS) (Chicago Tribune, 1991a). *The Lancet* published a study indicating that two drinks of alcohol per day reduces the risk of heart attack in men (Chicago Tribune, 1991b). At the national meeting of the American Chemical Society, research was presented linking a decreased risk for some cancers to drinking green tea (Chicago Tribune, 1991c). Even the "Today Show" did a feature story on the ten years of research on the effects of coffee drinking on health. Most experts felt that it was still too early to draw definitive conclusions, and were still drinking coffee, even some of those who had reported ill effects. It must be pointed out, however, that none of the nutrition researchers were drinking in excess of a few cups per day. They were drinking coffee, but in moderation.

It is recognized that in a healthful diet, moderation is the key factor. There are no good or bad foods, no good or bad nutrients. For most foods, it is the amount consumed in relation to other foods and nutrients that is important. Other life-style factors, such as exercise, must also be considered in planning a healthful diet. Obviously a 6-foot tall, 25-year-old man who runs 20 miles a week can easily incorporate a kcalorie-rich candy bar or two per week into his diet without squeezing out better sources of essential nutrients. Unfortunately, the same is not true for most sedentary, older people. Healthful diets do change over time as scientific evidence indicates the need for such change; however, each piece of research information must be looked at carefully before dietary changes occur. Such changes need to be viewed in terms of a person's entire diet. They should never be extreme in nature. Eating a variety of foods in moderation is always the best plan.

In a preceding paragraph, three research studies released in September, 1991, were mentioned, and each has different implications for change. Since other studies of PMS have shown similar results, women of child-bearing age may want to act immediately to increase their intake of dairy products to a level that provides 1,300 mg of calcium per day. There are no known ill effects from this level of calcium intake for normal people, and these women may be decreasing their risk of osteoporosis later in life. Whether or not everyone should consume two drinks of alcohol per day is a more complex issue. Certainly, because this study involved more than 40,000 men, it is likely to apply to most men. Whether the results apply to women is unclear. Premenopausal women are protected from cardiac disease by the hormone estrogen, but if pregnant and taking two drinks a day, they run the risk of having a child with fetal alcohol syndrome. Finally, there is the question of the relationship between alcohol intake and breast cancer. The last study, showing a protective effect of green tea on certain cancers, is very preliminary work that was done on rats. The amount of tea administered was large, and it is much too soon to state definitely that this amount of green tea does no harm. At this time, it would not be wise to start drinking 20 cups of green tea per day. However, a person who normally drinks tea might decide to switch from a black tea to a green tea.

Food Groups

The four food groups, frequently referred to as the Basic Four, was developed by the U.S. Department of Agriculture as a tool for the public to use in planning an adequate diet. The most commonly used version of the four food groups has been the *Guide to Good Eating* produced by the National Dairy Council. Rather than tell consumers that specific foods should be eaten each day, foods providing similar nutrients were grouped together. The result was the four food groups, Milk, Meat, Fruit and Vegetable, and Grain. Each food group has leader or target nutrients—foods that supply significant amounts of those nutrients qualify for inclusion in that group. In all, there are 10 leader nutrients, and it is assumed that if an individual obtains the proper amount of these 10 nutrients by eating a variety of foods, all other required nutrients will be consumed in sufficient quantities. Eating the recommended number of servings from each group does not provide sufficient kcalories for most individuals, so additional services are required to meet caloric needs. Additional kcalories can also be provided by foods and condiments that do not meet the criteria for inclusion in any of the food groups. Foods supplying primarily kcalories, such as sugar and/or fat, are grouped together as "Others" in this system.

Milk Group

Leader nutrients: calcium, riboflavin (B_2), protein.
Other Nutrients: vitamin A and beta-carotene, vitamin D, vitamin B_{12}, phosphorus.

Although named the Milk Group, a number of other milk-based foods are found in it. Cream soup, if prepared with milk, is a member of this group, as are puddings and custards. Most other dairy foods are also included. However, butter and cream supply little calcium or protein, so these foods are excluded. It should be noted that eggs are not included in the Milk Group. In the 1950s, the USDA used a different system, dividing foods into seven food groups. In that system, all dairy products, butter, cream, cheese, and milk were part of the Dairy Group, and it included eggs.

Vitamins A and D are listed as minor nutrients since not all foods in the Milk Group provide them. Vitamin D is supplied by fortified milk, and nearly all milk sold in the United States is fortified. However, the milk used in making yogurt may or may not be fortified with vitamin D, and cheese rarely has vitamin D added to it. Vitamin A occurs naturally in butter fat, and it is added to skim milk, but low-fat yogurt and low-fat cheese are not usually good sources of this nutrient.

It is important to remember that the kcalorie value of foods in this group varies considerably. Milk can vary from 0 percent to 4 percent fat. Ice cream requires a minimum of 10 percent butterfat, but premium ice creams may be more than 20 percent fat. Flavored milks, such as chocolate milk, contain added sugar. Careful selection is necessary to limit foods high in saturated fat, cholesterol, and sodium.

Meat Group

Leader nutrients: protein, niacin, iron, thiamin (B_1).
Other nutrients: vitamin A, riboflavin (B_2), vitamin B_{12}, trace minerals (zinc and copper).

This group includes all animal flesh: beef, veal, pork, lamb, poultry, game, fin fish, and shell fish. It includes animal products such as eggs and organ meats. High-protein plant foods also belong in the Meat Group, including dried peas and beans, lentils, and nuts. In previous editions of the *Guide to Good Eating*, cheese was placed in the Meat Group because of its high protein content. Cheese, however, is very low in iron, causing it to be removed in the current edition.

There are some important differences between the meat and plant proteins in this food group. The plant proteins provide fiber, while the animal proteins do not. Furthermore, dried peas and beans are fair sources of calcium and iron, while meat contains little calcium, but is an excellent source of iron. The fat content of meat varies greatly, but all dried peas, beans, and lentils are low in fat. The fat content of nuts, however, is extremely high, adding considerably to their caloric value. An ounce of almonds contains 178 kcalories and 16 grams of fat. The minor nutrients, vitamins A and B_{12}, are not found in these plant foods, and their trace minerals are not well digested or absorbed.

The amount of saturated fat, cholesterol, and sodium in some animal foods makes them less desirable choices, and the manner of preparation can add a significant number of kcalories as well. Broiling chicken without the skin is preferable to deep-fat frying, and round steak is preferable to a prime grade strip steak. Grilled strip steak and fried chicken are tasty foods and being health conscious does not require eliminating them entirely; however, portions should be small, and they should not be frequent entree choices.

Fruit and Vegetable Group

Leader nutrients: beta-carotene, vitamin C.
Other nutrients: fiber, folacin, iron, vitamin K.

Nearly all commonly eaten fruits and vegetables are included in this group. A few, such as avocados and olives, are not included because of their high fat content. This is the only group that provides significant amounts of dietary vitamin C. While most individuals think of citrus fruits, especially oranges, as dietary necessities to provide adequate vitamin C, other fruits and vegetables can supply sufficient amounts of this nutrient. Strawberries, cauliflower, green pepper, broccoli, cabbage, and even potatoes are good sources of vitamin C. Sufficient fruits and vegetables to provide the recommended daily allowance (RDA) for vitamin C should be eaten daily.

Vitamin A is not found as a preformed vitamin in fruits and vegetables, but rather as a group of plant pigments, the carotenes, that are converted to vitamin A in the body. Beta-carotene, a yellow pigment, is the one that results in the most vitamin A formation. Dark-green leafy vegetables such as spinach, and bright yellow-orange vegetables such as sweet potato, winter squash, and carrots are good vegetable sources of the carotenes, while yellow-orange fruits such as cantaloupe, apricots, papaya, and persimmons are good fruit sources. Light-colored vegetables such as wax beans, green beans, and head lettuce are poor sources of this vitamin. Since vitamin A is stored in the liver, eating an excellent source every other day will supply the body's need for this nutrient.

Fiber is also supplied by most members of this group, but varies greatly depending on the food selected. Juices, such as apple and cranberry, are devoid of fiber, while fresh apples and cranberries contain considerable quantities. Folacin, unlike other members of the B vitamin group, is found primarily in plant foods. Leafy greens such as romaine lettuce and spinach are good sources of this nutrient. These same leafy greens are also the primary dietary source of vitamin K. Fruits and vegetables can be significant sources of trace minerals, but generally these nutrients are not as well absorbed as when supplied by animal foods. Although iron is listed as another significant nutrient, debate continues among nutritionists as to how well it is absorbed from foods like spinach. Excessive dietary fiber can interfere with iron absorption, as can oxalic acid, which is present in cranberries, rhubarb, and spinach.

Nearly all fruits and vegetables are low in calories, even the so-called "starchy" vegetables, corn and potatoes. It is the manner of preparation that adds considerable calories and may decrease the nutrient content of the food as well. A large baked potato contains only 145 kcalories and supplies 4.0 grams of protein and 31 mg of vitamin C. Three ounces of french fries contains 214 kcalories with half the kcalories supplied by fat and only a little vitamin C. The sour cream, butter, or bacon chips added at the table make a baked potato "fattening."

A few foods in this group actually provide little in the way of nutrition other than kcalories. Apple juice and applesauce are among these foods. Some brands of these foods do provide considerable vitamin C because ascorbic acid is added to preserve their color even if not labeled "vitamin C added." In the past, applesauce and apple juice always were sugar-sweetened, but most grocery stores have unsweetened brands available. It is important to eat a variety of foods from this group to assure that nutrients other than beta-carotene and vitamin C are being supplied.

Grain Group

Leader nutrients: complex carbohydrates, thiamin (B_1), iron, niacin.

Other nutrients: calcium, fiber, protein, riboflavin (B_2), trace minerals.

The Grain Group includes products made from whole grains and enriched or fortified grain products. It also includes certain other natural products (e.g., wild rice). When grains are refined, the germ and the bran are removed. These portions of whole grain contain most of the nutrients and fiber. Refined grain products such as unenriched white flour contain mainly starch and a little protein.

Enrichment of refined flour, farina, and cornmeal was started during World War II by the federal government to improve the nutritional status of the United State population. The standards for enrichment are set by the Food and Drug Administration (FDA), but enrichment does not make refined flour equivalent to whole wheat flour. The FDA requires that specific amounts of iron, thiamin, niacin, and riboflavin be added to refined grains to be considered enriched. Calcium and vitamin D are optional additives. Other B complex vitamins and trace nutrients lost in the refining process are not replaced, and refined grains are considerably lower in fiber than are whole grains. Cereals and other grain products that are fortified contain higher levels of certain nutrients than either enriched or whole-grain cereals. Frequently, these cereals contain nutrients not found in grains at all. While it is enticing to think that one bowl of fortified cereal can supply the RDA for vitamins and minerals, a bowl of cornflakes and a vitamin–mineral supplement tablet is of similar nutritional value, and as pointed out later in this chapter, not the best way to meet your nutritional needs.

For many years this food group was held in low regard by many Americans. Breads, cereals, and pasta were thought of as fattening and to be avoided at all costs. Actually, grains are low in kcalories and high in nutrients. Although grain products such as cakes, sweet rolls, coffeecakes, cookies, and donuts are high-kcalorie foods, the source of the kcalories is primarily the added sugars and fats rather than the flour used in their preparation. Despite the fact that these foods are grain products, they do not belong in the Grain Group because of their caloric density. However, other high-kcalorie grain products such as crackers and ready-to-eat cereals are still included. All crackers, even those supplying 50 percent of their kcalories as fat, are part of this food group along with many ready-to-eat cereals marketed to children that contain considerable amounts of sugar. Some of these products are also high in sodium. Many cereals are enriched or fortified, so they do supply the leader nutrients, and this information is frequently given a prominent place on the label. Reading the nutrition labeling and ingredient list to determine the amount of fat, sugar, sodium, and kcalories in ready-to-eat cereals and crackers is advisable.

Other Group

This group is composed of a wide variety of foods that supply mainly kcalories in the form of sugars and fats. Included in this group are condiments; chips and related snacks; fats and oils; sweets; alcoholic beverages; sugar-sweetened beverages; and miscellaneous foods such as bacon, avocado, and olives. These foods add interest and palatability to the diet as well as needed kcalories, but a number of them have been used to excess, contributing to problems of obesity, heart disease, and tooth decay. They need to be used judiciously even though some members of this group do provide important nutrients. Vegetable oils, for example, contain essential fatty acids and vitamin E, and butter supplies vitamin A. Fortified margarine is a source of vitamins A and D. Fat, itself, adds to the feeling of satiety after a meal. Desserts such as fig bars and custard pies, especially pumpkin or sweet potato, provide significant quantities of a number of nutrients, but even a small serving is very high in kcalories. Moreover, a regular Hershey's Milk Chocolate Bar with Almonds contains 4 grams of protein, 80 mg of calcium, and 0.17 mg of riboflavin, not an insignificant contribution.

Recommended Dietary Allowances

Recommended dietary allowances are the levels of intake of essential nutrients that, on the basis of scientific knowledge, are judged by the Food and Nutrition Board of the National Research Council to be adequate to meet the known nutrient needs of practically all healthy persons. The RDAs were first published in 1943 to provide standards serving as a goal for good nutrition. Their intended use was as a guide for planning and procuring food supplies for national defense. Since the RDAs were based on the best scientific knowledge available at the time, it was intended that they be reviewed at five-year intervals. This occurred until the mid-1980s when the Food and Nutrition Board did not accept the Report of the Committee on Dietary Allowances. As a consequence, the tenth edition of the *Recommended Dietary Allowances* was not available until October, 1989. With each new edition of the RDAs, their intended use has expanded to include interpreting food-consumption records of groups and evaluating the adequacy of food supplies in meeting nutritional needs; planning and procuring food supplies for groups and establishing guides for public food assistance programs; developing new food products by industry; and developing nutrition education programs. The seventh edition, published in 1968, was used by the FDA to develop the U.S. RDAs that are used for the nutritional labeling of foods. It is now considered legitimate to use the current RDAs to interpret food-consumption records of individuals.

As the intended uses continue to increase, it is important to understand how the RDAs are set and their limitations, especially with respect to individual situations. Estimation of physiological requirements is the first step in determining the RDA for a nutrient. Physiological requirements are based on the need for absorbed nutrients. This need then must be corrected for incomplete utilization of the nutrient and variability in individual requirements. Finally, a safety factor is included to compensate for differences in the bioavailability of the nutrient among the food sources. It must be remembered, however, that the physiological requirement for a nutrient is only an estimate based on limited data.

Ideally, the first step in developing a nutrient allowance would be to determine the average physiological requirements of a healthy and representative segment of each age and sex group according to stipulated criteria. Knowledge of the variability among the individuals within each group would make it possible to calculate the amount by which the average requirement must be increased to meet the need of virtually all healthy people. Unfortunately, experiments in humans are costly and time-consuming, and even under the best of conditions, only small groups can be studied in a single experiment. Moreover, certain types of experiments are not possible for ethical reasons. Thus, estimates of requirements and their variability must often be derived from limited information. (RDA, 1989)

Furthermore, experts on a given nutrient do not necessarily agree on the criteria for determining the physiological requirement. The criteria may be based on balance studies and maintenance of acceptable blood and tissue concentrations, the amount that will prevent failure of a specific function or the development of specific deficiency signs. In the use of some nutrients, such as vitamin C, more than one criterion is used in determining the RDA.

Dietary sources of nutrients are assumed to be the foods found in a normal diet; therefore, the effects of a number of dietary factors that influence the absorption and utilization of nutrients must be considered in determining the RDAs. This includes the digestibility of the foods typically providing a given nutrient in the U.S. diet. Some vitamins, such as vitamin A and niacin, are found as precursors as well as in their vitamin form. The efficiency with which the precursors are converted to the vitamin is of importance in setting RDAs for these nutrients. For many nutrients, only a portion of the ingested amount is absorbed. In young adults only 20 to 40 percent of ingested calcium is absorbed, while absorption is even less in the aged. The form of the nutrient can profoundly affect absorption; heme iron, from animal products, is far more absorbable than non-heme iron from plant products, and concomitant intake of organic acids such as vitamin C increases the absorption of nonheme iron.

If sufficient data are available, an RDA is set for an essential nutrient. However, some nutrients, especially trace elements, have known toxic levels of intake, and lack a sufficient data base to set an RDA. In 1980, the Food and Nutrition Board solved this problem by creating a new category of requirements, Safe and Adequate Intakes. Nutrient requirements in this category are given as ranges of intake with the stipulation that the upper levels should not be habitually exceeded. At the time, there were 12 nutrients in this category. In the current edition of the RDAs, vitamin K and selenium have been given RDA status, and the electrolytes (sodium, potassium, and chloride) are no longer listed. For these nutrients, the Food and Nutrition Board now lists only Estimated Minimum Requirements for Healthy Persons.

The RDAs are set for various age and sex groups based on the so-called Reference Individual for that group. The current Reference Individuals are the actual averages for heights and weights of the U.S. population between 1976 and 1980. The source of the information is the National Health and Nutrition Examination Survey (NHANES–II). While the real weight for height of United States men and women is used in determining the RDAs, this situation does not imply that the weights are ideal. It does not, for example, consider how much of that weight is body fat and how much is muscle.

Applying the RDAs

The RDAs should not be met by consuming vitamin–mineral supplements or foods that are highly fortified or enriched, but rather by eating a varied diet. A varied diet that meets the RDAs will probably be adequate in the nutrients for which there are insufficient data to set an RDA. However, meeting the RDAs must be done within the caloric limits that keep each individual at his or her ideal body weight. For a few nutrients, this is an extremely difficult goal to reach and commonly results in a deficiency of that nutrient. Iron deficiency in women of childbearing age is one example. In these situations, food fortification and individual supplementation are acceptable.

It must be remembered that the RDAs are a tool for planning and evaluating the typical American diet. They do not apply to the Japanese businessman spending a year in the United States if he continues to consume the typical Japanese diet, nor are they useful to judge the dietary adequacy of the Central American peasant who has recently emigrated to the United States. The World Health Organization has a set of nutrient-intake standards that are uncorrected for nutrient source, which would be useful in evaluating the diets of these individuals. Also, the RDAs do not consider the role of diet as a causal or contributing factor in chronic or degenerative disease. Such considerations can lead to recommendations that vary from the RDAs. For example, the *Surgeon General's Report on Nutrition and Health* (SGR, 1988) discusses the possible beneficial effects of limiting protein in the prevention of chronic renal disease. Prevention of other diseases may require more of some nutrients than the RDAs for those nutrients.

While the RDAs are set in terms of daily needs, it is not necessary to consume the RDA every day. For most nutrients, the RDAs are intended to be average intakes over at least 3 days. A few nutrients, such as vitamins A and B_{12}, can be stored by the body in relatively large quantities. For these, the RDAs can be averaged out over several months.

Individual Variations

It is important to remember that the summary table of the RDAs is presented in terms of the Reference Individuals. The amounts of some nutrients need to be adjusted if the individual varies from the reference person. For example, the need for thiamin is based on caloric intake; the actual RDA is 0.5 mg per 1,000 kcalories with a minimum of 1.0 mg per day recommended. Due to their higher caloric intake individuals who are larger than the reference person or very physically active require more thiamin than the 1.2 mg (men) listed in the summary table. The same is true of riboflavin; the actual RDA is 0.6 mg per 1,000 kcalories with a minimum daily intake of 1.2 mg per day for adults. For niacin, the RDA is 6.6 niacin equivalents per 1,000 kcalories with a daily minimum need of 13 niacin equivalents, since it, too, is related to caloric needs. Additionally, the need for some trace elements relates to body size. The RDA for zinc is 15 mg per day for men and 12 mg per day for women, because of their smaller size. People who are considerably larger than the Reference Individuals may need more zinc than the RDA.

A number of other factors need to be considered when attempting to apply the RDAs to individuals. As previously stated, the RDAs are based on the typical mixed diets of the U.S. population. Individuals whose diets vary from this pattern may need to consume more of certain nutrients than stated in the RDA to maintain good health.

For example, the absorption of both zinc and iron is markedly decreased when meat is missing from the diet. Vegetarians consuming little or no milk and eggs may need more of these nutrients if their diets are primarily grain based. Other nutrient needs vary with the amount of protein consumed. Since most individuals in the United States habitually consume more protein than the RDA, this has been considered in the requirement for vitamin B_6. People who consume only the RDA for protein, 50 g for women and 63 g for men, will meet their need for vitamin B_6 if their diets contain 0.016 mg per gram of protein.

It is also necessary to take into account the interaction between nutrients. For instance, while there is a separate RDA for both selenium and vitamin E, there is no question that each of these nutrients can partially replace the need for the other. Therefore, individuals consuming excess of vitamin E, for example, may consume somewhat less than the RDA for selenium without ill effects. Vitamin D is a special case, since it is also a hormone produced in the skin as a response to sunlight. Anyone with considerable exposure to sunlight may take in little dietary vitamin D and still not compromise their vitamin D status. Care must be taken, however, to ensure that these individuals consume adequate dietary calcium, as the major source of both nutrients in the U.S. diet is milk.

Applying the RDAs to older adults is a difficult task. At present there is only one set of RDAs for all people older than 50 years. The committee considered establishing a separate set for people 70 years of age and above, but concluded that there are still insufficient data to do so for this group. In applying the RDAs to older individuals, it is necessary to remember that persons may be physiologically younger or older than their ages in years. Older people are also more likely to suffer from chronic diseases and undergo long-term drug therapies that affect nutritional needs. Such needs are not considered in the RDAs as they are planned for healthy persons. Defining health in older individuals is very difficult. Most experts would not consider an older person with either mild hypertension or arthritis as being in ill health, yet such individuals do not meet the criteria used in setting the RDAs. Each of these situations could require more than the RDA for some nutrients, depending on the drug therapy each is receiving. While the RDAs need to be adjusted for chronic disease and long-term illness, no adjustment is needed for a brief illness. Contrary to popular belief, short-term illnesses such as colds, flu, sore throat, or even a fractured arm do not increase nutritional needs above the RDAs in otherwise normal, healthy people.

Dietary Guidelines

The three most commonly used dietary guidelines for healthy people are the *Guide to Good Eating* developed by the National Dairy Council; the *1990 Dietary Guidelines* developed by the U.S. Departments of Agriculture and Health and Human Services; and *The American Heart Association Diet*. Superficially, these three sets of dietary guidelines appear to be different, but in practice, diets planned using them are similar.

The American Heart Association Diet (AHA, 1985, 1991) is an eating plan designed for all healthy Americans to decrease the risk of heart attack and is recommended for everyone older than 2 years. Goals of the diet are

1. Meet your daily needs for protein, vitamins, minerals, and other nutrients.
2. Achieve and maintain your best weight.
3. Reduce your total fat intake to about 30 percent of kcalories.
4. Avoid eating too many foods containing saturated fat and cholesterol.
5. Substitute polyunsaturated and monounsaturated fat for saturated fat wherever possible and yet do not eat too much of any kind of fat.
6. Make these changes gradually over a period of several months so they become a natural part of your permanent eating pattern.

Guidelines 4 and 5 translate into limiting saturated fat intake to less than 10 percent of total daily kcalories and cholesterol intake to less than 300 milligrams per day. Polyunsaturated fat is limited to no more than 10 percent of total kcalories. These goals are the same as the National Cholesterol Education Program Step I Diet/American Heart Association Diet for reduction of elevated cholesterol levels.

To control the amount and kind of fat eaten, the American Heart Association recommends

1. Limiting the intake of meat, poultry, and seafood to no more than six ounces per day.
2. Use chicken or turkey (without skin) or fish in most main meals.
3. Choosing lean cuts of meat, trimming all of the visible fat, and throwing away the fat that cooks out of the meat.
4. Substituting meatless or low-meat main dishes for regular entrees.
5. Using no more than a total of 5 to 8 teaspoons of fats and oils per day for cooking, baking, and salads.

To control the intake of cholesterol-rich foods

1. Use no more than three to four egg yolks a week, including those used in cooking.
2. Limit the use of organ meats, shrimp, and lobster.

Although there are no goals for fiber in the American Heart Association Diet, in essence, it is a high-fiber diet. Fruits and vegetables are emphasized, at least 5 servings per day, as are whole-grain breads. Dried peas and beans are recommended as meat alternatives. Limiting sodium to 3000 mg (3 grams) per day is a dietary guideline of the 1991 version of this diet. In the past, this was not a stated dietary objective, but ways to reduce sodium were suggested for each food category. Although limiting alcohol is not a stated dietary goal, no more than two drinks per day of wine, beer, or liquor are recommended. Sugar intake is not included in these guidelines in a straightforward manner, but low-sugar foods are recommended over high-sugar foods.

The third edition of the *Dietary Guidelines for Americans* (Table 10.1) was published in late 1990 (USDA and USDH & HS, 1990). This edition represents the first time the Dietary Guidelines Advisory Committee made specific dietary recommendations in terms of serving size and number of servings per day (Table 10.2) to meet the Dietary Guidelines. A range is given to accommodate variations in body size and activity level so that total nutritional and caloric needs for most individuals may be met using the Daily Food Guide. The

Table 10.1. Dietary Guidelines for Americans

Eat a variety of foods.
Maintain a healthy weight.
Choose a diet low in fat, saturated fat, and cholesterol.
Choose a diet with plenty of vegetables, fruits, and grain products.
Use sugars *only* in moderation.
Use salt and sodium *only* in moderation.
If you drink alcoholic beverages, do so in moderation.

Daily Food Guide is derived from the Basic Four Food Groups, so there is no recommended amount for fats and oils, but using fats and oils sparingly is advised. Following the Daily Food Guide results in a high-fiber diet, even though no specific recommendation for fiber is given. Sugar is limited because of its role in tooth decay and its low nutrient content. These guidelines are designed to meet recommendations found in *The Surgeon General's Report on Nutrition and Health* and *Diet and Health: Implications for Reducing Chronic Disease Risk*, as well as the tenth edition of the *Recommended Dietary Allowances*. The goal is to decrease the high rate of obesity in the United States and the incidence of heart disease, high blood pressure, stroke, diabetes, and some forms of cancer.

In spring 1992, the U.S. Department of Agriculture announced the development of the *Food Guide Pyramid* (USDA 1992) (Figure 10.1).

Table 10.2. Daily Food Guide

Food group	Suggested servings[a]
Vegetables	3 to 5 servings
Fruits	2 to 4 servings
Breads, cereals, rice, and pasta	6 to 11 servings
Milk, yogurt, and cheese	2 to 3 servings
Meats, poultry, fish, dry beans and peas, eggs, and nuts	2 to 3 servings

[a]Most people should have at least the lower number of servings suggested from each group. Some people may need more because of their body size and activity level. Serving sizes are similar to those in the Basic 4 Food Groups.

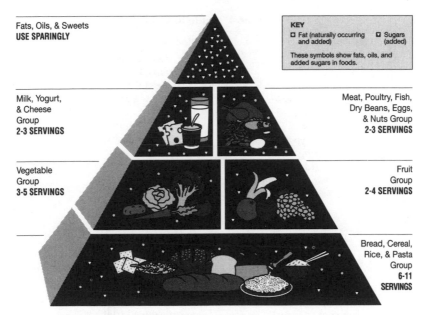

Fats, Oils, & Sweets
USE SPARINGLY

KEY
◻ Fat (naturally occurring ◻ Sugars
   and added)   (added)

These symbols show fats, oils, and added sugars in foods.

Milk, Yogurt,
& Cheese
Group
2-3 SERVINGS

Meat, Poultry, Fish,
Dry Beans, Eggs,
& Nuts Group
2-3 SERVINGS

Vegetable
Group
3-5 SERVINGS

Fruit
Group
2-4 SERVINGS

Bread, Cereal,
Rice, & Pasta
Group
6-11
SERVINGS

10.1. Food Guide Pyramid. *A Guide to Daily Food Choices* (USDA, 1992).

This is a pictorial version of the *Daily Food Guide*. A pyramid design was selected because the relative importance of various food groups can easily be illustrated in a graphic format. Breads, cereals, rice, and pasta form the base of the pyramid, since their six to eleven servings per day are the foundation of a healthy diet, and fats, oils, and added sugars are at the "use sparingly" point.

The fifth edition of the National Dairy Council's *Guide to Good Eating* (Table 10.3) became available in early 1990 (NDC, 1990). As in past editions, it is based on the U.S. Department of Agriculture's Four Food Groups and still advises, "Every day eat a wide variety of foods from the Four Food Groups in moderation." The number of servings recommended from each food group remains the same as in the fourth edition, but the serving size for a number of foods has changed. In the past, portion sizes were set so that equivalent amounts of the leader nutrient were provided. In the milk group, for example, one cup of milk and two cups of cottage cheese supply

Table 10.3. Basic 4: Guide to Good Eating

Milk Group	Meat Group
1 cup milk	3 oz. cooked lean meat
1 cup yogurt	3 oz cooked fish
1 oz cheese	½ whole chicken breast
½ cup cottage cheese	1 chicken leg and thigh
½ cup ice cream	1 egg
½ cup ice milk	½ cup cooked, dried peas
½ cup frozen yogurt	½ cup cooked, dried beans
½ cup pudding	¼ cup nuts
½ cup custard	¼ cup seeds
½ cup cream soup	2 Tbsp peanut butter

Servings

2	2
4	4

Grain Group	Fruit–Vegetable Group
1 slice bread	½ cup fruit juice
½ English muffin	½ cup vegetable juice
½ hamburger or hot dog bun	¼ large cantaloupe
1 oz ready-to-eat cereal	¼ cup dried fruit
½ cup cooked cereal	½ cup cooked fruit
½ cup cooked grits	1 large peach
½ cup cooked rice	1 medium apple or orange
1 tortilla	1 cup raw vegetables
1 roll	½ cup cooked vegetables
1 muffin	1 medium ear of corn

about the same amount of calcium. In the fifth edition, the serving size of cottage cheese has been reduced to ½ cup to keep the amount of fat and kcalories low. In the meat group, cheese has been eliminated as an alternative. The serving size of eggs has been reduced from two to one, and the serving size of cooked dried beans and peas has been decreased from one cup to ½ cup. The rationale for this last change is unclear, as dried beans and peas are low-kcalorie, high-fiber foods. According to the fifth edition of the guide, a ½-cup serving of dried peas or beans provides about half the protein that is present in a 2 to 3-oz serving of lean, cooked meat.

Following the *Guide to Good Eating* provides the core of a balanced diet, supplying about 1,200 kcalories. Additional servings are needed to provide required kcalories and in some cases nutrients. This diet can be used as the basis for limiting fat, cholesterol, kcalories, and sodium, as well as increasing fiber. For the first time, typical serving sizes are given for combination foods and the Other foods. Other foods are those that supply primarily kcalories from fat and/or sugar with few other nutrients provided. Other foods are not recommended.

Putting Dietary Guidelines into Practice

The first step in planning a diet requires knowledge of the number of kcalories that must be eaten daily to maintain ideal body weight. This can be done easily using a few simple calculations (Table 10.4). Ideally, women should weigh 100 pounds for the first five feet of height and five pounds for each additional inch, while men should weight 106 pounds for the first five feet of height and six pounds for each additional inch. Therefore, a 5'5" woman should weigh about 125 pounds, while a six foot tall man should weigh approximately 178 pounds. These weights can vary by 10 percent, resulting in a weight range for the woman of 112.5 to 137.5 pounds and 160 to 196 pounds for the man. Next, these ideal body weights are multiplied by 10 to determine the kcalories needed to supply basal energy requirements (see Chapter 8). Then a factor is added to supply kcalories for the day's activities. This moderately active female

---

Table 10.4. Calculation of Caloric Needs

1. Basal calories: desirable body weight × 10 = _____
2. Activity calories:
   Sedentary: desirable body weight × 3   = _____
   Moderate: desirable body weight × 5   = _____
   Strenous: desirable body weight × 10   = _____
3. Total calories to maintain ideal body weight:
   Basal calories + activity calories   = _____

needs 1,875 kcalories to maintain ideal body weight, while the man needs 3,650 because of participation in strenuous exercise five days per week. If either of these individuals needs to lose weight, 500 kcalories per day would be subtracted from these totals.

Once ideal body weight and the required number of kcalories per day have been determined, a decision can be made as to which set of dietary guidelines to follow. Usually, people who are overweight as well as individuals with high intakes of cholesterol and saturated fat do better with a more structured dietary plan such as the National Cholesterol Education Program Diet.

A person who is not overweight may simply want to estimate the number of kcalories needed to maintain his or her weight and then determine how many grams of fat make up 30 percent of kcalories. There is a shorthand way to do this that is accurate to within a gram or two of fat. For example:

> 2000 kcalories per day
> Drop the last zero = 200
> Divide by 3 = 67

An individual who needs 2000 kcalories per day should consume no more than 67 grams of fat. Dividing the grams of fat (67) by 3 will determine the amount of saturated fat permitted, in this case, 22 grams. Then by reading nutrition labels and U.S. Department of Agriculture tables, the amount of fat consumed can be determined. A person using this method also needs to remember the American Heart Association dietary guidelines presented earlier and to emphasize low-fat methods of food preparation (Table 10.5). Frying should be avoided, and foods that are boiled, roasted–baked, poached, steamed, and stir-fried should be emphasized. Meats should be trimmed of visible fat, and the skin of poultry needs to be removed before cooking. Low-fat dairy products should replace whole milk, high-fat cheese as well as premium ice creams. One important caveat for using this method is to make sure that any decrease in the number of kcalories coming from fatty foods is replaced by kcalories from other types of foods to maintain body weight. It is preferable to select complex carbohydrates to make up for any lost kcalories. Foods that are rich in complex carbohydrates include dried peas and beans, pasta, cereals, bread, rice, vegetables, and some fruits.

For those desiring a more formal diet plan, the National Cholesterol Education Program Step I Diet (NCEP, 1987) can be used. It is essentially the same as the American Heart Association Diet for the public. The major difference is that the NCEP Diet limits egg yolks to three per week, while the AHA Diet for normal healthy people permits three to four yolks per week. The NCEP Diet also has preset meal patterns for a number of caloric levels. A dietary plan for a person requiring 2000 kcalories per day to maintain ideal body weight would include the following:

Food Group	Daily Servings
Meat, poultry, seafood	6 ounces, cooked
Eggs, whole	3 per week
Dairy products	3 servings
Fat and oil	7 servings
Bread, cereal, pasta and starchy vegetables	7 servings
Vegetables	5 servings
Fruit	6 servings

Serving sizes are similar to those of the Basic Four Food Groups. A typical day's menu would be

Breakfast

Orange juice, 1 cup	2 servings fruit
Cornflakes, 1 cup	1 serving bread
Milk, 1%, 1 cup	1 serving dairy
Muffin (fat-modified recipe) 1	1 serving (each) bread and fat
Margarine, 1 teaspoon	1 serving fat

Lunch

Roast beef sandwich	
Roast beef, 3 ounces	3 ounces meat
Whole wheat bread, 2 slices	2 servings bread
Mayonnaise, 2 teaspoons	1 serving fat
Lettuce, 2 leaves	free
Carrot and celery sticks, 1 cup	1 serving vegetable

Table 10.5. Dietary Suggestions to Decrease Fat and Cholesterol

	Choose	Decrease
Fish, chicken, turkey, and lean meats	Fish; poultry without skin; lean cuts of beef, lamb, pork, or veal; shellfish	Fatty cuts of beef, lamb, or pork; spare ribs; organ meats; regular cold cuts; sausage; hot dogs; bacon; sardines; roe
Skim and low-fat milk, cheese, yogurt, and dairy substitutes	Skim or 1% fat milk (liquid, powdered, evaporated), buttermilk	Whole milk (4% fat); regular, evaporated, condensed; cream; half and half; 2% fat milk; imitation milk products; most nondairy creamers; whipped toppings
	Nonfat (0% fat) or low-fat yogurt	Whole-milk yogurt
	Low-fat cottage cheese (1% or 2% fat)	Whole-milk cottage cheese (4% fat)
	Low-fat cheeses; farmer or pot cheeses (all of these should be labeled no more than 2 to 6 g of fat per ounce)	All natural cheeses (e.g., blue, roquefort, camembert, cheddar, Swiss); low-fat or "light" cream cheese; low-fat or "light" sour cream; cream cheese; sour cream
	Sherbet, sorbet	Ice cream
Eggs	Egg whites (2 whites equal 1 whole egg in recipes); cholesterol-free egg substitutes	Egg yolks

Fruits and vegetables	Fresh, frozen, canned, or dried fruits and vegetables	Vegetables prepared in butter, cream, or other sauces
Breads and cereals	Homemade baked goods using unsaturated oils sparingly; angel food cake; low-fat crackers; low-fat cookies	Commercial baked goods; pies, cakes, doughnuts, croissants, pastries, muffins, biscuits, high-fat crackers, high-fat cookies
	Rice, pasta	Egg noodles
	Whole-grain breads and cereals (oatmeal, whole wheat, rye, bran, multigrain, etc.)	Breads in which eggs are a major ingredient
Fats and oils	Baking cocoa	Chocolate
	Unsaturated vegetable oils: corn, olive, rapeseed (canola oil), safflower, sesame, soybean, sunflower	Butter; coconut oil; palm oil; palm kernel oil; lard; bacon fat
	Margarine or shortenings made from one of the unsaturated oils listed above; diet margarine	
	Mayonnaise; salad dressings made with unsaturated oils listed above; low-fat dressings	Dressings made with egg yolk
	Seeds and nuts	Coconut

SOURCE: NCEP, 1987.

Sliced tomato, 1 medium with fresh basil	1 serving vegetable
Peach, fresh, 1 large	1 serving fruit
Dinner	
Baked chicken breast, 3 ounces	3 ounces meat
Steamed snow peas with tomato wedges and onion slices, 1½ cups	2 servings vegetables
Rice with mushrooms, 1 cup	2 servings bread
Margarine, 1 teaspoon	1 serving fat
Tossed green salad with carrot curls and dressing (olive oil, 2 teaspoons and vinegar)	1 serving vegetable 2 servings fat
Banana, 1	2 servings fruit
Ice milk, 1 cup	2 servings, dairy
Snack	
Graham crackers, 2	1 serving bread
Margarine, 1 teaspoon	1 serving fat
Apple juice, ½ cup	1 serving fruit

Convenience Foods for Fat-, Cholesterol-, and Kilocalorie-Controlled Diets

Although this diet does not require the purchase of any special foods, many people do enjoy them. These products add interest to the diet, and they are frequently used for their convenience. When selecting these foods, it is advisable to read the nutrition information on the label as some manufacturers use deceptive practices in labeling and advertising their products. For example, unreasonably small serving sizes are frequently used, such as a one ounce, raw weight serving of pork sausage. Another practice is to state the percentage of fat-free weight per 100 grams of the product. Seeing 94% Fat Free on a label is very enticing, but is meaningless in terms of the percentage of kcalories supplied by fat. The percentage of kcalories supplied by fat is the information the consumer really needs to know. At present, the term *cholesterol free* has a legal definition, i.e., the product has no cholesterol. However, the term cholesterol free provides no information about the amount and type of fat in a food, both of which can influence blood-cholesterol levels. Foods containing enormous quantities of fat, such as potato chips, are commonly labeled cholesterol free.

To eliminate such deceptive labeling practices, Congress passed the Nutrition Labeling and Education Act of 1990. The act required the FDA and the Department of Agriculture to devise a new nutrition label that would emphasize the fat, sodium, cholesterol, and sugar content of processed foods as well as their caloric values as both a typical portion and average daily kcalorie needs for adults, i.e., 2,000 kcalories for a woman and 2,500 kcalories for a man. Of greater importance, this act required the defining of numerous terms commonly used on the labels of processed foods. After considerable disagreement between then Secretary of Agriculture, Edward Madigan, and the FDA on the format of the new labels, President George Bush forged a compromise in December 1992, but implementation of the act was delayed (Chicago Tribune, 1992).

The new rules on food labeling contain 2,000 pages of regulations and definitions, and food manufacturers are required to follow them by May 1994 (Chicago Tribune, 1992). For the first time, terms such as free, low, reduced, less, and light/lite will have a legal definition. "Light" can appear on a label only if the fat content of the food has been reduced by 50 percent when compared to the standard product. However, foods such as bacon and mayonnaise are virtually all fat. Even a "light" version would still be considered a high-fat food. Low-calorie foods must have less than 40 kcalories per serving, and they can help in controlling total caloric intake, but the caloric source may be mostly fat. Reduced-calorie foods have one third less kcalories than a comparable standard product. Again, if the original food such as a chocolate torte is high fat, the reduced-kcalorie version can still contain considerable fat kcalories. Fortunately, much progress is being made in producing commercial bakery goods that are both shelf stable and palatable, and yet low in fat and cholesterol. Foods in these categories can do much to make a low-fat, low-cholesterol, and/or kcalorie-controlled diet more interesting. However, it must be remembered that they are not kcalorie free and cannot be eaten in unlimited quantities. Furthermore, they must not be eaten in place of fruits and vegetables or breads and cereals. Similar advice applies to the labeling of sodium-altered foods as well.

Why We Eat What We Eat

Why we eat what we eat is a complex issue, and we like certain foods and dislike others for even more complicated reasons. One fact is certain, knowledge of good nutritional habits does not guarantee that nutritious foods will be eaten. Food selection can be influenced by finances; state of health; lack of knowledge of food-preparation methods; mood, especially loneliness and anxiety; seasons of the year; convenience and availability; and even time. Although these factors can override food likes and dislikes in determining which foods are eaten, food preference is the most important factor in long-term dietary habits for most people.

Changing to a more healthful diet often involves substituting a disliked or less desirable food for a preferred one. In other words, food dislikes must be changed to food likes, and the desire for liked foods must be decreased. In order to change your food likes and dislikes, it is necessary to know why people have preferences in the first place. If asked the major reason for liking or disliking specific foods, most individuals reply that it is the flavor of the food that is the key. Psychological research indicates other factors are far more important. Additional facts cast doubt on flavor's importance to food preference: (1) Some adults and many children commonly decide they dislike foods before tasting them, and in some cases, before even seeing them; and (2) Often sensory qualities that are liked in the absolute are felt to be unfavorable qualities in food. Blue foods are highly undesirable, even though blue is a highly preferred color. In fact, blue is so distasteful when associated with food that many people find blue dinnerware unpleasant.

The development of food likes and dislikes is influenced by social and cultural mores; the individual's personality; the food's physical characteristics; and food's associations and meanings. Food meanings and associations represent attitudes toward the food itself, toward its sensory qualities, or toward the physical and social context in which it is served, including other people who serve or eat it. Most food dislikes develop because we think we dislike the food due to associations and ideas about the food rather than the way it tastes. The key to changing food preferences is changing our attitudes toward foods. Changing attitudes is difficult, but not impossible. The best way to accomplish this is to create new, positive associations for disliked foods (Lyman, 1989).

The advertising industry and many diet book authors are masters at finding positive associations that apply to large numbers of people. Despite the fact that oat bran had been on the market for some years, and research linking it with cholesterol reduction was published in *The Lancet* as long ago as 1963, it was not a very popular food until the book, *The 8-Week Cholesterol Cure* (Kowalski, 1987) was published. Oat bran is not a particularly eye-appealing or tasty food; it can cause gastrointestinal distress, and yet it was made appealing to several million Americans. Changing associations works best if individuals can personalize the new positive image. Trying to convince yourself to eat more fish by recalling the tasty fish dinners you had in Florida last year probably will not be successful if your trip was cut short by a hurricane. Associating fish with more pleasant memories such as eating freshly caught fish while on a family fishing trip is better than recalling a good fish dinner in an unpleasant situation.

Foods are disliked for at least four other reasons, three of which are relatively unimportant in avoiding foods. (1) A food may become boring and overly familiar if eaten very often. This applies to only a few foods and individuals. Fortunately it does not happen with most foods consumed frequently. Consider the number of times per week or per day that foods such as bread, potatoes, or orange juice are eaten without creating a dislike. (2) Some people develop a dislike for foods that cause allergic or other negative reactions; however, foods in this group are liked just as often as not. (3) A very few individuals may develop an intense dislike for foods associated with a physical illness or emotional–physical trauma. In this situation the food did not cause the problem, but accompanied the unpleasant experience by chance.

(4) The fourth reason foods are disliked, while not as important as food associations and meanings, is relatively important to eating

habits. Food is disliked after being tried because of taste or some other characteristic that results from the way in which it was prepared. If the food had been prepared and/or served in a different manner, it is very likely that the result would have been enjoyment rather than dislike. Plain boiled cauliflower is not a highly liked vegetable, but served raw with a dip, or breaded and french fried, cauliflower may be much more enjoyable. Even the notoriously despised liver is a delicatessen favorite when sold as chopped chicken livers or liver sausage. Failure to take into account this reason for food dislikes can result in major barriers to changing dietary habits.

If you are cutting down on salty snacks and high-fat foods, replacing them with fruits and vegetables is a desirable alternative. These replacements need to be made interesting to the palate. Avoiding overcooking, and adding flavor by using herbs, spices, and other flavoring agents such as wine and lemon juice are critical to success in substituting vegetables for porterhouse steak.

11

Can Nutrition Alter
the Aging Process?

The idea of increasing the life span elicits an interesting response from most people. In fact, the life span for Americans has increased significantly since 1900, due to the development of vaccines and antibiotics and changing life-styles that decrease the risk of death from heart disease, stroke, lung cancer, and infectious disease. Improvements in medical technology and earlier detection of some diseases have also contributed to increasing longevity. Despite much recent research on what our life span might be, the question remains unanswered, and at present it appears that there is little that can be done to repeat the dramatic increases in life span that occurred when bacterial infections were conquered in the early 1900s.

In the 1960s, much public attention was paid to the supposed longevity of a number of population groups that lived without modern medical science. The peasants of the Republic of Georgia were one such group. It was believed that many of these people lived to well over one hundred years of age, and the men regularly fathered children into their 90s. The key to their longevity was thought to be the amount of yogurt they consumed. The story of the Georgians was used to promote a national yogurt brand, and yogurt quickly moved into American supermarkets. Scientists began to take a closer look at the Georgians and quickly realized that they grossly exaggerated their ages. A typical Georgian died in his early 80s. Both the lay public and the scientific community lost interest in the life-style of these people.

Today we realize that scientists should not have abandoned their scrutiny of the Georgians so quickly. They were, in fact, living several years longer than Americans at the time, and the older members of the population were healthier than their American counterparts. It is now evident that the life-style of this group, i.e., exercise combined with a high-fiber, low-fat diet, contributed significantly to their freedom from chronic diseases that were thought to be an inevitable part of the aging process.

A number of health problems are still felt to be a "normal" part of aging. Bone loss and senile cataracts are thought to be inevitable at least for some people, but predicting which individuals and at what age is nearly impossible. Therefore, it would seem that as yet unrecognized factors influence the development of these and other typical problems of aging. The interrelationships among diet, nutritional status, and the aging process need to be explored. As a result, the U.S. Department of Agriculture funded the Human Nutrition Research Center on Aging at Tufts University in 1977. The first research efforts were begun in 1979, and Tufts has since become a major research center for nutrition and aging in the United States. The information presented in this chapter is based to a large extent on the research that has been conducted at Tufts, although other significant investigations have been included as well.

Cataracts

In testimony before the Congressional Subcommittee on Health and Long Term Care in October, 1985, the annual costs of cataract extractions and associated visits to physicians were estimated to be $3 to 5 billion. Each year more than 541,000 cataract extractions are performed in the United States, and with our aging population, the number and cost of these surgeries are rising and will continue to do so. The U.S. Department of Health and Human Services has estimated that if cataract development could be delayed by ten years, the need for lens extraction could be cut 50 percent. Furthermore, productivity and quality of life would be improved for individuals over 50 years of age.

The three major causes of cataracts in the United States are trauma, diabetes mellitus, and senile cataract. Obviously, influencing the public to wear protective eyewear when necessary, and individuals with diabetes to maintain control of their blood glucose, can decrease the risk of developing cataracts. Senile cataract, however, does not have a clear-cut cause, but many experts have attributed it to long-term exposure to ultraviolet rays present in sunlight. The ultraviolet light causes destruction of the proteins in the lens. Eventually, the proteins precipitate, forming the opacities known as cataracts.

Several nutrients are known to function as antioxidants. They have been studied both in terms of overall nutritional status and activity within the lens to determine their relationship to the incidence of cataract. One of the most promising of these nutrients is the carotenoid group (Jacques, 1988). Carotenoids are yellow-orange pigments, found in fruits and vegetables, that can be transformed into active vitamin A in the body. Beta-carotene, the best known of these pigments, is found in carrots, winter squash, and other vegetables. Individuals with higher serum levels of carotenoids are apparently protected against cataract development, but once a level of 3.3 micromoles/L (a very minute amount) is reached, no further protection is conferred (Taylor, 1989). The old advice that carrots are good for vision needs to be remembered in this connection.

Other antioxidant nutrients, such as vitamin C, vitamin E, and glutathione, appear to work together to delay cataract development (Taylor, 1989). Investigators who have studied each of these antioxidants independently have not produced consistent results, probably because they failed to allow for the actions of the others. Animal experiments show that liberal supplements of vitamins E or C confer protection against cataracts due to injury by ultraviolet light. However, excess vitamin C may increase the long-term risk of a rarely occurring type of cataract usually found only in diabetics (Bunce and Hess, 1988). Epidemiologic evidence does not indicate that there is an association between the serum levels of these nutrients and the risk of cataract development other than for individuals with vitamin C deficiency. However, at least two experts in the field believe that the serum levels of vitamin E in these studies were too low to influence the risk of cataract development. Bunce and Hess (1988) suggest that a supplement of more than 100 mg per day will help to delay the onset and slow the advance of cataracts. The current recommended daily allowance (RDA) for vitamin E is 10 mg, so some experts on vitamin E would not consider 100 mg per day to be a physiologic amount.

Glutathione is synthesized in the body from the nonessential amino acid, glutamic acid. The young lens is able to synthesize glutathione, but its level in cataracts is lower than that in the normal lens. Dietary intake of glutathione does not appear to increase the levels in the lens (Taylor, 1989). It is found in many foods, since it is present in most animal tissues and in yeast and plants.

Selenium is a nutrient closely related to the function of the antioxidant nutrients, especially glutathione. Research in the 1930s showed that selenium deficiency in animals caused cataracts, and selenium deficiency has also been associated with cataract development in humans. Surprisingly, recent epidemiologic evidence linked high levels of selenium to an increased risk of cataract development (Jacques et al., 1988). A second nutrient associated with the functioning of glutathione, riboflavin, has at times been linked to cataract development in both animals and humans. Early animal studies of the 1930s purported to use diets deficient in riboflavin to induce cataract development, but the diet was actually deficient in B-complex (Bunce and Hess, 1988). Recent epidemiologic research did not find an association between lower levels of riboflavin and cataract development, but did find an increased risk for individuals with high serum levels of B_6 (Jacques et al., 1988). Additionally, higher levels of vitamin D appear to decrease the risk of cataract development (Jacques et al., 1988).

Curiously, one deficiency offers protection from cataracts. Caloric restriction delays cataract formation in rats, increases the life span, and offers protection from a number of other diseases (Bunce and Hess, 1988). It appears that caloric restriction benefits people, too, as blood glucose levels are lower in these individuals (Taylor, 1989). People with the problem of lactose intolerance (see Chapter 5) appear to have an increased risk of developing cataracts. Some persons with primary lactose maldigestion absorb significant quantities of undigested lactose (Jacques *et al.*, 1988). One study even links excessive milk consumption with an increased risk of cataracts due to the absorption of large quantities of galactose, which is one of the two sugars present in lactose (Natow and Heslin, 1986). Both lactose and galactose may cause damage to the lens by drawing water into the lens.

Current research indicates that there is a relationship between diet, nutrient intake, serum levels of some nutrients, and the onset of senile cataracts. It is too early to advise the public to ingest large quantities of supplemental nutrients to prevent cataracts, but it is not too soon to follow the Dietary Guidelines for Americans, which states, "Choose a diet with plenty of vegetables, fruits and grain products," and "Maintain a healthy weight."

Osteoporosis and Bone Health

Loss of bone or osteoporosis is known to occur as the result of menopause (Type I) or aging (Type II). The loss occurs primarily in the hip, spine, forearms including the wrist, and handbones, and predisposes to a high incidence of fractures. Estrogen enhances calcium absorption and improves conservation of calcium by the kidney. Estrogen also affects calcium within the bone; it slows the breakdown that normally occurs as bone is remodeled, and it stimulates the secretion of calcitonin. Calcitonin is a hormone produced by the thyroid gland, which lowers serum calcium by slowing release of calcium from bone. At menopause, estrogen levels decrease dramatically, resulting in loss of calcium from the bone. Type I or postmenopausal osteoporosis occurs during the first five to ten years after menopause. There is greater loss of trabecular bone than of cortical bone and a low rate of bone turnover. In theory, most research has focused on this type of osteoporosis, but the later half of postmenopausal osteoporosis can overlap with Type II or senile osteoporosis. Type II usually occurs in individuals over 75 years of age. Both sexes are equally affected, and both trabecular and cortical bone is lost. Incidence rates nearly double every five years between 70 and 90 years of age (Paganini-Hill *et al.*, 1991).

Osteoporosis affects 24 million Americans and is responsible for 1.3 million bone fractures a year. It affects one-third to one-half of all postmenopausal women and nearly half of all elderly people older than 75. Because it is so common in postmenopausal women and in elderly persons of both sexes, osteoporosis is now a major public health problem (Kelsey, 1987).

Calcium

The amount of calcium needed to maintain healthy bone in postmenopausal women and all individuals over 50 years of age has been a controversial subject since the mid-1970s (Heaney, 1993a,b). Scientific evidence from numerous studies conducted into the early 1980s indicated that the RDA for calcium was too low for older individuals. Many experts on calcium nutrition expected the 1989 RDA to be set in the 1,000 to 1,500 mg per day range. This did not occur, because the Committee believed that osteoporosis is a medical rather than a nutritional problem. Because few longitudinal studies addressed the effects of calcium supplementation on bone loss directly, the Committee weighed heavily a 1987 study conducted in Denmark in which calcium supplements as high as 2,000 mg per day failed to prevent bone loss (Riis et al., 1987). There are a number of problems with attempting to apply this study to the U.S. population. As is the case with cardiovascular disease, osteoporosis is a multifactorial disease. Genetics and heredity are involved. Some individuals will develop the disease despite life-styles that decrease the risk, but their disease may occur later in life or be less severe than if they failed to follow a prudent life-style.

Scandinavian ancestry is a risk factor for developing osteoporosis in the United States. Scandinavians residing in their native countries have dietary patterns and life-style habits that are known to improve calcium nutriture and bone health. Calcium intake throughout life is considerably higher in Denmark than it is in the United States. The women in the Danish study were consuming an average of 950 mg of calcium per day before entry into the study. Conceivably, these women were already at their optimal intake of calcium. Additionally, physical activity and weight-bearing exercise were not considered in this study. Sedentary individuals are known to lose bone regardless of calcium intake, so it is vital to know the activity level of the study participants before attempting to apply these research findings to other population groups.

In the late 1970s, Heaney and his colleagues published numerous studies on calcium balance, i.e., the amount of calcium needed to replace losses from urine, feces, and sweat; (Heaney *et al.*, 1977, 1978, 1982; Recker *et al.*, 1977). Postmenopausal women needed 1,500 mg of calcium per day to replace these losses, while premenopausal women and estrogen-treated postmenopausal women required 1,000 mg per day to compensate for losses. Studies carried out on elderly individuals also have shown calcium needs of 1,000 mg or more per day.

Relating bone loss to calcium intake has been more difficult, but it must be remembered that early research showed that estrogen was unimportant to bone health. In 1987, Dawson-Hughes showed that healthy middle-aged women with low calcium intake lost more bone from the spine than women with calcium intakes greater than 777 mg per day. Although individuals with calcium intakes as high as 1000 mg per day still lost spinal bone, Dawson-Hughes's research does not demonstrate the inevitability of bone loss even with higher calcium intakes (Dawson-Hughes *et al.*, 1987, 1988). Vitamin D intake was inadequate in some participants, but vitamin D status was not assessed. Assessment of any other factor known to influence calcium nutrition or bone health was not done. In a follow-up study, published in 1990, Dawson-Hughes was able to increase the amount of bone in late-menopausal women by supplementing the diet with 500 mg of calcium (Dawson-Hughes *et al.*, 1990). In these women, only the spine continued to lose bone, but the amount of bone lost was considerably below the expected rate of one percent per year. Furthermore, these women were shown to be somewhat physically active, but no assessment of weight-bearing exercises was done. In 1989, Smith *et al.* found that four years of supplementation with 1.5 g calcium carbonate per day reduced bone loss in postmenopausal women. However, only the bones of the arm were used to determine bone mineral status. The results may not apply to the spine (Smith *et al.*, 1989). Comparing these studies is difficult due to the difference in bones used, and these differences are the basis for a major controversy in osteoporosis research.

A study that has largely been ignored because it monitored only forearm bone showed increasing calcium intake from 700 mg per day to 1400 mg per day stopped bone loss (Polley et al., 1987). This study is significant because the investigators attempted to address some of the complex issues involved in bone loss. First, they monitored all participants for nine months to make sure that they were losing bone at a comparable and significant rate. Then they used several different forms of calcium supplementation including dairy products, which increase vitamin D intake as well. The subjects were told to consume the supplements in a manner that ensured optimal absorption. Additionally, one group was placed on sodium restriction as high-sodium intake increases calcium excretion. Finally, the participants were closely monitored for compliance. The one problem with this study was the fact that the participants not receiving supplements stopped losing bone during part of the study. This occurred because a number of the participants were ten years postmenopausal. Having this situation occur makes it very difficult to demonstrate the effectiveness of additional calcium. Nonetheless, the investigators were able to make the following recommendation: normal postmenopausal women within ten years of menopause, and whose calcium intake is below 1,000 mg daily, on increasing the intake to about 1,400 mg, almost certainly reduced the rate of bone loss in the forearm.

This study illustrates a major problem with research into bone loss, namely, selection of the calcium source. Calcium carbonate is frequently used because it contains the most calcium, 40 percent, is inexpensive, and is readily available. However, calcium carbonate in large amounts causes unpleasant gastrointestinal side effects that lead to questions of compliance among study participants. Furthermore, it requires hydrochloric acid from the stomach if it is to be absorbed. As many elderly individuals lack gastric acid, the absorbability of calcium carbonate becomes a problem. Additionally, there are differences in dissolvability between brands (Sheikh and Fordtan, 1990). Some manufacturers have so compressed the tablets to make them easier to swallow, that they pass through the gastrointestinal tract undigested. Recently, a new calcium supplement became available, calcium citrate malate. It is superior to calcium carbonate in absorbability, and in postmenopausal women with low calcium intakes, it was also superior in halting bone loss (Miller, 1988; Dawson-Hughes, 1990).

In a study conducted in New Zealand, Reid et al. (1993), found that white women who had reached menopause more than three years earlier and who took 1,000 mg of calcium a day in addition to what they were getting in their food, reduced bone loss at multiple sites by one-third to one-half. The calcium was in the form of 5.24 g of calcium lactate–gluconate and 0.8 g of calcium carbonate, formulated as an effervescent tablet.

Dietary Calcium and the Risk of Kidney Stones

About 10 percent of men and 3 percent of women have a kidney stone during their adult life. About 80 percent of all stones are composed of calcium oxalate alone or with a nucleus of calcium phosphate (apatite).

For years, physicians have urged victims to avoid milk and other products that are rich in calcium. This situation presents a dilemma for adults who, on the one hand, are advised to avoid large intakes of calcium to offset kidney stone formation and, on the other hand, to increase their intake to offset osteoporosis. Now, however, in a study of 45,619 men, 40 to 75 years of age, who had no prior history of kidney stones, dietary calcium intake was found to be inversely associated with the risk of stone formation (Curhan et al., 1993). In other words, a high calcium intake decreases the incidence of kidney stones.

Although the tests involved men only, the authors state that they see no reason to believe that the relationships would be different for women, younger men, or men who have had a previous kidney stone.

Vitamin D

The RDA for vitamin D is set at 5 mg (200 IU) for all individuals above 24 years of age. This is based on limited data involving the treatment of individuals with clinical vitamin D deficiency and presumes that most people have enriched stores due to regular exposure to sunlight at least during certain times of the year (RDA, 1989). It also assumes that individuals are the same at 80 years of age as they are at 51, and that previous intake of vitamin D has been adequate. In fact, most individuals in the United States consume less than desirable amounts of vitamin D. Females typically consume less vitamin D than do males. The average adult female consumes 1.5 mg (60 IU) according to the United States Department of Agriculture, and older females consume even less (RDA, 1989). A 1982 study of 60- to 93-year-old women showed that older women take in only 1.35 mg (54 IU) of vitamin D per day (Omdahl *et al.*, 1982). Fifteen of these women had plasma levels of 25-(OH)D, (a metabolite of vitamin D formed in the liver), which is suggestive of deficiency. Some investigators believe that older individuals have difficulty converting 25-(OH)D to the active form of the vitamin. If this is true, the actual number of women with vitamin D deficiency is considerably higher.

Typically, vitamin D deficiency causes osteomalacia, a form of rickets in adults. According to the 1989 RDA Committee, this is a rare occurrence in the United States. However, there is evidence linking vitamin D deficiency to occult osteomalacia and the hip fractures that are characteristic of one form of osteoporosis. In Great Britain, 30 to 40 percent of the elderly are deficient in vitamin D at the time they experience their first hip fractures (Webb *et al.*, 1988). Similar observations have been made in Boston. Individuals living in Boston (42.2° N latitude) are not exposed to sufficient ultraviolet light from November through April to synthesize adequate amounts of vitamin D in the skin. The further north one lives, the more months there are with insufficient ultraviolet light. At 52° N latitude, which includes Edmonton, Alberta, Canada, the period extends from October through March. Ultraviolet light is sufficient during the winter months to synthesize vitamin D as far north as 34° N latitude, but older individuals need increased exposure to sunlight to form sufficient vitamin D_3 to make up for low dietary intake. The skin of older individuals has less 7-DHC (7-dehydrocholesterol) for conversion to vitamin D_3 (cholecalciferol) than the skin of younger people (Webb *et al.*, 1988). As a result, older individuals with limited exposure to sun tend to have low levels of 25-(OH)D. More research needs to be done before determining whether increasing the exposure to ultraviolet light is more desirable than increasing the dietary intake.

Research studies conducted on animals show that both the lack of estrogen and aging per se decrease the kidney's ability to activate vitamin D. Giving supplements of the active form of vitamin D does increase calcium absorption and the body's store of calcium, but its effect on osteoporosis remains to be demonstrated. Supplementation may not increase the amount of bone, but rather improve the quality. Some studies on individuals with fractures due to osteoporosis have demonstrated a decrease in the number of fractures without increasing the amount of bone present. In addition to increasing calcium absorption, activated vitamin D has a direct effect on bone. At low doses it stimulates formation of new bone, but at high doses, bone is broken down. This latter effect may be the reason that the 150,000 IU per week commonly given to osteoporosis patients 15 years ago did not improve their disease (SGR, 1988).

In an editorial in the *New England Journal of Medicine*, Heaney (1993b) states "It therefore seems prudent to increase the intake of calcium and vitamin D in most postmenopausal women—calcium to at least 1,000 mg and preferably to 1,500 mg per day and vitamin D to 400 to 800 IU daily—without waiting for more information."

Other Nutrients

Recent studies have shown that pharmacological doses of fluoride (50 mg per day) have a role in the treatment of women with spinal osteoporosis (Pak *et al.*, 1989). Women given a slow-release form of sodium fluoride on a cyclic basis for five years showed a marked increase in the amount of spinal bone. Surprisingly, the women in the study who were also given active vitamin D did not do as well, but both groups avoided the serious complications that can accompany fluoride therapy, such as hip fracture. Fluoride's role in the prevention of osteoporosis is less clear as higher levels of calcium intake block absorption of fluoride. The interactions of fluoride with the many other minerals found in bone have yet to be defined. These interactions may explain the conflicting reports on the incidence of osteoporosis in areas with naturally fluoridated water.

High sodium intake increases the excretion of calcium in the urine, but only a few studies have assessed the relationship between sodium intake and bone loss (SGR, 1988). These studies indicate an association with bone loss. Like sodium, zinc, silicon, and copper also influence the metabolism of calcium and bone mineralization (RDA, 1989). Whether or not deficiencies of these nutrients are important in the development of osteoporosis remains to be investigated. Boron deficiency may prove to be a risk factor for osteoporosis, especially when combined with low intakes of calcium, magnesium, and vitamin D. Boron increases calcium absorption and conservation by the kidneys. Giving boron supplements to postmenopausal women increased the serum estrogen levels and improved their calcium status. Depriving older individuals of boron for 63 days resulted in decreased serum levels of calcitonin and 25-(OH)D (Nielsen, 1988, 1990). At present, there is no RDA for boron because too little is known about human needs, but researchers believe that 1 mg per day will assure optimal health. Boron is found in foods of plant origin, fruits, leafy vegetables, nuts, and legumes.

Immune Function

Immune function declines as part of the aging process. This decline can contribute to the increased occurrence of infectious disease and cancer observed in the elderly. Furthermore, other diseases commonly thought of as age-associated degenerative diseases, such as rheumatoid arthritis, may be related to changes in the way in which the immune system functions. Early studies on the interrelationship between nutrition and immune function in the elderly looked at the occurrence of various nutritional deficiencies known to cause problems with the functioning of the immune system. Although some elderly people do have low intakes of a number of nutrients known to be necessary for a healthy immune system, in most instances the deficiency is not severe enough to produce a significant decline. More current research has focused on using diet and nutrition as a practical approach to intervening in age-related declines in immune function (Meydani et al., 1989a). Individual nutrients with known or potential roles in the immune system are being investigated to determine whether altering their intake can affect immune function. In the process, as yet unrecognized nutritional influences on the immune system are being elucidated, and new insights are being made into the interactions among nutrients. At present, most of this research is still at the level of basic scientific understanding rather than clinical application.

Large amounts of the nutrient being studied are used to keep the group being studied small and to look for unknown adverse reactions, or for effects that are druglike rather than nutritional. Positive research findings are not an indication that the investigator is suggesting that all older individuals should be consuming that amount of the nutrient. However, positive research findings are indications that individuals should be consuming adequate amounts of the nutrient being studied.

Research studies using animals have shown that restricting kcalories, if begun at a young age, delays many age-related changes. Life span is increased by as much as 50 percent, and chronic diseases common in laboratory animals occur later in their lives (Lipschitz, 1990). One of the prominent features of the longevity of these animals is the preservation of the immune system and the accompanying delay in the appearance of tumors. While most experts agree caloric restriction is of benefit to people, demonstrating the effect is difficult if not impossible. In Third World nations, where caloric intake is low, many individuals suffer from malnutrition, which adversely affects immune function. In the United States, few people voluntarily restrict kcalories. The studies that have been done use body weight as an indication of calorie intake. Recent data compiled by the National Institute on Aging (Elsasser, 1991), showed that being a bit above average weight is desirable. In fact, body weight is determined by a number of factors in addition to kcalories, including the amount of exercise and the presence of latent disease. Furthermore, it is possible to be of desirable weight and still be malnourished. A University of Texas physiologist, Roger McCarter, discussed the weight studies at a Washington, DC conference on "Diet and Health—Where is America Going?" He said, "We believe there is strong evidence that in the presence of a nutritionally adequate diet, body weight is not the critical factor for health and longevity, rather, daily caloric input is" (Elsasser, 1991).

Much promising research is being done using antioxidant nutrients to improve immune function. These same nutrients appear to delay the aging of other cells as well. Vitamin E levels are known to decrease with age (Meydani *et al.*, 1989a). Supplementation of healthy elderly individuals improves their serum levels of vitamin E and results in improvement in T cell–mediated immune responses

(Meydani, 1988, 1989b). The degree of improvement was not the same for all individuals. Some showed no improvement at all. Glutathione levels are known to decrease in body tissues as part of the aging process. Some investigators believe that these low levels may be responsible for some aspects of the aging process including partial responsibility for declines in the immune system (Meydani *et al.*, 1989a,c). It is not believed to be an essential nutrient because the body makes it from the sulfur-containing amino acids, but it may be essential for older persons. Glutathione supplementation increases tissue levels and improves immune function (Meydani *et al.*, 1989c). Selenium is required for the glutathione-containing enzyme to perform its antioxidant function, and selenium deficiency causes impaired function of the immune system. Giving laboratory animals supplements of selenium improves their ability to fight infectious disease and has an antitumor effect (Sherman and Hallquist, 1990).

The absorption and metabolism of selenium is tied to vitamin C (Martin, 1989). Apparently its absorption is not regulated by the selenium status of the individual and is influenced by the presence of or lack of vitamin C. Selenium absorption and retention were decreased when dietary vitamin C was limited to 20 mg per day. Supplementing the diet with one gram of ascorbic acid per day increased its absorption and resulted in a larger metabolic pool of selenium. But other researchers believe that this much vitamin C is detrimental to selenium absorption (Robinson *et al.*, 1985). One study showed that selenium absorption was improved by giving a selenium supplement with 200 ml of orange juice. That is about ¾ cup of juice containing approximately 60 mg of ascorbic acid, the current RDA for vitamin C. The key to how much vitamin C is needed to assure optimal absorption of selenium appears to be the individual's nutritional status with regard to vitamin C. If vitamin C intake has been adequate, 60 mg of vitamin C enhances selenium intake. But if the diet has been deficient in vitamin C for some time, extra vitamin C may be needed, and individuals who have been using large amounts of the vitamin for extended periods may be adversely affecting the absorption of selenium (Martin *et al.*, 1989).

Declines in the immune system that occur with aging and with zinc deficiency are similar, but most older individuals appear to have adequate zinc stores to prevent problems with immune function.

Attempts to improve immune function in older individuals have been successful when very high doses of zinc were given (Meydani *et al.*, 1989c). At present this appears to be a druglike effect (see Chapter 9), but there are other possible explanations. Perhaps the high doses of zinc needed to improve immune function compensate for the deficiency of other nutrients with which zinc interacts. More research is needed to determine how zinc supplementation improves immune function in older persons.

Exercise

Many age-related chronic diseases such as hypertension, cardiovascular disease, and non–insulin-dependent diabetes are influenced by both diet and exercise. As knowledge of the aging process continues to expand, it is becoming apparent that the increase in body fat and decrease in muscle that accompany aging are not a normal part of the aging process. Body composition changes are, rather, the result of deconditioning due to voluntary declines in physical activity (Evans, 1989). This deconditioning negatively affects the quality of life of elderly individuals and can affect their capacity to lead independent lives. Studies have shown that individuals who have exercised throughout their life live longer and suffer less from the debilitation of aging. Recent research shows that elderly individuals who have spent years living a sedentary life-style can benefit from aerobic and strength training (Fiatarone *et al.*, 1989).

Older individuals have nearly the same ability to respond to aerobic exercise training as younger individuals. Twelve weeks of aerobic changes produced significant increases in aerobic capacity in elderly men and women without increasing the amount of muscle or decreasing total body fat content (Meredith *et al.*, 1989). Both young and old individuals increase oxygen consumption by the same amount after similar training, despite the fact that older sedentary individuals use less oxygen than younger sedentary individuals. Younger persons increase their aerobic capacity by increasing the amount of blood pumped by the heart. Older people, however, increase their aerobic capacity by improving the muscle's ability to extract oxygen from the vascular system. The increased use of oxygen by muscle occurs as the muscle increases in ability to store glycogen and to utilize it for energy.

Despite the age-related differences in the way the body increases the capacity to perform oxygen-requiring work, older individuals have the same capacity to respond to aerobic conditioning as younger people. They also retain the ability to respond to strength conditioning. Subjecting 12 healthy, untrained older men to 12 weeks of resistance training increased both the size and strength of their muscles (Frontera *et al.*, 1988). Similar results have occurred even in frail, chronically institutionalized persons over 90 years of age. After resistance training of thigh muscles, these individuals had improved ability to walk, as well as increased muscle strength and size.

Exercise may improve the functioning of the immune system. Many of the body's responses to infectious agents are similar to those that occur in the first few hours after exercise (Cannon *et al.*, 1989). Plasma proteins and hormones are altered to patterns like those occurring with infection. Certain leukocytes are mobilized and activated. One of these is the natural killer cell, a type of lymphocyte important in cell-mediated immunity. The chemical mediators with which leukocytes communicate and influence metabolism increase. Increases in interferon activity have been observed. Unaccustomed exercise that results in next-day muscle pain and stiffness is the result of exercise-induced muscle damage. Such damage causes an inflammatory response within the muscle that is similar to one induced by infectious agents. The muscle becomes edematous, certain leukocytes that digest cellular debris congregate in the area, and the chemical mediators of this process increase within the muscle. While the whole-body response to exercise lasts only hours, immune system activity within the muscle can last for days. Research demonstrating whether or not exercise can bolster the immune system's ability to prevent infection in the elderly remains to be done, but numerous well-trained, young athletes report fewer episodes of upper respiratory tract infections and flu as well as briefer recovery times. Perhaps the effect of exercise on the immune system is the source of their better health.

Exercise affects hormone levels and bone health in older people (Nelson *et al.*, 1988). Endurance training of women increases their aerobic capacity while decreasing their body weight and body fat.

Additionally, their estrogen and parathyroid hormone levels are lower than those in sedentary individuals. Although these two latter factors are known risk factors for osteoporosis, their bone mineral density is greater not only in the femur and lower spine, which are the weight-bearing bones, but also in the radius bone of the arm. The increase in bone density is believed to be due to higher levels of 1-25(OH) vitamin D, somatomedin-C, and growth hormone that result from the endurance training. In addition, calcium absorption may have been improved by the extra kcalories consumed as carbohydrates by these women.

References

Chapter 1

American Association of Retired Persons (AARP). *A Profile of Older Americans: 1985.* AARP Publication PF3049 (1085), D996. Amer. Assoc. Retired Persons, Washington, DC, 1985.

Barinaga, M. How long is the human life span? *Science* 254:936–938, 1991.

Barinaga, M. Mortality: Overturning received wisdom. *Science* 258:398–399, 1992.

Birren, J.E. Research on the psychology of aging: Principles and experimentations, in *Handbook of Psychology of Aging*, (J.E. Birren and K.W. Schaie, eds.), Van Nostrand Reinhold Co., New York, 1977.

Bray, G.A. Obesity, in *Present Knowledge in Nutrition*, 6th ed. (M.L. Brown, ed.), International Life Sciences Institute, Nutrition Foundation, Washington, DC, 1990, p. 26.

Brody, J.A. Epidemiological and statistical characteristics of the United States elderly population, in *Handbook of the Biology of Aging* (C.E. Finch and E. Schneider, eds.), Van Nostrand Reinhold, New York, 1985, pp. 3–26.

Carey, J.R. *et al.* Slowing of mortality rates at older ages in large medfly cohorts. *Science* 258:457–461, 1992.

Chatfield, W.F. Economic and sociological factors influencing life satisfaction of the aged. *J. Gerontol* 32:593–599, 1977.

Chauhan, J. *et al.* Age-related olfactory and taste changes and interrelationships between taste and nutrition. *J. Am. Diet Assoc.* 87(11):1543–1550, 1987.

Chicago Tribune. Chicago, IL, business section, Mar. 22, 1991.

Cutler, R.G. Antioxidants and aging. *Am. J. Clin. Nutr.* 53:373S–379S, 1991.

Davidson, S. *et al.* The nutrition of a group of apparently healthy aging persons. *J. Clin. Nutr.* 10:191–199, 1962.

Fanelli, J.T. Nutrient intakes and health status of older Americans: Data from NHANES II. *Ann. N.Y. Acad. Sci.* 561:94–103, 1989.

Garetz, F.K. Breaking dangerous cycle of depression and faulty nutrition. *Geriatrics* 31:73–75, 1976.

Hall, E. Acting one's age: New rules for the old. *Psychol. Today* 9(1):66, 1980.

Harmon, D. Free radical theory of aging: Role of free radicals in the origination and evolution of life, aging and disease process, in *Free Radicals, Aging and Degenerative Diseases*, (J.E. Johnson, Jr., R. Walford, D. Harmon, and J. Miquel, eds.), Alan R. Liss, Inc., New York, 1986.

Hathcock, J. Nutrient–drug interactions. *Clin. Geriatr. Med* 3(2):297–308, 1987.

Hayflick, L. Current theories on biological aging. *Fed. Proc.* 34(1):9, 1975.

Holden, D.C. Poverty and living arrangements among older women: Are changes in economic well-being underestimated? *J. Gerontol.* 43:S22–S27, 1988.

Hurd, M.D. The economic status of the elderly. *Science* 244:659–664, 1989.

Kane, R.L. Long-term care: Policy and reimbursement, in *Geriatric Medicine*, Vol. 2, (C.K. Cassel and J.R. Walsh, eds.), Springer-Verlag, New York, 1984, pp. 380–396.

Kowall, N.W. *et al.* An in vivo model for the neurodegenerative effects of beta-amyloid and protection by substance P. *Proc. Natl. Acad. Sci. U.S.A.* 88:7247–7251, 1991.

Letsov, A.P. and Price. Health, aging and nutrition: An overview. *Clin. Geriatric Med.* 3(2):253–260, 1987.

Masoro, E.J. Nutrition and aging—a current assessment. *J. Nutr.* 115:842–848, 1985.

Mayer, J. Aging and nutrition. *Geriatrics* 29(5)57–59, 1974.

McCay, C.M. *et al.* The effect of retarded growth upon the length of the lifespan and upon the ultimate body size. *J. Nutr.* 10:63–79, 1935.

McGandy, R.B. Nutrition and the aging cardiovascular system. Bristol-Meyers Nutrition Symposium, 1986, in *Nutrition and Aging*, Vol. 5 (M. Hutchinson and H.N. Munro, eds.), Academic Press, Orlando, FL, 1986, pp. 263–275.

National Center for Health Statistics (NCHS). *Characteristics of Nursing Home Residents, Health Status and Care Received*: National Nursing Home Survey. Vital Health Statistics, Series 13, No. 51. PHS Publication No. 81–1712, 1981.

National Center for Health Statistics (NCHS). *Blood Pressure Levels in Persons 18–74 Years of Age in 1976–1980 and Trends in Blood Pressure from 1960–1980 in the United States*. Vital and Health Statistics, Series 11, PHS Publication No. 234, 1986.

National Center for Health Statistics (NCHS). *Health, United States, 1987*. DHHS Publication No. (PHS)88–1232, U.S. Government Printing Office, Washington, DC, 1988.

National Institute on Aging (NIA). *Differential Diagnosis of Dementing Diseases*. National Institutes of Health Consensus Development Conference Statement, Vol. 6, No. 11, July 6–8, 1987.

Nielsen, J. *et al.* Follow-up 15 years after a geronto-psychiatric prevalence study. *J. Gerontol* 32:554–561, 1977.

Olshansky, S.J. *et al.* In search for Methuselah: Estimating the upper limits to human longevity. *Science* 250:634–640, 1990.

Russell, R.M. Implications of gastric atrophy for vitamin and mineral nutriture. Bristol-Meyers Nutrition Symposia, 1986, in *Nutrition and Aging*, Vol. 5, (M. Hutchinson and H.N. Munro, eds.), Academic Press, Orlando, FL, 1986, pp. 56–59.

Sandman, P. *et al.* Nutritional status and dietary intake in institutionalized patients with Alzheimer's disease and multi-infarct dementia. *J. Am. Geriatr. Soc.* 35:31–38, 1987.

Slesinger, D.P. *et al.* Food patterns in an urban population: Age and sociodemographic correlates. *J. Gerontol* 35:432–438, 1980.

Smith, E.L. *et al.* Diet, exercise and chronic disease patterns in older adults. *Nutr. Rev.* 46(2): 52–61, 1988.

Strehler, B.L. *Time, Cells and Aging*, 2nd ed. Academic Press, New York, 1977.

Todhunter, E.N. Lifestyle and nutrient intake in elderly. *Curr. Concepts Nutr.* 4:119–127, 1976.

U.S. Bureau of the Census. *Statistical Abstract of the United States*, ed. 108, p. 77, Government Printing Office, Washington, DC, 1988.

U.S. Department of Health, Education and Welfare (DHEW). *Preliminary Findings of the First Health and Nutrition Examination Survey. United States, 1971–72. Dietary intake and biochemical findings.* DHEW Publication No. (HRA) 74-1219-1, Government Printing Office, Washington, DC, 1974.

U.S. Senate. 1987/88. U.S. Senate Special Committee on Aging—1988. *Aging America: Trends and Projections.* LR3377(188), D12198. Dept. of Health and Human Services, Washington, DC, 1988.

Weindruch, R. *The Retardation of Aging and Disease by Dietary Restriction.* Thomas, Springfield, IL, 1988.

Widgor, B. and Morris. A comparison of 20-year medical histories of individuals with depressive and paranoid states: A preliminary note. *J. Gerontol.* 32:160–163, 1977.

World Health Organization (WHO). *Statistical yearbook*, 1991.

Yankner, B.A. *et al.* Neurotrophic and neurotoxic effects of amyloid beta protein: Reversal by tachykinin neuropeptides. *Science* 250:279–282, 1990.

Zarit, S.H. *Aging and Mental Disorders: Psychological Approaches and Assessment and Treatment.* The Free Press, New York, 1980.

Chapter 2

Bowman, B.B. Assessment of nutritional status of the elderly. *Am. J. Clin. Nutr.* 35:1142–1151, 1982.

Chauhan, J. *et al.* Age-related olfactory and taste changes and interrelationships between taste and nutrition. *J. Am. Diet Assoc.* 87(11):1543–1550, 1987.

Cheng, A.H.R. *et al.* Comparative nitrogen balance study between young and aged adults using three levels of protein intake from a combination wheat–soy–milk mixture. *Am. J. Clin. Nutr.* 31:12–22, 1978.

Clydesdale, F.M. Meeting the needs of the elderly with the foods of today and tomorrow. *Nutr. Today* 26(5):13–20, 1991.

Frisancho, A.R. New standards of weight and body composition by frame size and height for assessment of nutritional status of adults and the elderly. *Am. J. Clin. Nutr.* 40:808–819, 1984.

Gersovitz, M. *et al.* Human protein requirements; assessment of the adequacy of the current recommended dietary allowance for dietary protein in elderly men and women. *Am. J. Clin. Nutr.* 35:6–14, 1982.

Guthrie, H.A. Nutrient requirements of the elderly, in *Health Promotion and Disease Prevention in the Elderly* (R. Chernoff and D. Lifschitz, eds.), Raven Press, New York, 1988, pp. 33–43.

Irwin, M.I. A conspectus of research on protein requirements of man. *J. Nutr.* 101:387–429, 1971.

Morley, J.E. Nutritional status of the elderly. *Am. J. Med.* 81:679–695, 1986.

Munro, H.N. *et al.* Protein nutriture of a group of free-living elderly. *Am. J. Clin. Nutr.* 46:568–592, 1987.

National Research Council (NRC). *Diet and Health: Implications for Reducing Chronic Disease Risk.* Report of the Committee on Diet and Health, Food and Nutrition Board, 750 pp. National Academy Press, Washington, DC, 1989.

Ostlund, R.E. *et al.* The ratio of waist-to-hip circumference, plasma insulin level, and glucose intolerance, as independent predictors of the HDL_2 cholesterol levels in older adults. *N. Engl. J. Med.* 322(4):229–234, 1990.

Recommended Dietary Allowances (RDA), 10th ed. Food and Nutrition Board, National Research Council, National Academy Press, Washington, DC, 1989.

Smith, E.L. *et al.* Diet, exercise, and chronic disease patterns in older adults. *Nutr. Rev.* 46(2):52–61, 1988.

Surgeon General's Report on Nutrition and Health (SGR). U.S. DHHS, (PHS) publication No. 88-50210; U.S. Government Printing Office, Washington, DC, 1988.

Uauy, R. *et al.* The changing pattern of whole body protein metabolism in aging humans. *J. Gerontol.* 33:663–671, 1978a.

Uauy, R. *et al.* Human protein requirements: Nitrogen balance response to graded levels of egg protein in elderly men and women. *Am. J. Clin. Nutr.* 31:779–785, 1978b.

U.S. Department of Agriculture (USDA). *Nutrient Intakes; Individuals in 48 States, Year 1977–78.* Report No. 1–2. Consumer Nutrition Division, Human Nutrition Information Service, Hyattsville, MD, 1984.

U.S. Department of Health and Human Services (DHHS). *Dietary Intake Source Data. United States, 1976–80.* Vital and Health Statistics, Series 11, No. 231. DHHS Publication No. (PHS)83-1681, 1983.

U.S. Department of Health, Education, and Welfare (DHEW). *Dietary Intake Source Data: United States, 1971–74.* DHEW Publication No. (PHS) 79-1221. U.S. Government Printing Office, Washington, DC, 1979.

Wright, H.S. *et al.* The 1987–88 nationwide food consumption survey: An update on the nutrient intake of respondents. *Nutr. Today* 26(3):21–27, 1991.

Zanni, E. *et al.* Protein requirements for elderly men. *J. Nutr.* 109:513–524, 1979.

Chapter 3

Altchul, Z. *et al.* Influences of nicotinic acid on serum cholesterol in man. *Arch. Biochem. Biophys.* 54:558–559, 1955.

Blumberg, J.B. cited in *AARP Bull.* 31(3):8, March, 1990.

Blumberg, J.B. Changing nutrient requirements in older adults. *Nutr. Today* 25(5):15–20, 1992.

Canner, P.L. *et al.* Fifteen-year mortality in Coronary Drug Project patients: Long-term benefit with niacin. *J. Am. Coll. Cardiol.* 8:1245–1255, 1986.

Chandra, R.K. Effect of vitamin and trace element supplementation on immune response and infection in elderly subjects. *Lancet* 340:1124–1127, 1992.

Cohen, L.A. Diet and cancer. *Sci. Am.* 257(5):42–48, 1987.

Dallman, P.R. *et al.* Prevalence and causes of anemia in the United States, 1976–1980. *Am. J. Clin. Nutr.* 39:437–445, 1984.

DeMaeyer, E. *et al.* The prevalence of anemia in the world. *World Health Stat. Q.* 38:302–316, 1985.

Funk, C. *State Medicine* 20:341, 1912; see reprint of this paper on p. 145 of Goldblith, S.A. and Joslyn, M.A. *Milestones in Nutrition*, Avi Publishing Co., Westport, CT, 1964.

Funk, C. *Die Vitamine*, Wiesbaden, Germany, 1914; republished in English, 1922. See, also, Todhunter, E.N., *J. Am. Diet. Assoc.* 52:432, 1968.

Gillooly, M. *et al.* The effects of organic acids, phytates and polyphenols on the absorption of iron from vegetables. *Br. J. Nutr.* 49:331–342, 1983.

Hopkins, F.G. Feeding experiments illustrating the importance of accessory factors in normal dietaries. *J. Physiol. (London)* 44:425–460, 1912.

Horwitt, M.K. *et al.* *Investigations of Human Requirements for B-Complex Vitamins.* Bulletin of the National Research Council No. 116. Report of the Committee on Nutritional Aspects of Aging, Food and Nutrition Board, National Academy of Sciences, Washington, DC, 1948.

Iber, F.I., *et al.* Thiamine in the elderly—relation to alcoholism and to neurological degenerative disease. *Am. J. Clin. Nutr.* 36:1067–1082, 1982.

Intersalt Cooperative Research Group. Intersalt: An international study of electrolyte excretion and blood pressure: Results for 24-hour urinary sodium and potassium excretion. *Br. Med. J.* 297:319–328, 1988.

Lunin, N. Dissertation, Univ. Dorpat, Estonia, 1880 (see p. 204 in McCollum, E.V. *A History of Nutrition*. Boston, Houghton Mufflin Co., 1957). Published (German) *Z. Physiol. Chemie* 5:31, 1881.

Mayer, J. Aging and nutrition. *Geriatrics* 29(5):57–59, 1974.

National Research Council (NRC). *Selenium in Nutrition*, rev. ed., National Academy Press, Washington, DC, 1983.

Page, L.B. Epidemiologic evidence on the etiology of human hypertension and its possible prevention. *Am. Heart J.* 91:527–534, 1976.

Page, L.B. Hypertension and atherosclerosis in primitive and acculturating societies,

Hypertension Update, Vol. 1 (J.C. Hunt, ed.), Health Learning Systems, Lyndhurst, NJ, 1979, pp. 1–12.

Pauling, L. *How to Live Longer and Feel Better.* W. H. Freeman and Co., New York, 1986.

Pilch, S.M. *Assessment of the Iron Nutritional Status of the U.S. Population Based on the Data Collected in the Second National Health and Nutrition Survey, 1976–1980.* Federation of American Societies for Experimental Biology, Bethesda, MD, 1984, p. 65.

Recommended Dietary Allowances (RDA), 10th ed. Food Nutrition Board, National Research Council, National Academy Press, Washington, DC, 1989.

Schneider, E.L. *et al.* Recommended dietary allowances and the health of the elderly. *N. Engl. J. Med.* 314:157–160, 1986.

Selby, J.V. and Friedman. Epidemiologic evidence of an association between body iron stores and risk of cancer. *Int. J. Cancer* 41:677–682, 1988.

Shamburger, R.F. Selenium metabolism and function. *Clin. Physiol. Biochem.* 4(1):42–49, 1986.

Shamburger, R.F. *et al.* Antioxidants and cancer. Part VI. Selenium and age-adjusted human cancer mortality. *Arch. Environ. Health* 31:231–235, 1976.

Stevens, R.G. *et al.* Body iron stores and the risk of cancer. *N. Engl. J. Med.* 319;1047–1052, 1988.

Surgeon General's Report on Nutrition and Health (SGR). U.S. Department of Health and Human Services, Public Health Service, DHHS (PHS) Publication No. 88-50210, U.S. Government Printing Office, Washington, DC, 1988.

Suter, P.M. Vitamin requirements for the elderly. *Am. J. Clin. Nutr.* 45:501–12, 1987.

Verlangieri, A., cited in *Insight* 6(11):46, March, 12, 1990.

Chapter 4

Arnaud, C.D. Mineral and bone homeostasis, in *Cecil Textbook of Medicine*, 18th ed. (J.B. Wyngaarden, L.H. Smith, Jr., and F. Plum, eds.), W.B. Saunders, Philadelphia, PA, 1988, pp. 1469–1479.

Basu, T.K. The conditioning effect of large doses of ascorbic acid in guinea pigs. *Can. J. Physiol. Pharmacol.* 63:427–430, 1985.

Beaton, G.H. Nutritional assessment of observed nutrient intake; an interpretation of recent requirement reports, in *Advances in Nutritional Research*, vol. 7 (H.H. Draper, ed.), Plenum, New York, 1985, pp. 101–128.

Bendich, A. Safety of oral intake of vitamin E. *Am. J. Clin. Nutr.* 48:612–619, 1988.

Bhuyan, K.C. *et al.* The role of vitamin E in therapy of cataract in animals. *Ann. N.Y. Acad. Sci.* 393:169–171, 1982.

Bidlack, W.R. *et al.* Nutritional requirements of the elderly. *Food Tech.* 40(2):61–71, 1986.

Blumberg, J.B. Changing nutrient requirements in older adults. *Nutr. Today* 25(5):15–20, 1992.

Bouillon, R.A. *et al.* Vitamin D status in the elderly: Seasonal substrate deficiency causes 1-25 dihydroxycholecalciferol deficiency. *Am. J. Clin. Nutr.* 45:755–63, 1987.

Bowman, B.B. *et al.* Assessment of nutritional status of the elderly. *Am. J. Clin. Nutr.* 35:1142–1151, 1982.

Burton, G.W. *et al.* Beta-carotene: An unusual type of lipid antioxidant. *Science* 224: 69–73, 1984.

Chavance, M. *et al.* Immunological and nutritional status among the elderly, in *Nutrition, Immunity and Illness in the Elderly*, (R.K. Chandra, ed.), Pergamon Press, New York, 1985, pp. 137–142.

Cross, C.E. et al. Oxygen radicals and human disease. *Ann. Intern. Med.* 107:526–545, 1987.

Dawson-Hughes, B. *et al.* A controlled trial of the effect of calcium supplementation on bone density in postmenopausal women. *N. Engl. J. Med.* 323:878–883, 1990.

DeMaeyer, E. *et al.* The prevalence of anemia in the world. *World Health Stat. Q.* 38:302–316, 1985.

Faizallah, R. *et al.* Alcohol enhances vitamin C excretion in the urine. *Alcohol Alcohol.* 21:81–84, 1986.

Frisancho, A.R. New standards of weight and body composition by frame size and height for assessment of nutritional status of adults and the elderly. *Am. J. Clin. Nutr.* 40:808–819, 1984.

Gallup Organization. *The Gallup Study of Vitamin Use in the United States.* Survey 6, Vol. 1, Princeton, NJ, 1982.

Garry, P.J. *et al.* Nutritional status in a healthy population: Vitamin C. *Am. J. Clin. Nutr.* 36:332–339, 1982a.

Garry, P.J. *et al.* Nutritional status in a healthy elderly population: Dietary and supplemental intakes. *Am. J. Clin. Nutr.* 36:319–331, 1982b.

Garry, P.J. *et al.* Longitudinal assessment of iron status in a group of elderly, in *Nutrition Immunity and Illness in the Elderly*, (R.K. Chandra, ed.), Pergamon, New York, 1985, pp. 77–83.

Garry, P.J. *et al.* Biochemical assessment of vitamin status in the elderly: Effects of dietary and supplemental intakes. Bristol-Myers Nutrition Symposia, in *Nutrition and Aging*, Vol. 5 (M. Hutchinson and H.N. Munro, eds.), Academic Press, Orlando, Fl, 1986.

Garry, P.J. *et al.* Vitamin A intake and plasma retinol levels in healthy elderly men and women. *Am. J. Clin. Nutr.* 46:989–994, 1987.

Gersovitz, M. *et al.* Human protein requirements: Assessment of the dietary adequacy of the current recommended daily allowances for dietary protein in elderly men and women. *Am. J. Clin. Nutr.* 35:6–14, 1982.

Gerster, H. *et al.* Is high-dose vitamin C intake associated with systemic conditioning? *Nutr. Res.* 8:1327–1332, 1988.

Haeger, K. Long-term treatment of intermittent claudication with vitamin E. *Am. J. Clin. Nutr.* 27:1179–1181, 1974.

Herbert, V. *et al.* Destruction of vitamin B_{12} by ascorbic acid. *JAMA* 230:241–242, 1974.

Holick, M.F. Vitamin D synthesis by the aging skin. Bristol-Meyers Symposia 1986, in *Nutrition and Aging*, Vol. 5 (M. Hutchinson and H.N. Munro, eds.), Academic Press, Orlando, FL, 1986, pp. 45–58.

Horwitt, M.K. Data supporting supplementation of humans with vitamin E. *J. Nutr.* 121:424–429, 1991.

Jacques, P.F. *et al.* Antioxidant status in persons with and without senile cataract. *Arch. Ophthalmol.* 106:337–340, 1988a.

Jacques, P.F. *et al.* Nutritional status in persons with and without senile cataract: Blood vitamin and mineral levels. *Am. J. Clin. Nutr.* 48:152–158, 1988b.

Kallner, A. *et al.* Steady-state turnover and body pool of ascorbic acid in man. *Am. J. Clin. Nutr.* 32:530–539, 1979.

Kirsch, A. *et al.* Nutrition and the elderly: Vitamin status and efficacy of supplementation. *Nutrition* 3(5):305–314, 1987.

Knekt, P. *et al.* Serum vitamin E and risk of cancer among Finnish men during a 10-year follow-up. *Am. J. Epidemol.* 127:28–41, 1988.

Koplan, J.P. *et al.* Nutrient intake and supplementation in the United States (NHANES II). *Am. J. Public Health* 76:287–289, 1986.

Kuhn, I.N. *et al.* Observations on the mechanism of iron absorption. *Am. J. Clin. Nutr.* 21:1184–1188, 1968.

Leggott, P.J. *et al.* The effect of controlled ascorbic acid depletion and supplementation on periodontal health. *J. Periodontol.* 57:480–485, 1986.

Mann, B.A. *et al.* Effect of daily multivitamin supplementation on vitamin blood levels in the elderly: A randomized double-blind, placebo-controlled trial. *J. Am. Geriatr. Soc.* 35(4):302–306, 1987.

Marcus, M. *et al.* Stability of vitamin B_{12} in the presence of ascorbic acid in food and serum: Restoration by cyanide of apparent loss. *Am. J. Clin. Nutr.* 33:137–143, 1980.

McDonald, J.T. Vitamin and mineral supplement use in the United States. *Nutrition* 5(1):27–33, 1986.

Medeiros, D.M. *et al.* Long-term supplement users and dosage among adult Westerners. *J. Am. Diet. Assoc.* 91(8):980–982, 1991.

Melethil, S. *et al.* Dose-dependent absorption and excretion of vitamin C in humans. *Int. J. Pharm.* 31:83–89, 1986.

Menkes, M.S. *et al.* Serum beta-carotene, vitamins A and E, selenium, and the risk of lung cancer. *N. Engl. J. Med.* 315:1250–1254, 1986.

Meydani, S.N. *et al.* Vitamin E supplementation enhances cell-mediated immunity in healthy elderly subjects. *Am. J. Clin. Nutr.* 52:557–563, 1990.

Monsen, E.R. Iron nutrition and absorption: Dietary factors which impact iron bioavailability. *J. Am. Diet. Assoc.* 88:786–790, 1988.

Newmark, H.L. *et al.* Stability of vitamin B_{12} in the presence of ascorbic acid. *Am. J. Clin. Nutr.* 29:645–649, 1976.

Omdahl, J. *et al.* Nutritional status in a healthy elderly population: Vitamin D. *Am. J. Clin. Nutr.* 36:1225–1233, 1982.

Piatkowski, J. *et al.* Ascorbic acid in chronic alcoholics. *Int. J. Vitam. Nutr. Res.* 56:421, 1986.

Pierson, R.M. Jr. *et al.* Aspirin and gastrointestinal bleeding. Chromate 51 blood loss studies. *Am. J. Med.* 31:259–265, 1961.

Pilch, S.M. *et al.* F.R. *Assessment of the iron nutritional status of the U.S. population based on* the data collected in the Second National Health and Nutrition Survey, 1976–1980; p. 65. FASEB, Bethesda, MD, 1984.

Rank, P. et al. Preventable dental disease. *West. J. Med.* 139:545–546, 1983.

Recker, R.R. The effect of milk supplements on calcium metabolism, bone metabolism and calcium balance. *Am. J. Clin. Nutr.* 41:254–263, 1985.

Recommended Dietary Allowances (RDA), 10th ed. National Research Council, National Academy Press, Washington, DC, 1989.

Rivers, J.M. Safety of high-level vitamin C ingestion. *Ann. N.Y. Acad. Sci.* 498:445–454, 1987.

Roberts, L.J. Beginnings of the recommended dietary allowances. *J. Am. Diet. Assoc.* 34:903–908, 1958.

Scheider, C.L. et al. Prevalence of vitamin and mineral supplement use in the elderly. *J. Fam. Pract.* 17:243–247, 1983.

Schorah, C.J. et al. Clinical effects of vitamin C in elderly inpatients with low blood-vitamin-C levels. *Lancet* 1:403–405, 1979.

Smith, J.L. Serum levels of vitamin C in relation to dietary and supplemental intake of vitamin C in smokers and nonsmokers. *Ann. N.Y. Acad. Sci.* 498:144–152, 1987.

Subar, A.F. Use of vitamin and mineral supplements: Demographics and amounts of nutrients consumed. *Am. J. Epidemiol.* 132(6):1091–1101, 1990.

Surgeon General's Report on Nutrition and Health (SGR). U.S. Dept. of Health and Human Services; Public Health Service; DHHS(PHS) Publication No. 88-50210, U.S. Government Printing Office, Washington, DC, 1988.

Suter, P.M. et al. Vitamin requirements of the elderly. *Am. J. Clin. Nutr.* 45:501–512, 1987.

Taylor, A. Associations between nutrition and cataract. *Nutr. Rev.* 47:225–234, 1989.

U.S. Department of Health, Education and Welfare (DHEW, 1972). *III Clinical Anthropometry, Dental; IV Biochemical; V Dietary. Ten-State Nutrition Survey 1968–1970.* DHEW Publication Nos. (HSM)72-8131; 8132; 8133. Centers for Disease Control, Atlanta, GA, 1972.

VanderJagt, D.J. et al. Ascorbic acid intake and plasma levels in healthy elderly people. *Am. J. Clin. Nutr.* 46:290–294, 1987.

Yip, R. et al. The roles of inflammation and iron deficiency as causes of anemia. *Am. J. Clin. Nutr.* 48:1295–1300, 1988.

Zauber, N.P. et al. Hematological data of healthy very old people. *JAMA* 257:2181–2184, 1987.

Chapter 5

Allen, F.M. *Studies Concerning Glycosuria and Diabetes*. W.M. Leonard, Boston, MA, 1913.

Anderson, J.W. Dietary fiber and diabetes, in *Medical Aspects of Dietary Fiber* (G.A. Spiller and R.M. Kay, eds.), Plenum Medical Book Co., New York, 1980.

Bamforth, C.W. Barley beta-glucans, their role in malting and brewing. *Brewers Dig.* 22:22, 1982.

Bell, L.P. *et al.* Cholesterol-lowering effects of psyllium hydrophilic mucilloid. *JAMA* 261:3419–3423, 1989.

Burkitt, D.P. *et al.* Dietary fiber and disease. *JAMA* 229:1068–1074, 1974.

Chen, W.J.L. Hypocholesterolemic effects of soluble fibers, in *Dietary Fiber: Basic and Clinical Aspects* (G.V. Vahouny and D. Kritchevsky, eds.), Plenum Press, New York, 1986.

Cheng, A.H.R. *et al.* Long-term acceptance of low-lactose milk. *Am. J. Clin. Nutr.* 32:1989–1993, 1979.

Chernoff, R. Physiological aging and nutritional status. *Nutr. Clin. Pract.* 5:8–13, 1990.

Chernoff, R. *et al.* Assessment of the nutritional status of the geriatric patient. *Geriatr. Med. Today* 3:129–141, 1984.

de Groot, A.P. Cholesterol lowering effect of rolled oats. *Lancet* 2:203, 1963.

Deutsch, R.M. *The New Nuts among the Berries.* Bull Publishing Co., Palo Alto, CA, 1977.

Gershoff, S.N. *The Tufts University Guide to Total Nutrition.* Harper & Row, New York, 1990.

Hull, C. *et al.* Alleviation of constipation in the elderly by dietary fiber supplementation. *J. Am. Geriatr. Soc.* 28:410, 1980.

Humble, C.G. Oats and cholesterol: The prospects for prevention of heart disease. *Am. J. Public Health* 81(2):159–160, 1991.

Kirby, R.W. *et al.* Oat bran intake selectively lowers serum low-density lipoprotein cholesterol. *Am. J. Clin. Nutr.* 34:824, 1981.

Kritchevsky, D. Dietary fiber. *Annu. Rev. Nutr.* 8:301–328, 1974.

National Academy of Sciences (NAS), Assembly of Life Sciences, Committee on Diet, Nutrition and Cancer. *Diet, Nutrition and Cancer*, Chapt. 8, National Academy Press, Washington, DC, 1982.

National Research Council, Committee on Diet and Health, Food and Nutrition Board. *Diet and Health: Implications for Reducing Chronic Disease Risk.* National Academy Press, Washington, DC, 1989.

Newman, R.K. *et al.* An *in vivo* model for predicting hypocholesterolemic properties of cereal grains. *Fed. Proc.* 2:A1419, 1988.

Newman, R.K. *et al.* The hypocholesterolemic function of barley beta-glucans. *Cereal Foods World* 34(10):883–885, 1989.

Nix, J. *et al.* Food and Fitness. Price, Stern and Sloan, Inc., Los Angeles, CA, 1988.

Raymond, L.R. *et al.* The interaction of dietary fibers and cholesterol upon the plasma lipids and lipoproteins, sterol balance and bowel function in human subjects. *J. Clin. Invest.* 60:1429–1437, 1977.

Recommended Dietary Allowances, 10th Ed. National Research Council, National Academy Press, Washington, DC, 1989.

Ribakove, B. Private enemies: Gas. *Health* 15:44, 1983.

Scala, J. *The Physiologic Effects of Dietary Fiber*, A.C.S. Symposium Series, Lippincott, Philadelphia, PA, 1975.

Surgeon General's Report on Nutrition and Health. Superintendent of Documents, U.S. Government Printing Office, Washington, DC, 1988, p. 203.

Swain, J.F. *et al.* Comparison of the effect of oat bran and low-fiber wheat on serum lipoprotein levels and blood pressure. *N. Engl. J. Med.* 322(3):147–152, 1990.

Trowell, H.C. *Refined Carbohydrate Food and Disease: Some Implications of Dietary Fibre* (D.P. Burkitt and H.C. Trowell, eds.), Academic Press, London, 1975.

Trowell, H.C. Definition of dietary fiber and hypothesis that it is a protective factor in certain diseases. *Am. J. Clin. Nutr.* 29:417–427, 1976.

Trowell, H.C. *et al. Western Diseases: Their Emergence and Prevention.* Harvard University Press, Cambridge, MA, 1981.

Van Horn, L. *et al.* Effects on serum lipids of adding instant oats to usual American diets. *Am. J. Pub. Health* 81(2):183–188, 1991.

Williams, S.R. *Nutrition and Diet Therapy*, 6th ed., Times Mirror-Mosby, St. Louis, MO, 1989, pp. 146–147.

Wood, P.J. Oat beta-glucan: Structure, location and properties, in *Oats: Chemistry and Technology* (F.H. Webster, ed.), Amer. Assoc. Cereal Chem., St. Paul, MN, 1986.

Wood, P.J. *et al.* Physiological effects of beta-D-glucan rich fractions from oats. *Cereal Foods World* 34(10):878–882, 1989.

Wood, P.J. *et al.* Comparisons of viscous properties of oat and guar gum and the effects of these and oat bran, on glycemic index. *J. Agric. Food Chem.* 38(3):753–757, 1990.

Chapter 6

Atherosclerosis

Alderman, M.H. *et al.* Association of the renin–sodium profile with the risk of myocardial infarction in patients with hypertension. *N. Engl. J. Med.* 324:1098–1104, 1991.

Allred, J.B. *et al.* Elevated blood cholesterol: A risk factor for heart disease that decreases with age. *Am. Diet Assoc.* 90(4):574–576, 1990.

American Heart Association. *1988 Heart Facts* (Item 55-0351). American Heart Association, Dallas, TX, 1988.

Anderson, J.W. *et al.* Hypercholesterolemic effects of oat and bean products. *Am. J. Clin. Nutr.* 48:749–753, 1988.

Anderson, K.M. *et al.* Cholesterol and mortality: 30 years of follow-up from the Framingham Study. *JAMA* 257(16):2176–2180, 1987.

Bonanome, A. and Grundy, S.M. Effect of dietary stearic acid on plasma cholesterol and lipoprotein levels. *N. Engl. J. Med.* 318:1244–48, 1988.

Bortz, W.M. The pathogenesis of hypercholesterolemia. *Ann. Inter. Med.* 80:738, 1974.

Brunner, H.R. *et al.* Renin as a risk factor in essential hypertension: More evidence. *Am. J. Med.* 55:295–302, 1973.

Castelli, W.P. *et al.* Incidence of coronary heart disease and lipoprotein levels: The Framingham Study. *JAMA* 256(20):2835–2838, 1986.

Council on Scientific Affairs, Advisory Panel, AMA. Dietary and pharmacological therapy for the lipid risk factors. *JAMA* 250:1873, 1983.

Diokno, A.C. *et al.* Sexual function in the elderly. *Arch. Intern. Med.* 150:197–200, 1990.

Enstrom, J.E. *et al.* Vitamin C intake and mortality among a sample of the U.S. population. *Epidemiology* 3(3):194–202, 1992.

Fihn, S.D. A prudent approach to control of cholesterol levels. *JAMA* 258:2416, 1987.

Frezza, M. *et al.* High blood alcohol level in women: The role of decreased gastric alcohol dehydrogenase activity and first-pass metabolism. *N. Engl. J. Med.* 322:95–99, 1990.

Friedman, M., and Rosenman, R. *Type A Behavior and Your Heart*, Knopf, New York, 1974.

Garber, A.M. *et al.* *Costs and Effectiveness of Cholesterol Screening in the Elderly.* Office of Technological Assessment, Washington, DC, April, 1989.

Goldberg, R.B. Dietary modification of cholesterol levels. *Consultant* 28(suppl.):35–41, 1988.

Gordon, T.P. *et al.* Predicting coronary heart disease in middle-aged and older persons. The Framingham Study. *JAMA* 238:497, 1977.

Grobbee, D.E. *et al.* Coffee, caffeine, and cardiovascular disease in men. *N. Engl. J. Med.* 323:1026–1032, 1990.

Grundy, S.M. Cholesterol and coronary heart disease: A new era. *JAMA* 256:2849–2858, 1986.

Grundy, S.M. Monounsaturated fatty acids, plasma cholesterol, and coronary heart disease. *Am. J. Clin. Nutr.* 45:1168, 1987.

Hammond, E.C. *et al.* Smoking and death rates: Report on 44 months of follow-up on 187,783 Men. Total Mortality. II Death rate by cause. *JAMA* 116:1159–1172, 1294–1308, 1958.

Harris, T. *et al.* Proportional hazards analysis of risk factors for coronary heart disease of individuals aged 65 or older. *J. Am. Geriatr. Soc.* 36:1023, 1988.

Hegsted, D.M. *et al.* Diet, alcohol and coronary heart disease. *J. Nutr.* 118:1184–1189, 1988.

Kannel, W.B. *et al.* for the MRFIT Research Group. Overall and coronary heart disease mortality rates in relation to major risk factors in 325,348 men screened for the MRFIT. *Am. Heart J.* 112(4):825–836, 1986.

Katz, L.N. and Stamler, J. *Experimental Atherosclerosis*, Charles C Thomas, Springfield, IL, 1953, p. 3.

Kinsella, J.E. Effect of polyunsaturated fatty acids as factors related to cardiovascular disease. *Am. J. Cardiol.* 60:23G–32G, 1987.

Kromhout, D. *et al.* The inverse relation between fish consumption and 20-year mortality from coronary heart disease. *N. Engl. J. Med.* 312:1205–1209, 1985.

Lipid Research Clinics Program. The Lipid Research Clinics Coronary Primary Prevention trial results. I. Reduction in incidence of coronary heart disease. *JAMA* 251:351–364, 1984.

Lipid Research Clinics Program. The Lipid Research Clinics Coronary Primary

Prevention trial results. II. The relationship of reduction in incidence of coronary heart disease to cholesterol lowering. *JAMA* 251:365–374, 1984.

Mattson, F.H. Comparison of effects of dietary saturated, monounsaturated and polyunsaturated fatty acids on plasma lipids and lipoproteins in man. *J. Lipid Res.* 26:194–202, 1985.

McNamara, D.J. Effects of fat-modified diets on cholesterol and lipoprotein metabolism. *Annu. Rev. Nutr.* 7:273–290, 1987.

Musliner, T.A. Lipoprotein subspecies and risk of coronary disease. *Clin. Chem.* 34: B78–B83, 1988.

Nakoshima, T. *et al.* A study of human aortic distensibility with relation to atherosclerosis and aging. *Angiology* 22:477–490, 1971.

National Institutes of Health Consensus Conference. Lowering blood cholesterol to prevent heart disease: Consensus Conference. *JAMA* 253:2080, 1985.

National Institute of Health Consensus Development Panel on the Health Implications of obesity. National Institute of Health Consensus Development Conference statement. *Ann. Intern. Med.* 103(6, Part 2):1073–1077, Dec. 1985.

Pooling Project Research Group. Relationship of blood pressure, serum cholesterol, smoking habit, relative weight and ECG abnormalities to incidence of major coronary events: Final report of the Pooling Project. *J. Chronic Dis.* 31:201–306, 1978.

Report of the National Cholesterol Education Program Expert Panel on Detection, Evaluation, and Treatment of High Blood Cholesterol in Adults. *Arch. Intern. Med.* 148:36–69, 1988.

Rimm, E.B. *et al.* Prospective study of alcohol consumption and the risk of coronary disease in men. *Lancet* 338:464–468, 1991.

Roine, R. *et al.* Aspirin increases blood alcohol concentrations in humans after ingestion of ethanol. *JAMA* 264:2406–2408, 1990.

Rosenberg, I.H. Dietary saturated fatty acids and blood cholesterol. *N. Engl. J. Med.* 318:1270–1271, 1988.

Salonen, J.T. *et al.* High stored iron levels are associated with excess risk of myocardial infarction in eastern Finnish men. *Circulation* 86:803–811, 1992.

Stamler, J. *et al.* Is the relationship between serum cholesterol and risk of premature death from coronary heart disease continuous and graded? *JAMA* 256:2823–2828, 1986.

Stephens, R. Cholesterol study focuses on elderly. *AARP Bull.* 32(2):8, Feb., 1991.

Sullivan, J.L. Iron and the sex difference in heart disease risk. *Lancet* 1:1293–1294, 1981.

Sullivan, J.L. The iron paradigm of ischemic heart disease. *Am. Heart J.* 117:1177–1188, 1989.

Superco, H.R. *et al.* Lipoprotein and alipoprotein changes during a controlled trial of caffeinated and decaffeinated coffee drinking in men. *Circulation* 80(suppl. II):II-86, 1989 [Abstract].

Surgeon General's Report on Nutrition and Health (SGR). U.S. Dept. of Health and Human Services. Public Health Service, U.S. Government Printing Office, Washington, DC, 1988.

Diabetes Mellitus

American Diabetes Association (ADA). Nutritional recommendations and principles for individuals with diabetes mellitus: 1986. *Diabetes Care* 10:126–132, 1987a.

American Diabetes Association (ADA). Use of non-caloric sweeteners (Position Statement). Diabetes Forecast 40 (Sept.): 15, 1987b.

American Diabetes Association Task Force on Nutrition and Exchange Lists. Nutritional recommendations and principles for individuals with diabetes mellitus: 1986. *Diabetes Care* 10:126–132, 1987c.

American Dietetic Association (ADA). Position of the American Dietetic Association: appropriate use of nutritive and non-nutritive sweeteners. *J. Am. Diet. Assoc.* 87:1687–1694, 1987d.

Anderson, J.W. *et al.* Hypolipemic effects of high-carbohydrate, high-fiber diets. *Metabolism* 29:551–558, 1980.

Bantle, J.P. *et al.* Postprandial glucose and insulin responses to meals containing different carbohydrates in normal and diabetic subjects. *N. Engl. J. Med.* 309:7–12, 1983.

Bantle, J.P. *et al.* Metabolic effects of dietary fructose and sucrose in type I and type II diabetic subjects. *JAMA* 256:3241–3246, 1986.

Canadian Diabetes Association (CDA). Special report: Committee guidelines for the nutritional management of diabetes mellitus. *J. Can. Diet. Assoc.* 42:110–118, 1981.

Coulston, A.M. *et al.* Deleterious metabolic effects of high carbohydrate, sucrose containing diets in patients with NIDDM. *Am. J. Med.* 82:213–220, 1987.

Coulston, A.M. *et al.* Persistence of the hypertriglyceridemic effect of high-carbohydrate, low-fat diets in patients with type 2 diabetes mellitus. *Diabetes Care* 12:94–101, 1989.

Crapo, P.A. Use of alternative sweeteners in diabetic diet. *Diabetes Care* 11:174–182, 1988.

Garg, A. *et al.* Comparison of a high-carbohydrate diet with high-monounsaturated fat diet in patients with non-insulin-dependent diabetes mellitus. *N. Engl. J. Med.* 319:829–834, 1988.

Glauber, H. *et al.* Adverse metabolic effects of omega-3 fatty acids in non-insulin dependent diabetes mellitus. *Ann. Intern. Med.* 108:663–668, 1988.

Harris, M.J. *et al.* Prevalence of diabetes and impaired glucose tolerance and plasma glucose levels in U.S. population aged 20–74 years. *Diabetes* 36:523–534, 1987.

Hollenbeck, C.B. *et al.* The effects of variations in percent of naturally occurring complex and simple carbohydrates on plasma glucose and insulin response in individuals with non-insulin-dependent diabetes mellitus. *Diabetes* 34:151–155, 1985.

Hollenbeck, C.B. *et al.* To what extent does increased dietary fiber improve glucose and lipid metabolism in patients with non-insulin-dependent diabetes mellitus (NIDDM). *Am. J. Clin. Nutr.* 43:16–24, 1986.

Hollenbeck, C.B. *et al.* Effect of variation in diet on lipoprotein metabolism in patients with diabetes mellitus. *Diabetes Metab. Rev.* 3:669–689, 1987.

Jenkins, D.J.A. *et al.* Unabsorbable carbohydrates and diabetes. Decreased postprandial hyperglycemia. *Lancet* 2:172–174, 1976.

Karlstom, B. *et al.* Effects of an increased content of cereal fiber in the diet of type 2 (non-insulin-dependent) diabetic patients. *Diabetologia* 26:272–277, 1984.

Kiehm, T.G. *et al.* Beneficial effects of a high carbohydrate, high fiber diet on hyperglycemic diabetic men. *Am. J. Clin. Nutr.* 29:895–899, 1976.

Kromhout, D. *et al.* The inverse relation between fish consumption and 20-year mortality from coronary heart disease. *N. Engl. J. Med.* 312:1205–1209, 1985.

Liu, G. *et al.* Moderate weight loss on non-insulin-dependent diabetes mellitus. *Arch. Intern. Med.* 145:665–669, 1985.

National Diabetes Data Group (NDDG). International Work Group. Classification and diagnosis of diabetes and other categories of glucose intolerance. *Diabetes* 28:1039–1057, 1979.

Newburgh, L.H. *et al.* A new interpretation of diabetes mellitus in obese, middle-aged persons: Recovery through reduction in weight. *Trans. Assoc. Am. Physicians* 53:245–257, 1938.

Riccardi, G. *et al.* Separate influences of dietary carbohydrate and fiber on metabolic control of diabetes. *Diabetologia* 26:116–121, 1984.

Schechtman, G. *et al.* Effect of fish oil concentration on lipoprotein composition in NIDDM. *Diabetes* 37:1567–1573, 1988.

Simpson, H.C.R. *et al.* High carbohydrate leguminous fibre diet improves all aspects of dietary control. *Lancet* 1:1–5, 1981.

Slama, G. *et al.* Sucrose taken during a mixed meal had no additional hyperglycemic action over isocaloric amounts of starch in well-controlled diabetes. *Lancet* 2:122–125, 1984.

Surgeon General's Report on Nutrition and Health (SGR). U.S. Dept. of Health and Human Services, Public Health Service. DHHS (PHS) Publication No. 88-50210, U.S. Government Printing Office. Washington, DC, 1988.

Toma, R.B. Dietary fiber: Its role for diabetics. *Food Technol.* 40(2):118–123, 1986.

Uusitupa, M. *et al.* Metabolic and nutritional effects of long-term use of guar gum in the treatment of non-insulin-dependent diabetes of poor metabolic control. *Am. J. Clin. Nutr.* 49:345–351, 1989.

Wing, R.R. *et al.* Long-term effects of modest weight loss in type II diabetic patients. *Arch. Intern. Med.* 147:1749–1753, 1987.

Wood, F.C. New concepts in diabetic dietetics. *Nutr. Today*, May/June:4–12, 1972.

Wood, P.J. *et al.* Physiological effects of beta-D-glucan rich fractions from oats. *Cereal Foods World* 34(10):878–882, 1989.

Cancer

Albanes, D. Total calories, body weight and tumor incidence in mice. *Cancer Res.* 47:1987–1992, 1987.

American Cancer Society (ACS). *1990 Facts and Figures*, Atlanta, GA, 1990.

Armstrong, B. Environmental factors and cancer incidence and mortality in different countries, with specific reference to dietary practices. *Int. J. Cancer* 15:617–631, 1975.

Bingham, S. *et al.* Dietary fibre and regional large-bowel cancer mortality in Britain. *Br. J. Cancer* 40:456–463, 1979.

Burkitt, D.P. and Trowell, H.C. *Refined Carbohydrate Foods and Disease. Some Implications of Dietary Fibre*. Academic Press, London, New York and San Francisco, 1975.

Burton, G.W. Beta carotene: An unusual type of lipid antioxidant. *Science* 224:569–573, 1984.

Byers, T. Diet and cancer: Any progress in the interim? *Cancer* 62:1713–1724, 1988.

Byers, T.E. *et al.* Diet and lung cancer risk: Findings from the Western New York Diet Study. *Am. J. Epidemiol.* 125:351–363, 1987.

Carroll, K.K. Fat and cancer. *Cancer* 58:1818–1824, 1986.

Cerutti, P.A. Peroxidant status and tumor promotion. *Science* 227:375–381, 1985.

Cohen, L.A. Diet and cancer. *Sci. Am.* 257:42–48, 1987.

Combs, G.F. and Combs, S.B. *The Role of Selenium in Nutrition*, Academic Press, Orlando, FL, 1986.

Connett, J.E. Relationship between carotenoids and cancer: The multiple risk factor intervention trial (MRFIT) study. *Cancer* 64:126–134, 1989.

Decarli, A. *et al.* Vitamin A and other dietary factors in the etiology of esophageal cancer. *Nutr. Cancer* 10:29–37, 1987.

Desmond, S. Diet and cancer: Should we change what we eat? *West. J. Med.* 146:73–78, 1987.

Diet, Nutrition and Cancer (DNC). Committee on Diet, Nutrition and Cancer, Assembly of Life Sciences, National Research Council, National Academy Press, Washington, DC, 1982.

Doll, R. The causes of cancer: Quantitative estimates of avoidable risks of cancer in the United States today. *J. Natl. Cancer Inst.* 66:1191–1308, 1981.

Enstrom, J.E. *et al.* Vitamin C intake and mortality among a sample of the U.S. population. *Epidemiology* 3(3):194–202, 1992.

Fiddler, W. *et al.* Inhibition of the formation of volatile nitrosamines in fried bacon by the use of alpha-tocopherol. *J. Agric. Food Chem.* 26:653–656, 1978.

Friedman, L. *et al.* Toxic response of rats to cyclamates in chow and semi-synthetic diets. *J. Natl. Cancer Inst.* 49:751–764, 1972.

Gey, K.F. *et al.* Plasma levels of antioxidant vitamins in relation to ischemic heart disease and cancer. *Am. J. Clin. Nutr.* 45:1368–1377, 1987.

Glatthaar, B.E. *et al.* The role of ascorbic acid in carcinogenesis. *Adv. Exp. Med. Biol.* 206:357–377, 1986.

Graham, S. *et al.* Diet in the epidemiology of cancer of the colon and rectum. *J. Natl. Cancer Inst.* 51:709–714, 1978.

Gridley, G. *et al.* Vitamin supplement use and reduced risk of oral and pharyngeal cancer. *Am. J. Epidemiol.* 135(10):1083–1092, 1992.

Hanck, A.B. Vitamin C and cancer. *Prog. Clin. Biol. Res.* 259:307–320, 1987.

Harvey, E.B. *et al.* Alcohol consumption and breast cancer. *J. Natl. Cancer Inst.* 76:657, 1987.

Ingold, K.U. *et al.* Vitamin E remains the major lipid-soluble, chain-breaking antioxidant in human plasma even in individuals suffering severe vitamin E deficiency. *Arch. Biochem. Biophys.* 259:224–225, 1987.

Katsouyanni, K. *et al.* Diet and breast cancer: A case control study in Greece. *Int. J. Cancer* 38:815–820, 1986.

Katsouyanni, K. *et al.* Risk of breast cancer among Greek women in relation to nutrient intake. *Cancer* 61:181–185, 1988.

Kinzler, W. *et al.* Identification of FAP locus genes from chromosome 5q21. *Science* 253:661–665, 1991.

Kritchevsky, D. *et al.* Caloric effects in experimental mammary tumorigenesis. *Am. J. Clin. Nutr.* 45:236–242, 1987.

Kune, G.A. *et al.* Serum levels of beta-carotene, vitamin A and zinc in male lung cancer cases and controls. *Nutr. Cancer* 12:169–176, 1989.

Kune, S. *et al.* Case-control study of dietary etiological factors: The Melbourne colorectal cancer study. *Nutr. Cancer* 9:21–42, 1987.

La Vecchia, C. *et al.* Dietary factors and the risk of breast cancer. *Nutr. Cancer* 10:205–214, 1987.

Lavender, O.A. A global view of human selenium nutrition. *Annu. Rev. Nutr.* 7:227–250, 1987.

LeMarchand, L. *et al.* Vegetable consumption and lung cancer risk: A population-based case-control study in Hawaii. *J. Natl. Cancer Inst.* 81:1158–1164, 1989.

Lemoyne, J.E. *et al.* Breath pentane analysis as an index of lipid peroxidation. A functional test of vitamin E status. *Am. J. Clin. Nutr.* 46:267–272, 1987.

Marx, J. Zeroing in on individual cancer risk. *Science* 253:612–616, 1991.

McMichael, A.J. *et al.* Dietary and endogenous cholesterol and human cancer. *Epidemiol. Rev.* 6:192–216, 1984.

Mettlin, C. Milk-drinking, other beverage habits and lung cancer risk. *Int. J. Cancer* 43:608–612, 1989.

Mcydani, S.N. *et al.* Vitamin E supplementation enhances cell-mediated immunity in healthy elderly subjects. *Am. J. Clin. Nutr.* 52:557–563, 1990.

Mirvish, S.S. Effects of vitamins C and E on N-nitroso compound formation, carcinogenesis and cancer. *Cancer* 58:1842–1850, 1986.

National Academy of Sciences (NAS). *The Health Effects of Nitrate, Nitrite and N-Nitroso Compounds.* Part 1 of a 2-part study by the Committee on Nitrate, Nitrite and Alternative During Agents in Food. National Academy Press, Washington, DC, 1981.

National Research Council (NRC). *Selenium in Nutrition*, rev. ed. Report of the Subcommittee on Selenium, Committee on Animal Nutrition, Board on Agriculture. National Academy Press, Washington, DC, 1983.

Nishisho, I. *et al.* Mutations of chromosome 5q21 genes in FAP and colorectal cancer patients. *Science* 253:665–669, 1991.

Nomura, A.M.Y. *et al.* Serum vitamin levels and the risk of cancer of specific sites in men of Japanese ancestry in Hawaii. *Cancer Res.* 45:2369–2372, 1985.

Nomura, A. *et al. Helicobacter pylori* infection and gastric carcinoma among Japanese Americans in Hawaii. *N. Engl. J. Med.* 325:1232–6, 1991.

Parsonnet, J. *et al. Helicobacter pylori* infection and the risk of gastric carcinoma. *N. Engl. J. Med.* 325:1127–1131, 1991.

Pilch, S.M., ed. *Physiological Effects and Health Consequences of Dietary Fiber*, Fed. Amer. Soc. Exptl. Biol., Bethesda, MD, 1987.

Roe, F.J.C. *et al.* Feeding studies in sodium cyclamate, saccharin and sucrose for carcinogenic and tumour-promoting activity. *Food Cosmet. Toxicol.* 8:135–145, 1970.

Rogers, A.E. Alcohol and cancer, in *Essential Nutrients in Carcinogenesis* (L.A. Porier, P.M. Newberne, and M.W. Pariza, eds.), Plenum Press, New York, 1985, p. 473.

Rogers, A.E. Biology of disease. Dietary and nutritional influences on cancer; a review of epidemiologic and experimental data. *Lab. Invest.* 59:729–759, 1988.

Rohan, T.E. *et al.* A population-based case-control study of diet and breast cancer in Australia. *Am. J. Epidemiol.* 128:478–489, 1988.

Romney, S.L. *et al.* Plasma reduced and total ascorbic acid in human uterine cervix dysplasias and cancer. *Ann. N.Y. Acad. Sci.* 498:132–143, 1987.

Rothman, K.J. *Modern Epidemiology*. Little, Brown and Company, Boston, MA, 1986.

Salonen, J.T. *et al.* Risk of cancer in relation to serum concentrations of selenium and vitamins A and E: Matched case-controlled analysis of prospective data. *Br. Med. J.* 290:417–420, 1985.

Schapira, D.V. *et al.* Abdominal obesity and breast cancer risk. *Ann. Intern. Med.* 112:182–186, 1990.

Selby, J.V. *et al.* Epidemiologic evidence of an association between body iron stores and risk of cancer. *Int. J. Cancer* 41:677–682, 1988.

Shekelle, R.B. *et al.* Dietary vitamin A and risk of cancer in the Western Electric Study. *Lancet* 2:1185–1189, 1981.

Stevens, R.G. *et al.* Body iron stores and the risk of cancer. *N. Engl. J. Med.* 319:1047–1052, 1988.

Summerfield, F.W. and Tappel. Effects of dietary polyunsaturated fats and vitamin E on aging and peroxidation damage to DNA. *Arch. Biochem. Biophys.* 233:408–416, 1984.

Surgeon General's Report on Nutrition and Health (SGR). U.S. Dept. of Health and Human Services, Public Health Service, DHHS (PHS) Publication No. 88-50210, U.S. Government Printing Office, Washington, DC, 1988.

Tannenbaum, A. The dependence of tumor formation on the degree of caloric restriction. *Cancer Res.* 5:609–615, 1945.

Tannenbaum, S.R. Inhibition of nitrosamine formation by ascorbic acid. *Ann. N.Y. Acad. Sci.* 498:364–388, 1987.

Trickler, D. and Shklar. Prevention by vitamin E of experimental oral carcinogenesis. *J. Natl. Cancer Inst.* 78:165–169, 1987.

Van Gossum, A. *et al.* Decrease in lipid peroxidation measured by breath pentane output in normals after oral supplementation with vitamin E. *Clin. Nutr.* 7:53–57, 1988.

Wald, N.J. *et al.* Serum beta-carotene and subsequent risk of cancer: Results from the BUPA study. *Br. J. Cancer* 57:428–433, 1988.

Watson, R.R. *et al.* Selenium and vitamins A, E and C: Nutrients with cancer prevention properties. *J. Am. Diet. Assoc.* 86:505–510, 1986.

Wattenberg, L.W. Inhibition of polycyclic hydrocarbon-induced neoplasia by naturally occurring indoles. *Cancer Res.* 38:1410–1413, 1978.

Weinhouse, S. The role of diet and nutrition in cancer. *Cancer* 58:1791–94, 1986.

Weisburger, J.H. *et al.* Inhibition of carcinogenesis. Vitamin C and the prevention of gastric cancer. *Prev. Med.* 9:352–361, 1980.

Willett, W.C. *et al.* The search for the causes of breast and colon cancer. *Nature* 338:389–394, 1989.

Willett, W.C. *et al.* Diet and cancer—an overview. *N. Engl. J. Med.* 310:633–638, 1984; 310:697–703, 1984.

Willett, W.C. Selenium and cancer. *Br. Med. J.* 297:573–574, 1988.

Willett, W.C. *et al.* Relation of meat, fat and fiber intake to the risk of colon cancer in a prospective study among women. *N. Engl. J. Med.* 323:1664–1672, 1990.

Willett, W.C. *et al.* Dietary fat and fiber in relation to risk of breast cancer. An 8-year follow-up. *JAMA* 268:2037–2044, 1992.

Zhang, Y. *et al.* A major inducer of anticarcinogenic protective enzymes from broccoli: Isolation and elucidation of structure. *Proc. Natl. Acad. Sci. U.S.A.* 89:2399–2403, 1992.

Arthritis and Gout, and Nutritional Anemias

Bollet, A.J. Nutrition and diet in rheumatic disorders, in *Modern Nutrition in Health and Disease*, 7th ed. (M.E. Shils and V.R. Young, eds.), Lea & Febiger, Philadelphia, PA, 1988, Chapt. 68.

Coleman, N. Nutrition and blood disorders, in *The Mt. Sinai School of Medicine Complete Book of Nutrition* (V. Herbert and G.J. Subak-Sharpe, eds.), St. Martin's Press, New York, 1990, pp. 507–517.

Denman, A.M. Joint complaints and food allergic disorders. *Ann. Allergy* 51(2 Pt. 2):260–263, 1983.

Drum, D.E. Elevation of serum uric acid as a clue to alcohol abuse. *Arch. Intern. Med.* 14(4):447–449, 1981.

Hunt, J.R. *et al.* Ascorbic acid: Effect on ongoing iron absorption and status in iron-depleted young women. *Am. J. Clin. Nutr.* 51(4):649–655, 1990.

Kalman, E. Can diet help in the fight against arthritis? *Environ. Nutr. Newsl.* 4(4):1, 1981.

Leming, P.D. Magnesium carbonate pica: An unusual case of iron deficiency. *Ann. Intern. Med.* 94(5):660, 1981.

Lindenbaum, J. et al. Neuropsychiatric disorders caused by cobalamin deficiency in the absence of anemia or macrocytosis. *N. Engl. J. Med.* 318(26):1720–1728, 1988.

Meydani, S.N. *Fatty Acids and Immune Function.* Presented at ASPEN fall course: Nutrient modification of disease process. Chicago, IL, Sept. 12–13, 1991a.

Meydani, S.N. *et al*. Fish oil and tocopherol induced changes in natural killer cell mediated cytotoxicity and PGE_2 synthesis in young and old mice. *J. Nutr.* 118:1245–1252, 1988.

Meydani, S.N. *et al*. Oral N-3 fatty acid supplementation suppresses cytokine production and lymphocyte proliferation: Comparison in young and older women. *J. Nutr.* 121:547–555, 1991b.

Natow, A.B. and Heslin, A. *Nutritional Care of the Older Adult*. Macmillan Publishing Co., New York, 1986.

Parke, A.L. *et al*. Rheumatoid arthritis and food: A case study. *Br. Med. J.* 282(6281):2027–2029, 1981.

Recommended Dietary Allowances, 10th ed. National Research Council, National Academy Press, Washington, DC, 1989.

Roe, D.A. *Geriatric Nutrition*, 2nd ed., Prentice-Hall, Englewood Cliffs, NJ, 1983.

Rosenberg, I.H. *et al*. Folate nutrition in the elderly. *Am. J. Clin. Nutr.* 36:1060–1066, 1982.

Sahud, M.A. Effect of aspirin ingestion on ascorbic acid level in rheumatoid arthritis. *Lancet* 1(7706):937–938, 1971.

Schilling, R.F. Pernicious anemia (questions and answers). *JAMA* 253(1):94, 1985.

Simson, K.B. Study design/sample questioned for osteoarthritis research. [Letter to the Editor]. *J. Am. Diet. Assoc.* 89:1586–1588, 1989.

Surgeon General's Report on Nutrition and Health, Superintendent of Documents, U.S. Government Printing Office, Washington, DC, 20402, 1988.

Vreugdenhil, G. *et al*. Anaemia in rheumatoid arthritis: The role of iron, vitamin B_{12} and folic acid deficiency, and erythropoietin responsiveness. *Ann. Rheum. Dis.* 49(2):93–98, 1990.

Vreugdenhil, G. Prediction and evaluation of the effect of iron treatment in anemic patients. *Clin. Rheumatol.* 8(3):352–362, 1989.

White-O'Connor, B.W. *et al*. Dietary habits, weight history and vitamin supplement use in elderly osteoarthritis patients. *J. Am. Diet. Assoc.* 89:378–82, 1989.

Zeller, M. Rheumatoid arthritis—Food allergy as a factor. *Ann. Allergy* 7(2):200–205, 1949.

The relationship of disorders of the digestive tract to anemia. (Reprint from *JAMA* 97:904–906, 1931). *Nutr. Rev.* 47(9):262–266, 1989.

Chapter 7

American Dental Association (ADA). *Accepted Dental Therapeutics*. American Dental Association, Chicago, IL, 1984, pp. 399–402.

American Public Health Association (APHA). PHS reports on fluoride. *The Nation's Health* 21:3, May–June, 1991.

Bowden, J.W. Current concepts of fluoride. *N. C. Dent. J.* 60:21–26, 1977.

Dennison, C.I. Diet and dental caries, in *Diet, Nutrition and Dentistry* (P.A. Randolph and C.I. Dennison, eds.), C.V. Mosby Co., St. Louis, MO, 1981, pp. 200–223.

Diesendorf, M. The mystery of declining tooth decay. *Nature* 322:125–129, 1986.

Gustafson, B.E. *et al.* The Vipeholm dental caries study. *Acta Odontol. Scand.* 11:232, 1954.

Kaplan, A. *et al.* Nutrition and dental disease, in *The Mount Sinai School of Medicine Complete Book of Nutrition* (V. Herbert and G.J. Subak-Sharpe, eds.), St. Martin's Press, New York, 1990, pp. 611–626.

Nizel, A.E. *Nutrition in Clinical Dentistry*, 3rd ed. W.B. Saunders Company, Philadelphia, PA, 1989.

Patoka, G. *et al.* Effects of eating dairy products on plaque calcium and phosphorus. *Dent. Res.* (special issue) 70:404, 1991.

Pollack, R.L. *et al. Nutrition in Oral Health and Disease.* Lea & Febiger, Philadelphia, PA, 1985.

Recommended Dietary Allowances (RDAs). 10th ed. National Academy Press, Washington, DC, 1989, p. 267.

Rubinoff, A.B. *et al.* Vitamin C and oral health. *Can. Dent. Assoc. J.* 55:705–707, 1989.

Shaw, J.H. Nutrition and dental caries, in, *A Survey of the Literature of Dental Caries* (G. Toverud, G.J. Cox, S.B. Finn, C.F. Bodecker, and J.H. Shaw, eds.), National Research Council, Washington, DC, 1952, pp. 207–415, 417–507.

Shaw, J.H. *et al.* Nutrition in relation to dental medicine, in, *Modern Nutrition in Health and Disease*, 5th ed. (R.S. Goodhart, and M.E. Shills, eds.), Lea & Febiger, Philadelphia, PA, 1968, pp. 766–769.

Surgeon General's Report on Nutrition and Health (SGR). U.S. Government Printing Office, Washington, DC, 1988.

Chapter 8

Anderson, R.A. *et al.* Acute effects of chromium, copper, zinc, and selected clinical variables in urine and serum of male runners. *Biol. Trace Elem. Res.* 6:327–336, 1984.

Berdanier, C.D. Weight loss—weight regain: a vicious cycle. *Nutr. Today* 26(5):6–12, 1991.

Bjorntorp, P. Adipose tissue in obesity, in *Recent Advances in Obesity Research IV* (J. Hirsch and T.B. Van Itallie, eds.), Libbey, London, 1983, pp. 163–170.

Blair, S.N. *et al.* Comparison of nutrient intake in middle aged men and women runners and controls. *Med. Sci. Sports Exerc.* 13:310–315, 1981.

Blair, S.N. *et al.* Physical fitness and all-cause mortality. A prospective study of healthy men and women. *JAMA* 262:2395–2401, 1989.

Blumenthal, J.A. *et al.* Failure of exercise to reduce blood pressure in patients with mild hypertension. *JAMA* 266:2098–2104, 1991.

Bouchard, C. Is weight fluctuation a risk factor? *N. Engl. J. Med.* 324:1887–1889, 1991.

Bray, G.A. *The Obese Patient. Major Problems in Internal Medicine.* W.B. Saunders, Philadelphia, PA, 1976.

Bray, G.A. Obesity, in *Present Knowledge in Nutrition*, 6th ed. (M. L. Brown, ed.), International Life Sciences Institute, Nutrition Foundation, Washington, DC, 1990, p. 26.

Brotherhood, J.R. Nutrition and sports performance. *Sports Med.* 1:350–389, 1984.

Brownell, K.D. *et al.* The effects of repeated cycles of weight loss and regain in rats. *Physiol. Behav.* 38:459–464, 1986.

Buskirk, E.R. Some nutritional considerations in the training of athletes. *Annu. Rev. Nutr.* 1:319–350, 1981.

Buskirk, E.R. Health maintenance and longevity: exercise, in *Handbook of the Biology of Aging* (C.E. Finch and E.L. Schneider, eds.), Van Nostrand Reinhold, New York, 1985, pp. 894–931.

Buskirk, E.R. Exercise, in *Present Knowledge in Nutrition*, (M. L. Brown, ed.), International Life Sciences Institute, Nutrition Foundation, Washington, DC, 1990, p. 343.

Campbell, W.W. *et al.* Effects of aerobic exercise in training on the trace minerals chromium, zinc and copper. *Sports Med.* 4:9–18, 1987.

Chow, R. *et al.* Effect of two randomized exercise programmes on bone mass of healthy postmenopausal women. *Br. Med. J.* 295:1441–1444, 1987.

Dennis, B.H. *et al.* Nutrient intakes among selected North American populations in the Lipid Research Clinics Prevalence Study: Composition of energy intake. *Am. J. Clin. Nutr.* 41:312–329, 1985.

Deuster, P.A. *et al.* Nutritional survey of highly trained women. *Am. J. Clin. Nutr.* 44:954–962, 1986.

Gohil, K. *et al.* Effect of exercise training on tissue vitamin E and ubiquinone content. *J. Appl. Physiol.* 63:1638–1641, 1987.

Goodrich, G.K. *et al.* Why treatments for obesity don't last. *J. Am. Diet. Assoc.* 91:1243–1247, 1991.

Koplan, J.P. *et al.* Physical activity, physical fitness and health: Time to act. *JAMA* 262:2437, 1989.

Krotkiewski, M. *et al.* Impact of obesity on metabolism in men and women: Importance of regional adipose tissue distribution. *J. Clin. Invest.* 72:1150–1162, 1983.

Lapidus, L. *et al.* Distribution of adipose tissue and risk of cardiovascular disease and death: A 12-year follow-up study of participants in the population study of women in Gothenburg, Sweden. *Br. Med. J.* 288:1259–1261, 1984.

Larsson, B. *et al.* Abdominal adipose tissue distribution, obesity and risk of cardiovascular disease and death. A 13-year follow-up of participants in the study of men born in 1913. *Br. Med. J.* 288:1401–1404, 1984.

Lemoyne, M. *et al.* Breath pentane analysis as an index of lipid peroxidation: A functional test of vitamin E status. *Am. J. Clin. Nutr.* 46:267–272, 1987.

Lissner, L. *et al.* Variability of body weight and health outcomes in the Framingham population. *N. Engl. J. Med.* 324:1839–1844, 1991.

Martin, J.E. *et al.* Controlled trial of aerobic exercise in hypertension. *Circulation* 81:1560–1567, 1990.

Martin, R.J. *et al.* The regulation of body weight. *Am. Scient.* 79(6):528–541, 1991.

McDowell, H. *et al.* *Plan and Operation of the Second National Health and Nutrition Examination Survey, 1976–1980.* Vital and Health Statistics, Series 1, No. 15. DHHS publication No. (PHS)81-1317, 1981.

National Center for Health Statistics (NCHS). *Health, United States, 1986*. DHHS publication No. (PHS)87-1232, Hyattsville, MD: National Center for Health Statistics, 1986.

National Center for Health Statistics (NCHS). *Anthropometric Reference Data and Prevalence of Overweight, United States, 1976–1980*. National Health Survey, Series 11, No. 238. DHHS publication No. (PHS)87-1688, Hyattsville, MD, National Center for Health Statistics, 1987.

National Cholesterol Education Program (NCEP). Expert panel on detection, evaluation and treatment of high blood cholesterol in adults. *Arch. Intern. Med.* 148:36–39, 1988.

National Research Council (NRC). Obesity and eating disorders, in *Diet and Health: Implications for Reducing Chronic Disease Risk*. National Academy Press, Washington, DC, 1989, pp. 563–592.

Ostlund, R.E. *et al.* The ratio of waist-to-hip circumference, plasma insulin level, and glucose intolerance as independent predictors of HDL_2 cholesterol level in older adults. *N. Engl. J. Med.* 322:229–234, 1990.

Owen, O.E. *et al.* A reappraisal of the calorie requirements of men. *Am. J. Clin. Nutr.* 46:875–885, 1987.

Packer, L. Vitamin E, physical exercise and tissue damage in animals. *Med. Biol.* 62:105–109, 1984.

Paffenbarger, R.S. *et al.* Physical activity, all-cause mortality, and longevity of college alumni. *N. Engl. J. Med.* 314:605–613, 1986.

Paganini-Hill, A. *et al.* Exercise and other factors in the prevention of hip fractures: The Leisure World Study. *Epidemiology* 2:16–25, 1991.

Pender, N.J. *Health Promotion in Nursing Practice*. Appleton & Lange, Norwalk, CT, 1987.

Pincemail, J. *et al.* Pentane measurement in man as an index of lipoperoxidation. *J. Electroanal. Chem.* 232:117–125, 1987.

Pincemail, J. *et al.* Tocopherol mobilization during intensive exercise. *Eur. J. Appl. Physiol.* 47:189–191, 1988.

Ravussin, E. *et al.* Determinants of 24-hour energy expenditure in man. Methods and results using a respiratory chamber. *J. Clin. Invest.* 78:1568–1578, 1986.

Ravussin, E. *et al.* Reduced rate of energy expenditure as a risk factor for body-weight gain. *N. Engl. J. Med.* 318:467–472, 1988.

Schoene, R.B. *et al.* Iron repletion decreases maximal exercise lactate concentrations in female athletes with minimal iron deficiency anemia. *J. Lab. Clin. Med.* 102:306–312, 1983.

Segal, K.R. *et al.* Lean body mass estimation by bioelectrical impedance analysis: A four-site cross-validation study. *Am. J. Clin. Nutr.* 47:7–14, 1988.

Simon-Schnass, I. *et al.* Effect of vitamin E on exercise parameters in high altitude mountaineering (Ger.) *Deutsch Z. Sportmedi.* 38:200–206, 1987.

Stephenson, M.H. *et al.* 1985 NHIS findings: Nutrition knowledge and baseline data for the weight-loss objectives. *Public Health Rep.* 102:61–67, 1987.

Stern, J.S. Diet and exercise, in *Contemporary Issues in Clinical Nutrition*, vol. 4 (M.R.C. Greenwood, ed.), Churchill Livingston, New York, 1983, pp. 65–84.

Stern, J.S. Is obesity a disease of inactivity? in *Eating and Its Disorders* (A.J. Stunkard and E. Stellar, eds.), Raven, New York, 1984, pp. 131–139.

Stricker, E.M. Biological basis of hunger and satiety: Therapeutic implications. *Nutr. Rev.* 42:333–340, 1984.

Stunkard, A.J. Conservative treatments for obesity. *Am. J. Clin. Nutr.* 45:1142–54, 1987.

Stunkard, A.J. *et al.* A twin study of human obesity. *JAMA* 256(1):51–54, 1986a.

Stunkard, A.J. *et al.* An adoption study of human obesity. *N. Engl. J. Med.* 314(4):193–198, 1986b.

Surgeon General's Report on Nutrition and Health (SGR). DHHS (PHS) Publication No. 88-50210, U.S. Government Printing Office, Washington, DC, 1988.

Van Itallie, T.B. Health implications and obesity in the United States. *Ann. Intern. Med.* 103:983–988, 1985.

Wickham, C.A.C. *et al.* Dietary calcium, physical activity and risk of hip fracture: A prospective study. *Br. Med. J.* 299:889–892, 1989.

Wiley, R.L. *et al.* Isometric exercise training lowers resting blood pressure. *Med. Sci. Sports Exerc.* 24(7):749–754, 1992.

Williamson, D.F. *et al.* The 10-year incidence of overweight and major weight gain in U.S. adults. *Arch. Intern. Med.* 150:655–672, 1990.

Chapter 9

AMA Drug Evaluation, 4th ed. American Medical Association, Chicago, IL, 1981.

AMA Drug Evaluations Annual, 1992. American Medical Association, Chicago, IL, 1992.

Federal Food, Drug and Cosmetic Act, as Amended and Related Laws. U.S. Government Printing Office, 1–2, Washington, DC, 1985.

Feinman, L. Absorption and utilization of nutrients in alcoholism. *Alcohol, Health Res. World* 13:207–210, 1989.

Fried, R. *et al.* The effect of filtered-coffee consumption on plasma lipid levels. *JAMA* 267:811–815, 1992.

Hester, F.G. Take your medicine, but carefully. *Chicago Tribune*, Sec. 1, p. 22, Jan. 11, 1991.

Leonard, T.K. *et al.* The effects of caffeine on various body systems: A review. *J. Am. Diet. Assoc.* 87:1048–1053, 1987.

Lieber, C.S. Alcohol and nutrition: An overview. *Alcohol, Health Res. World* 13:197–205, 1989.

Manual of Clinical Dietetics. The American Dietetic Association, Chicago, IL, 1988.

Mastrangelo, M.R. and Moore. Spontaneous rupture of the stomach in a healthy adult man after sodium bicarbonate ingestion. *Ann. Intern. Med.* 101:649,1984.

McCormick, D.B., Niacin, in *Modern Nutrition in Health and Disease*, 6th ed. (M.E. Shils and V.R. Young, eds.), Lea & Febiger, Philadelphia, PA, 1988, pp. 370–375.

Mullin, G.E. *et al.* Hepatic failure after ingestion of sustained release nicotinic acid. *Ann. Intern. Med.* 111:253–255, 1989.

Murray, J.J. *et al.* Drug–mineral interactions: A new responsibility for the hospital dietitian. *J. Am. Diet. Assoc.* 91:66–73, 1991.

Natow, A.B. and Heslin, J. *Nutritional Care of the Older Adult*. Macmillan Co., New York, 1986.

Physicians' Desk Reference (PDR). Medical Economics Data, Oradell, NJ, 1991.

Recommended Dietary Allowances (RDAs). 10th ed. National Academy Press, Washington, DC, 1989.

Requirements of Laws and Regulations Enforced by the U.S. Food and Drug Administration. U.S. Government Printing Office, Washington, DC, 1984.

Roe, D.A. *Drug-Induced Nutritional Deficiencies*, 2nd ed. AVI Publishing Co., Westport, CT, 1985.

Roe, D.A. *Geriatric Nutrition*, 2nd ed. Prentice-Hall, Englewood Cliffs, NJ, 1987.

Roe, D.A. Diet, nutrition and drug reactions, in *Nutrition in Health and Disease*, 6th ed. (M.E. Shils and V.R. Young, eds.), Lea & Febiger, Philadelphia, PA, 1988, p. 631.

Roe, D.A. *Handbook on Drug and Nutrient Interactions*. The American Dietetic Association, Chicago, IL, 1989a.

Roe, D.A. *Diet and Drug Interactions*. Van Nostrand Reinhold, New York, 1989b.

Spallholz, J.E. *Nutrition: Chemistry and Biology*. Prentice-Hall, Englewood Cliffs, NJ, 1989.

Stone, N. and McDonald, A. *Cholesterol Handbook*. Publications International, Ltd., Lincolnwood, IL, 1989.

The Hypercholesterolemia Handbook. Merck, Sharp, and Dohme, West Point, PA, 1989.

Surgeon General's Report on Nutrition and Health (SGR). U.S. Government Printing Office, Washington, DC, 1988.

Williams, S.R. *Nutrition and Diet Therapy*, 6th ed. Times Mirror/Mosby College Publishing, St. Louis, MO, 1989, pp. 671–688.

Editorial. *Alcohol, Health and World Research* 13:195, 1989.

Chapter 10

American Heart Association (AHA). *The American Heart Association Diet: An Eating Plan for Healthy Americans*. American Heart Association, Dallas, TX, 1985 and 1989.

Calcium gets new support as aid for PMS. *Chicago Tribune*, Chicago, IL. Sect. 1, p. 4, Sept. 4, 1991a.

Green tea may reduce some cancers. *Chicago Tribune*, Chicago, IL. Sect. 1, p. 3, Aug. 27, 1991c.

Kowalski, R.E. *The 8-week Cholesterol Cure*. Harper and Row, New York, 1987.

Lyman, B. *A Psychology of Food*. AVI, Van Nostrand Reinhold, New York, 1989.

National Dairy Council (NDC). *Guide to Good Eating*, 5th ed. National Dairy Council, Rosemont, IL, 1989.

National Cholesterol Education Program (NCEP). *Dietary Treatment of High Blood Cholesterol*. National Cholesterol Education Program of the National Heart, Lung, and Blood Institute, Washington, DC, 1987.

New rules on food labeling. *Chicago Tribune*, Chicago, IL, Sect. 1, Dec. 3, 1992.

Recommended Dietary Allowances (RDAs), 10th ed. National Academy Press, Washington, DC, 1989.

Surgeon General's Report on Nutrition and Health (SGR). U.S. Government Printing Office, Washington, DC, 1988.

Two drinks per day may prove beneficial to heart care, new study shows. *Chicago Tribune*, Chicago, IL. Sect. 1, p, 20, Aug, 23, 1991b.

Dietary Guidelines for Healthy Americans. U.S. Dept. of Agriculture and U.S. Dept. of Health and Human Services (USDA and USDH & HS), U.S. Government Printing Office, Washington, DC, 1990.

Food Guide Pyramid. A Guide to Daily Food Choices (USDA). U.S. Government Printing Office, Washington, DC, 1992.

Chapter 11

Cataracts

Bunce, G.E. Cataract—What is the role of nutrition in lens health? *Nutr. Today* 23(6):6–12, 1988.

Jacques, P.F. *et al.* Nutritional status in persons with and without senile cataract: Blood vitamin and mineral levels. *Am. J. Clin. Nutr.* 48:152–158, 1988.

Natow, A.B. and Heslin, J. *Nutritional Care of the Older Adult.* Macmillan Co., New York, 1986.

Taylor, A. Associations between nutrition and cataract. *Nutr. Rev.* 47:225–234, 1989.

Osteoporosis and Bone Health

Curhan, G.C. *et al.* A prospective study of dietary calcium and other nutrients and the risk of symptomatic kidney stones. *N. Engl. J. Med.* 328:833–838, 1993.

Dawson-Hughes, B. *et al.* Dietary calcium intake and bone loss from the spine in healthy postmenopausal women. *Am. J. Clin. Nutr.* 46:685–687, 1987.

Dawson-Hughes, B. *et al.* Calcium intake and bone loss. *Nutr. Rev.* 46:123–125, 1988.

Dawson-Hughes B. *et al.* A controlled trial of the effect of calcium supplementation on bone density in postmenopausal women. *N. Engl. J. Med.* 323:878–883, 1990.

Heaney, R.P. Nutritional factors in osteoporosis. *Annu. Rev. Nutr.* 13:287–316, 1993a.

Heaney, R.P. Thinking straight about calcium. An editorial. *N. Engl. J. Med.* 328:503–505, 1993b.

Heaney, R.P. *et al.* Calcium balance and calcium requirements in middle-aged women. *Am. J. Clin. Nutr.* 30:1603–1611, 1977.

Heaney, R.P. *et al.* Menopausal changes in calcium balance performance. *J. Lab. Clin. Med.* 92:953–963, 1978.

Heaney, R.P. *et al.* Calcium nutrition and bone health in the elderly. *Am. J. Clin. Nutr.* 36(suppl.):986–1013, 1982.

Kelsey, J.F. Epidemiology of osteoporosis and associated fractures, in *Bone and Mineral Research*, Vol. 5 (W.A. Peck, ed.), Elsevier, New York, 1987, pp. 409–444.

Miller, J.Z. *et al*. Calcium absorption from calcium carbonate and a new form of calcium (CCM) in healthy male and female adolescents. *Am. J. Clin. Nutr.* 48:1291–1294, 1988.

Nielsen, F.H. Boron—an overlooked element of potential nutritional importance. *Nutr. Today* 23:4–7, 1988.

Nielsen, F.H. Ultratrace minerals: Mythical elixirs or nutrients of concern? *Contemp. Nutr.* 15:1–2, 1990.

Omdahl, J.L. *et al*. Nutritional status in a healthy adult population: Vitamin D. *Am. J. Clin. Nutr.* 36:1225–1233, 1982.

Paganini-Hill, A. *et al*. Exercise and other factors in the prevention of hip fracture. *Epidemiology* 2:16–25, 1991.

Pak, C.Y. *et al*. Safe and effective treatment of osteoporosis with intermittent slow release of sodium fluoride: Augmentation of vertebral bone mass and inhibition of fractures. *J. Clin. Endocrinol. Metab.* 68:150–159, 1989.

Polley, K.J. *et al*. Effect of calcium supplementation on forearm bone mineral content in postmenopausal women. A prospective, sequential controlled trial. *J. Nutr.* 117:1929–1935, 1987.

Recker, R.R. *et al*. Effect of estrogens and calcium carbonate on bone loss in postmenopausal women. *Ann. Intern. Med.* 87:649–655, 1977.

Recommended Dietary Allowances (RDAs), 10th ed. Vitamin D. National Academy Press, Washington, DC, 1989.

Reid, I.R. *et al*. Effect of calcium supplementation on bone loss in postmenopausal women. *N. Engl. J. Med.* 328:460–464, 1993.

Riis, B. *et al*. Does calcium supplementation prevent postmenopausal bone loss? *N. Engl. J. Med.* 316:173–177, 1987.

Sheikh, M.D. Calcium bioavailability from two calcium carbonate preparations. *N. Engl. J. Med.* 323:921, 1990.

Smith, E.L. *et al*. Calcium supplementation and bone loss. *Am. J. Clin. Nutr.* 50:833–842, 1989.

Surgeon General's Report on Nutrition and Health (SGR). U.S. Government Printing Office, Washington, DC, 1988.

Webb, A.R. *et al*. Influence of season and latitude on the cutaneous synthesis of vitamin D: Exposure to winter sunlight in Boston and Edmonton will not promote vitamin D_3 synthesis in human skin. *J. Clin. Endocrinol. Metab.* 67:373–378, 1988.

Immune Function

Elsasser, G. Food debate: As consumer group turns 20, controversy continues on diet and health. *Chicago Tribune*, Sec. 7, p. 3, June 13, 1991.

Lipschitz, D.A. Impact of nutrition on the age-related decline in immune and hematologic function. *Contemp. Nutr.* 15:102, 1990.

Martin, R.F. *et al.* Ascorbic acid–selenite interactions in humans studied with oral dose of $^{74}SeO_3^{2-}$. *Am. J. Clin. Nutr.* 49:862–869, 1989.

Meydani, S.N. *et al.* Fish oil and tocopherol-induced changes in natural killer cell-mediated cytotoxicity and PGE_2 synthesis in young and old mice. *J. Nutr.* 118:1245–1252, 1988.

Meydani, S.N. *et al.* Beneficial effect of dietary antioxidants on the aging immune system, in *Oxygen Radicals in Biology and Medicine* (M.G. Simic *et al.*, eds.), Plenum Press, New York, NY, 1989a, pp. 621–625.

Meydani, S.N. *et al.* Effect of vitamin E supplementation on immune responsiveness of the aged. *Ann. N.Y. Acad. Sci.* 570:283–290, 1989b.

Meydani, S.N. *et al.* Nutrition and immune function in the elderly, in *Human Nutrition: A Comprehensive Treatise, vol. 6, Nutrition, Aging, and the Elderly* (N.H. Munro and D.E. Danford, eds.), Plenum Press, New York, 1989c, pp. 61–87.

Robinson, M.F. *et al.* Effect of a megadose of ascorbic acid, a meal and orange juice on the absorption of selenium as sodium selenite. *N.Z. Med. J.* 96:627–629, 1985.

Sherman, A.R. Immunity, in *Present Knowledge in Nutrition*, 6th ed. (M.L. Brown, ed.), Nutrition Foundation, Washington, DC, 1990, pp. 463–476.

Exercise

Cannon, J.G. *et al.* Increased interleukin 1B in human skeletal muscle after exercise. *Am. J. Physiol.* 257:R451–455, 1989.

Evans, W.J. Exercise and aging. *Med. Sci. Sport Exerc.* 21(2 suppl.):S1, 1989.

Fiatarone, M.A. *et al.* High intensity strength training in nonagenarians: Effects on skeletal muscle. *Clin. Res.* 37:330A, 1989.

Frontera, W.R. *et al.* Strength conditioning in older men: Skeletal muscle hypertrophy and improved function. *J. Appl. Physiol.* 64:1038–1044, 1988.

Meredith, C.N. *et al.* Peripheral effects of endurance training in young and old subjects. *J. Appl. Physiol.* 66:2844–2849, 1989.

Nelson, M.E. *et al.* Hormone and bone mineral status in endurance-trained and sedentary postmenopausal women. *J. Clin. Endocrinol. Metab.* 66:927–933, 1988.

Appendix

A. Unisex Table of Suggested Weights
for Adults

Height[a]	Weight in pounds[b]	
	19 to 34 years	35 years and older
5'0"	97–128[c]	108–138
5'1"	101–132	111–143
5'2"	104–137	115–148
5'3"	104–141	119–152
5'4"	111–146	122–157
5'5"	114–150	126–162
5'6"	118–155	130–167
5'7"	121–160	134–172
5'8"	125–164	138–178
5'9"	129–169	142–183
5'10"	132–174	146–188
5'11"	136–179	151–194
6'0"	140–184	155–199
6'1"	144–189	159–205
6'2"	148–195	164–210
6'3"	152–200	168–216
6'4"	156–205	173–222
6'5"	160–211	177–228
6'6"	164–216	182–234

[a]Without shoes; [b]Without clothes; [c]The higher weights in the ranges generally apply to men, who tend to have more muscle and bone; the lower weights more often apply to women, who have less muscle and bone.

The table shows higher weights for people 35 years and older than for younger adults. This is because recent research suggests that people can be a littler heavier as they grow older without added risk to health.

SOURCE: *Nutrition and Your Health: Dietary Guidelines for Americans*, 3rd ed. U.S. Dept. of Agric., U.S. Dept. of Health and Human Services. Garden Bulletin No. 232. Washington, DC, 1990.

B. Median Heights and Weights and Recommended Energy Intake

Category	Age (years) or Condition	Weight (kg)	(lb)	Height (cm)	(in)	REE[a] (kcal/day)	Multiples of REE[d]	Average Energy Allowance (kcal)[b] Per kg	Per day[c]
Infants	0.0–0.5	6	13	60	24	320		108	650
	0.5–1.0	9	20	71	28	500		98	850
Children	1–3	13	29	90	35	740		102	1,300
	4–6	20	44	112	44	950		90	1,800
	7–10	28	62	132	52	1,130		70	2,000
Males	11–14	45	99	157	62	1,440	1.70	55	2,500
	15–18	66	145	176	69	1,760	1.67	45	3,000
	19–24	72	160	177	70	1,780	1.67	40	2,900
	25–50	79	174	176	70	1,800	1.60	37	2,900
	51+	77	170	173	68	1,530	1.50	30	2,300
Females	11–14	46	101	157	62	1,310	1.67	47	2,200
	15–18	55	120	163	64	1,370	1.60	40	2,200
	19–24	58	128	164	65	1,350	1.60	38	2,200
	25–50	63	138	163	64	1,380	1.55	36	2,200
	51+	65	143	160	63	1,280	1.50	30	1,900
Pregnant	1st trimester								+0
	2nd trimester								+300
	3rd trimester								+300
Lactating	1st 6 months								+500
	2nd 6 months								+500

[a]Calculation based on FAO (Food and Agriculture Organization) equations, then rounded.
[b]In the range of light to moderate activity, the coefficient of variaton is ± 20 percent.
[c]Figure is rounded.
[d]Resting Energy Expenditures.
SOURCE: *Recommended Dietary Allowances*, 10th ed., © 1989 by National Academy of Sciences, National Academy Press, Washington, DC. Used with permission.

C. Food and Nutrition Board, National Academy of Sciences—National Research Council Recommended Dietary Allowances,[a] Revised 1989

Designed for the maintenance of good nutrition of practically all healthy people in the United States

Category	Age (years) or Condition	Weight[b] (kg)	Weight[b] (lb)	Height[b] (cm)	Height[b] (in)	Protein (g)	Fat-Soluble Vitamins Vitamin A (µg RE)[c]	Vitamin D (µg)[d]	Vitamin E (mg α-TE)[c]	Vitamin K (µg)
Infants	0.0–0.5	6	13	60	24	13	375	7.5	3	5
	0.5–1.0	9	20	71	28	14	375	10	4	10
Children	1–3	13	29	90	35	16	400	10	6	15
	4–6	20	44	112	44	24	500	10	7	20
	7–10	28	62	132	52	28	700	10	7	30
Males	11–14	45	99	157	62	45	1,000	10	10	45
	15–18	66	145	176	69	59	1,000	10	10	65
	19–24	72	160	177	70	58	1,000	10	10	70
	25–50	79	174	176	70	63	1,000	5	10	80
	51+	77	170	173	68	63	1,000	5	10	80
Females	11–14	46	101	157	62	46	800	10	8	45
	15–18	55	120	163	64	44	800	10	8	55
	19–24	58	128	164	65	46	800	10	8	60
	25–50	63	138	163	64	50	800	5	8	65
	51+	65	143	160	63	50	800	5	8	65
Pregnant						60	800	10	10	65
Lactating	1st 6 months					65	1,300	10	12	65
	2nd 6 months					62	1,200	10	11	65

	Water-Soluble Vitamins							Minerals						
Vitamin C (mg)	Thiamin (mg)	Riboflavin (mg)	Niacin (mg NE)[f]	Vitamin B$_6$ (mg)	Folate (µg)	Vitamin B$_{12}$ (µg)	Calcium (mg)	Phosphorus (mg)	Magnesium (mg)	Iron (mg)	Zinc (mg)	Iodine (µg)	Selenium (µg)
30	0.3	0.4	5	0.3	25	0.3	400	300	40	6	5	40	10
35	0.4	0.5	6	0.6	35	0.5	600	500	60	10	5	50	15
40	0.7	0.8	9	1.0	50	0.7	800	800	80	10	10	70	20
45	0.9	1.1	12	1.1	75	1.0	800	800	120	10	10	90	20
45	1.0	1.2	13	1.4	100	1.4	800	800	170	10	10	120	30
50	1.3	1.5	17	1.7	150	2.0	1,200	1,200	270	12	15	150	40
60	1.5	1.8	20	2.0	200	2.0	1,200	1,200	400	12	15	150	50
60	1.5	1.7	19	2.0	200	2.0	1,200	1,200	350	10	15	150	70
60	1.5	1.7	19	2.0	200	2.0	800	800	350	10	15	150	70
60	1.2	1.4	15	2.0	200	2.0	800	800	350	10	15	150	70
50	1.1	1.3	15	1.4	150	2.0	1,200	1,200	280	15	12	150	45
60	1.1	1.3	15	1.5	180	2.0	1,200	1,200	300	15	12	150	50
60	1.1	1.3	15	1.6	180	2.0	1,200	1,200	280	15	12	150	55
60	1.1	1.3	15	1.6	180	2.0	800	800	280	15	12	150	55
60	1.0	1.2	13	1.6	180	2.0	800	800	280	10	12	150	55
70	1.5	1.6	17	2.2	400	2.2	1,200	1,200	320	30	15	175	65
95	1.6	1.8	20	2.1	280	2.6	1,200	1,200	355	15	19	200	75
90	1.6	1.7	20	2.1	260	2.6	1,200	1,200	340	15	16	200	75

[a]The allowances, expressed as average daily intakes over time, are intended to provide for individual variations among most normal persons as they live in the United States under usual environmental stresses. Diets should be based on a variety of common foods in order to provide other nutrients for which human requirements have been less well defined. See text for detailed discussion of allowances and of nutrients not tabulated.

[b]Weights and heights of Reference Adults are actual medians for the U.S. population of the designated age, as reported by NHANES II. The median weights and heights of those under 19 years of age were taken from Hamill *et al.* (1979). The use of these figures does not imply that the height-to-weight ratios are ideal.

[c]Retinol equivalents. 1 retinol equivalent = 1 µg retinol or 6 µg β-carotene. See text for calculation of vitamin A activity of diets as retinol equivalents.

[d]As cholecalciferol. 10 µg cholecalciferol = 400 IU of vitamin D.

[e]α-Tocopherol equivalents (TE). 1 mg d-α tocopherol = 1 α-TE. See text for variation in allowances and calculation of vitamin E activity of the diet as α-tocopherol equivalents

[f]1 NE (niacin equivalent) is equal to 1 mg of niacin or 60 mg of dietary tryptophan.

SOURCE: *Recommended Dietary Allowances*, 10th ed. © 1989 by National Academy of Sciences, National Academy Press, Washington, D.C. Used with permission.

D. Summary Table: Estimated Safe and Adequate Daily Dietary Intakes of Selected Vitamins and Minerals[a]

Category	Age (years)	Vitamins	
		Biotin (μg)	Pantothenic Acid (mg)
Infants	0–0.5	10	2
	0.5–1	15	3
Children and	1–3	20	3
adolescents	4–6	25	3–4
	7–10	30	4–5
	11+	30–100	4–7
Adults		30–100	4–7

Category	Age (years)	Trace Elements[b]				
		Copper (mg)	Manganese (mg)	Fluoride (mg)	Chromium (μg)	Molybdenum (μg)
Infants	0–0.5	0.4–0.6	0.3–0.6	0.1–0.5	10–40	15–30
	0.5–1	0.6–0.7	0.6–1.0	0.2–1.0	20–60	20–40
Children and	1–3	0.7–1.0	1.0–1.5	0.5–1.5	20–80	25–50
adolescents	4–6	1.0–1.5	1.5–2.0	1.0–2.5	30–120	30–75
	7–10	1.0–2.0	2.0–3.0	1.5–2.5	50–200	50–150
	11+	1.5–2.5	2.0–5.0	1.5–2.5	50–200	75–250
Adults		1.5–3.0	2.0–5.0	1.5–4.0	50–200	75–250

[a]Because there is less information on which to base allowances, these figures are not given in the main table of RDA and are provided here in the form of ranges of recommended intakes.
[b]Since the toxic levels for many trace elements may be only several times usual intakes, the upper levels for the trace elements given in this table should not be habitually exceeded.
SOURCE: *Recommended Dietary Allowances*, 10th ed. © 1989 by National Academy of Sciences, National Academy Press, Washington, DC. Used with permission.

Glossary

adenoma Tumor composed of glandular tissue.

ad libitum At pleasure or as much as is wanted.

aerobic exercise Exercise during which energy needed is supplied by the oxygen inspired. Required for long periods of hard work and vigorous athletic activity. Involves significant kcalories, and the heart and lungs are exercised as well.

amino acid Building blocks of proteins and the products of their digestion.

anaerobic exercise Exercise during which energy needed is provided without utilization of inspired oxygen. Limited to short bursts of vigorous activity. Uses little energy and primarily stretches and builds skeletal muscle.

analgesic A medicine or drug that relieves pain.

analog In chemistry, a compound that is structurally similar to another, but differs in that an atom or radical has been replaced by a different one.

anecdotal A short account or story of a particular incident, experience, or occurrence of an interesting nature; unpublished.

anemia Reduction in number of red blood cells.

angina pectoris Pain and oppression about the heart; caused by an insufficient flow of blood to the heart muscle.

antioxidant Substance able to chemically protect other substances from oxidation, e.g., vitamins C and E; beta-carotene.

Apo-B   Part of a lipoprotein that helps regulate how it is metabolized.

arrhythmia   Literally, without rhythm; any abnormal heartbeat.

atrophy   A wasting away of any part; reduction in size of a structure after having come to full functional maturity.

balance studies   Determination of the amount of a nutrient required to replace losses on a daily basis.

beriberi   Deficiency disease from a lack of sufficient thiamin, vitamin B_1.

biliary system   The system produces bile and delivers it to the small intestine.

bioavailability   The amount of an ingested nutrient that becomes available for absorption.

blood serum   Colorless fluid portion of blood that separates when it clots.

carcinogen   A chemical, physical, or biological agent that increases the incidence of cancer.

carcinoma   Cancer in an external epithelial tissue (mainly skin and linings of the gastrointestinal tract, lungs, and cervix) and internal epithelia (which line glands such as the breast, pancreas, and thyroid).

cardiomyopathy   Any disease that affects the myocardium.

cariogenic   Conducive to caries formation.

case study   An in-depth investigation of an individual, group or institution. The researcher attempts to analyze the variables important to the history, development, or care of the subject or his problems.

catalyst   A substance that increases the rate of a chemical reaction without being used up. In living things, these are called enzymes.

cataract   Opacity or clouding of the lens of the eye, or its capsule, or both.

causal relationship   A relationship between two variables such that the presence or absence of one variable (the "cause") determines the presence, absence, or value of the other (the "effect").

cell   Smallest structural unit of living material.

chelation   From the Greek "chela," meaning claw; chelation products supposedly combat atherosclerosis by grabbing the calcium in the plaques that clog arteries, causing the plaques to disintegrate.

chromosome   Microscopic, threadlike bodies within the nucleus of a cell that bear the genes of an organism.

cirrhosis   Liver function and structural changes from diffuse liver cell death.

citric acid cycle   An intricate series of reactions in the body involving oxidation and the liberation of energy. The main pathway of oxidation for carbohydrates, fats, and proteins.

CNS   Central nervous system.

cohort   A group of people with a defined history of exposure who are studied for a specific time to determine disease incidence or mortality, e.g., cancer.

colorectal cancer   Malignant neoplastic disease of the large intestine, characterized by black, tarry stools, changes in bowel habits, and passing blood.

compound   A substance containing two or more elements, chemically combined in a definite proportion by weight and by atoms, e.g., water, H_2O.

coronary thrombosis   Blockage of one or more of the coronary arteries.

correlation study   A relationship between two variables that may be negative (inverse), positive, or curvilinear; a curvilinear trend is one in which a graphic representation of the data yields a curved line.

cortical bone   Compact densely packed bone that gives strength to the long bones of the body, e.g., the bones of the leg.

cross-sectional study   A study based on observations of different age or developmental groups at a point in time for the purpose of inferring trends over time.

cytoplasm   Substance enclosed within the cell membrane, exclusive of the nucleus.

DNA   Deoxyribonucleic acid; a compound in living cells that contains all genetic information; the chemical of a gene.

double-blind technique   Neither the subject nor the investigator working with the subject or data knows what treatment, if any, the subject is receiving.

dyspepsia   Any form of indigestion.

edema   Swelling of any part of the body due to fluid accumulation outside the blood vessels.

EDTA   Ethylenediamine tetraacetate, a chelating agent. Used, for example, in the treatment of poisoning due to heavy metals, e.g., lead.

efficacy   As used medically, a term for effectiveness.

electrolyte   A substance that forms an electrically conducting solution when dissolved in water.

embolus   A blood clot traveling within the vascular system.

endogenous   Produced or arising from within a cell or organism.

endometrium   The mucous membrane lining the inner surface of the uterus.

enzyme   A catalyst, protein in nature, produced by living cells. It can accelerate the speed of a chemical reaction, thus making an otherwise too slow life process happen at a reasonable rate.

epidemiology   The study of the occurrence, distribution, and causes of health and diseases in humans.

epithelium   The layer of cells forming the epidermis or outer layer of the skin and the surface of mucous membranes.

esophagus   The muscular passageway from the throat to the stomach.

etiology   The study of the causes of diseases.

exogenous   Developed from external causes.

flatulence   Excessive intestinal gas.

flatus   Intestinal gas.

free radical   Highly reactive, electrically charged, fragments of molecules. Arise from spontaneous attack of oxygen on polyunsaturated fatty acids in membranes, or from the impact of cosmic rays. When a cosmic ray strikes a molecule in a cell of the body, free radicals may be born.

gastrointestinal   Pertaining to the organs of the gastrointestinal tract, from mouth to anus; GI tract.

gene   Hereditary determiner on chromosomes of a cell, consisting of DNA.

glucose tolerance   The ability of the body to maintain normal blood glucose levels after consuming a quantity of glucose.

glucosuria   The appearance of glucose in the urine.

goiter   Enlargement of the thyroid gland, seen as a swelling in front of neck.

heat   The form of energy transferred between two objects in contact that initially have different temperatures.

hemoglobin   The oxygen carrier in blood; found in red blood cells (erythrocytes).

hepatoma   A tumor of the liver.

hormone   Chemical substance, originating in an organ or gland, carried by the blood to another part of the body, stimulating it to increased activity, e.g., insulin, secreted in the pancreas.

hyperglycemia   A greater-than-normal amount of glucose in the blood.

hyperinsulinemia   A greater-than-normal amount of insulin in the blood.

hypertension   A condition in which the blood pressure is higher than normal.

hypertriglyceridemia   A greater-than-normal amount of triglyceride in the blood.

hyperuricemia   Excess uric acid in the blood.

hypoglycemia   A blood glucose level below normal.

hypolipemia   A lower-than-normal level of lipids present in the blood.

incidence   Frequency of occurrence of an event over a time and in relation to the population in which it occurs, e.g., incidence of a disease.

infarct   An area of tissue in an organ or part of the body that undergoes necrosis as a result of the blood supply being cut off.

ingest   The process of taking food in through the mouth.

inverse relationship   See "negative relationship."

ischemia   Local and temporary anemia due to blocking of circulation to a part.

ketone bodies   A group of compounds produced during the oxidation of fatty acids, including acetoacetic acid, beta hydroxybutyric acid, and acetone.

larynx   The organ of voice that is part of the air passage connecting the pharynx with the trachea; evident as an enlargement in the neck; the Adam's apple.

lipoprotein   Simple protein combined with cholesterol, phospholipid, triglyceride, or lecithin. May be chylomicrons, high-density lipoproteins (HDL), low-density lipoproteins (LDL), very-low density lipoproteins (VLDL).

longitudinal study   A study designed to collect data at more than one point in time, in contrast to a cross-sectional study.

melanoma   A cancer of the cells that produce the pigment melanin.

menopause   That period that marks the permanent cessation of menstruation.

metastasis   The spread of a malignancy to distant body sites by cancer cells transported in the blood or lymph system.

microsomal oxidizing system   The enzyme system by which the liver metabolizes a number of drugs, toxins, and alcohol.

mg   Milligram; one thousandth of a gram.

morbidity   The number of sick persons or cases of disease in relationship to a specific population.

mortality   The death rate; the ratio of the number of deaths to a given population.

multiple myeloma   A malignant neoplasm of plasma cells usually arising in the bone marrow.

mutagen   A chemical or physical agent that causes a permanent, transmissible change in the genetic material of a cell.

mutant   An animal or plant with inheritable characteristics that differ from those of the parents.

myocardial infarction   Formation of dead tissue resulting from an obstruction of the blood vessels supplying the myocardium, e.g., following occlusion (blockage) of a coronary artery.

myocardium   The thick contractile muscle, the middle layer that forms the bulk of the heart wall.

necrosis   Death of areas of tissue or bone surrounded by healthy parts.

negative (or inverse) relationship   A relationship between two variables in which there is a tendency for higher values of one variable to be associated with lower values of the other.

neoplasm   A new growth of tissue with the potential for uncontrolled and progressive growth; may be benign or malignant.

nephropathy   Disease of the kidney.

neuropathy   Any disease of the nerves.

NHANES   The National Center for Health Statistics conducted the first National Health and Nutrition Examination Survey (NHANES) in 1971–1974 to measure the Nutritional Status of the

U.S. population. This was followed by NHANES–II in 1976–1980, Hispanic Hanes in 1982–1984, and NHANES–III in 1988.

organic acids   Any acid containing one or more carboxyl groups (–COOH), e.g., acetic, lactic, and all fatty acids.

oxyradical   Any of a number of chemically active oxygen species arising from unfavorable side reactions of normal biologic processes. Implicated as a cause of aging.

pancreatitis   Inflammation of the pancreas.

peptic   Referring to the upper gastrointestinal tract or to the stomach and/or first part of the small intestine connecting with the stomach.

pH   The symbol, pH, represents a convenient scale (0–14) used to indicate the acidity (or hydrogen ion concentration) and basicity (or hydroxide concentration) of aqueous solutions. A value of 7 indicates a neutral solution, e.g., pure water. Any number less than 7 indicates an acidic solution, and the smaller the number, the more acidic it is. A number greater than 7 indicates a basic (or alkaline) solution, and the greater it is, the more basic is the solution.

pharmacology   The study of drugs and their origin, nature, properties, and effects on living systems.

placebo   Inactive substance used in studies of drugs, accessory food factors, etc. The placebo is given to one group of persons and the active substance to another similar group; results from the two groups are then compared.

plasma   The liquid part of the blood.

platelet   Oval disks found in the blood of vertebrates; less than half the size of red cells; do not contain hemoglobin; have an important role in blood clot formation following an injury to a blood vessel.

PMS   Premenstrual syndrome; nervous tension, irritability, weight gain, edema, headache, breast pain, depression, and lack of coordination occurring during the last few days of the menstrual cycle preceding the onset of menstruation.

polydipsia   Excessive or abnormal thirst.

polypharmacy   Use of multiple drugs concurrently.

polyuria   Excessive secretion and discharge of urine.

postmenopausal   After menopause.

postprandial   Following a meal.

premenopausal   Before menopause.

prevalence   The number of cases of a disease present in a specified population at a given time.

proportional   Relation between two quantities such as A and B, e.g., directly proportional: if A increases, B also increases; inversely proportional: if A increases, B decreases.

prospective study   Study designed to determine the relationship between a condition and a characteristic shared by some members of a group. The population is healthy at the beginning of the study. Some members of the group share a particular characteristic (e.g., cigarette smoking). The investigator follows the population group over a period and notes the rate at which a condition such as lung cancer occurs in the smokers and the nonsmokers.

protoplasm   A semifluid viscous solution, the essential living matter of all animal and plant cells.

provitamin   Substances in particular foods that may be changed to vitamins in the body, e.g., beta-carotene may be changed to vitamin A.

pulmonary   Concerning or involving the lungs.

quartile   From Latin, quartus, a fourth. In statistics, one of the two middle values of each half of a series of variables.

radical   A group of atoms acting as a single unit, passing without change from one compound to another, but not able to exist in the free state.

randomization   Involves the assignment of subjects to groups in a completely random manner, that is, a manner determined entirely by chance.

renal   Pertaining to the kidneys.

renin   An enzyme made by the kidneys; functions in regulating blood pressure.

retinol   A particular form of vitamin A; found in the retinas of mammals.

retinopathy   Any disorder of the retina (the innermost coat of the back part of the eyeball, on which the image is formed).

retrospective study   Search for a relationship between a current condition and another that occurred in the past.

RNA   Abbreviation for ribonucleic acid. In the cytoplasm, RNA functions in the assembly of proteins.

satiety   State of being full to satisfaction, especially of food.

scurvy   A disease resulting from a deficiency of vitamin C; marked by abnormal formation of bones and teeth, bleeding gums, and subcutaneous hemorrhages.

Sjögren's syndrome   An autoimmune disease that causes dry eyes, dry mouth, and, in women, dry vagina.

SLE   Systemic lupus erythematosus. An autoimmune disease in which an individual makes antibodies to his own DNA, resulting in damage to the small blood vessels throughout the body.

somatomedin   Plasma factors that mediate growth and are dependent on growth hormone.

squamous cell carcinoma   A slow-growing tumor found on the skin; firm, red, or scaly, painless nodule; often the result of overexposure to the sun.

steatorrhea   Greater than normal amounts of fat in the feces.

subcutaneous   Situated or occurring beneath the skin.

sublingually   Under the tongue.

syndrome   Group of signs or symptoms that collectively characterize a particular disease or abnormal condition.

synergistic   Working together; for example, an interaction between drugs causing each to exert its effect more powerfully than either one would alone.

synthesis   In chemistry and biochemistry, the union of elements or parts of compounds to produce new compounds.

T-cell mediated immune response   T cells are a type of lymphocyte (white blood cell) that attacks microorganisms directly. Another type, B cells, produce antibodies in response to bacteria entering the body.

thermogenesis   The production of heat, especially in the body.

thrombus   A blood clot that obstructs a blood vessel or a cavity of the heart.

trabecular bone   Also referred to as cancellous bone; spongy in appearance; provides strength and elasticity; the spine is primarily trabecular bone.

trend studies   Investigations in which samples from a general population are studied over time with respect to some phenomenon.

triglyceride   Combination of glycerol with three fatty acids, most often stearic, oleic, and palmitic. Most animal and vegetable fats are triglycerides.

tumor   A spontaneous new growth of tissue forming an abnormal mass that performs no physiologic function.

tumorigenic   To produce tumors, especially malignancies; oncogenic.

vascular system   The heart, blood vessels, lymphatics, and their parts considered collectively.

1-25(OH) vitamin D   The active form of vitamin D; produced by the kidneys.

vegan   An extreme vegetarian who omits all animal protein from the diet.

ventricle   Either of two lower chambers of the heart which, when filled with blood, contract to propel the blood into the arteries.

Index